KU-576-909

THE GERMAN OCCUPATION OF
THE CHANNEL ISLANDS

The views expressed in this book are those of the author. They do not necessarily reflect the views of the Trustees of the Imperial War Museum.

CHARLES CRUICKSHANK

The German Occupation of The Channel Islands

*Published for the Trustees of
the Imperial War Museum
by*

OXFORD UNIVERSITY PRESS

LONDON   NEW YORK   TORONTO   MELBOURNE

1979

Oxford University Press, Walton Street, Oxford OX2 6DP

OXFORD LONDON GLASGOW
NEW YORK TORONTO MELBOURNE WELLINGTON
NAIROBI DAR ES SALAAM CAPE TOWN
KUALA LUMPUR SINGAPORE JAKARTA HONG KONG TOKYO
DELHI BOMBAY CALCUTTA MADRAS KARACHI

ISBN 0 19 285087 3

© The Trustees of the Imperial War Museum, 1975

First published by Oxford University Press, London 1975
First issued as an Oxford University Press paperback 1979

All rights reserved. No part of this publication may be reproduced, stored in a retrieval system, or transmitted, in any form or by any means, electronic, mechanical, photocopying, recording, or otherwise, without the prior permission of Oxford University Press

Printed in the Channel Islands by The Guernsey Press Co. Ltd.

CONTENTS

ILLUSTRATIONS

PLATES
Between pages 84 *and* 85

MAPS

DIAGRAMS

FOREWORD

THE States of the Island of Jersey and the States of Deliberation of the Island of Guernsey, with the full support of the States of Alderney and the Chief Pleas of Sark, agreed, in 1970, the year in which the twenty-fifth anniversary of the Liberation of the Channel Islands from German Occupation occurred, that this event should be commemorated by the commissioning of a history of the German Occupation of the Islands which commenced on 30 June 1940.

The appropriate Committees of both States, who from the outset have benefited greatly from the advice and assistance of the Director of the Imperial War Museum, Dr. Noble Frankland, D.F.C., selected Dr. Charles Cruickshank to be the historian to whom the work should be entrusted, the selection being ratified by each Committee's respective States.

The author was given a free hand in the way in which he undertook his task and it is he who is responsible for the history and for the views which he has expressed.

The work has been published under the auspices of the Trustees of the Imperial War Museum as they regard it as a very valuable contribution to the history of the 1939–45 War.

The Committees of the two States wish to express their thanks to those officials of the Imperial War Museum who have throughout been concerned with assisting the author in the execution of his task.

C. S. Dupré

President
States of Jersey
Liberation Anniversary Committee

C. H. de Sausmarez

President
States of Guernsey
History 1939–45 Committee

PREFACE

THE occupation of the Channel Islands by the Germans may have been a small episode in the Second World War, but it confronted the individual Islander with exactly the same problems which faced men and women in the larger occupied countries – how far to collaborate with the enemy, what to do about resistance and sabotage, how to endure isolation from friends and allies, how to tolerate extreme hunger and cold, how to face illness with inadequate medicines, how year after year to sustain morale when there was no certainty that they would ever be liberated.

For the Germans the capture of the Islands was their first conquest of British soil and therefore had great propaganda value. They saw it as a step towards the occupation of Britain, and even went so far as to make a special study of the Channel Islanders' behaviour under military government to learn how best they could in due course govern Britain. Before long, however, they were a millstone round Hitler's neck. His insistence that they should be fortified far more heavily than was immediately necessary led to the commitment of huge quantities of materials and weapons which would have been better used to strengthen the Atlantic Wall on the mainland of Europe; and he locked up a reinforced infantry division for the whole of the war.

For the British the loss of the Islands had little strategic significance, but their demilitarization and partial evacuation were so clumsily handled that had the facts been known to the British people at the time it would have weakened their faith in the government's ability to win the war. Happily the more serious mistakes were successfully covered up. It is easy enough, however, to be wise when the fog of war has dispersed and the catastrophic events of 1940 are at a comfortable distance.

The author has had access to sources hitherto unused, the most important being a large number of military government files left by the Germans in Guernsey and Jersey; the Islands' own wartime files;

British government papers preserved in the Public Record Office, which were opened to the public at the beginning of 1972; and captured German documents microfilmed by the American Historical Association and the British Ministry of Defence. These sources are listed on pages 347–53. The inferences drawn from them are, of course, the author's own.

The author would like to thank collectively those who provided information about personal experiences – their names are in the list on pages 353–4 – and many others in all the Islands who helped in different ways, including the members of the two Island Committees, officials of both bailiwicks, of the Occupation Societies, of the Islands' libraries, and of the Société Jersiaise, the Société Guernesiaise, and the Alderney Museum. To these must be added numerous colleagues in Whitehall.

Perhaps this army of helpers will forgive him if he singles out a few for special mention: the Secretaries of the two Committees, Miss Mary Newcombe in Jersey and Mr. Vernon Luff in Guernsey, for their cheerful compliance with his outrageous demands during the years that the book was in preparation, and for looking after his material comfort on his visits to the Islands; Mr. John D. Lawson of the Ministry of Defence whose scholarship and expert guidance through the records of the Naval Historical Branch were invaluable; Mr. Leonard Matchan, the hospitable lord of the Island of Brecqhou, for his generous provision of aerial transport which made it possible to photograph places where the Commandos landed; and above all his twin guiding spirits, Senator C. S. Dupré in Jersey and Deputy C. H. de Sausmarez in Guernsey, whose inspired intellectual union gave birth to this History, and for whose help and encouragement the author is profoundly grateful.

Finally, he acknowledges the debt due to his wife for her painstaking translation of many hundreds of pages of German records – on paper and microfilm – without which the book could not have been written.

C.G.C.

INTRODUCTION

THE Channel Islands belonged to the Duchy of Normandy from 933 A.D., and when William became King of England in 1066 he continued to rule them as Duke of Normandy. The mainland of Normandy was lost to England in the thirteenth century but the Islands remained loyal to King John. After 1453 Calais was the only English possession in Europe (except for the French city of Tournai, which Henry VIII occupied between 1513 and 1519), but in 1558, the last year of Mary Tudor's reign, the lethargy of the English government allowed the French to recapture Calais. The Channel Islands, however, were steadfastly loyal through the centuries, in spite of their nearness to France and periodic attacks by the French.

The four main Islands are Jersey, Guernsey, Alderney, and Sark. They lie to the west of the Cherbourg or Cotentin peninsula with which they have a close geological affinity. Alderney is the nearest to the mainland of both England and France; but while its most northerly point is more than 60 miles from Weymouth, the closest English seaport, its most easterly promontory is only 10 miles from Cap de la Hague.

The shallow bay in which the Islands find themselves with their satellites – Herm and Jethou, three miles east of Guernsey, and Lihou to the west; Brecqhou, off the west coast of Sark, separated only by a narrow channel; and Burhou, west of Alderney – contains a number of rocky islets subject to British sovereignty. These are the Casquets, west of Alderney; the Ecréhous, midway between Jersey and the French coast; and the Minquiers, due south of Jersey on the route to St. Malo. The islets, adjacent reefs, and the swift tidal currents which flow between them – for example, the Great Russel Strait dividing Sark from the Islands to the west, the Little Russel separating Herm and Jethou from Guernsey, and the Race of Alderney between that Island and France – make navigation hazardous at all seasons.

Jersey, 12 miles by 7 at its greatest breadth, is a rough oblong of 45 square miles. The capital, St. Helier, is on the south coast at the eastern end of the magnificent St. Aubin's Bay. The seabed in the vicinity slopes gently and it has been impossible to provide a deep-water harbour. An attempt to build breakwaters in the nineteenth century failed because of severe storms. Guernsey is a triangle of about 24 square miles. The capital, St. Peter Port on the east coast, has a fine harbour. It is dominated by Castle Cornet, a splendid fortress dating from the earliest times, which has the no less splendid Elizabeth Castle as its counterpart off St. Helier. Alderney, $3\frac{1}{2}$ by $1\frac{1}{2}$ miles, is just under 2,000 acres, and Sark just over 1,000 acres.[1]

In 1939 there were about 50,000 people in Jersey, 40,000 in Guernsey, 1,500 in Alderney, and 600 in Sark. The great majority were natives of the Islands, but there were some thousands from the United Kingdom who had made their home in the Islands because of the better climate and the financial advantages. There was a seasonal ebb and flow of other nationalities: Irish and French (mainly Bretons) to help with the potato crop in Jersey, and French, Spaniards, and Italians to man the hotels during the tourist season. A small number of Frenchmen who were originally seasonal workers had settled in the Islands either as managers of farms or, in some cases, as proprietors. There were a few Jews, most of whom had wisely retreated into England on the outbreak of war, or when the German armies began to sweep across France. The handful who remained in June 1940 were mainly domestic servants.

The Island of Jersey is a self-contained bailiwick. The bailiwick of Guernsey includes the adjacent Herm, Jethou, and Lihou, and also the more distant Islands of Alderney, Sark, and Brecqhou. In 1939 each bailiwick had its own Lieutenant-Governor and Commander-in-Chief, the personal representative of the Crown, and official channel of communication between the Island governments and the government of the United Kingdom.

The machinery of government in Jersey and Guernsey is broadly similar but there are nevertheless important differences. The representative bodies are both known as the States (the Assembly of the States in Jersey and the States of Deliberation in Guernsey).[2] They are presided over by the Bailiff, who is appointed by the Crown and who

---

[1] **The acreage of the smaller Islands is: Herm, 320; Brecqhou, 200 ; Jethou, 44; and Lihou, 38.**

[2] For the origin of the States see J. H. Le Patourel, *The Medieval Administration of the Channel Islands* (Oxford, 1937), pp. 117–18.

in 1939 held office during the Sovereign's pleasure.[1] He is the link between the administrative departments and the Lieutenant-Governor. The Law Officers (Attorney General and Solicitor General),[2] who are also appointed by the Crown, had in 1939 the right to address the assembly in Jersey, and in Guernsey they had the right both to speak and to vote.

There were in the States of Deliberation in Guernsey eighteen Deputies of the People elected by parishes by persons of full age (i.e. 20 years). The Deputies correspond broadly to members of the House of Commons in the United Kingdom, except that they are not elected on the basis of their political views. There were also the ten parish Rectors, who held their appointments from the Crown, six elected representatives from the parish of St. Peter Port, and one each from the other nine parish councils or *Douzaines*. Finally, there were twelve Jurats chosen by an electoral college known as 'the States of Election', which in 1939 comprised the Bailiff, Law Officers, Jurats, Rectors, Constables, Deputies, and the 180 *Douzeniers*. The office of Jurat, which is very ancient, was originally judicial, but with the passage of time it was widened, and in 1939 it combined legislative and administrative functions with judicial. The Jurats – British subjects who could be neither brewers, publicans, nor Roman Catholics – held office for life.[3]

In the States of Jersey there were in addition to the Bailiff and Law Officers twelve Jurats elected for life by the ratepayers of each parish. As in Guernsey, Roman Catholics (and also Jews and Freethinkers) were ineligible for the office, but it was open to brewers and publicans. The other members were the twelve Rectors; twelve Constables elected triennially by popular vote; seventeen Deputies; and the *Vicomte*. The last – the chief executive of the courts in Jersey, who acted as sheriff – was a member who had no right to speak or vote.[4] In Guernsey the functions of the *Vicomte* were carried out by the

[1] There is also now an age limit of 70.

[2] On occasion alternative forms are used: in Jersey, *Procureur-Général* or *Procureur du Roi* (Advocate General), and *Avocat-Général* or *Avocat du Roi* (Solicitor General); and in Guernsey *Procureur* (Attorney General), and Comptroller (Solicitor General).

[3] It was decided in 1948 that the Jurats and Rectors should no longer sit in the States of Deliberation and provision was made for the inclusion of twelve *Conseillers*. The number of Deputies was increased to thirty-three. The terms of the Jurat's oath made it impossible for brewers, publicans, and Roman Catholics to hold office.

[4] For changes made in the constitutions of Guernsey and Jersey after the Second World War see the *Report of the Committee of the Privy Council on Proposed Reforms in the Channel Islands* (Cmd. 7074, 1947); and Resolutions on Guernsey *Billets d'État* Nos. XVI and XXII of 1947.

Prévôt, who was chosen by the States of Election but was not a member of the States of Deliberation.

Although they were part of the bailiwick of Guernsey, Alderney and Sark had a large measure of independence in 1939. Sark was – and still is – a hereditary Seigneurie with her own predominantly feudal constitution. Her 'Chief Pleas' corresponded to the States in the other Islands. Alderney also had a representative assembly, the States of Alderney.[1]

The constitutional position of the Islands is admirably summed up by Professor Le Patourel in his essay on their development from the earliest times:

Before the German occupation in 1940 the Channel Islands had achieved a high degree of self-government. They could not be classified as dominions, for they had no international status, yet they had greater powers of self-government than any of the colonies. Nor, indeed, could they profitably be compared with those territories within the British Commonwealth whose government is intermediate between those of the dominons and the colonies, for their whole process of development has been so different. Their constitutions have not been given them at any time by an act of the Crown or by an act of Parliament. These constitutions are both home-made and *sui generis*. This is perhaps the one thing about the government of the Channel Islands that is really important. Though conditions have, on the whole, been made favourable to them; though they have through the centuries enjoyed the protection of the English armed forces; though successive governments at Westminster, recognizing the strategic importance which the Islands possessed until very recently, have shown themselves generous, tolerant, and helpful; and although the Islands owe a great deal to the facts that they were never sovereign communities, and could call for assistance to higher authority when local problems grew so tangled that they could not be solved locally, yet, when all such allowances have been made, it must be conceded that the Channel Islands have achieved self-government chiefly as a result of their own efforts.[2]

Since the Islands are legally outside the United Kingdom, acts of the United Kingdom parliament apply to them only by express provision. This is exceptional. It has for so long been customary for the States to initiate local legislation, and so much reponsibility has been entrusted to

[1] The governments of Guernsey and Alderney are now linked for some purposes. Guernsey is responsible for the education and health services on Alderney and for the upkeep and management of the airport. Alderney contributes to the revenue of the two Islands, which have the same level of taxation; and Alderney sends two members to the representative assembly of Guernsey.

[2] J. H. Le Patourel, 'The political development of the Channel Islands,' *Transactions of La Société Guernesiaise* (1946), pp. 27–34.

them, that the United Kingdom parliament does not legislate on matters with which they can deal, unless for some special reason a United Kingdom act is necessary. In certain United Kingdom acts, such as those dealing with exchange control, merchant shipping, and civil aviation, there are clauses applying to the Islands; but the more usual procedure is to enact that the provisions of United Kingdom statutes may, where necessary, be extended to the Islands by Order in Council. This is preferred by the States because it gives them the opportunity of arguing their cases before a Committee of the Privy Council, should they find it necessary to raise an objection to some aspect of the legislation. It is also convenient because provisions in a United Kingdom statute may have to be modified to fit them into the Islands' administrative systems. The necessary modifications can be made very simply by means of an Order in Council.

Although there is no written constitution, the fields in which the Crown and the States legislate are clearly established by many years of precedent. In 1946 the Attorney General of Guernsey, speaking in the States of Deliberation, observed: 'In relation to our domestic affairs we are virtually an independent democracy, but I would remind the States that the legislature of this Island in regard to such matters is not the States alone, but His Majesty, His Majesty's Privy Council, and the States.' It was the Privy Council, not any individual, and certainly not the United Kingdom parliament that the Islanders recognized as the authority responsible for decisions on their affairs. This was also the position in Jersey, and it obtained in both bailiwicks in 1939.

In Guernsey and Jersey *Projets de Loi* are sent to the Privy Council after approval by the States – in the former by the Bailiff through the Lieutenant-Governor, and in the latter by the Greffier of the States – and the measures are considered by the Committee of the Privy Council for the affairs of Jersey and Guernsey, after advice has been sought from interested United Kingdom departments. When they are approved they become the subjects of Orders in Council. These go to the Royal Courts to be registered. There are, however, some spheres in which the States have no right to initiate legislation. In these it is the Sovereign who is seen by the Islanders to exercise the legislative function, and not the parliament at Westminster.

In both bailiwicks the day-to-day management of affairs is carried on by departments staffed by permanent civil servants. Their work is directed by Committees drawn from members of the States, and subject to the direction of the States, which between them cover the whole range of governmental activity. The Committees evolve policy, making use of the advice of the appropriate civil servants, and they lay proposals before the States for discussion and embodiment in legislation. They derive their being, powers, and duties from the States, whose servants they are. Some of them are standing Committees, while others are set up to carry out a specific task. They are given terms of reference which may not be departed from without the approval of the States.

In Jersey, local government is in the hands of the twelve parish assemblies. These are presided over by the Constable, the principal officer of the parish, except that the Rector presides when ecclesiastical matters are under discussion. The other parish officers are the *Centeniers* (honorary policemen); the *Procureurs de Bien Publique* (Public Trustees); the Churchwardens; the *Vingteniers*, who collect the parish rates and assist the *Centeniers* in their police duties; the Constable's officers; and finally, the Almoners.[1]

In Guernsey the management of each of the ten parishes is in the hands of the Senior and Junior Constables, plus twelve *Douzeniers*, except in St. Peter Port, which has twenty and the Vale, which has sixteen. Since the *Douzaines* are represented at the meetings of the States of Deliberation there is a link between local and central government. There is a corresponding link in Jersey, where the twelve Constables are *ex officio* full members of the States.

The law of the Channel Islands originated in the Duchy of Normandy. It has been modified by local precedent and custom during a thousand years, in which changes in England and later the United Kingdom have made little impact because of the different bases of the two legal systems, the extreme difficulty of communication, and the independent disposition of the Islanders. In some respects it still differs materially from the law of the United Kingdom.

The Royal Courts in Jersey and Guernsey had in 1939 full power to determine civil and criminal causes. They constituted the final court of appeal, except that if sufficient cause was shown leave might be granted to appeal to the Judicial Committee of the Privy Council. This was an expensive procedure, and seldom used. There was a right of appeal to Guernsey from the Court of Alderney, and from the Court of the Seneschal of Sark.

The Royal Court in Guernsey has three divisions: the Full Court comprising the Bailiff and at least seven Jurats; the Ordinary Court (the

[1] F. de L. Bois, *A Constitutional History of Jersey* (Jersey, 1970), p. 9.

Bailiff and at least two Jurats); and the Matrimonial Causes Division (the Bailiff and four Jurats). The Full Court deals with all indictable offences, and registers Orders in Council. The Ordinary Court has jurisdiction in all civil matters and hears appeals from the Magistrate's Court. The last has summary jurisdiction in criminal matters and in minor civil matters.

In Jersey the Royal Court sitting as 'the Superior Number', consisting of the Bailiff and at least seven Jurats, has jurisdiction in both criminal and civil matters, and can act as a Court of Appeal from 'the Inferior Number', which comprises the Bailiff and two Jurats. It is this latter Court which registers Orders in Council. The Assize Court, also presided over by the Bailiff, sits four times a year to hear criminal cases. At least seven Jurats sit with the Bailiff, and there is also a Jury. The Police and Petty Debts Courts are presided over by Stipendiary Magistrates.[1]

In 1939 the economy of the Channel Islands was almost entirely based on agriculture, horticulture, and tourism. In Jersey the principal crop was potatoes. The breeding and export of the world-famed Jersey cattle were important. Guernsey cattle were also exported in 1939, but then as now the Island's main sources of overseas exchange were early flowers and vegetables, and tomatoes grown in heated greenhouses. Tourism was important to both Islands, but particularly to Jersey. The Islands had one market and one supplier – the United Kingdom – but their customs duties and taxation were independent of the United Kingdom, as they still are.[2]

So it was that the Channel Islands awaited the Second World War. Two densely-populated bailiwicks, close to France, still using French for some purposes, and patois in the country districts, but loyal to the United Kingdom for a thousand years; virtually self-governing, except for the King in Council standing benevolently in the wings, and taking the stage only to consider the wishes of the Island legislatures; each with the machinery of an independent state, but sometimes incapable of making quick decisions because of their relationship with the Privy Council; dependent on selling their produce to Britain, and on visitors from Britain, but with their taxpayers more gently treated than those of

[1] Since 1964 each bailiwick has had its own Court of Appeal, comprising a panel of ordinary judges (who serve both bailiwicks) and the Bailiff. In Jersey the Deputy Bailiff also sits.

[2] Trade between the Channel Islands and the United Kingdom is now regarded as 'United Kingdom home trade' for the purpose of United Kingdom trade statistics.

the United Kingdom; defended by historical monuments of great magnificence which were unable to afford protection against the weapons of the twentieth century; strategically no longer of importance to the United Kingdom, which was nevertheless formally responsible for their defence; and maintaining small militias which had no positive role in the coming struggle against Europe's latest dictator.

It is against their constitutional background, which the Germans did not understand, and with due regard to the even more incontrovertible facts of their geography and economy that the occupation of the Channel Islands must be examined.

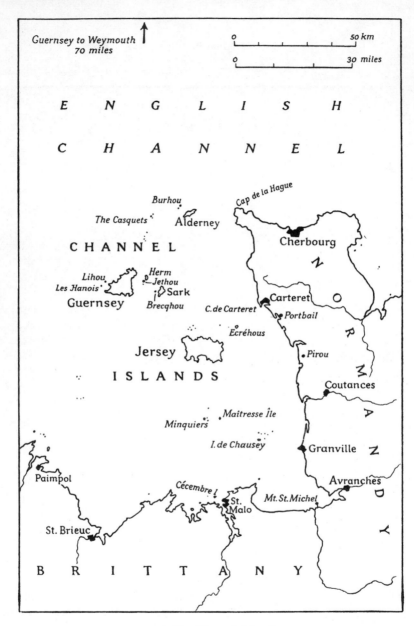

Guernsey to Weymouth
70 miles

0   50 km

0   30 miles

E   N   G   L   I   S   H

C   H   A   N   N   E   L

Burhou

The Casquets · Alderney

Cap de la Hague

C   H   A   N   N   E   L

Cherbourg

Lihou · Herm
Les Hanois · Jethou
Brecqhou · Sark

Guernsey

C. de Carteret · Carteret
· Portbail

Ecréhous

Jersey · Pirou

I   S   L   A   N   D   S

Coutances

Maitresse Île

Minquiers

I. de Chausey · Granville

Avranches

Paimpol

Cécembre !
St. Malo · Mt. St. Michel

St. Brieuc

N   O   R   M   A   N   D   Y

B   R   I   T   T   A   N   Y

1. *The Channel Islands*

1

Preparation for War

THE first step taken by the Islands to contribute to the defeat of Hitler was the embodiment of their militias. On 1 September 1939 both Lieutenant-Governors,[1] aware of the need for speed, but without positive instructions from London, ordered that all ranks should be called up next day.

On 3 September the Home Office and War Office were still corresponding about the proper procedures. The former explained to their colleagues across Whitehall that 'the militia in these Islands may be embodied according to circumstances, by Royal Proclamation, Order in Council, or by an order of the Lieutenant-Governor, and Sir Samuel Hoare will. be glad to know whether Mr. Secretary Hore-Belisha concurs in the Lieutenant-Governors of the Channel Islands being approached at this stage with a view to embodying the militia now'. Four days and one Secretary of State later[2] the reply came: 'I am commanded by the Army Council to acquaint you for the information of Secretary Sir John Anderson that they concur with the proposal that the Channel Islands' militia should be embodied.'

On the same day news that the militias had already been called up reached the Home Office. The official concerned tried to telephone it to the War Office, without success. He therefore wrote a further letter saying that that Department must now be aware of the position. This was a false assumption.

In acknowledging the letter on 10 September the War Office admitted that they had no idea what was happening in the Channel Islands. Stranger still, in spite of the fact that Britain was responsible for the

---

[1] Major-General J. M. R. Harrison (Jersey) and Major-General A. P. D. Telfer-Smollet (Guernsey).
[2] Sir John Anderson succeeded Sir Samuel Hoare on 4 September 1939.

defence of the Islands, they were unsure 'about the machinery by which we communicate with the Lieutenant-Governors of Jersey and Guernsey in their capacity of General Officers Commanding'. Could one deal with them direct, or had all communications to go through the Home Office? This curious transaction, which suggests that the United Kingdom authorities had begun to muddle through the Second World War almost before it had started, ended happily on 11 September when the Home Office told the War Office that there was no objection to their getting in touch with the Lieutenant-Governors – who, as serving soldiers, were responsible to the Army Council.[1]

The militias were the least of the problems facing the Island authorities. They were intended only for defence. The men of the Channel Islands had for centuries been exempt from service in the armed forces of the Crown, unless they were required to rescue the sovereign from the enemy; but they have never sheltered behind this right. Many from all the Islands volunteered during the First World War, and when the United Kingdom introduced conscription the Islands followed suit. They did so again in the Second World War.

On 16 September the States of Jersey passed a resolution assuring His Majesty of their loyalty and devotion, and placing all their resources at the disposal of the Crown.[2] Both bailiwicks introduced a law to make their men available for the United Kingdom forces and consequential measures to re-shape their militias. The Lieutenant-Governor of Jersey wrote to the Home Office in September about their proposed National Service Bill. He was sure that the services in Britain would welcome it since it would give them all the fighting men who could safely be released. The National Service Law empowering the States to direct British subjects in Jersey between 18 and 41 into His Majesty's forces was registered in the Royal Court on 20 January 1940. The complementary Insular Defence Corps Law reorganizing the militia – which could, of course, no longer rely on men fit for overseas service – was registered the same day. It set up a new Defence Corps for service within the Island – the Royal Militia Island of Jersey (Defence Unit) – into which men could be directed under the National Service Law.[3]

[1] WO 79/HD/952.
[2] 'Fière de ses traditions et de son passé d'attachement loyal et inbranlable au trône d'Angleterre et resolue à tous sacrifices pour aider la Mêre Patrie à vaincre l'ennemi commun...' JF W 12.
[3] HO 45/18589(827872/2 and 4).

According to the usual practice, the Bailiff, Mr. Alexander Coutanche (later Lord Coutanche), should have submitted these laws to the Lieutenant-Governor for transmission to London, and the Home Secretary would have returned them for a report by the Law Officers (who were servants of the Crown) before passing them on to the Privy Council. In view of the urgency, however, the Law Officers, Mr. C. W. Duret Aubin (Attorney General) and Mr. Cecil Harrison (Solicitor General), sensibly provided their report when the measures were first sent to the Home Office. They were satisfied that His Majesty might properly be advised to approve them.[1]

So far so good. Guernsey was no less forthcoming. On 27 September 1939 the States passed a resolution that 'for the period of the duration of the present war, in which the liberties of mankind are at stake, our constitutional rights and privileges in respect of military service overseas, while being formally reserved in perpetuity, should be waived'. The Island's men would be placed at the disposal of His Majesty for service overseas, subject only to the needs of their own essential industries and defence.

This was followed by a loyal address recording that 'for centuries past by authority of Princely writ we have been exempt from military service out of the Islands, unless it be to accompany Your Majesty in person for the recovery of England, or that the person of Your Majesty should be taken prisoner by the enemy. Your Majesty's Norman subjects earnestly trust that their services may never be needed by reason of the happening of either of these calamitous events which render them obligatory.' Men from the bailiwick were already serving in every branch of the armed forces; but the legislatures of Guernsey, Alderney, and Sark 'yield back, freely and gladly, then, to Your Majesty, for the duration of this struggle, those exemptions from military service overseas which Your Majesty's noble predecessors conferred in times past'.

On 15 December 1939 the Home Office, stirred by a telephone call from Guernsey, agreed that the Island's proposals were acceptable, and belatedly offered help in working out the details. Eight weeks later – on 19 February 1940 – the Guernsey National Service Law was sent to London for comment. Now a major difficulty appeared. The legislation made Guernseymen liable for compulsory service in the United Kingdom armed forces, under Guernsey law. It transpired, however, that if a Guernseyman was invited to complete the United Kingdom

[1] HO 45/19783(827873/2).

attestation form (which asked, for example, 'Are you willing to be enlisted for general service?') all he need do to escape conscription was to say 'No', and that was the end of the matter. The Attorney General of Guernsey, Major (later Sir) Ambrose Sherwill, pointed out that this could lead to a complete breakdown of the law. Further, if Guernsey's difficulty was resolved by an act of the United Kingdom parliament, it would draw attention to the fact that Jersey's parallel legislation, which was now on the statute book, was subject to the same fundamental weakness.

It was hinted in the correspondence which followed that the authorities in Jersey had been careless. This was quickly disposed of by their Attorney General, Mr. C. W. Duret Aubin. The law had been designed to meet the wishes of the War Office, in spite of Jersey's misgivings. The Home Office agreed that the service departments had accepted Guernsey's draft, and the Attorney General of Guernsey wrote with considerable restraint: 'We have reason to think that it was correctly settled in accordance with the wishes and the technical requirements of the Service Departments. I mention this in order that you may not think that we are the cause of any muddle which may have arisen in this respect.' The Lieutenant-Governor added that 'it appears to us that the War Office have put us in an impossible position which can only be put right by act of parliament'.[1]

The Islands were handsomely exonerated in a Whitehall memorandum. It made no bones about the blunder over the Jersey law, for which the War Office was mainly responsible. Jersey's original draft was right and the Home Office (acting under pressure from the War Office) should not have had it amended. It was obvious that dual legislation was needed. In the words of the memorandum: 'What was referred to as "a cunning device" for evading legislation at Westminster naturally had the effect of transferring the difficulties to the Islands, and it has not been successful.' By following the Jersey legislation the Guernsey authorities had unwittingly fallen into the trap laid by War Office officials trying to avoid the drudgery of piloting a bill through the United Kingdom parliament; and at the same time they had exposed the existence of the trap.

On 20 May 1940, more than eight months after the outbreak of war, the War Cabinet considered the National Service (Channel Islands) Bill. They were not told it was designed to paper over cracks created by the War Office. A memorandum by the Home Secretary explained

[1] HO 45/19783(827873/4).

that 'the Jersey States have passed, and the Guernsey States will shortly pass local laws similar to the National Service (Armed Forces) Act, 1939; but these local acts cannot operate outside the insular jurisdiction, and in order to make enlistments under the insular legislation valid for all purposes outside the Islands further legislation by the parliament at Westminster is necessary'. He drew a discreet veil over the reasons why it had taken so long for this small bill to appear.

Things could now start moving again. On 3 June Sherwill reported to London that the States had approved the national service law and that the States of Alderney had concurred in its application to their Island. He hoped that the measure would be brought before the Privy Council at the earliest opportunity. Next day *The Times*, with a fine disregard for the constitutional niceties, reported that 'the new bill awaits the ratification of the Home Office'. The King 'by and with the advice of His Privy Council' approved and ratified the *Projet de Loi* on 26 June – ten months after the outbreak of war, and two days before the German attack on the Channel Islands made the law a dead letter.

While this slow-moving comedy of administrative errors was being played out, the Guernsey States instituted an inquiry into their militia's wartime role. Many members were volunteering for the United Kingdom forces, and it was therefore necessary to establish a defence force consisting of men unqualified for service overseas. The Island would continue to be defended by men owing service under the ancient militia law. The new force, which must retain the honourable name of the Royal Guernsey Militia, would be a source of pride for every inhabitant. It was assumed that there would be plenty of volunteers, but if there were not, there would have to be conscription. Finally, there was the question of the band. As an economy measure it had not been embodied at the beginning of the war, but it was now proposed that it should continue in being in its present establishment of 41 musicians. The consistent improvement in its performance in recent years and the keenness of its personnel warranted the support of the Island.[1]

Neither the reorganized Royal Guernsey Militia nor Jersey's Insular Defence Corps had a chance to play a part in the defence of the Islands. The former was still under discussion when the Germans invaded, and the latter awaited the appointment of officers. The Lieutenant-Governor told the Bailiff that it was impossible to get suitable senior

[1] *Billet d'État* No. XV, 1939.

officers of experience at the original rate of pay proposed.[1] Further, the number of volunteers was not large, and it was considered in May 1940 that it would be necessary to call men up. Thus for most of the nine months between the declaration of war and demilitarization the existing militias had to carry on, their numbers being steadily depleted as members went into the United Kingdom forces.

Earlier the Channel Islands had been invited to participate in the United Kingdom Civil Air Guard Scheme. Light aeroplane clubs were to train pilots who would offer their services in the event of an emergency. Coutanche saw no constitutional difficulty, so long as Jersey did not re-introduce compulsory service, but he wanted something more ambitious. Jersey must play her part in imperial defence; even after the militia had been reorganized there would still in his view be Jerseymen with no chance to serve the Empire, 'in strong contrast to what is happening in England at this time'. An Auxiliary Air Force Unit would give them this chance. The Air Ministry were discouraging, since they considered that the Islands could not support such a unit. They suggested instead a Volunteer Reserve Centre at which pilots could be trained. Coutanche agreed. He was sure that there would be plenty of volunteers.

The Guernsey authorities welcomed the Civil Air Guard Scheme and offered to start a flying club. Their new airport would not be ready until the following summer but members could be given theoretical training during the winter months. The winter months came and went and there was no further news from London. When the Lieutenant-Governor asked what was happening he was told that the Air Ministry had not reached a decision. By the outbreak of war nothing had been done, and a Guernsey file recorded that 'now presumably nothing *will* be done'.[2]

The Lieutenant-Governors of Jersey and Guernsey, both military men, studied the defences of the bailiwicks before the war began, but failed to arouse much interest in the United Kingdom. This was not surprising. Whitehall knew that the strategic importance of the Islands had been reduced; was equally conscious of the desperate shortage of weapons in Britain; and was seemingly oblivious of the United Kingdom's formal responsibility for the defence of the Islands. In September 1939 Jersey asked for two 4·7-inch coastal defence guns, four Bofors

[1] JF W 19/2.   [2] GF 85/38.

anti-aircraft guns, and twelve Bren guns. The War Office received the order without enthusiasm and the official handling the transaction made an ungenerous marginal note: 'Perhaps when the States are informed of the cost (about £40,000) and its effect on their income tax, they may review their requirements.' The formal reply was that coastal guns might be delivered in August 1940 but that it was impossible to quote a date for Bofors, production of which had only just started, or for Bren guns. The War Office airily told the Home Office that the possibility of an attack on Jersey was 'somewhat remote', and the Army Council hinted that the weapons asked for might be more useful elsewhere. The best that Jersey could do for the Empire Defence Problem (the Army Council's capitals) would be to protect the airfield from low-flying attacks. They recommended Lewis guns, 'which are at present the most general weapon in use at Home'.[1]

In October 1939 the Lieutenant-Governor faced up to the inevitable. He said, humbly, that Jersey realized that the Imperial Armed Forces must have priority. Two months later he retreated further. He wrote to the Home Office: 'As the possibility of obtaining the equipment asked for in sufficient time for it to be of any use in the present war is remote, and as the situation may have materially changed by the time the equipment is available', the States wished to cancel the order, except for seven Bren guns. The War Office gratefully noted this change of heart and replied that there was no chance of supplying anything in 1940.

In April 1939 the Lieutenant-Governor of Guernsey, Major-General Sir Edward Broadbent, in his capacity of Officer Commanding, Guernsey and Alderney District, reported to the Bailiff that he had examined 'with some anxiety' the question of the defence of the Island in the event of war. The Channel Islands were not of primary strategical importance but might have to face minor raids from the sea or the air. An artillery unit to man coastal and air defence weapons and an infantry unit would therefore be needed – about 270 officers and men. Weapons could not be provided for 12 to 18 months and would be costly. It seemed to him sensible to train the militia to a higher standard before buying sophisticated equipment. Major-General Telfer-Smollett, who succeeded Broadbent as Lieutenant-Governor, agreed that the shape of the militia should be changed on these lines; but suggested that in view of the long delivery dates two Bofors and two 4·7 inch coastal guns should be ordered right away.

Expert advice was needed before the sites for the coastal guns could

[1] WO 106/2956.

be chosen, but the War Office could not spare anyone. Further, the guns could be supplied only at the expense of more important commitments.[1] On 4 October the Lieutenant-Governor told the Bailiff that he fully agreed with the decision to buy guns, but that war had come before they could be installed and gunners trained. He now recommended that the States should rely solely on Lewis guns – the advice the War Office had already given Jersey. The modest attempts by the two bailiwicks to take care of themselves had come to naught.

They could, however, make a financial contribution to the common cause. In the summer of 1939 the States of Guernsey voted £180,000 towards the cost of the Island's defence, which meant doubling income tax from 9d. to 1s. 6d. in the pound. This money was to be used to buy British government securities, which would be returned for cancellation. In Jersey the States decided unanimously in March 1940 to raise a loan of £100,000, which would be given to Britain as a first instalment. Lord Portsea, doughty champion of the Channel Islands all through the war, drew attention to the relative munificence of this gift in a letter to *The Times*.[2] He calculated that a proportionate amount from the United Kingdom would be £118,000,000.

In June 1938 – three months before the Munich crisis – the Home Office considered how to put the Channel Islands on to a war footing, if war came. Defence regulations would have to be brought in at short notice, and the Island authorities were asked to list what they were likely to need. Discussion of these matters should be restricted to the Bailiffs and the Attorney Generals. If too many people knew what was going on there might be alarm and despondency.

Munich, if it made war inevitable, also bought some time in which the Channel Islands, in common with the United Kingdom, could press on with their preparations. In April 1939 the Home Office proposed delegating to the States of Jersey and the Royal Court of Guernsey the power to make their own defence regulations. In the First World War these had been framed in the United Kingdom and sent, usually by post, to the self-governing territories; but it was now considered necessary to decentralize and to allow the territories to make their own regulations. There was every probability that the normal legislative processes in the Channel Islands, in which the Privy Council played an essential part, would be interrupted. The United Kingdom Emergency Powers (Defence) Act therefore provided that it should be extended to

[1] WO 106/2956.   [2] *The Times*, 19 March 1940.

the Islands. Under this act the States of Jersey and the Royal Court of Guernsey were substituted for the King in Council as the regulation-making authority. Both bailiwicks could now make their own defence regulations for the duration.[1]

However, they still had to give effect to some general United Kingdom regulations – for example, those relating to merchant shipping, trading with the enemy, and import and export control. Admiralty wartime measures had to be introduced. Navigation lights on ships had to be dimmed, and their other lights made invisible outboard. The necessary modification of lighthouse beacons made it difficult for the Channel Island mail steamers to operate; harbour masters were given discretion to provide whatever light they deemed essential, so long as the beacons did not act as reference points for enemy aircraft. Again, orders made by the United Kingdom Postmaster General controlling the ownership and use of radio transmitters were applied to the Islands.

Royal Proclamations were also used to keep the Islands' wartime arrangements in step with those of Britain, including the calling out of officers and men of the Royal Naval Reserve, and the specification of articles to be treated as contraband of war.

There was some purely local defence legislation. In Jersey, for example, protected areas were designated; racing and homing pigeons had to be notified to the authorities; Constables were authorized to take possession of any sand within their parishes for use in making sandbags; vehicles were banned from beaches during the hours of darkness; and driving between midnight and 5 a.m. was forbidden except under special licence.

Thus the Channel Islands were gradually put on a war footing by a blend of legislation: United Kingdom acts of parliament, given effect in the bailiwicks through Orders in Council, or by special clauses in the acts; United Kingdom defence regulations; Royal Proclamations, duly registered in the records of the Islands and publicly proclaimed; and their own defence regulations.

Planning to safeguard the Islands' food supplies and other essential needs in time of war began in 1938. The United Kingdom Food (Defence Plans) Department, which became the Ministry of Food, took

[1] Lord Coutanche, 'The Government of Jersey during the German Occupation', *Bulletin of the Société Jersiaise*, Vol. XIX (1965), pp. 33–53. The authorities differed for historical reasons. In Jersey the Royal Court ceased to legislate in 1771. In Guernsey in 1940 the Royal Court still had power to pass ordinances.

account of the needs of the Channel Islands in their overall plans. Reserves in Britain were intended to meet the requirements of all the surrounding Islands. Supplies would be sent through normal trade channels under a food controller. The Island authorities might nevertheless consider it prudent to build stocks of food for defence purposes, which would help to make the national position more secure. Details of the organization proposed for food distribution in the United Kingdom were sent in the hope that the Islands might make similar arrangements.[1]

It was left to the bailiwicks to decide what they needed. The Food Department offered technical advice and asked to be kept informed about their proposals so that they might be brought into the general plan for south-west England. They observed with cheerful optimism that the interruption of supplies through interference with shipping might cause anxiety in regard to foodstuffs, but as any hold-up would be temporary the less vital products could be shipped at convenient opportunities.[2]

The Islands were asked by the Home Office if they wanted to follow Britain's lead in increasing food production. If so, what additional quantities of equipment and fertilizers would they need? Jersey replied that given their methods of cultivation 'no endeavours to increase production in time of war would be necessary' – a strange assessment in the light of the sweeping changes forced on the Island by occupation. Guernsey said that her soil was already intensively cultivated and that there was little room for the expansion of arable farming. Most of her pastureland was needed for cattle for milk, butter, and meat. She proposed, however, to increase her use of fertilizers by one-fifth, although she agreed with Jersey that there was no scope for using more agricultural machinery.[3]

It was accepted that the two bailiwicks would adopt common standards with the United Kingdom in their wartime plans, but the Guernsey authorities maintained that they had no clear idea as to what was happening in Britain. They asked the Board of Trade what they should do 'so as to be in consonance with the British arrangements'. At first there was some confusion. A cargo of Canadian wheat destined for the Islands was detained in London because it was not realized that for the purposes of food distribution they were reckoned to be within the south-west region. The wheat was released only after an appeal to the Ministry of Food. That department, a few days old and properly

[1] HO 45/18650(900418).   [2] HO 45/18650(900418/4).
[3] HO 45/18650(900418); GF 1/2/4.

sensitive about its infant image, apologized, and ordered its many subordinate bodies not to make the same sort of mistake.

The Ministry pointed out at this time that it would help to have regular information about the needs of the Islands. They had asked that a joint committee should supply this, and while Guernsey had submitted figures, nothing had come from Jersey. This elicited a programme which indicated that for rationing purposes the population was being taken as 55,000 – a generous figure about 10 per cent above the usual estimate. It was not, however, challenged by the Ministry. Guernsey's estimate for the whole bailiwick was 42,600, which was rather more realistic.[1]

Special arrangements also had to be made to safeguard supplies of fuel and raw materials. The Mines Department in Britain was confident that there would be no problem over coal. If the enemy interrupted deliveries from one coalfield an alternative source would be found, but again it would be sensible to build stocks to tide the Islands over a temporary dislocation of deliveries. Fuel rationing would be introduced in Britain, and the Islands readily agreed to follow suit. They would be included in the petrol distribution scheme for south-west England. Supplies would come from Southampton. If the enemy put that port out of action another would be substituted. Britain planned to reduce usage by not less than one-third and it was assumed that the Islands would make a similar saving. The United Kingdom plans for government purchase and storage of metals and other raw materials made provision for the needs of the Islands, but, as in the case of food, they were advised to accumulate their own reserves.

Close collaboration between the two bailiwicks was desirable although their needs differed and could not readily be centralized. They could share the same shipping programme, however, and the Home Office suggested that the Insular authorities in Guernsey might consult with those of Jersey with a view to setting up a joint committee to handle their shipping arrangements.[2] It was also necessary to have parallel import controls with the United Kingdom. The Order prohibiting imports into Britain except under licence – to conserve shipping space – did not at first apply to the Islands, which was quickly spotted by those in Britain who could not get licences for Swiss watches, French agricultural machinery, shrubs from Belgium, and so on. To cope with this the Island authorities had to evolve their own control scheme, which came into force at the end of May, a month before all

[1] HO 45/18650(900418/5).　　　　[2] HO 45/18650(900418/4a).

B

leakages into the United Kingdom were effectively stopped by the German invasion.

In Jersey essential materials were controlled by a law of April 1939[1] based on the corresponding United Kingdom act. It covered commodities which the Island Defence Committee thought necessary as food for man, forage for animal, or fertilizer for land; and petrol, oil, coal and timber. This measure shows how slow the legislative machinery could be. It was passed by the States on 11 April, but it was not until 3 June that the Order in Council giving effect to it was registered. Thus nearly two months had elapsed between an urgent decision of the States and its implementation.

Air Raid Precautions, first studied in 1936, followed the United Kingdom pattern. Those in charge attended courses in Britain and passed on the techniques to volunteer wardens and fire-fighters. First aid and ambulance services were organized. Warning sirens were erected, a blackout imposed, gas masks issued – and, as in the United Kingdom, very soon ignored by their owners – emergency hospital accommodation planned, and decontamination centres established. Fire engines and trailer pumps were bought. It was arranged that air raid warnings in one bailiwick would be passed on to the other. A proposal that the Islands should have the benefit of the French air raid warning system was turned down on grounds of cost.[2]

However the United Kingdom authorities may have regarded the strategic importance of the Islands and their responsibility for defending them, they were surely under an obligation to include them in any general arrangements made for the safety of the people in Britain. Yet it was only when Island officials attended the A.R.P. Staff School in England that they learned that the special code which was to alert the A.R.P. services throughout Britain when war was imminent did not include the Channel Islands. This illustrates the sort of difficulty in which the two bailiwicks found themselves when making preparations for war in fields where their powers were not sovereign.

[1] Essential Commodities Reserves (Jersey) Law, 1939.
[2] JF W 5/1; 5/3.

2

Demilitarization

IN THE years between the world wars the United Kingdom authorities satisfied themselves that the Channel Islands had virtually no strategic value for Britain.

They were wide open to attack from France by sea and air. To defend them adequately would be costly, perhaps impossible. To defend them inadequately would expose the people to the horror and privation of war for no good reason. If they were captured by an enemy operating from France he would gain no strategic advantage but rather an economic liability. The two battalions of regular United Kingdom troops in the Islands suffered from lack of facilities for combined training because of their isolation; and it might be difficult to extricate them in time of war. In short, there was no strategic reason for maintaining a regular garrison there. Thus the Chiefs of Staff in the academic calm of 1925. The battalion was withdrawn from Jersey, but United Kingdom troops did remain in Guernsey until 1939.[1]

In 1928 the Committee of Imperial Defence accepted a War Office recommendation that there was no military reason for helping to finance the Island militias. This was a blow, and from time to time the Island authorities appealed for renewal of United Kingdom support in this field, but to no avail. The British government would not change its mind. The Channel Islands had no military value and the British taxpayer would not foot the bill for their therefore unnecessary defence.

With the Blitzkrieg sweeping irresistably across Europe the Chiefs of Staff now suddenly found that the academic memoranda of their

[1] The Second Battalion The Queen's Own Royal West Kent Regiment was withdrawn from Guernsey in 1930 and was not replaced until 1935, when the Second Battalion The Sherwood Foresters was stationed there. They remained until 1938 and were replaced by the First Battalion The Royal Irish Fusiliers, which was withdrawn in 1939.

predecessors were to be put dramatically to the test. Surprisingly, the Channel Islands might be lost to the Allied cause. Would it really matter? Were they truly worthless from the military, naval, and air point of view as had been contended for many years? The Lieutenant-Governor of Jersey had provided the War Office with an assessment of the situation on 28 May 1940. If his Island and the cable which now connected it – and therefore England – to France were of any importance, trained troops should be sent there from Guernsey, Alderney, or the mainland. He had at his disposal only about 150 members of the militia and a party of 50 naval ratings who had been sent to guard the airport. The ratings were all 'mechanicians'. Some had never handled a rifle. In any case he had been informed that they might be recalled to England at any moment. True, the local defence force was now being established, but only half of them would have rifles. The Island was virtually defenceless.[1]

On 5 June the Chief of the Imperial General Staff, General Sir John Dill, submitted a paper to the Chiefs of Staff Committee of the War Cabinet based on the Lieutenant-Governor's assessment. It is a document remarkable for its leisurely approach at a time when every second counted. It begins with the unhurried observation that the existence of armed forces in the Channel Islands is of great antiquity. As long ago as 578 A.D. both Jersey and Guernsey furnished bodies of armed men to fight the Bretons, and ever since they have periodically found themselves in conflict with the French, the most notable occasion being in 1781. The paper then examines the contribution of the Islanders in the First World War.[2]

So much for the historical survey. The questions that really matter are now answered. Possession of the Channel Islands will give the Germans bases of some importance which could be used to develop attacks on British lines of communication, on the areas in France still held by British forces, on the south coast of England, and on Eire. There is no immediate danger of full-scale invasion, but raids by motor torpedo boats are possible since the enemy now holds the coast of France less than 200 miles from the Channel Islands. His immediate target could be the cable to France, the destruction of which will cause great embarrassment. The only other remaining links with France are radio telephone between the Isle of Wight and Cherbourg and telegraph between Cuckmere and Le Havre. In both Jersey and Guernsey the cable is laid along the shore and is therefore vulnerable. It must be kept

[1] WO 106/2956.   [2] CAB 80/12; WO 106/2956.

open as long as possible, and both Lieutenant-Governors have been instructed to prevent sabotage, although it is admitted that their troops are incapable of dealing with even the smallest of raids. The memorandum concludes with lordly self-confidence: 'If the enemy effected a landing on these Islands, it would be essential to eject him as a matter of prestige.'

While the Chief of the Imperial General Staff was lucubrating on thirteen centuries of Channel Islands' military history and demonstrating that they had no strategic value, except for the cable, the Islands themselves were becoming increasingly aware of the impending danger. On 10 June the Lieutenant-Governor of Jersey sent a personal letter to Mr. C. G. Markbreiter, the Assistant Secretary at the Home Office concerned with Channel Islands affairs, 'written in an awful hurry to catch the post'. He confessed that he could not hazard an opinion about the strategic importance of the Islands, although he supposed that their fate would have little bearing on the winning of the war. If communications were vital, and if the port of St. Malo came into prominence, it was essential to retain them; but if the Germans reached Cherbourg, which they were now bombing, they would hardly leave the Channel Islands alone. The most Jersey could do was to deal with paratroops, saboteurs, and raiders from submarines and troop-carrying aircraft – and then only if they came in small numbers. If any sort of defence was called for he must have men and equipment.

He had discussed with the Bailiff what would happen if Jersey fell to the Germans. They assumed that the Bailiff would be required to carry on the administration under German orders, which Coutanche thought would betray his oath of allegiance. The Lieutenant-Governor disagreed. It would be better for the people as a whole if the Bailiff remained in office. He ended his letter with a grumble about being kept too much in the dark: 'One doesn't even know if the powers that be have considered at all what might happen to the Channel Islands, and if so what action they would be likely to take if they had any views. I think we ought to be taken into their confidence. We are British Isles, though too far away for much protection.'

Two days later – on the morning of 12 June – the Chief of the Imperial General Staff presented his paper to the War Cabinet. He reaffirmed the view that the Channel Islands had no great strategic importance. Nevertheless he considered that a certain measure of defence was desirable in Jersey and Guernsey. Indeed, because of the urgency of the situation the Chiefs of Staff had taken it upon themselves to order a battalion to each Island.[1] There had been no time to get the Prime Minister's prior approval but at least he had been informed. After discussion the War Cabinet gave covering approval to the despatch of the two battalions, and they also agreed that when they arrived in the Islands the training establishments there should be withdrawn. The Minister of Home Security was invited to prepare for the destruction of all facilities that might be of value to the enemy.

The Lieutenant-Governor of Jersey would no doubt have derived some comfort from the knowledge that his Island had been considered by the War Cabinet, but he had no inkling of what was happening in Whitehall. He continued to write officially to the War Office about the vulnerability of his position, and personally to Markbreiter in the hope that the Home Office would press the military authorities to provide 'some sort of defence in this Island'. Otherwise he could not guarantee to hold out against more than the smallest raid. At the airport, for example, he had only a few machine guns to oppose an enemy bombing attack.

In fact his gratification would have been short-lived, for the War Cabinet met again in the afternoon of 12 June and further discussed the Channel Islands, among other matters. The Secretary of State for War reminded his colleagues of their decision that morning to send two battalions to the Islands, and suggested that since the enemy would soon reach the French coast the decision should be reconsidered. This was agreed.

Next day the Chief of the Imperial General Staff provided a new appraisal on the assumption that the French coast was in enemy hands. The Islands would definitely cease to have any strategic importance. The cable would be useless, since the French end would be controlled by the Germans, who would also control important airfields on the mainland of France a short flying distance away. It was therefore pointless to risk losing the two battalions earmarked for the Islands, particularly as they might soon be sorely needed for the defence of Britain. He now advised that they should not go; that the remaining British troops[2] should be withdrawn at once; that the local forces should concern themselves solely with security and anti-sabotage measures; and that the preparation for the destruction of facilities should be pressed on with, so that

[1] CAB 80/12.

[2] Guernsey and Alderney District: 341st Machine Gun Training Centre (1,500 men); Detachments of R.E., R.A.S.C., and R.A.M.C. Jersey District: Army Technical School (Boys) (250); Detachments of R.E., R.A.S.C., Military Hospital.

it could readily be carried out in the event of invasion. He added that if his recommendations were approved by the War Cabinet the Lieutenant-Governors should be instructed to surrender if the Germans landed, to avoid useless bloodshed.[1]

The continued lack of guidance from the War Office and Home Office now began to worry the Lieutenant-Governor of Jersey. He and the Bailiff telephoned the Home Office on 14 June and were dismayed to learn that there was no news, except that the possibility of demilitarization was still under consideration by the War Cabinet. The Bailiff found this most unsatisfactory. If the Islands were to be defended many would want to leave and others would have to be evacuated on military grounds. For the next two days the Home Office tried to find out what was happening, without success.

The decision that the Islands should be left undefended was for all practical purposes taken on Saturday 15 June. The War Office, on the assumption that no troops would be sent from England to protect the airfields on Jersey and Guernsey, ordered that the personnel of the Machine Gun Training Centre (which was stationed on Alderney, where the airfield was of relatively little importance) should be used for their defence.[2] This would release a Canadian unit which had been standing by. Telegrams to both Lieutenant-Governors were drafted telling them that the policy was to protect the airfields so that the R.A.F. might use them as long as possible in supporting land operations in north-west France – while these continued. 'Thereafter the policy of demilitarization will rule.'[3]

On the same day the Admiralty made a small but negative contribution to clarifying the situation in the Islands. An official of that department, replying to the Lieutenant-Governor of Jersey's letter of a week earlier, was 'commanded by My Lords Commissioners of the Admiralty to inform you that, as the Fleet Air Arm has no further interest in Jersey, you have complete freedom, so far as My Lords are concerned, to take any measures you consider necessary for the immobilization of aircraft landing facilities in the Island.' It is not clear from the records whether a copy of this single-minded missive was sent to the Air Ministry, which still had a strong interest in keeping the airfields operational, having regard to the needs of Bomber and Fighter Commands.

On Sunday 16 June the Lieutenant-Governor of Jersey's patience began to run out. He sent a peevish signal to the War Office saying that

[1] CAB 79/5; WO 106/2956.   [2] WO 106/2956.   [3] WO 106/2957.

he presumed he would be told when to destroy the cable to France. His irritation cannot have been much assuaged by the laconic reply. He was told not to worry. The Admiralty and the Post Office had the matter well in hand. His opposite number in Guernsey asked if the aerodrome at Alderney, which was, of course, in his bailiwick, was to be destroyed. He too was not to worry. The Air Ministry had that in hand.[1]

The Lieutenant-Governors were also informed that a battery of Bofors guns was being sent to provide one troop each for the aerodromes in Jersey and Guernsey, and a third troop which could be used either at Jersey aerodrome or in St. Helier. A section of a Royal Engineers construction company was being moved to Guernsey from Gosport[2] – all this in spite of the earlier intention to leave the protection of the airfields to the Machine Gun Training Centre. The Admiralty might want to use the Channel Islands as staging posts for troops embarked from St. Malo, should the arrangements already made for their evacuation turn out to be inadequate. The Lieutenant-Governors were asked to assemble as many sea-going boats as possible and to have them ready to sail when the signal came – which it did later in the day, but only to Jersey. Guernsey was too far from St. Malo to be able to help at such short notice.

The Bailiff of Jersey asked the Commodore of St. Helier Yacht Club to send as many yachts as possible to St. Malo as soon as possible; four left almost at once. Fourteen more, which were laid up, followed 24 hours later. The first four reached St. Malo on the morning of Monday 17 June and began to ferry troops from the shore to the transports. By the time the others had arrived early on Tuesday morning most of the men had been successfully embarked, but they stood by and helped to take off the demolition parties. All the yachts returned safely to Jersey in the early hours of Wednesday, despite a strong wind and heavy seas. On 25 June the Commodore received a signal from the Admiralty thanking the Yacht Club for their contribution to the highly successful evacuation operation.[3]

[1] WO 106/2956.   [2] Ibid.

[3] Major C. E. Carrington, who was in command of No. 10 Air Intelligence Liaison Section, escaped to Jersey on 17 June and reported to the airport from which Blenheim fighters were still reconnoitring the German advance in France. He was asked by Cherbourg to bomb the coastal road, and found that the only way he could communicate with London was from a telephone kiosk. The only number he could remember was that of the War Office. He found a friend there – 'who happily had not gone to lunch' – and asked him to contact the Air Ministry. After the war he learned that this informal procedure had in fact proved effective.

Jersey and Guernsey were at least able to communicate with White-hall, and they had the minor satisfaction of knowing that the Home Office was trying to keep them in touch with events. But Mr. F. G. French, the Judge (Chief Administrator) of Alderney had no direct link with London. He did, however, see at first hand what was happening to the troops in his Island, without knowing exactly what was behind it. His own account, compiled shortly after he arrived back in England, vividly reflects the chaos prevailing in Alderney from the middle of June.

Orders came to evacuate the troops at 5 a.m. on 16 June, and in less than two hours the men were moving to the transports. There was a great deal of alarm and despondency, especially among the soldiers' wives. French consulted the commanding officer and it was agreed that he (French) should address the people in church – it being Sunday – to discount the inevitable rumours. He told the congregation that the withdrawal of the troops was perfectly normal, although admittedly it was being carried out rather hastily. The men were simply crossing to Jersey and Guernsey. The implication that the Island nearest to the advancing enemy was being left to its fate cannot have been reassuring, and the general alarm increased in the afternoon when the evacuation of the troops was suddenly speeded up.

Next day the departure of the troops became even more obviously an emergency measure, and panic further increased among the civilian population. Morale was also lowered by the arrival of boatloads of French soldiers and sailors who had escaped from the Cherbourg peninsula in a state of utter exhaustion. The main body of troops sailed after midnight, French (who had been unable to communicate satis-factorily with Guernsey) having asked them to explain Alderney's plight to the Lieutenant-Governor. The last party left on 18 June. Large quantities of military stores were abandoned on the quayside and in the arsenal, including the complete equipment of the new military hospital. French gathered a party of civilians to destroy them and to dispose of the remaining stocks of petrol and diesel oil.

Although the formal decision about demilitarization had still to be taken by the War Cabinet, on 16 June the Home Office followed the War Office's lead by concluding that the Islands must inevitably be demilitarized. They invited Jersey and Guernsey to send representa-tives to London immediately to discuss the implications. Next day, Sir Alexander Maxwell, the Permanent Under-Secretary, took the matter up with Sir James Grigg, his opposite number in the War Office. The

Islands were to be demilitarized 'at an early date'. Those concerned in the War Office were no doubt applying their minds to the position of the Lieutenant-Governors thereafter. Each was General Officer Commanding, in addition to being Lieutenant-Governor appointed by Royal Warrant. The Home Office thought it would be best to recall them when the last combatant units had left. The Bailiffs were Deputy Governors by virtue of their office and would carry on such civilian functions as remained. So far as the Home Office was concerned, they would be able to do all that was needed. One alternative – to divest the Lieutenant-Governors of their military function and leave them in the Islands as civil governors – seemed to have no advantage from any point of view.

A file note by Markbreiter on Monday 17 June records that although the Chiefs of Staff were still merely aiming at demilitarization, the meeting with the Islands' representatives had been arranged on the assumption that demilitarization would certainly take place. In the event Jurat E. A. Dorey of Jersey represented both Islands. Most of the discussion centred on whether evacuation should follow demilitarization. If so, what form should it take? There were 3,000 young men who had just become liable for service. It was agreed that they should be sent to the United Kingdom. There was also the problem of the 500 Irish labourers who had gone to the Islands to lift potatoes. It was felt that in spite of the security risk which they posed as not particularly friendly aliens they should also go to the United Kingdom. Otherwise they would probably cause trouble.

An open session of the Jersey States (there had been a series of secret sessions) was held on Wednesday 19 June. The Lieutenant-Governor said there was no need to remind the House how serious the situation was. All British troops had left France: in the final stages small craft from the Islands had rendered noble service in ferrying men to the transports. Although there was as yet no decision about demilitarization he himself thought it was inevitable. He had orders to send the troops under his command to Britain as soon as possible. Some had gone, and the rest would follow. He too might be ordered to leave, which he would do with the greatest reluctance. If the enemy did occupy the Islands the British government hoped that it would not be for long. Later in the session he was called to the telephone to take a message from London. The decision had been taken. The Islands were to be demilitarized.

In the War Cabinet the Prime Minister had not liked the paper recommending this. He said, it may be presumed with force, that British naval power could frustrate the invasion of the Islands. It was repugnant to abandon territory held by the Crown since the Norman Conquest. If there was the slightest chance of a successful resistance the Royal Navy must give battle. The Vice-Chief of Naval Staff, Vice-Admiral T. S. V. Phillips, pointed out, however, that the Islands could not be defended. It was impossible to provide them with the anti-aircraft guns and fighter planes needed without weakening the essential defences of the United Kingdom. They were too far from Britain and too near the enemy bases at Brest and Cherbourg for the navy to prevent invasion by sea. This the War Cabinet accepted. The Islands must be abandoned.

Dorey visited Guernsey on his return from London to brief the authorities there, and the Bailiff announced in the evening newspaper of 19 June that the United Kingdom government had decided to de-militarize the bailiwick. This meant the immediate demobilization of the Royal Guernsey Militia and the Defence Volunteers. Uniforms and equipment were to be handed in and all men to proceed quietly to their homes. Civilians should surrender arms in their possession to the Constable of their parish.[1]

In Jersey the States met again on 20 June, mainly to hear an account of Dorey's meetings in London. He had little to say about demilitariza-tion but spoke in glowing terms of the efforts which the Home Office officials had been making on behalf of the Islands, in particular Sir Alexander Maxwell and Markbreiter.

As soon as the War Cabinet decision was taken the War Office sent formal instructions to the Lieutenant-Governors. Once all the regular troops and training establishments had been withdrawn no attempt would be made to defend the Channel Islands against external invasion by sea or air. The S.S. *Biarritz* arrived at Guernsey at 4 a.m. on Thurs-day 20 June to embark the last of the troops there. The S.S. *Malines* arrived at Jersey at 8 a.m. on the same day with only two hours to com-plete embarkation if she was to leave on the same tide. The authorities in Jersey were instructed to cut the cable to France in consultation with the Post Office. Finally, the Lieutenant-Governors were told that when the troops had gone their function as Commanders-in-Chief would lapse. They would return to the United Kingdom.[2]

The evacuation of military personnel went according to plan. The *Biarritz* left punctually at 8 a.m. with roughly 1,000 troops. She also

---

[1] *The Guernsey Press.*   [2] WO 106/2956.

carried 85 French naval ratings and 91 civilians. The *Malines* left Jersey two hours later. The Lieutenant-Governor told the War Office that when the last man had gone he would await further instructions. They should be sent in plain language, as he would then have no one to decipher a coded message.[1]

The two Lieutenant-Governors duly departed on 21 June on naval vessels. Next day the Imperial General Staff were told that the military evacuation was complete. The Chiefs of Staff should ask the Foreign Office to inform the German government that the Islands had been demilitarized and declared undefended areas.[2] The Home Office, alive to the peculiar danger in which the Islands now stood – undefended but presumably regarded by the enemy as legitimate military targets – drafted a press notice declaring that it had been decided to demilitarize the Channel Islands; that all service personnel had been withdrawn; and that the civil government was being administered by the Bailiffs. This notice, prepared on 22 June, was withheld on the ground that it would be picked up by the Germans and regarded as an invitation to move into the Islands.

Two days later the Bailiffs received a message from the King. It ran:

For strategic reasons it has been found necessary to withdraw the armed forces from the Channel Islands. I deeply regret this necessity and I wish to assure my people in the Islands that in taking this decision my Government has not been unmindful of their position. It is in their interest that this step should be taken in present circumstances. The long association of the Islands with the Crown and the loyal service the people of the Islands have rendered to my ancestors and myself are guarantees that the link between us will remain unbroken and I know that my people in the Islands will look forward with the same confidence as I do to the day when the resolute fortitude with which we face our present difficulties will reap the reward of victory.

The Home Secretary, who had had no time to consult the Prime Minister before advising the King to send a message, told him after it had gone that everything possible had been done to ensure that it attracted no publicity outside the Islands. In his covering letters to the Bailiffs he said that the message was 'for communication to the people in such manner as may seem to you advisable having regard to the interests of national security'.[3]

This choice morsel of gobbledygook presumably meant that the widespread publication of the message in the Islands might bring it to

[1] Ibid.   [2] WO 106/2957.   [3] JFW 12.

the notice of the Germans, and that they would guess they had been demilitarized. That the Bailiffs did not read this into the covering letter was no doubt because they firmly believed that demilitarization had already been announced to the world. Had they realized that the reference to 'the interests of national security' meant keeping demilitarization dark, and therefore leaving the Islands exposed to any bombing attacks which the Luftwaffe might launch, the Bailiffs would have demanded that they be declared an open city.

The result of this unfortunate letter was that the King's message was not allowed to have the impact it deserved, for which the Island authorities were blamed.[1] If they were at fault it was for failing to see the inwardness of the letter and for not enquiring of the Home Office what the Home Secretary really meant.

Nothing more happened until the Chiefs of Staff considered a paper on 26 June repeating the suggestion that the Foreign Office should inform Germany that the Islands were undefended. The point was again made that this would be an invitation to the enemy to walk in, although it would save the civilian population from bombardment from the air. It was also suggested that the Germans were certain to know the position through their own intelligence channels. Although there was no advantage from the strictly military point of view in announcing demilitarization, some declaration might be advisable on humanitarian grounds. Having come to this conclusion they agreed, without any hint of urgency, to instruct the Secretary to draw the attention of the Foreign Office to the demilitarization of the Islands and to suggest that no declaration of demilitarization should be made by them unless they felt it advisable.[2]

On 28 June it was still the government's policy to maintain silence. A member of parliament put down a question about the evacuation of the civil population and was asked to withdraw it on the grounds of national security. The Home Secretary wrote to him: 'We have been at pains to prevent any publicity being given to the fact that a measure of evacuation from the Channel Islands has been carried out; and the newspapers in this country have been asked not to publish any statements which would indicate that this evacuation had taken place. There are military reasons for this which I would rather not put in writing.' The Home Secretary went on to say that it would be most inexpedient in the interests of the

[1] Cf. F. W. Falla, *The Silent War* (London, 1967), p. 14.
[2] CAB 79/5.

Channel Islands that any public statement should be made at the present time. He would be happy to explain the reasons to the member in private.

What he should have said was that it was essential in the interests of the Channel Islands to make a public statement about demilitarization at the earliest possible moment.

Later on the same day the Luftwaffe exposed the futility of the ultra-cautious line of the Chiefs of Staff and the pointless attempt of the Home Secretary to cover up demilitarization. They carried out bombing raids first on Guernsey and shortly afterwards on Jersey and met virtually no opposition. Sherwill, the Attorney General of Guernsey and President of the Controlling Committee, was speaking on the telephone to the Home Office in London when the attack on St. Peter Port began. He suggested, to the accompaniment of exploding bombs and with considerable restraint, that the announcement of the demilitarization of the Channel Islands might be broadcast as soon as possible. But the damage was done.

The United Kingdom authorities could do no more than try to save something from the wreck. That evening the B.B.C. nine o'clock news carried an announcement from the Home Office that in view of the German occupation of the parts of France nearest to the Channel Islands it had been decided to demilitarize them. All armed forces and equipment had been withdrawn. There was no reference to the German raids which had forced the belated announcement about demilitarization, although there was time enough to include the item in the same news bulletin.

It was not until the morning of 29 June that the Home Office released the news of the bombing, in what may seem to be a rather tendentious press notice. After giving details of the casualties the announcement concluded: 'As stated last night, the Channel Islands have been demilitarized and all armed forces and equipment have already been withdrawn.' The implication clearly was that the Germans had been outwitted. They had launched their attack after the British troops had made good their escape to the mainland.

It had now been forcibly brought home to the inhabitants that in the absence of an earlier formal declaration they were having the worst of both worlds. They had no means of defending themselves – not a single trained soldier, not a single effective weapon – and yet so far as the Germans were concerned they might have had a powerful garrison ready to fight to the last ditch. At a meeting of the Controlling Committee of Guernsey a member asked the pertinent question 'had the

British government informed the German government that Guernsey had been demilitarised?' There was no satisfactory answer. The members of the Committee must all have been aware that the news of demilitarization had been broadcast from London the night before, but a news item can hardly be regarded as a formal declaration by one government to another.[1] Until such a declaration had been made, the Islands were sitting ducks.

In the course of the discussion in the Committee it was suggested that if Guernsey guaranteed to abandon all export trade she might in turn be allowed by the Germans to receive one or two ships a month with the essentials of life. The President of the Committee was asked to take this up with his opposite number in Jersey, in the hope that an agreed plan might be put to the Home Office on behalf of both Islands.[2] But events soon made all thought on these lines academic.

The last act came on 30 June when the Foreign Office addressed a communication to the United States Ambassador in London, Mr. Joseph P.Kennedy. He was asked to be good enough to transmit as soon as possible through the United States Embassy in Berlin the following message for the German government:

The evacuation of all military personnel and equipment from the Channel Islands was completed some days ago. The Islands are therefore demilitarized and cannot be considered in any way as a legitimate target for bombardment. A public announcement to this effect was made on the evening of June 28.

The German government and their commanders in the field did not know for certain that the Islands were undefended when the raids were carried out on 28 June. Now at least they could not pretend ignorance.

Two points call for comment: the belated decision not to defend the Islands; and the delay in announcing it.

Why did the Chiefs of Staff take so long to arrive at the conclusion which their predecessors had come to over and over again – that the Islands had no strategic value? It can be said in their defence that the earlier studies did not assume that a British expeditionary force would be bundled unceremoniously into the sea, partly in the neighbourhood of the Channel Islands. Indeed, if those who made their earlier assessments had based their conclusions on this possibility, their qualification for high rank might have been called in question.

The situation which the Chiefs of Staff faced had important new

[1] CCM 29 June 1940.   [2] Ibid.

elements. One was the cable link with France through the Channel Islands, which became more vital as the Germans moved westwards and broke other lines of communication. The extension of the cable from Le Fliquet in Jersey to Pirou in the Cherbourg peninsula had been completed only on 1 August 1939. On the outbreak of war it was decided to duplicate the whole system. The leg connecting Pirou to the main French network at St. Lô was begun in January 1940, the work being directed by the British Post Office. The job was still unfinished when the German advance cut off the Channel ports from Britain, which meant that supplies of cable had to come 150 miles by road from St. Malo. Nevertheless, on 10 June the land system was completed and linked with the submarine cable from Jersey. On 15 June the Post Office engineers withdrew, leaving a brand new communications link which the Germans gratefully took over a fortnight later.[1] Had this link with France existed when the Chiefs of Staff made their earlier studies they would have rated more highly the importance of the Islands.

Secondly, the airfields, which were of little use for general operational purposes (although Jersey was once used as a staging post for a raid on Italy), assumed temporary importance during the final stages of the rout in France. It would have been foolish to deny the R.A.F. even a tiny port in a storm that was raging.

Thirdly, the Islands provided an escape route from France, especially for the British troops who had been swept to the neighbourhood of St. Malo. It was essential to keep them available so long as there was still a chance that troops would have to come through them.

There was therefore for a few days a case for keeping up the pretence that the Islands were defended; but most of the troops escaped from St. Malo by 17 June, and the last few were brought out on the following day.[2] The regular troops had all left the Islands by 21 June. The civilian evacuation ended on 23 June. Demilitarization should have been announced at the very latest on 24 June.

The idea that keeping the Germans in the dark would serve some useful purpose was nonsense. According to earlier studies, occupation of the Islands would bring an enemy no strategic advantage but rather an

---

[1] W. R. Tyson, 'Channel Islands Communications and the War', *The Post Office Electrical Engineers' Journal*, vol. 38 (1946), pp. 102–4.

[2] 'Meanwhile embarkation had also been proceeding at St. Malo, whence the 1st Canadian Division sailed for home on the 16th. By the evening of the 17th 21,474 men had been embarked without loss and, early next day, the final search was made for stragglers.' S. W. Roskill, *The War at Sea 1939–1945* (London, 1954–61), vol. i, p. 233.

economic liability. If so, the sooner they were saddled with it the better. To conceal that the Islands were undefended would at best restrain the invading forces for a few days, without affecting the long-term course of events; and it could well have exposed the civilian population to a devastating attack against which they had no defence. If the German High Command had concluded that the Islands were heavily fortified – as some of their advisers believed – the consequences could have been very serious.

The Chiefs of Staff made an almost unbelievable error at their meeting on 26 June when they accepted that 'it was almost certain that Germany would have learned of the demilitarisation through intelligence channels and would therefore be unlikely to waste her resources in bombarding the Islands'.[1] The same mistake was made in a debate in the House of Commons, when it was argued that demilitarization had been effectively announced to the world when the newspapers printed the Lieutenant-Governor's speech to the States in Jersey. One member said: 'I have seen a copy of the paper, and it certainly has a full report of the States meeting and the announcement of the Lieutenant-Governor. The German authorities must have got possession of papers from the Islands fairly early and known that they were demilitarised and that therefore it was open to them to occupy the Islands. Demilitarisation was thus announced on 19 June.'[2] This may have been a reasonable assumption, but in fact the Germans knew nothing of the newspaper report.[3] The British government was right to keep silent until the voluntary evacuation was completed on 23 June, but after that the Islanders were left at the mercy of the Luftwaffe for no good reason.

In replying to the debate the Under-Secretary of State for the Home Department, Mr. O. Peake, said: 'To have announced the demilitarisation at that stage (i.e. 19 June) publicly in this country, or over the wireless, would have been to invite the Germans to take immediate possession of the Islands, and for that reason no announcement was made.'[4] True enough of 19 June, but had the House known the timing of the related events Peake's argument would have been torn to shreds. It was madness not to inform the German government as soon as it could be done safely, simply on the assumption that their High Command were regular subscribers to the Islands' newspapers.

---

[1] CAB 79/5.
[3] See Chapter IV.
[2] Hansard (Commons) vol. 363, col. 1357.
[4] Hansard (Commons) vol. 363, col. 1363.

The Home Office was left with the difficult task of presenting the sequence of events in the best possible light. The strategic withdrawal from the Channel Islands had to be revealed as a sensible and successful plan. It was no doubt for this reason that the news of the air raids was held up until after the belated announcement of demilitarization, in the expectation that the public would gain the impression that the Luftwaffe had launched a cowardly attack as soon as they knew the Islands were undefended. Whether or not this was done deliberately, the truth – that the declaration that the troops had left had been forced out by the German attacks – did not become obvious.[1]

In reporting the air raids the following day *The Times* took its cue from the Home Office statements, perhaps with a little encouragement. It said that the German air force had murdered 33 civilians in the Channel Islands, 'which had been made and declared a demilitarised area some days previously'. This was just not true. The Islands had been made a demilitarized area on 21 June; and they were declared to be un-defended on 28 June, but only in a news broadcast. It was not until 30 June that the formal process of notifying the German government began.

This did not prevent the newspaper from going on to argue that morally speaking the attack was worse even than those made on columns of refugees in France. They at least were in an area of military operations, whereas in the Channel Islands the victims were not. 'It was as if Paris had been bombed after having been declared an open town and after the armies had retired to the south of it.'[2] In a leading article a few days later this error was compounded when it was observed that demilitarization had not saved the Channel Islands from a particularly barbaric attack.[3]

It was just as well that the newspapers did not carry an accurate account of the way the Chiefs of Staff had handled this small element in the struggle. It would have raised one more doubt in the minds of the British people about the mastery with which the war effort was being managed at this chaotic moment in their history.

[1] Mr. Emanuel Shinwell, M.P. (later Lord Shinwell) asked the Home Secretary on 18 July about the intervals between demilitarization and the air raids, and the demilitarization decision and its announcement. The reply was a masterpiece of misleading half-truth: 'There was an interval of some days between the date when arrangements were put into operation for demilitarizing the Islands and the date on which demilitarization was publicly announced. To have made the public announcement earlier would have been tantamount to inviting the enemy to occupy the Islands or to attack the ships engaged in the evacuation operations.' Hansard (Commons) vol. 363, col. 390.

[2] *The Times*, 1 July 1940.   [3] *The Times*, 5 July 1940.

3

Preparation for Occupation

THE possibility that the Channel Islands might have to be evacuated had been considered immediately before the war. The Foreign Office studied the problem of bringing British subjects from Europe but the Channel Islands' evacuation was seen merely as part of the total obscure picture. It was estimated that the mail steamers normally serving the Islands could carry 6,400 people to England every 24 hours.[1] This was based on peacetime standards of safety. In an emergency many more could be carried.

There was no further attempt at contingency planning. The control of movement between the Islands and the United Kingdom introduced at the beginning of the war was relaxed in March 1940 when the Home Secretary said that it was no longer necessary to restrict travel.[2] His announcement on the eve of the holiday season carried the clear implication that the government saw no reason why people should not flock in their accustomed thousands to enjoy a peaceful holiday in Jersey, Guernsey, Alderney, or Sark.

It may seem strange that at a time when the evacuation of government departments in Britain had been planned to the uttermost detail – a single whispered codeword could instantly move a whole Ministry, armbanded and labelled, complete with files, typewriters and other paraphernalia from Whitehall to a relatively safe castle in the depths of the country – no thought had been devoted to the Channel Islands or to British holiday-makers there. It meant that when the War Cabinet considered demilitarization they had no brief on the related question of evacuation. The Minister of Home Security was anxious to study whether women and children should be brought out on a free and

---

[1] HO 45 18650(900418/3).
[2] Hansard (Commons) vol. 358, col. 1367.

voluntary basis. He thought that the true inhabitants would not take advantage of such an offer, and that the well-to-do settlers would fend for themselves. If general evacuation was wanted it would have to be organized by the Islands.

On 10 June the Lieutenant-Governor of Jersey wrote to Markbreiter: 'They are beginning to fuss about the evacuation of children, but I take it you agree with me that it is really ought [sic] of the question from here.' The letter was written in his own hand by an exhausted man. He concluded by saying: 'Don't worry over this letter, it is private to you just to see if you can find out anything about Policy or Strategy. I'm quite serene and don't care too [sic] hoots except for the big thing.' He was probably trying to say that the people as a whole thought that children should be sent to England, and that this would have to be arranged from London.

The Chiefs of Staff thought at first on the same lines. They decided on 11 June that troops must be sent to the Islands to secure them against minor raids. It followed that women and children should be given a chance to leave at once 'since we cannot contemplate the evacuation of large numbers of civilians under heavy air attack'. But when they met again and reversed the recommendation about sending troops they advised that 'as the Islands will have been demilitarised it will be unnecessary and undesirable to evacuate women and children, and that the Ministry of Home Security should be so informed'.[1]

On 14 June Harrison and Coutanche telephoned Markbreiter but he could only say that the War Cabinet were still considering evacuation. Coutanche thought that Jersey should arrange to send away those of the native population who wanted to leave – he too believed that the 'settlers' could look after themselves. He accepted, however, that the decision must wait until the strategic role of the Islands had been determined. Markbreiter sounded him out on the question of costs, and gathered that he considered that Jersey should foot the bill only if people left voluntarily. By 16 June the Home Office assumed that the Islands must be abandoned to their fate, and began to examine evacuation seriously. Yet when Sherwill asked if the United Kingdom government would evacuate Guernsey's children, simply because they might suffer through food shortage, the Ministry of Food replied that his fears were groundless.

When Home Office officials met Jurat Dorey of Jersey (representing both bailiwicks) on 18 June he stated that in addition to men of military

[1] CAB 79/5.

age there were about 30,000 women and children who should leave; he was told that the Home Secretary would agree to this. He at once telephoned Jersey and Guernsey so that the necessary arrangements could be put in hand. Next day the War Cabinet took the formal decision not to defend the Channel Islands, and the Home Secretary said that the Islanders must be given the chance of coming to Britain. The arrangements would be made by their own governments. Further, for the taxpayer must not be forgotten even when Armageddon is only just around the corner, they – the Islands – would bear the cost. The War Cabinet agreed that the evacuation of women and children should be considered, in spite of the earlier advice that it was 'unnecessary and undesirable'.[1]

There was still a good deal of confusion among the United Kingdom authorities as to what the policy really was. For example, the Director of Sea Transport told the Commander-in-Chief, Portsmouth, in whose area the evacuation ships would have to be found, that 'the Home Office have decided that it is not the policy to evacuate the Channel Islands'. The Lieutenant-Governor of Jersey, on the other hand, announced that the British government hoped to evacuate the bulk of those who wanted to go; but he felt that many who had their roots in the soil would not want to leave.[2]

The Permanent Under-Secretary at the Home Office informed the Lieutenant-Governors in both bailiwicks that if they were recalled the government wanted the Bailiffs to discharge the duties of Lieutenant-Governor, which would now be purely civil. The Bailiffs and the Crown Officers should stay at their posts – whether or not they were in a position to receive instructions from His Majesty's Government. In short, occupation was now seen to be inevitable, although no one said it in so many words, and it was up to the Bailiffs to make their preparations in such a way that there would be the least disruption to the lives of the people.[3]

In Jersey, Dorey's message about the possibility of evacuation caused consternation throughout the Island, partly, in Coutanche's view, because the people believed that Jersey was going to be defended by the troops who had escaped there from St. Malo. Had there been time to evolve even a makeshift plan an orderly evacuation would have been possible; but the rumour that the Island was to be abandoned spread and panic became general. On 20 June the Lieutenant-Governor reported to the War Office by telephone that things were rather difficult.

[1] WO 106/2956. [2] *The Morning News*, 20 June 1940. [3] NG 01/3.

Many people were doing their best to get away, and they were inclined to panic.[1]

In the States in Jersey on 20 June Dorey said that English people might well want to leave; but he did not understand why those of old Norman stock who should be rooted to the soil were so anxious to get out. The House should express their utter contempt for them. Men of military age should be sent to England. They had an honourable mission and should not be mixed up with rabbits and rats. He hoped that everything would be done to prevent the latter from leaving.

The Bailiff, Crown Officers, and Jurats declared that they were all remaining at their posts. Coutanche addressed a huge crowd in the Royal Square. They had one duty – to keep calm. He knew that many wanted to leave, and it was up to each to act according to his conscience. 'I will never leave, and my wife will be by my side.' He would do his duty, as would the Crown Officers and the members of the States. He then called on the crowd to join with him in singing the national anthem, which they did with great fervour. Later he wrote: 'He would have been a brave man who at that moment of the evacuation would have taken responsibility of advising any person to go or stay. All that could be done was to show a good example.'

It was announced in the press on 19 June that the United Kingdom government was providing ships to evacuate women and children, men between 20 and 33 who wanted to join the forces, and, so far as accommodation permitted, for other men. Names had to be handed in before 10 a.m. the next day, by which time about 8,800 had registered, including 434 volunteers for the forces. The final figure for registrations was just over 23,000, but many, impressed by Coutanche's resolution, changed their minds. The total number who left was under 10,000.

Much the same general line was followed in Guernsey, yet the end result was very different. It was announced on 19 June that children of school age, younger children accompanied by their mothers, men of military age, and 'all others' would have to register for evacuation that evening. It was thus open to the whole population to leave. The sudden announcement caused panic, for there was little time for families to consider what they should do. In the Royal Court next day the Attorney General tried to calm things down. He denied a rumour that the Bailiff and Royal Court members had left. The run on the banks was quite unnecessary, and must stop. Arrangements had been made for 2,000 to leave, and more ships were on the way from England. He then said,

[1] WO 106/2956.

surprisingly, that after the mothers and children and the men of military age had gone 'it is improbable that any more people will be evacuated'. This added to the confusion as it had been implied earlier that anyone who wanted to leave could do so.

Sherwill tried to clarify the position on 21 June by asking the Home Office for authority to evacuate the wives of men leaving to join the forces (presumably with the same priority as their husbands). He added, in spite of his statement in the Royal Court, that he proposed to evacuate others, including men, to the extent that there was room for them. The Home Office then compared notes with the Bailiff of Jersey. Had he allowed the wives of volunteers to go? Coutanche said yes. His evacuation was now almost complete. Few had left, and Jersey was calm. The Home Office then spoke again to Sherwill, who revealed that he had decided not to announce that men other than volunteers could leave. The Bailiff endorsed this line on the same day: 'It is impracticable for others [i.e. those not covered by the special classes] to hope to be evacuated.'

In their attempts to dispel panic the authorities in Guernsey carried out a powerful anti-evacuation campaign, which had much less impact than Coutanche's speech in the Royal Square in St. Helier. Their attitude seemed strange to at least one neutral observer. The commander of H.M.S. *Sabre* sent a signal to the Admiralty informing them that much confusion was being caused in Guernsey by anti-evacuation propaganda. 'Suggest this should be exposed as being of enemy origin and a vigorous counter-propaganda campaign instituted.' A member of the States broadcast each evening on a public address system 'doing his best to dispel rumour and furnish the public with the truth', which to him meant that it was better for everyone to remain in the Island.[1]

The truth, as seen by the doctors in Guernsey, was different. Mr. John Leale said in the States on 21 June: 'I met the local doctors this morning, and they assured me – I asked them the question – that we can maintain health on milk and vegetables.' Two days later the doctors told the Attorney General that total evacuation was necessary.[2] Under occupation there would be a real danger of epidemics. It would be

[1] CCM 25 June 1940.
[2] In his unpublished memoirs Sherwill gives an account of his meeting with the doctors: 'One of them argued that total evacuation was necessary to avoid starvation . . . I had never before, nor have I since, felt waves of panic emanating from a person near me. They were affecting my own judgement and, but for politeness sake, I would have asked the source of them to go and sit at the other end of the room. In contrast I well remember the resolution of the oldest doctor of them all, Dr Arderne Wilson, who argued that despite grave hardships we should survive.'

difficult to keep the water supply pure, food would be scarce, and there would be inadequate heating in winter. Sherwill believed that even if they were right, total evacuation was now impracticable. Nevertheless he sent one of their number, Dr. W. J. Montague, to the Home Office to ask them to consider it.

Montague told Markbreiter that Sherwill thought that everybody should leave Guernsey, and that others agreed with him. This surprised Markbreiter. He immediately telephoned Sherwill, who said that if they were occupied they would have an unpleasant time and would find living very hard; but if it was inevitable they could get by. Leale, who was with him, agreed, but added that both could do more useful work in Britain. They found it difficult to assess the feeling in the bailiwick as a whole. They reaffirmed that they would have preferred total evacuation; but if the British government thought it wrong they would not press the matter. The doctors would accept the decision of the Island authorities, although they – the doctors – still thought that everyone should leave.

The letter which Montague carried said that he was being directed to go to England for racial reasons and that he must not come back until after the war. He was an able doctor of sterling character, who had volunteered to remain in Guernsey in spite of the special dangers which German occupation would hold for him.

The evacuations were handled very differently in Jersey and Guernsey. Coutanche firmly grasped the nettle and was never in any doubt as to the proper course. After the initial panic he succeeded in imposing his will on the people. He thought that most should remain, and remain they did. There is little doubt that if he had come to the conclusion that all should go the great majority would have left.

In Guernsey, however, although the authorities at first thought that people should not leave, they had no single-minded leader of the calibre of Coutanche to carry the Islanders with him. The Bailiff was not strong, and it was left to Sherwill to decide policy; but he did not have the weight of the Bailiff's office behind him, and he may have been inhibited from recommending without hesitation what he thought was right. In fact he was far from certain what *was* right and perhaps his indecision communicated itself to his colleagues and to the people. To begin with he seemed to be opposed to total evacuation; but later, influenced by the doctors, he decided that the more who went the better. By this time it was too late to organize wholesale evacuation.

One factor probably contributed to the different line in the two Islands. The Lieutenant-Governor of Jersey had been in office for a year. He had learned a great deal about the Island and worked in close co-operation with Coutanche, who probably derived additional strength from their association. The Lieutenant-Governor of Guernsey took office only on 7 June 1940, and clearly had no time to master the problems of the bailiwick or to strike up an understanding with the authorities. Some of the uncertainty in Guernsey must have stemmed from this.

The evacuation problem in Alderney was smaller, since there were just over 1,000 people there. The Island, as part of the bailiwick of Guernsey, looked to the Bailiff for guidance on important matters; but in the weeks before the Germans arrived there was little communication between Guernsey and Alderney. On 12 and 13 June fishing boats began to arrive from France with refugees from Boulogne and St. Valéry. This had its effect on the people, who began to hire boats to take them to Guernsey to join the mail steamer for the United Kingdom. The crews brought back disturbing rumours about affairs on other Islands. Alarm increased on 17 June when it became known that the troops were to be recalled to England. All work on the farms stopped. The mailboat was due, but never turned up. More refugees arrived from France in a state of utter exhaustion.

As Judge French drove round St. Anne his car was stopped by 'groups of Island men in obvious panic' demanding that he should arrange to evacuate them. He telegraphed Guernsey for permission to handle the situation as he saw fit, but received no reply. He sent a second telegram and this time was told to do nothing without the approval of the Alderney States. But the States could not remain in constant session and the situation was changing from hour to hour. On 18 June the *Courier* took off the families of soldiers and brought the alarming news that civilians were leaving Guernsey. The ruthless abandonment of all military stores heightened the alarm, and the clamour that something must be done increased.

Then on 19 June a telegram came from the Lieutenant-Governor in Guernsey giving French discretion to do whatever seemed necessary. He at once formed an Executive Committee with the only three Jurats who remained unshaken and himself as President. It was now possible to make some progress but as it turned out the next ship to arrive, the *Glen Tilt*, was under instructions to take only French troops. Then came the *Sheringham*, which was supposed (on whose authority it was not clear) to take only children of school age, accompanied by teachers but *not* their mothers, and men of military age. This caused great distress, but French insisted that the ships should carry only the special categories which the masters stipulated.

Next day he despatched a fishing boat to Guernsey with urgent mail and a request that Alderney should have the same evacuation facilities as Guernsey. It returned on 21 June with a letter from Sherwill promising to send supplies for as long as possible. French deduced from the letter, perhaps unfairly, that Guernsey was doing nothing to help Alderney, and after consulting his Executive Committee decided to appeal direct to the Admiralty for a ship to evacuate anyone who wanted to leave. He may have been influenced by Sherwill's statement that 'we have evacuated masses of our population and expect to complete it by tomorrow night' (i.e. 22 June), which French took to mean that everybody would have gone, although in fact it only meant that the planned evacuation would be completed.

The Trinity House ship *Vestal* arrived at Alderney on 22 June to take off the lighthouse personnel and their families. The captain offered to take 150 civilians as well. French refused the offer lest there should be a dangerous rush in which people might be injured. He did, however, ask the captain to ensure that ships would come to evacuate the whole of the population. He summoned the people and told them what he had done. If ships came promptly the authorities in the United Kingdom must regard the position as serious. If none came, there was no danger.

Early next morning it became evident that French's request for ships had borne fruit. Six arrived with instructions to embark all who wanted to go; and it was concluded on the basis of the Judge's formula that *everybody* must go. Embarkation began at 10 a.m. People, seeing that there was plenty of room, proceeded on board in a 'very orderly and obedient fashion'. French went on the first ship as he wanted to supervise the reception arrangements. The last, carrying considerable quantities of stores abandoned by the troops, sailed at noon. Only 20 of the 1,100 still on the Island remained behind. The airfield was left obstructed with barbed wire and *chevaux de frise*, and the wireless transmitter was destroyed.[1]

The *Courier* called at the Island on the evening of 27 June and found volunteers from Guernsey rounding up livestock. The master had been given the keys of the church so that he could bring away the plate and records. He also loaded more of the abandoned military stores before sailing for Guernsey next evening, to pick up stores left

[1] GF 1/1/16.

there; but he soon saw signs of the German air raid on St. Peter Port. He decided to return to Alderney to take off the few people still there, and then make for St. Sampson's on the east coast of Guernsey; but on the way they spotted the silhouettes of the *Isle of Sark* and the *Sheringham*, apparently bound for England undamaged, and they assumed that St. Peter Port must now be safe. When they got there they found that the stores had been destroyed in the raid. The master judged that the morale of the Islanders had been badly shaken by the bombing. 'Many tales of "hate of England" came to my ears for leaving them unprotected.' These, he thought, were undoubtedly boosted by a fifth column – a strange echo of the comment by the commander of H.M.S. *Sabre*.

Later French explained why the evacuation of Alderney happened as it did. The people were influenced by the sudden departure of the military, the panic evacuation of soldiers' wives, the ruthless destruction of military stores, tales of French refugees, the signs of war on the Cherbourg peninsula, the reported evacuation of Guernsey, and the feeling that the Guernsey authorities were either panicking and incapable of dealing with the situation, or that they were 'deliberately seeing after themselves and their own people'.

Sherwill's version of Guernsey's share in these events (written many years later) puts it in a different light. Communication was difficult because the radio telephone was banned on security grounds. He assumed that Alderney, like Sark, would stay put, but he nevertheless sent the *Sheringham*, 'which could at a pinch have brought away the whole population', to evacuate anyone who wished to leave. In the event the master took only children, teachers, and men of military age. When the ship came back to Guernsey with only a handful of refugees other than these classes, Sherwill concluded that no one wanted to leave, or that something approaching panic had engulfed those in authority. He therefore asked the Ministry of Shipping to send more ships to Alderney; he believed that this rather than French's request made it possible to complete the evacuation.

It is now apparent that the misunderstandings were due to poor communications and the fact that Sherwill and French were under extraordinary pressures. Sherwill was led to believe that French was panic-stricken, and French thought that Sherwill was either panicking or deliberately looking after Guernsey's interests at the expense of those of Alderney. Had it been possible for them to talk calmly to each other there would almost certainly have been no problem. Each blamed the other, but the verdict must be that neither was to blame.

Sark also had the right to expect some guidance from Guernsey. *La Dame de Serk* (Mrs. Robert Hathaway),[1] the Island's feudal ruler since 1926, had an easier job than Judge French. Sark was near enough to Guernsey for her to find out what was going on. Her control over the people, whom she ruled with a rod of benevolent iron, and whom she knew intimately, was greater than that of either the Guernsey or Alderney authorities.

She summed up the situation in a letter of 24 June. She had been in Guernsey when the panic started there. 'No one took any lead and *explained*.' The Islands had been demilitarized, so there was no danger of attack. Whatever happened in Guernsey 'we stay and see this Island through'. Mrs. Hathaway also kept the Home Office in the picture. Work was proceeding normally. Not one native had left. There had been panic when the news of evacuation first came but now all was quiet. The English residents had gone and 471 people were left. The crops were good, there were plenty of cattle and pigs, and a fair amount of wheat. 'Officially Guernsey has forgotten us, and we have not had any instructions as regards the situation at all. The responsibility of advising people to go or remain falls on me and I should be thankful for any assurance or hints from you. Personally I remain unless ordered to leave, and all the Sarkese remain also.' The English in Sark had asked whether they should go or stay. She told them that if they had somewhere to go in England they must make up their own minds. If they had nowhere to go they were welcome to stay in Sark.

In his unpublished memoirs Sherwill observes: 'In Sark, under the leadership of La Dame, calm reigned. We had offered them a ship to bring away those wishing to leave. Our offer was declined. Scarcely anyone left or sought to leave. Such is the effect of leadership.'

Contemporary accounts of the evacuation reveal how chaotic the whole operation was. In Jersey:

Twenty-three thousand people out of a population of fifty thousand, queued up at the Town Hall to register their names for embarkation, but such was the disorganisation that the next day people who had registered were bundled on to the boats indiscriminately with those who had not, whilst hundreds more waited on the quays in the glaring sun with their

[1] *La Dame* married Mr. Robert Hathaway in 1929, her second marriage. Mr. Hathaway was an American who served with the Royal Flying Corps in the First World War and later became a naturalized British subject. He died in 1954. Mrs. Hathaway, who was appointed D.B.E. in 1965, died in 1974.

weeping and hungry children for twelve to twenty-four hours before they were taken aboard small boats, mail boats, coal boats and potato boats. Without food, without water, these poor devils endured sea passages ranging from six to twenty-four hours.

Bars, cinemas, and shops were closed. Stray dogs were shot by the hundred. Cattle were turned loose. Cars were abandoned on the jetty. The rumour spread that Alderney was completely evacuated. There was a run on the banks. 'The queue to the Southern Railway Company's offices stretched right down the streets and people waited all day to book accommodation. The queues outside the post offices were prodigious . . . In all this chaos we managed to get berths on the *Isle of Sark*, the mailboat for Friday 28th June.'

The mailboat called as usual at St. Peter Port in Guernsey and was on the point of sailing in the evening when:

Three planes with their engines shut off swooped out of the sun . . . There was a terrific explosion as the first bomb fell, splinters rattled on to the deck and a man standing next to my small boy sagged on to the deck with the blood pouring from a wound in the groin . . . some ran to get below, but others less lucky, chose to panic down the gangway plank and make for the sheds and warehouses on the wharf. They were caught by a raking machine gun fire from the second and third Nazi planes and went down in rows like ninepins. The policeman taking the tickets on the gangway was blown into pieces and the sheds went up in flames.[1]

In Jersey, Sinel recorded: 'Unfortunately the suddenness of the decision flung the Island into a panic and long queues were formed by people waiting to register at the Town Hall for accommodation on the boats. This was indeed a severe testing time for many folk who were faced with making perhaps the greatest decision of their lives . . . Hundreds of houses and farms are abandoned, also cars, cycles, and domestic animals.'[2] Ralph Mollet, also writing of Jersey, says:

When this information [the news about demilitarization] reached the public, a considerable amount of panic ensued . . . The telephones were working without cessation, trunk calls and telegrams were very long in transmission. Everyone was asking his neighbour what he was going to do. Many buried their valuables. Thursday 20th. The panic was at its height. Long queues of cars were waiting to take their occupants to board the government ships.[3]

Ralph Durand has left a graphic picture of the position in Guernsey:

[1] Mrs. R. J. Stephen, in *King-Hall Newsletter*, 2 August 1940.
[2] L. P. Sinel, *The German Occupation of Jersey* (Jersey, 1945), p. 11.
[3] R. Mollet, *Jersey Under the Swastika* (Jersey, 1945), p. 17.

In the country, the panic was worse than in the town. . . . Some farmers killed cattle that in the months to come could ill be spared. Some people before abandoning their homes turned their pet animals out of doors to fend for themselves; some with still less humanity left fowls and rabbits shut up without food or water. Some houses were left open, beds un-made and the remains of a hurried morning meal on the table. Other houses were so securely locked that men authorized soon afterwards to collect perishable food from abandoned houses had difficulty in entering. A tobacconist gave away his entire stock before closing his premises and a publican before leaving invited his neighbours to go into his bar and help themselves to the liquor there. Panic is bad enough when the panickers are otherwise sober, but panic inflamed by drunken-ness degenerates into sheer madness.[1]

The transport of the evacuees, first to Weymouth and then on to their wartime homes further north, was well managed considering how short the notice was. The first stage was much less comfortable than the normal mail steamer trip; but there was a war on – a war which at that point Britain looked like losing. Three States' officials accompanied the Guernsey contingents and worked with the civic authorities in Wey-mouth, and with officials of the Ministry of Health. There were doctors to look after the sick and ambulances to take serious cases to hospital. The evacuees were given a meal before being sent by special trains to three main destinations – Lancashire, Yorkshire, and Scotland. Those of independent means left to find friends or relatives, some of whom had moved to safer areas and could not be found.[2] The Controlling Com-mittee in Guernsey received a satisfactory report about the reception of the evacuees.[3] The United Kingdom authorities had provided relief in a small number of cases; but the States in both Islands had already agreed to support those evacuees who could not support themselves.

An account of life in England as an evacuee is given by Mr. E. J. Hamel, a Post Office employee at St. Peter Port. He makes the common complaint that 'except for advising men of military age to leave the island, officialdom gave no lead. It neither said you should go, nor did it advise you to stay'. After much heart-searching he decided that he and his family should go, and they found themselves at Weymouth on the evening of 22 June. Only stretcher cases and their relatives were allowed

---

[1] R. Durand, *Guernsey under German Rule* (Guernsey, 1946), p. 14.

[2] GF 1/1/16. The official evacuation from all Islands was as follows: 20 June, 4 ships with 2,687 passengers; 21 June, 26 ships with 14,143 passengers; 22 June, 7 ships with 1,672 passengers; and 23 June, 7 ships with 1,700 passengers – in all 44 ships with 20,202 passengers. But of course others left with the regular mail steamer service, which continued to run until the eve of occupation.

[3] CCM 25 June 1940.

to disembark that night. Eventually, after a journey of more than 36 hours, they reached their destination – Bradford – in the small hours, and were put up for what was left of the night on camp beds in a hall. They were well received, but at least to the author of this account Bradford was less attractive than Guernsey. 'I just couldn't tell these kind folk that I thought I'd been dropped in the Black Hole of Calcutta, could I?'

The things which helped to make life tolerable for the evacuees included a guide to the Channel Islands, which was borrowed over and over again by the evacuees in Bradford; the arrival of Red Cross messages in March 1941 after nine months of silence, 'which gave us the morale booster we needed'; the weekly meetings of the Bradford Channel Islands Society; church services in which prayers were offered for the Channel Islands; and the *Channel Islands Review*. In spite of his first reaction, Hamel, like thousands of others, came to accept his wartime home. Indeed he says: 'Could it have been foreseen that the occupation would last five years there can be little doubt that many thousands more would have left the Island.'[1]

At the beginning of July leading Channel Islanders in Britain, in consultation with the Home Office, set up the Channel Islands Refugees Committee, which went into action with commendable speed. It did invaluable work during the whole of the occupation by caring for those who needed help, and by providing a focal point for the many thousands dispersed throughout the length and breadth of the United Kingdom. It made it possible for them to maintain a sense of community without which their reassimilation into the Islands at the end of the war would have been much more difficult.

Lord Justice du Parcq, a Jerseyman, was chairman of the Committee and his deputy was Mr. C. T. Le Quesne, KC, also a Jerseyman, in whose rooms in the Temple the first meeting of the Committee was held. They appealed for funds, first through the columns of *The Times* and then in a B.B.C. broadcast, and within a few months had collected nearly £25,000. The sudden removal of many thousands to a strange if not entirely foreign country inevitably created problems. The United Kingdom authorities were responsible for housing those of the refugees who had no friends in Britain – the great majority – and on the whole the arrangements worked well. The voluntary organizations in the towns where the refugees were did noble work in helping them to feel at home, especially in the early weeks.

The Refugees Committee found itself operating in four main fields:

[1] E. J. Hamel, *X-Isles* (unpublished typescript).

the relief of distress, on which £14,000 was spent in the first six months; helping people to find jobs; card indexing the refugees and those who had elected to remain in the Islands, so that friends might keep in touch; and counselling individual refugees on their special problems. The Committee also helped Channel Islanders in the services. The main driving force behind its work was the Director General, Mr. M. E. Weatherall, a Guernseyman, who was instrumental in arranging for the transfer of Islanders with particular skills to places in Britain where they could most usefully contribute to the war effort.

Evacuation was not the only problem which the Island authorities faced on the eve of invasion. It implied probable occupation, and it was accepted that this would call for a change in the administrative machinery. A 'Superior Council' was set up in Jersey, and a 'Controlling Committee' in Guernsey, which were both intended to give more room for manoeuvre *vis-à-vis* the Germans than would have been possible with the more cumbersome machinery of the States.[1]

There was little time to transact business between the establishment of the Superior Council and the Controlling Committee and the arrival of the Germans; but at least both were going concerns and likely to be accepted as they stood by the invaders. If special administrative arrangements were needed for the duration it was better that they should be introduced by the Islanders themselves, and not dictated by the occupying power. In the few days before the invasion both the Council and the Committee held meetings at which their members did their best to see into the future.

The Committee was largely concerned with financial matters. It discussed existing methods of taxation which might no longer be appropriate because of the departure of large numbers of taxpayers. New sources of revenue might be necessary, but a change of this sort needed the sanction of the King in Council. The Committee, with occupation in mind, felt that someone should be empowered to exercise locally the authority of the King in Council.[2]

The Committee also considered the banking system, on which the evacuation had imposed a great strain. Thousands of customers – evacuees and volunteers for the United Kingdom forces – had suddenly wanted to withdraw cash, to arrange for the transfer of funds to Britain, and to recover securities deposited with the banks. It had seemed

[1] See Chapter 6 for the origin and constitution of these bodies.
[2] CCM 28 June 1940.

inevitable that the supply of cash would run out, despite the limitation on withdrawals. This was not so serious in Guernsey, where the States issued their own currency, but in Jersey £300,000 in cash had to be brought from the United Kingdom. In sending this sum the banks took a calculated risk, since there was a chance that the Germans would be in occupation before the money could be issued; but this did not happen.

A greater danger was that the invaders would fall heir to the many millions of pounds worth of securities and bearer bonds held by the banks on behalf of their customers. At first it was thought that they should be burned, but by superhuman effort the officers of the banks listed and packed into sacks 'documents worth millions of pounds in sterling, which at that period could have been negotiated had they fallen into enemy hands . . . Altogether eighty sacks of securities were shipped and safely delivered in London by officials, unshaven and weary after their long hours and hazardous journey: at one stroke the savings of thousands of customers had been preserved and the enemy frustrated.'[1]

In Guernsey the Controlling Committee decided on 25 June that the banks could return to normal working. At the same time the Committee considered the general financial arrangements in the event of occupation. The banks had instructions to freeze all credits, which would obviously paralyse the whole life of the Island. It was agreed that the States would have to make available to creditors amounts equal to their bank balances, and to ensure that at the end of the war the States were reimbursed before the frozen credits were released. Expert advice would have to be sought from Britain before any scheme was worked out. It was also pointed out that Gresham's Law was bound to make itself felt under occupation. Silver and copper coins would be driven out by whatever form of money the Germans introduced, and it would be necessary to put into circulation some form of other money of small denomination.

In the event, however, the banking system was left more or less undisturbed. In the days before the occupation the Treasury in the United Kingdom and the Bank of England were considering what should be done about the Channel Islands banks. The Bank of England wanted guidance 'now that these Islands have been declared open and a considerable portion of the population is . . . being evacuated'. In reply the Treasury said that they had conferred with the Home Office and that they accepted their view that the banks should carry on as usual, retaining whatever staffs they deemed necessary for the reduced volume of business. It would be wrong for any bank to close without

[1] John Wadsworth, *Counter Defensive* (London, 1946), pp. 41–2.

C

the approval of the Island authorities. The Bank of England agreed, and told the headquarters of the banks in London so that they might know the official view.

The sudden departure of large numbers of people meant that for the moment there was too much food. In Guernsey the Essential Commodities Committee suspended the rationing of butter, bacon, and ham, on the understanding that sales would be restricted to the customer's normal requirements. It was appreciated that this situation would not last for ever, and the sale of canned goods was limited to prevent people from stocking up. The export of food, with the exception of tomatoes, was prohibited.

The Controlling Committee received representations from the medical profession about control of the sale of liquor. There were vast stocks of spirits in the Island, and it was feared that if there was no restriction on consumption it would lead to trouble when the Germans arrived. It was decided not to change the licensing hours but simply to ask the Licensed Victuallers Association to ensure that their members served customers with discrimination. The reduced population also meant a surplus of milk. Should it be turned into butter, of which there was already too much, or should cattle be slaughtered to reduce the production of milk? A request was sent to the Ministry of Agriculture in the United Kingdom for advice on this problem – which was to come up again when the Islands were under siege in 1944.[1]

The Prime Minister personally interested himself in the food position in the Islands, having in mind the desirability of denying food to the Germans rather than the importance of keeping the Islanders well fed. He issued a curious and un-Churchillian edict to the effect that all 'edible food' must be got away from the Islands. It was assumed that he meant normal exports of tomatoes and potatoes, and not supplies for the people, which the Home Office said must continue as long as possible. The Minister of Food minuted him saying that he presumed that the stocks of food in the Islands were not to be interfered with. He would therefore take no action 'unless and until you decide that the population is to be evacuated, in which case we will arrange to lift the stocks in the wholesale warehouses and principal shops . . . tell me your wishes if there is any further step we should take'.[2]

It was important that the petrol in the Islands should be denied to the enemy. The United Kingdom authorities had planned to destroy it well in advance of a German invasion, but the Home Office, anxious to keep

[1] CCM 25 June 1940.   [2] HO 45/19782(819311/12).

life in the Islands as normal as possible for as long as possible, suggested that it should be destroyed by the Island authorities at the last moment. On 25 June it was decided that no more petrol would be issued for private purposes after 7 July; and on 28 June the Controlling Committee discussed how best to dispose of motor spirit before the arrival of the Germans. The best course seemed to be to burn it, but it was agreed to seek the advice of the Petroleum Board in Southampton. There was also discussion about coal supplies, which seemed to be low. Merchants were hesitating to order, and it was resolved that the States should buy on their own account.[1]

It was only after the German success in France that aliens began to be interned – four Germans in Guernsey on 18 May, another eight on 29 May, and others at intervals until 11 June, when seven Italians were interned.[2] It was obvious that the occupying forces would release these people, and it was sensible to free them as soon as occupation was seen to be inevitable. On 19 June eight Germans were, however, taken from internment and escorted to Southampton;[3] and in due course the invaders took a great interest in their fate. They had ostensibly been removed to England because it was thought that they would seek revenge on those responsible for their internment.[4] Four days after the Lieutenant-Governor had left the Island the Government Secretary in Guernsey asked that all aliens should be released. At the beginning of June the authorities in Jersey imposed a curfew on aliens between the ages of 16 and 60. Further, they were forbidden to possess bicycles, motor vehicles, or sea-going craft without special permission.[5] On the eve of the occupation sixteen – four Germans and 12 Italians – were removed to England.

There were other last-minute measures. The Island defence force in Jersey, which had had the briefest of careers, was formally disbanded by an act of the States on 20 June. On the same day the militiamen who were still left in the Island sailed in a body for Southampton on the S.S. *Hodder*. In Guernsey the remaining members of the militia left in groups on the ships carrying out the general evacuation, and on 29 June servicemen on leave in the Island from the United Kingdom were instructed to wear uniform, lest they be regarded as spies when the enemy came, and to surrender their weapons until arrangements could be made to transport them back to their units in Britain. The Controlling

[1] CCM 28 June 1940.   [2] GF 7/1/19.
[3] NG 01/3.   [4] GF 7/1/19.
[5] Defence (Aliens) (No. 5) (Jersey) Regulations, 1940.

Committee considered whether people living in vulnerable areas should be moved, and there was a discussion about a ban on the sale of property for the duration. It was pointed out that this would need an Order in Council, which would take far too long. There was nothing for it but to wait patiently for the invader.[1]

On 26 June, three days after the official evacuation had ended and two days before the German attack, Sir Alexander Maxwell summed up for the benefit of the Home Secretary. The government had facilitated the departure from the Islands of certain classes of people, and allowed the departure of others; encouraged the population to stay; and told the Crown Officers that it was their duty to stay. There had been grave objections to inviting or encouraging all the Islanders to leave. It would be difficult to absorb them, and it might become necessary to resort to compulsion because too few would be left behind to sustain communal life. The last point may seem strange in retrospect. There was plenty of evidence that life under German occupation was not the happiest state; and in the event the viable communities which the British government left provided many essential services for the occupation troops.

The Home Secretary recorded on the file on 29 June that his Department had taken the right line about evacuation, and added that even if they had been wrong the matter was now academic. The German attack had effectively stemmed the flow of evacuees, willing or unwilling. Markbreiter telephoned Sherwill to say that the British government felt that there was nothing more to be done, and got the impression that the Attorney General fully accepted this.

At a Ministerial meeting on the same day the Minister of Health, Mr. Malcolm MacDonald, said that he understood that there was a proposal to evacuate the whole of the population, to which the Home Secretary replied that there was now no question of further large-scale evacuation.[2] Yet on 30 June the Prime Minister minuted the Minister of Food, Lord Woolton:

I think it will be necessary to evacuate the whole of the population, as the Germans will soon steal all the food left from the 80,000 remaining, and we shall have to feed them from here, the food again being stolen.

He had been imperfectly briefed on the state of affairs in the Islands, and went on:

I do not know in what circumstances 90,000 have been selected to come home, and 80,000 left. It would seem inevitable that all should go, and

[1] CCM 25 and 29 June 1940.   [2] HO 45/19782(819311/12).

everything worth moving be taken away as soon as possible. A few watchers and scouts might be left to report any happenings. Fishermen would be good for this.[1]

This gives some idea of the chaos in Whitehall. The Home Secretary had written off the possibility of further evacuation; but the Prime Minister (presumably unaware of the Home Secretary's decision) still thought that total evacuation was possible and desirable.

The evacuation was debated in both houses of parliament. In the Lords on 9 July Lord Portsea drew attention to the financial plight of the refugees and generally deprecated the fact that the Islands had been abandoned to the enemy. Others enlarged on the same theme. The withdrawal, coming so soon after another evacuation – from Narvik – was most disturbing. Would it not have been better to move more quickly, to take away the civilians, and to leave the fighting men to stand a siege? To abandon a fief of the Crown held for 800 years, without firing a shot – that was what hurt, without firing a shot! – required explanation. The government was at fault in not explaining the situation to the Islanders and making the evacuation compulsory. A more moderate speaker suggested that the Islands were indefensible, and that if they *had* been defended they would have been devastated.

The Lord Chancellor, Viscount Simon, replied. The evacuation might have been badly handled – he was not prepared to say. After dealing with the banking arrangements made for the evacuees he asked leave to say a few words about the Islands. If they had been saved from terrible and continuous bombardment from the air, as he thought they had been by the withdrawal of the garrison, the evacuees might count it as some compensation for their temporary separation from their homeland.[2] He acknowledged that the Islanders had contributed, in peace and in war, most significantly to the service and to the strength of Britain.

On 11 July the Home Secretary, Sir John Anderson, was showered in the Commons with questions about the evacuation. What was the present position? What neutral representatives were looking after British interests in the Islands? Could the Islanders communicate with their friends and relatives in Britain? Why had no adequate plans been made for evacuation? What percentage of the population had come to Britain? How were the refugees being looked after? Had a clearing-house for information about them been set up? Anderson replied that when it was decided for strategic reasons to demilitarize the Islands the information before the government indicated that substantial numbers of the

[1] PREM 3/87.   [2] Hansard (Lords) vol. 116, cols. 835–54.

inhabitants would be unwilling to leave their homes. In any case it would have been impracticable and undesirable to remove the whole of the population. It had been recognized, however, that facilities should be provided for those who wanted to leave. Priority had been given to women and children and to men of military age who, under the Island laws, were liable to serve with the forces. The government believed that those who had remained in the Islands were being reasonably treated, and the Ministry of Health and the Ministry of Labour were helping those who had come to Britain.[1]

This was not enough to satisfy the House, however, and three weeks later there was an adjournment debate, in which Mr. C. G. Ammon,[2] member for Camberwell North, raised 'a matter of vital importance'. For the first time in history, British territory had been invaded without resistance. The whole House must deprecate the fact. A few days before evacuation, military equipment was poured into the Islands. Suddenly there was a violent change. The Lieutenant-Governors were the first to leave, abandoning the civil authorities and the unfortunate people to their fate. Worse, news of the event had been suppressed. The Ministry of Information had fallen down on the job. Indeed, there was some doubt whether in certain quarters there was real earnestness in going on with the war. There had been great vacillation on the part of the government, and confusion in the Islands. Other members took the same line. Had there been any policy at all about evacuation? Farmers who had been in the Islands for generations might well want to stay, but the government should have ordered everybody else out.

Inevitably, the speakers were ill-informed, and the facts did not support all their angry criticism. But there was no doubt that Britain had suffered a humiliating defeat and that, whatever the reasons, the British government and the Island authorities had lost control of the situation to an extent that puzzled and worried the layman, no less than members of parliament.

In defence of the government the Under-Secretary of State for the Home Department pointed out that all the advice they had had from the Islands showed that compulsory evacuation would be unpopular. The government had therefore given a lead by providing all the ships they could lay their hands on. The Island administrations, for their part, could not encourage people who held important posts to leave. Had they done so, those left behind would have been in an impossible position. Very different views had been taken in the two main Islands.

[1] Hansard (Commons) vol. 362, cols. 1331–5.   [2] Later Lord Ammon.

Only 6,600 out of 50,000 left Jersey, but 17,000 out of 42,000 left Guernsey. In short, the British government had nothing whatever to reproach itself with. 'I wish that on all matters the Government and the Home Office had as perfectly clear a conscience as they have on this question'.[1]

[1] Hansard (Commons) vol. 363, col. 1369.

4

Invasion

THE phoney war ended on 10 May. The Germans had for the time being settled affairs on their eastern front and could now direct their energies against the west. Army Group A under General von Rundstedt and Army Group B under General von Bock sprang into life and moved forward with unprecedented speed along a front stretching from Holland to Luxembourg. At the end of May the British Expeditionary Force was driven back to the beaches at Dunkirk. Paris fell on 14 June. Eight days later the French government capitulated. The German armies poured unopposed into the vacuum left in Western France and at leisure consolidated their positions along the whole coastal area from Calais to Bordeaux. Seemingly irresistible, they looked eagerly across the English Channel to a Britain standing alone, and across the narrower stretch of water that separated them from the Channel Islands – tiny, but since they were British, of special importance.

Long before they attacked Poland in 1939 the Germans had calculated that it might be necessary to occupy the Islands as part of their general strategy. In July 1938 they had at least one agent there. He travelled to Guernsey from Germany via Ostend, London, and Weymouth; and returned via Southampton. He reported that a month before his visit 'the Navy Minister, Duff Cooper',[1] was in the Islands to evaluate their military potential, and that he had decided to enlarge the airfield and establish a submarine base in Guernsey. The agent confirmed from his own observation that the enlargement of the airfield, which he estimated to be twice the size of that at Cologne, was making good progress. He saw no submarines but considered that the Islands would make a good base because of their granite cliffs and well-concealed bays. He said that the garrison consisted of about 400 men living in barracks. They were all

[1] Mr. Duff Cooper was at this time First Lord of the Admiralty.

Islanders receiving military training.[1] He reckoned that 150 Germans lived in Guernsey, in addition to between 300 and 400 domestic servants who had lately been systematically replaced by Poles and Czechs.[2]

The agent identified 'a ditch covered by gorse bushes broken here and there by prepared gun positions' which ran round the whole Island; but he was unable to examine all the defences because there were several forbidden zones. There was a radio receiving station on Guernsey, but no transmitter. He guessed that the transmitter must be on Jersey, which he did not visit. In the granite quarries he spoke to many Irish workers, all of whom were very friendly to Germany.[3]

In the middle of June 1940, when the occupation of the Channel Islands seemed to be the logical conclusion of the Wehrmacht's progress westwards, this report and some others were put together by German naval intelligence into a comprehensive memorandum for the guidance of the *Oberkommando der Wehrmacht* (OKW).[4]

The coastal defences were probably nothing to worry about. There had been talk about modernizing the defences but on Jersey and Guernsey at least nothing had been done. There was an old fort guarding the harbour at St. Helier, apparently with seven guns facing south, and there were some other forts. On the north-west coast of Guernsey there were old defence works and barracks. St. Peter Port harbour was defended by Fort St. George,[5] where there was an armoury. But the military value of all these installations was presumed to be negligible.

Alderney, however, might have to be reckoned with. A newspaper report in 1939 spoke of its strategic value and of British plans for basing reconnaissance planes there. The need for strong defences had been stressed. The old forts on the north and west coasts, except for Fort Tourgis on its island, and Fort Albert on the Braye coast, were unarmed. An agent had reported a plan to use Alderney as a base for four U-boat chasers and also for motor torpedo boats; it was suggested that the presence of two dredgers (in July 1940) confirmed this. Alderney might therefore put up some resistance.

All three Islands had civil airports in regular use. The main one,

---

[1] Here he was confusing the regular troops stationed in the Island with the militia.
[2] MOD 584/593.
[3] Ibid.
[4] High Command of the Armed Forces.
[5] The intelligence officers wrongly canonized Fort George.

which was on Guernsey, had been opened in May 1939. The airfield on Alderney had been taken over by the R.A.F., and there was a bombing range on the Island. There were also radio masts, and in July 1939 two British naval flying boats had been observed there. Small peacetime garrisons were maintained on Jersey and Guernsey, and the Islands had rest camps for troops who had returned from overseas. In Guernsey there was a militia in which service was compulsory, and which provided infantry training. (The Royal Jersey Militia, it seems, escaped the notice of the German agents.)

Although little was known about the fortifications and the nature of the defending forces it was thought unlikely that Britain, in view of her secure position at the western end of the Channel, would have troubled to strengthen them at the beginning of the war; and events had moved so quickly in recent weeks that she had had no time to take emergency measures. It was known that 'apart from the natives who catch fish and tend cattle' the Islands were chiefly inhabited by well-to-do English people. It was therefore unlikely that any great action would be mounted against them by Britain after they had been occupied, and it followed that the Wehrmacht need not fortify them heavily. They could be defended without great expense by transferring captured coastal and anti-aircraft guns from France.[1]

The memorandum is perhaps evidence more of the Germans' interest in the Channel Islands than of the efficiency of their intelligence services, but the picture, although inaccurate in many respects, was near enough the truth for their purposes.

While OKW was deciding on the best way to take the Channel Islands, the Island governments were deciding how best to resist. On 16 May the civil aviation authorities in Britain warned them that the enemy might try to land troops on the airfields. They were advised to obstruct the runways from an hour before sunset to an hour after sunrise, using vehicles, farm implements, fencing, and even goal posts. The local police should arrange for detachments of troops 'to proceed at speed to the aerodrome to repel parachutists on receipt of a telephoned request for such assistance'. This eleventh-hour advice shows how naive British planning was at this stage of the war. Paratroops are most vulnerable in the few moments before and after they touch ground; the Germans were hardly likely to wait patiently while a message was solemnly relayed to the military – who were in any case so few as to be

[1] MOD 106/6–9; 584/572–3, 577.

virtually useless. At this time the Home Office suggested to the Lieutenant-Governors that they should use their discretion in restricting the movements of enemy aliens.

Next day the Admiralty assumed responsibility for anti-paratroop measures in Jersey. The Island authorities were told that they need no longer decorate the runways with farm carts and goal posts. But once again the arrangements were strangely haphazard. The civil aviation authorities told the Home Office about the Admiralty's decision; the Home Office told the Attorney General in Jersey; and the Attorney General told the Lieutenant-Governor, who was supposed to be in charge of the defences of the Island. In Guernsey the defences of the airfield were left almost to chance.

Although there was no dynamic guidance from Whitehall the Islanders were well aware of the impending danger and anxious to do what they could to meet it. An eminent Jerseyman wrote in *The Evening Post* at the beginning of June that 'a lightning attack on this Island is not out of the question, but if we keep our heads and act swiftly it is doomed to failure'. He was just as sure as the Prime Minister had been in the War Cabinet that if the enemy landed they would quickly be thrown out: 'We can comfort ourselves with the reflection that any occupation could only be very limited in extent and merely temporary while we have the navy and the R.A.F. close at hand to help us'. The writer also expected airborne attack, not only against the airfields but also against the golf courses. The royal and ancient game must be sacrificed, at least for the duration. Old wagons and piles of rocks must be left on all fairways.[1]

An informal letter of 12 June from the Lieutenant-Governor of Jersey to Markbreiter at the Home Office illustrates the general chaos. He understood that the Air Ministry intended to use Jersey airport for R.A.F. operations; but this was only a surmise based on the fact that 50 men of the Fleet Air Arm had been told by the Admiralty that the airfield was no longer available for them, and that they must return to the United Kingdom. Their departure, if it came about, would weaken the defences. If the Air Ministry needed the airfield they must formally take it over from the States. At the least, the R.A.F. should send an officer to look after refuelling, and accommodation and food for the air-crews. The Lieutenant-Governor asked that these matters should be taken up with the Air Ministry at once. He added: 'All sorts and conditions of aircraft roll up at odd hours' with some trouble or other. Planes

[1] *The Evening Post*, 4 June 1940.

might have to land at short notice but it took at least an hour to remove the obstructions, which had to be kept in position during the night. He thought that on balance it was better to leave the runways clear and chance a paratroop landing.

The same letter gives a vivid account of the activity at the airport. Eighteen Whitley bombers arrived on 11 June to refuel for raids on northern Italy. They planned to refuel again on the return journey, but because of engine trouble and bad weather many of them came back to Jersey soon after take-off. In the words of Mr. Charles Roche, the airport controller:

> Then the C.O. asked if we had airport lights. We had, I replied, but could not use them as the whole Island had been in a state of blackout for months. He gave me an order to switch them on as the airport was a military one, he said, while he was in command of a vitally important air attack. So I switched on, but within two or three minutes a very angry Lieutenant-Governor was on the phone ordering me to turn them off as I was inviting the whole Island to be bombed by the Germans. I managed to get the C.O. to talk to him and the lights remained on![1]

According to the Lieutenant-Governor in his letter to Markbreiter the airport beacon, which could be seen up to 40 miles away, was kept on for hours. 'That, combined with the aerodrome landing lights, Verey [sic] lights and flares produced a Brock's benefit which, if there were any Hun raiders over Cherbourg, must show them that this airport is a centre of activity.' This, he feared, could lead to a bombing attack, against which there was no defence.

He found this all the more worrying since the R.A.S.C. Boys' Technical School occupied the old infantry barracks adjoining the airfield. From the air the school looked like one of the airport buildings and was therefore very much at risk. He thought the boys should be transferred to a similar establishment in England. On the following day he pointed out to the War Office that if the airfield was going to be used to any great extent something must be done about its defence. Searchlights and anti-aircraft guns were essential. He made the point that the States of Jersey had put in a bid for defensive weapons but that it had been cancelled (except for seven Bren guns) because Jersey was far too low on the priority list. He understood that twelve Bren guns had been sent to Guernsey and, like a good Jerseyman, made it clear that Jersey must not be left behind.

Lastly, as a footnote, he mentioned that the English residents,

[1] Manuscript account by Mr. Charles Roche.

retired service people and so on 'who all get their money from home, are getting "windy" '. They were wondering what would become of them 'if the Hun arrived and they had nothing to live on'. But he had little sympathy for them. Most had settled in Jersey because of the financial advantages and they must now face up to taking the rough with the smooth.

It was so obvious that the Channel Islands would have to be occupied that on 18 June *Kommandierender Admiral Frankreich* (Admiral Commanding, France),[1] discussed with the operations staff of *Luftflotte* 2 how best to take them, and ordered a reconnaissance for the same day.[2] This was the first of a long series of reconnaissances, the main purpose of which was to reveal whether or not the Islands had been demilitarized. Two days later the naval staff in Berlin radioed to Schuster that the occupation of the Channel Islands was urgent and important. He was to arrange for a reconnaissance and to examine the feasibility of taking the Islands. The Admiral recorded, no doubt with satisfaction, since he had anticipated the wish of his superiors, that a reconnaissance had already been carried out and that it had revealed nothing of significance.[3] A further reconnaissance covering Jersey, Guernsey, Alderney, and Ushant was carried out on 21 June and the photographs sent to headquarters by courier plane for interpretation. The preliminary findings confirmed that there were no artillery installations on the Channel Islands.[4]

On 23 June Admiral Eugen Lindau, *Marinebefehlshaber Nordfrankreich* (Flag Officer, Northern France), made a report to Schuster based on a study of the reconnaissance photographs. There were numerous harbour and coastal fortifications, and in the harbour areas there were long columns of lorries, which pointed to the presence of troops. It seemed likely that the garrisons had been strengthened. In fact, of course, the opposite had happened. The last of the troops had left two days earlier and the vehicles shown in the photographs were carrying tomatoes (in Guernsey) and potatoes (in Jersey) to the docksides. Nevertheless, both *Luftflotte* 2 and the army considered that it would need a large force to take the Islands. There was no chance of success with anything less, since a surprise attack was out of the question. Moreover, it was essential that there should first be very heavy bombing raids.[5] At its first meeting on 24 June the Superior Council in Jersey stressed

[1] Admiral Karlgeorg Schuster, later head of the German naval historical branch.
[2] MOD 581/17.
[3] MOD 584/574.
[4] MOD 584/576, 586, 587.
[5] MOD 584/523, 584; 106/24–5.

the importance of ensuring that there were no large accumulations of vehicles in St. Helier.

Two reconnaissances on 24 June with an hour between them established that there were no aircraft on the airfield at Alderney, that there were no ships in the neighbourhood of Guernsey, and that there was a single freighter bound for Jersey from Guernsey.[1] Daily thereafter reconnaissance planes from *Luftflotte* 2 tried to answer the question that sorely puzzled Berlin,[2] and which the British Government ought to have answered for them on 23 June.[3] Were the Islands defended? As flight after flight was made without retaliation it seemed to be clear that all the troops had gone. The German pilots became bolder and on the afternoon of 27 June one flew round the coastlines at 200 metres 'without encountering any action whatsoever'.[4]

An attempt had now to be made to evaluate the defences as seen through the reconnaisance cameras and the eyes of the pilots, and how best to overcome them. Lindau reported to *Oberkommando der Kriegs-marine* (OKM)[5] that in the opinion of *Luftflotte* 2 and the local army commanders the Islands could not be taken, mainly because of the impossibility of surprise.[6] Admiral Schuster was equally pessimistic. The reports suggested that the three main Islands had defence installa-tions near the main harbours. There were also some forts 'surrounded by woodlands'. Although nothing was known of their state or even if they were manned, the possibility that they were defended could not be ignored. If they were, a raid was doomed to failure; and although the Admiral did not say so, failure was something the Führer would not stand for.[7] He noted in his War Diary that the fact that not a single shot had been fired 'could not by any means be taken to mean that the Islands had neither air nor sea defences'. If anything, the fact that the German pilots had seen nothing was highly suspicious.[8]

Meanwhile the plan of campaign against the Islands was being evolved. It was assumed that when the French coast had been completely occupied by German troops it would be necessary to occupy Jersey, Guernsey, and Alderney simultaneously. They represented an advance observation post of the enemy on the German flank, which threatened their sea and air operations in the middle and west Channel.[9] The

[1] T 314 444/200.
[2] MOD 584/584, 586, 592.
[3] See Chapter 2.
[4] MOD 581/34; 584/590.
[5] High Command of the Navy.
[6] MOD 584/581.
[7] MOD 581/32.
[8] MOD 581/35.
[9] MOD 584/577.

Island harbours, which could take small and medium craft, would be useful to the enemy, especially in winter; and they could be used as a base for attacks on the French coast. It was therefore necessary to deny their facilities to the British.[1] Even if there had been no military case for the occupation Hitler would certainly have insisted on it for propaganda purposes.

The assault was to be carried out by naval assault troops supported by the army and the Luftwaffe in a combined operation under the command of Lindau. The troops would be taken to the Islands in coastal craft and launches seized in the Cherbourg peninsula, and they would be equipped with light weapons to help to establish beachheads and to provide defence against enemy aircraft. They would also take captured French guns to strengthen their defences after landing.[2] The whole operation must be carried out with the greatest speed, and the enemy guns must be silenced at once.[3] Motor Torpedo Boat Operations were told to have craft ready on 25 June. Lindau would get in touch with them if it was decided to use their support.[4]

Schuster continued to be profoundly unhappy about the whole enterprise. Although it was thought in Berlin that the Islands could be captured by a small force, he was not so sure. On the basis of the reconnaissances it was arguable that only a large-scale attack would succeed. He considered that he must now intervene, although the orders to get on with the operation had been issued personally to Lindau. He proposed to send one of his staff officers to the latter to discuss the plan.[5]

Lindau was no less cautious than Schuster. His attitude is revealed by proposals put by him to OKM on 26 June. The preparatory measures which he deemed necessary included aerial reconnaissance along the south coast of England, cross-examination of French civilians familiar with the Islands, especially fishermen, clearing of mines, and aerial softening-up attacks several days before the assault. On the first day of the assault the Luftwaffe must patrol the Channel from dawn to intercept fighters from airfields in south-west England. The Island defences must be attacked by Stuka dive-bombers to prepare the way for the landing force, and Stukas must also cover the troops and deal with attacks by enemy motor torpedo boats. Strong fighter protection would be needed in the Cherbourg peninsula, where the assault force would embark.[6]

[1] MOD 106/8.   [2] MOD 584/578.   [3] MOD 106/19–21.
[4] MOD 584/576.   [5] MOD 581/27.   [6] MOD 106/27; 581/47–8.

The minimum needed was reckoned to be one infantry battalion for Alderney, two for Guernsey, and three for Jersey. All six would be equipped only with light weapons as it would be too difficult to man-handle heavy guns on the beaches. Two engineer companies would be required, as well as a naval assault detachment drawn from the *Abteilung Gotenhafen*. Because of shortage of shipping the assault would have to be spread over two days. The first wave would take Alderney and Guernsey, the second Jersey.[1]

Ships were going to be the key to the whole operation – perhaps the conclusion to be expected from a naval man. Large vessels could not be used because of the nature of the Island harbours, and only a small number of coastal craft and tugs were available. They were unarmed and their crews inexperienced. Competent commanders would have to be found, particularly in view of the navigational difficulties and expected enemy activity. The strength of the tidal currents meant that a minimum speed of 12 knots was desirable. Plans must be worked out to the last detail because many units drawn from all three branches of the Wehrmacht would be involved, and above all because there was no possibility of surprise.[2]

At 4 p.m. on 28 June *Luftflotte* 3 (which had taken over from *Luftflotte* 2) reported the result of a reconnaissance carried out at midday. In St. Helier two transports were alongside the quay, where there were also a number of vehicles. At St. Peter Port there was a single transport and about 150 vehicles on the quay.[3] It was still impossible to say if the Islands were defended. In the afternoon Schuster summed up the situation as he saw it. The Islands had been at least partially evacuated by either the military or the civilian population. Although the anti-aircraft defences were obviously weak it was nevertheless certain that the Islands were garrisoned, and they probably had artillery and mine defences. There was only one certain test. There must be an armed reconnaissance to force the silent batteries to reveal themselves, and to determine what form *Grüne Pfeile* ('Green Arrows'), as the operation was now called, should take.[4]

Squadrons of Heinkel 111s took off from Cherbourg late on the afternoon of 28 June to determine whether there was any foundation for Admiral Schuster's suspicions. If a fierce bombing attack provoked no retaliation it would be pretty conclusive. The raid was carried out from an altitude of 1,000 to 2,500 metres and about 180 bombs were dropped.

¹ MOD 106/27.   ² MOD 106/28.
³ MOD 581/35.   ⁴ MOD 584/599, 600.

The only opposition was light anti-aircraft fire, which the German aircrews thought came from Sark, although in fact it was from the mail steamer (oddly enough, the *Isle of Sark*) which was at that moment embarking passengers for England in the harbour at St. Peter Port. Direct hits were observed on the quay installations and on columns of vehicles at St. Helier. At St. Peter Port, where there were also heavy concentrations of lorries, several hits were seen. There were explosions, and large fires were started. As the Heinkels withdrew the Island was enveloped in smoke, which suggested that fuel storage tanks had been hit.[1]

The stage was set, at a cost of the lives of 44 Channel Islanders, for Operation *Grüne Pfeile* – although it now seemed likely to be no more than a triumphal entry. The main force was to be drawn from 216 Infantry Division, which the earlier operations had brought to St. Omer on 8 June, to St. Germain a week later, and finally to the neighbourhood of Cherbourg.[2] The naval assault detachment was attached to the Division and sent to Cherbourg on 21 June to await orders 'for a special task'.[3] On 25 June *Luftflotte* 3 was designated to support the operation.[4]

Schuster attended a conference about *Grüne Pfeile* at OKM in Berlin on 29 June and next morning told his staff what had happened. It had been agreed that the attack must be much more than a raid. Seaworthy vessels and experienced seamen were essential. It would be the first attempt to capture British territory and there could be no question of failure. It would have to be undertaken at once – before the British could put the airfields out of action. The estimate of the assault force needed was reduced from the six battalions proposed by Lindau. Only a single company would be needed for Alderney, a battalion for Jersey, and a battalion for Guernsey. The Luftwaffe would have to provide constant air cover.

OKM had suggested that the Islands might in fact have been evacuated, but the single-minded Schuster maintained 'in spite of the Daventry broadcast' (i.e. the announcement about demilitarization in the B.B.C. nine o'clock news, which was sent out in Reuter's international service at 10.30 p.m. on 28 June, picked up by the Germans, and passed on verbatim to *Admiral Frankreich* at 11.45 p.m.)[5] that careful reconnaissance was still essential.[6] When the three-dimensional photographs were studied at Schuster's headquarters on 29 June many

[1] MOD 581/35.   [2] T 314 445/468.
[3] MOD 584/575.   [4] MOD 106/22.
[5] MOD 106/30.   [6] MOD 581/38, 51.

artillery earthworks were clearly distinguishable. It remained an open question whether there were silent batteries. Schuster recorded in his War Diary that the situation was developing very quickly – this was strange, since in fact virtually nothing was happening – and he repeated the mistaken report that during the bombing of the harbours the only anti-aircraft fire came from Sark. He again referred to the B.B.C. demilitarization report, but asserted that the reconnaissance photographs showed all defence installations with their guns intact. He had to admit, however, that there was no sign of their crews.[1]

On the afternoon of 30 June he attended a meeting in Paris with Lindau and representatives of *Luftflotte* 3 to finalize the arrangements for *Grüne Pfeile*. The chief of staff of *Luftflotte* 3 said that the reconnaissances suggested that the Islands had been abandoned; but he confessed, perhaps in deference to Schuster's known views, that silent batteries might come into action if a landing was attempted. In any case more time was needed to find ships and sweep a mine-free channel.[2] During the meeting a report was brought in that the B.B.C. had announced that the Islands were undefended. The record implies that it was the first time those present had heard the report, which is curious since Schuster himself was aware of it and had discounted it.[3]

It was decided that a second armed reconnaissance should be carried out on 1 July and that a plane should land. If it met no opposition, naval and army units would be flown in. If there was opposition, a large-scale attack would be planned. A further meeting of the three services was fixed for 6 p.m. on 1 July at Deauville, when the results of the second armed reconnaissance would be available.[4]

After the conference had broken up news came through which finally made nonsense of the doubting Schuster's suspicion that the British were lying low, and indeed of the whole assault plan. Hauptmann Liebe-Pieteritz, who was carrying out a routine reconnaissance, anticipated the decision that the defences should be tested by landing an aircraft. Observing that the airfield at Guernsey was completely deserted he took it upon himself to land, leaving three other planes overhead to cover him; by so doing he established that Guernsey at least was undefended.[5] He had to beat a hasty retreat when three Bristol Blenheims appeared to engage his comrades, but he took off safely and rejoined them. Two of the Blenheims were shot down.[6]

[1] MOD 581/38.   [2] MOD 581/39.
[3] MOD 584/591.   [4] MOD 581/39.
[5] MOD 581/39-40, 43.   [6] MOD 581/41.

He reported his brief, unmolested visit to *Luftflotte* 3, who came to the conclusion that the Islands were undefended and were patiently awaiting invasion. That evening a platoon of soldiers of the Luftwaffe was flown into Guernsey by Junkers transports. The Wehrmacht's elaborate plans had been made redundant by the enterprise of one Luftwaffe pilot.[1]

It remained for Lindau, who had been charged with the task of capturing the Channel Islands, to save the navy's face by catching up with the Luftwaffe as speedily as possible. The exasperating news of Liebe-Pieteritz's exploit reached him at 6 p.m. on 30 June and he immediately recalled his army and Luftwaffe colleagues. They agreed that next day the naval assault troops and army units should fly from Cherbourg to Guernsey. Jersey and Alderney would be occupied on 2 and 3 July respectively.[2]

At 8.45 a.m. on 1 July Lindau telephoned to 216 Infantry Division saying that he proposed to occupy Guernsey that morning, as the weather forecast was good.[3] The naval assault detachment which had been intended to be the spearhead of the attack and which had been left at the post by the Luftwaffe, was at the airfield ready to board the aircraft;[4] but alas the Junkers transports were grounded by fog at their base and only a few of them got through to Cherbourg. They had been scheduled to leave for Guernsey at 9 a.m., but since not all the transport planes had arrived by 2 o'clock the operation was held up.[5]

Then news came through that the Island of Guernsey had 'officially surrendered' to the force which had landed there the day before. Any risk in sending a smaller number of troops than planned had vanished, and in the afternoon the first of the Junkers took off, ferrying in turn the naval assault troops, a light anti-aircraft unit to protect the airfield, and a company of Infantry Regiment 396. The operation was successfully completed by 8.30 p.m.[6] At the same time a few small vessels sailed from Cherbourg with equipment and stores.[7]

While Admiral Schuster and his colleagues were planning a massive assault on three small, defenceless Islands, the Islanders went about their daily business in blissful ignorance of the preparations being made against them only a few miles away. It was firmly in their heads that St. Peter Port and St. Helier were open towns. Most of them must have presumed

[1] MOD 581/514.
[2] MOD 581/39.
[3] T 314 445/447–8.
[4] MOD 584/589.
[5] T 314 445/446–6.
[6] MOD 584/514.
[7] MOD 581/44; MOD 584/515.

that by now this fact, which had been headline news in the Islands as long ago as 19 June, was known to the world at large, including the Germans. They were aware of the daily reconnaisance flights which were carried out at a great height, but it was difficult to identify the planes. It was not even certain that they were hostile. However, the low level reconnaissance on 27 June, when the markings on the German planes were clearly visible, revealed that the enemy were still very much interested in the Islands.

On the evening of 28 June, when the German dive bombers were taking off from their airfields in the Cherbourg peninsula, the problem that was exercising the minds of most of the Islanders was whether they had been right to remain behind when large numbers of their fellow citizens had gone to England. If a further chance of evacuation offered, should they take it? In Guernsey the Attorney General had just finished addressing an open-air meeting to reassure the people of St. Peter Port, when the German planes arrived overhead. In Jersey it had been

a quiet and uneventful day until about 6.45 p.m. when . . . bombs were dropped at La Rocque and in the Town Harbour vicinity, the planes sweeping over roads with their machine-guns blazing. Houses were wrecked at South Hill, stores were set on fire in Commercial Buildings and hundreds of panes of glass were shattered in the Weighbridge vicinity, stained-glass windows of the Town Church being damaged. Bombs also fell in the harbour itself, which was primarily the German objective, several small boats and yachts being destroyed. Eleven people were killed and nine injured, either by pieces of shrapnel or machine-gun bullets.[1]

Casualties in Guernsey were higher, simply because of ill-luck. Sherwill reported to the Home Office that 23 had been killed and 36 wounded.[2] Details of the casualties in Jersey were telegraphed by the Bailiff.

In spite of the raids, communication was maintained with London, and that part of the administrative machine in Whitehall which was concerned with the affairs of the Channel Islands ground ponderously on. The Home Office was informed on 29 June that the Casquets and Les Hanois navigational lights had been extinguished, and that all the lights in the Channel Islands were now out. An official of the Admiralty wrote to the Home Office about a proposal to establish a coastal watch in the Islands. He was commanded by The Lords Commissioners of the Admiralty 'to acquaint you for the information of the Secretary of

[1] Sinel, p. 12.
[2] The final figure for Guernsey was 33 killed. GF 7/1/3.

State for Home Affairs that in view of the present situation and policy regarding the Channel Islands They do not consider it necessary to pursue the matter further'. A sensible conclusion on which 'They' were to be congratulated. In Jersey the States met to adopt three new defence regulations, the curfew was reimposed, and the use of cars restricted.

In Guernsey the news of Liebe-Pieteritz's landing reached the Attorney General in a garbled form. He passed it on to the Home Office by telephone, saying that at about 2 p.m. four planes had landed. The crews got out, but quickly re-embarked and took off again. While they were on the airfield they had set up a machine gun and 'taken the ordinary precautions'. In fact, although there had been four planes, only one of them landed.

Inspector W. R. Sculpher, head of the police force, had on 27 June been armed with a letter in English addressed to 'the Officer Commanding German troops in Guernsey' and signed by the Bailiff which read: 'This Island has been declared an Open Island by His Majesty's Government of the United Kingdom. There are in it no armed forces of any description. The bearer has been instructed to hand this communication to you. He does not understand the German language.'[1] Sculpher went to the airport soon after noon on 30 June. When he got there the plane had gone, but he saw its wheel tracks in the grass.

In the evening the news came through that several planes had landed, and when the Inspector returned he found that the airport had been taken over by the Luftwaffe. He handed his letter to the senior officer, Major Lanz, who knew little more English than Sculpher knew German, and who merely asked to be taken to 'the chief man' of the Island. They went by police car to the Royal Hotel, where they were joined by the Bailiff, the President of the Controlling Committee, and senior officials. After an interpreter had been found Lanz announced that the Island was under German occupation. He dictated a number of regulations, which were put into English by Sherwill for publication next day.[2] Before he came out to meet the Germans Sherwill had called the Home Office to tell them that troop carriers had begun to land at 7.48 p.m. This time there was no doubt about the accuracy of his information.

The Post Office in London reported that the enemy appeared to have removed the relays in Guernsey, and so put the telegraph out of order; but they had not interfered with the telephones. They suggested that the Germans might have left them intact 'for some nefarious purpose'.

[1] GF 7/1/3.   [2] Sculpher's report of 3 July 1940.

They were therefore simply noting the Guernsey callers' numbers with a view to investigating the calls in due course. The Home Office agreed that this was right, but said that official calls should be allowed to come through. The Post Office were afraid that when the Germans took the exchange over they would be able to communicate with their agents in Britain. It was hardly likely that they would risk exposing their agents in this way, but at least it showed that the Post Office's heart was in the right place.

Guernsey was for all practical purposes occupied on the evening of 30 June. Jersey's turn came next day. Early on the morning of 1 July a message addressed to the Chief of the Military and Civil Authorities was dropped on the airfield calling on the Island to surrender. They were to signify their willingness by hanging out white flags and painting white crosses in prominent places, one of which was the Royal Square. If they surrendered peacefully, the life, property, and liberty of all peaceful citizens would be guaranteed. (This undertaking was to have significance more than two years later when the United Kingdom-born Islanders were being deported.) The tokens of surrender were duly displayed and a detachment of naval assault troops and a company of Infantry Regiment 396 were flown in, accompanied, as in the case of Guernsey, by a light anti-aircraft unit.[1] 'In the late afternoon troop-carriers arrive and German officials are met at the Airport by the Bailiff, Government Secretary, and the Attorney General. Soldiers are billeted at several hotels, anti-aircraft posts are established and many public buildings are visited. The Occupation has commenced.'[2]

Alderney posed a different problem. As the population had gone, there was no point in asking anyone to surrender. The Germans' first attempt to land troops there had to be abandoned when the pilots spotted that the landing field was obstructed with heavy lorries and wire entanglements. On 2 July two Fieseler Storch planes, which needed only a short landing strip, were called in, and their crews cleared the runway.[3]

Finally, on 4 July, a small detachment crossed from Guernsey to Sark, and the occupation of the Islands was complete.[4]

The Germans were quick to consolidate their position. By 2 July they had radio communication with the mainland, and shortly afterwards an air service was operating, first with three and later with six aircraft.[5]

[1] MOD 584/515. The first German to land in Jersey was Oberleutnant Kern.
[2] Sinel, p. 13.   [3] MOD 581/41.
[4] T 314 445/424.   [5] T 314 444/778; MOD 445/343; 584/603.

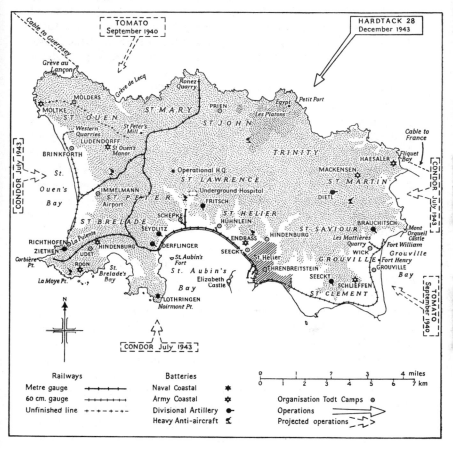

TOMATO
September 1940

HARDTACK 28
December 1943

Cable to Guernsey

Grève au
Lançon

Grève de Lecq

Ronez
Quarry.

MOLDERS

MOLTKE

ST OUEN

Western
Quarries

St Peter's
Mill

LUDENDORFF

St Ouen's
Manor

BRINKFORTH

St.
Ouen's
Bay

IMMELMANN

ST PETER

Airport

ST BRELADE

RICHTHOFEN
ZIETHEN
Corbière
Pt.

La Pulente

UDET

HINDENBURG

ROON

La Moye Pt.

St.
Brelade's
Bay

ST MARY

PRIEN

ST JOHN

Egypt

Petit Port

Les Platons

Cable to
France

TRINITY

Fliquet
Bay

HAESALER

MACKENSEN

Operational H.Q.

ST LAWRENCE

Underground Hospital

FRITSCH

SCHEPKE

SEYDLITZ

DERFLINGER

St. Aubin's
Fort

St. Aubin's

Bay

Elizabeth
Castle

HÜHNLEIN

ST HELIER

ENDRASS

HINDENBURG

SEECKT

St Helier

EHRENBREITSTEIN

DIETL

ST MARTIN

ST SAVIOUR

BRAUCHITSCH

Mont
Orgueil
Castle

Les Mattières
Quarry

Fort William

WICK

Fort Henry

GROUVILLE

GROUVILLE

Grouville
Bay

SEECKT

SCHLIEFFEN

ST CLEMENT

CONDOR July 1943

CONDOR July 1943

CONDOR July 1943

TOMATO
September 1940

N

LOTHRINGEN
Noirmont Pt.

CONDOR July 1943

Railways		Batteries	
Metre gauge	╬╬╬╬╬	Naval Coastal	✦
60 cm. gauge	++++++	Army Coastal	✪
Unfinished line	+-+-+-+-	Divisional Artillery	●
		Heavy Anti-aircraft	⅃

0   1   2   3   4 miles
0   1   2   3   4   5   6   7 km

Organisation Todt Camps ⊚
Operations →
Projected operations ⇢

2. *Jersey*

From noon on 4 July 2-cm anti-aircraft batteries were fully operational on both Jersey and Guernsey.[1] British servicemen who had been on leave were rounded up.[2] The Islands as a group were brought into the command area of X Army Corps, which placed them under 216 Infantry Division.[3] Some of the naval assault troops whose services had not been needed were pulled out for special duties in Paris[4] and those who remained were temporarily subordinated to 216 Division.[5] It was decided that it would be enough to send a detachment of harbour defence troops to Alderney, particularly as the airfield there was so small that it was difficult to send in an airborne force.[6]

OKW laid down that the forces occupying the Islands must be strong enough to withstand any attack that the British were likely to mount, although it was not expected that they would risk an offensive.[7] The coastal defences would be the responsibility of OKM.[8] Now that the Germans were able to make a close inspection of the forts in Jersey and Guernsey they saw that Schuster and Lindau had been wildly wrong in their interpretation of the aerial photographs. There were no fortifications, at least no modern fortifications, and there were no silent batteries. The only guns were museum pieces in the old forts, most of which had been silent for centuries. Further, the German spy who had suggested in 1938 that there were meaningful defences was shown to have been a long way off the mark.

Sea communications presented a problem. A small motor boat was enough for the journey between Guernsey and Sark, and the lifeboat was able to cope with the journey from Guernsey to Jersey; but after a week of the occupation there was still no satisfactory sea link between the Islands and the mainland. There were no suitable vessels, there was a shortage of experienced crews, and it was difficult to provide adequate protection on the route from the Islands to Cherbourg. Cherbourg and St. Malo were the only possible ports on the mainland of France. The ports on the west coast of the Cotentin peninsula were examined, but neither Carteret nor Portbail was of any use, since at low tide their harbours were dry.

In the short term it would be enough to provide a small vessel to carry troops and freight between Carteret and St. Helier, but for a long-term regular service something different was needed. It would have to

[1] T 314 445/427.
[2] T 314 445/427.
[3] T 314 444/758, 775.
[4] MOD 584/515.
[5] T 314 445/115.
[6] MOD 584/515, 604.
[7] MOD 584/604.
[8] MOD 584/602, 694.

carry heavy military equipment, including light and heavy anti-aircraft guns, troop replacements, and tomatoes and potatoes – for the Germans had their eye on the Islands' produce right from the beginning. The danger of attacks by submarines and motor torpedo boats at first ruled out a service between Cherbourg and the Islands, but the route from St. Malo to St. Helier was considered to be reasonably safe. British submarines were unlikely to operate there, and St. Malo had a good harbour.[1]

This then was how the Germans saw the occupation in the early days. They had no reason to suppose that their plans would not be implemented.

The most striking thing about the invasion is the extreme caution with which it was planned. The Germans have been given credit for their relatively humane treatment of the Channel Islanders during the occupation; and the caution which they exercised before they invaded may seem to be further evidence of their solicitude for the welfare of the inhabitants. In fact their only concern was to avoid embarking on an operation before they were certain it would succeed. The efficient capture of the Islands would put the finishing touch to a remarkably successful campaign. If they failed to capture them, or if they suffered heavy casualties on the eve of an operation as critical as 'Sealion' it could boost the morale of the British as they made their last-ditch stand on their own territory, and correspondingly lower the morale of the all-conquering Wehrmacht. Schuster and Lindau may have been thinking more of their own reputations in going so slowly but the fact remains that if *Grüne Pfeile* had been bungled the consequences might have been more serious than the intrinsic strategic value of the Channel Islands would suggest.

The reputations of the two leading men involved suffered, simply because of their caution; and the navy as a whole was seriously upset by the handling of the Channel Islands operation. Kapitänleutnant Hans Reinicke of naval staff operations later read Schuster's complacent comment of 18 June – that he had already carried out the reconnaissance asked for by his superiors, and that it had revealed nothing – he wrote in the margin: 'In that case *we* should have done something about it, and not waited until one Luftwaffe pilot landed there off his own bat.'[2]

That the Germans had landed in Jersey and Guernsey was announced

[1] MOD 650/146–7.   [2] MOD 584/17.

to the people of Britain in a brief statement from the Ministry of Information. It appeared in *The Times* on 2 July along with the news broadcast by the Germans: 'On June 30 the British Island of Guernsey was captured in a daring *coup de main* of the Luftwaffe. In an air fight a German reconnaissance aeroplane shot down two Bristol Blenheim bombers. On July 1 the Island of Jersey was occupied by surprise in the same manner.' Berlin radio followed this with German battle songs, including the *Englandlied* (*Wir fahren gegen England*). The German press made the most of the event. The Islands had been England's last continental outpost, and could not be held against the might of Germany. The panic evacuation of troops and equipment showed that England was finished. The enemy might claim that the Islands had no strategic importance, but why then had they planned to make a great fortress out of Alderney? Germany's total victory had forced England to abandon every bulwark near the French coast.[1]

When the occupation was a few weeks old the President of the Controlling Committee in Guernsey played into the hands of the Germans by recording a talk for their radio. His motive was to set at rest the minds of Channel Islanders in Britain. His contribution was harmless enough in isolation, although it may seem to be rather fulsome. He said there was no gun pointed at his head, nor was he reading from a typescript thrust into his hand by a German officer. He, the Bailiff, and the Island officials were being treated with the greatest courtesy by the German military authorities. The conduct of the German troops was exemplary and he was grateful for their correct and kindly attitude towards the Islanders. 'We have always been and will remain intensely loyal subjects of His Majesty; and this has been made clear, and is respected by the German commandant and his staff.'

Loyalty to the Sovereign, gratitude to the courteous invader. Had that been all no great harm would have been done. The real sting came in the remarks introducing the recording. A neutral correspondent had the day before broadcast an account of affairs in Jersey. Today, here was a companion piece about the other Island, 'a talk by the head of the administration of Guernsey, that little outpost of Great Britain now under German occupation'. Some listeners, anxious to hear about the wider aspects of the war, might consider the tomato crops of Guernsey small beer. To the speaker, however, it was highly symptomatic that 'a Guernsey alderman' should tell the world that life, social and economic,

[1] MOD 584/596.

was going on there, just as if there was no occupation. 'The few allusions he makes to German troops are so favourable and fair that he himself seemed to deem it necessary to emphasise that no pistol was pointed at him while he was speaking.' It had been by no means certain that the inhabitants would show themselves ready to cope with the situation – after all Britain had not been invaded since 1066 – or that the German officers and men would have the knowledge and tact to rule the Islands. The British had claimed that wherever the Germans went the Gestapo followed, bringing starvation, persecution, unrest, and dissatisfaction. 'They would have prophesied the same for Jersey and Guernsey if only they had had time to foresee that the Germans would land there. Therefore I think it is a happy coincidence that a prominent inhabitant of Guernsey whose voice you will hear presently has offered to make use of our wireless facilities and speak to his fellow-countrymen in England and overseas about his experience and his opinion of what British propaganda calls "German persecution" '.

This was insidious propaganda at its worst – or brilliant best. It moderately established that German troops now occupied British soil, that they had caught the British unawares, that the British allegations about German behaviour in the occupied countries were all lies, that the Channel Islanders – now that they knew what the Germans were really like – welcomed them, and that all this was vouched for by the head of the administration. It is difficult to believe that Sherwill would have made the recording had he known how cleverly it would be used.[1]

[1] Mr. Cecil de Sausmarez was Duty Officer at the Ministry of Information when Sherwill's broadcast was picked up by the B.B.C. He was able to draw attention to an error in the transcript, which began: 'This is the Guernsey potterer speaking.' 'Potterer' should of course have read 'Procureur'. He has placed on record that his own reactions to the broadcast at the time were very unfavourable, as were those of many Islanders who read the text in the German-controlled press next day.

5

Early Operations

THE occupation of the Channel Islands – whether or not they had any real military importance for either side – was the culminating humiliation for Britain. Her troops had been ignominiously bundled out of Europe by the Germans; and now the Germans were firmly established on British soil. The Prime Minister, having reluctantly accepted the advice of the Chiefs of Staff that it would be foolish to defend the Islands, was not long in seeking to hit back at the invading forces. He minuted General Ismay on 2 July, two weeks after he had agreed to let the Islands go without a fight:

If it be true that a few hundred German troops have been landed on Jersey or Guernsey by troop-carriers, plans should be studied to land secretly by night on the Islands and kill or capture the invaders. This is exactly one of the exploits for which the Commandos would be suited. There ought to be no difficulty in getting all the necessary information from the inhabitants and from those evacuated. The only possible reinforcements which could reach the enemy during the fighting would be by aircraft-carriers, and here would be a good opportunity for the Air Force fighting machines. Pray let me have a plan.[1]

A plan was quickly provided, too quickly as it turned out. It was given the code name 'Anger', perhaps by some staff officer who had noted the Prime Minister's mood in the preceding weeks.

The enterprise had no strategic value. It was not designed to win back the Channel Islands. It might, however, provide lessons for future amphibious operations, and if it succeeded it would be good news at a time when good news was scarce.

Late on the evening of 6 July, only four days after the Prime Minister's minute, Second Lieutenant Hubert Nicolle, formerly of the Royal Guernsey Militia, embarked in a submarine (H 43, Lieutenant G. R.

[1] Winston S. Churchill, *The Second World War* (London, 1948–54), vol. ii, p. 566.

Colvin) at Devonport to make a one-man reconnaissance of his native Guernsey, which had been chosen for the Prime Minister's 'exploit' since it was furthest from the French coast. The weather was fine and calm. They headed for the western point of Guernsey, escorted at first by H.M. Trawler *Lord Stanhope*. Then they followed a zig-zag course until 3.20 a.m. on 7 July, when they were 36 miles from Les Hanois. They dived to 60 feet and proceeded slowly, coming to periscope depth to take bearings from time to time. At 10 p.m. they were within four miles of their objective, Icart Point. They came up to periscope depth and fixed their position on cliffs silhouetted against the after-glow of sunset. It was high summer and the days were still long. They dived again to work out a plan of campaign; that the plan had to be evolved after the operation was well under way shows how weak 'Anger' was right from the start.[1]

The operation was divided into three phases, 'Anger' covering the first two, and 'Ambassador' the third.[2] As the Prime Minister had suggested, it was first necessary to get information about the state of affairs on the Islands. An agent must glean something useful about the numbers and disposition of the German forces. He would be picked up two days later when a second party landed to act as guides for a Commando raid. This ambitious sequence of interlocking operations looked well enough on paper; but it depended too much on careful timing and the weather over nearly a week to have a real chance of success – especially with inexperienced troops. But the Prime Minister had spoken.

Nicolle was to land in a collapsible two-seater canoe consisting of a folding wooden frame covered with a thick rubber skin and propelled by double paddles, bought for the operation in a London store – so well equipped was the navy at this stage of the war. He would paddle to Le Jaonnet beach on the south coast, and hide the canoe for the return journey three days later. After discussion with the submarine commander, however, he decided that the plan had little chance of success. The Germans were bound to find the canoe; and although he had experience of boats, he had no navigational training. It would be difficult to get back to the submarine in the dark. It was agreed that he should be accompanied by the submarine's navigational officer, Sub-Lieutenant J. L. E. Leitch, who would paddle the canoe back to the submarine.

An unforeseen difficulty arose when it was found that the canoe, like Robinson Crusoe's, was too big to be launched. It had gone through the

[1] ADM 199/278.
[2] Operation 'Ambassador' was provisionally named 'Collar II'.

forehatch all right in its packaged form – still in the wrappings in which it had been bought – but the assembled craft was too broad in the beam to go out. Further, it was too complicated to reassemble in the dark on the narrow forecasing. Hasty improvisation was necessary. Some of the cross-struts were removed and the framework was tied tourniquet-fashion to compress it enough to go through the hatch. At 11.30 p.m. the submarine surfaced; the half-assembled canoe was passed up and launched after the missing struts had been replaced. The submarine then moved slowly inshore, towing the canoe alongside.

The weather was still fine, too fine for the immediate purpose. The moonlit sky was cloudless and visibility dangerously good. If the Germans were keeping watch they would spot the submarine creeping slowly across the surface. The commander decided that it was too risky to go close in. Nicolle and his companion were faced with a two-mile trip, which started at 17 minutes past midnight. The calm sea made paddling easy at first; but almost at once the weather worsened. The sky clouded over and the night became darker. A breeze sprang up from the west and when it met the tide setting to westward it raised a short lop. What had been an easy paddle became difficult and exhausting.

Nevertheless the two men made good speed and although they capsized in the breakers Nicolle was successfully landed. There was no sign of the enemy. When the canoe was righted Nicolle moved inland and Leitch paddled back into the darkness. The return journey was much more arduous. Leitch had to contend with a choppy sea and a 3-knot cross-tide, with no one to help him. The submarine had taken advantage of the increased darkness to move in closer, but he missed it and paddled on southwards. It had been arranged that a light should be flashed to seaward and fortunately he spotted it over his shoulder. He was taken on board worn-out, having been away for just under two hours. The return trip to Devonport was uneventful. The party arrived at 6.45 p.m. on 9 July, leaving exactly 14 hours in which to prepare for the second leg of 'Anger'.

The submarine commander's report shows how hazardous the operation had been. They had been submerged for more than 40 out of $57\frac{1}{2}$ hours at sea. They had had to contend with the dangerous tides that sweep the Channel Islands. All navigational lights on Guernsey had been extinguished. The commander concluded that it would have been impossible to land anybody if the weather had been thick (although the clearer it was the greater the risk of detection); and he

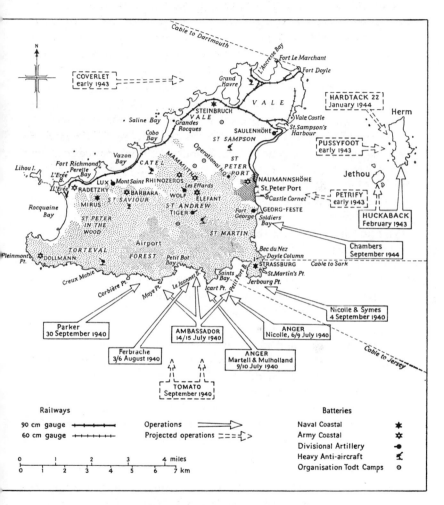

3. *Guernsey, Herm, and Jethou*

thought that it would have been more sensible to use a motor torpedo boat. But they were committed to a submarine, and the second leg of 'Anger' had to be faced.

It began on the evening of 9 July. The submarine set off for Guernsey, the initial escort this time being provided by H.M. Trawler *Indian Star*. On board were Second Lieutenant Philip Martel of the Hampshire Regiment and Second Lieutenant Desmond Mulholland of the Duke of Cornwall's Light Infantry, both of whom, like Nicolle, were formerly of the Royal Guernsey Militia. When they surfaced off Guernsey it was much darker than last time. The moon was screened by cloud; but the sea was calm with only a slight swell. Just before midnight the submarine's Berthon boat (necessary because three men had to be carried) was assembled and launched alongside. It was towed to a point about a mile from the shore and the men pulled away to Le Jaonnet beach. The round trip had to be completed inside the 60 minutes when the tide was turning, to avoid the violent cross-currents which Leitch had experienced on the first trip. He was ordered to be back no later than 1.30 a.m. – with or without Nicolle.

The only signs of life on the Island were a few dim lights, apparently from windows – in spite of the black-out and the lateness of the hour. The breakers again gave trouble. They were too much for the heavily-laden Berthon and swamped it a few yards from the beach. Nicolle was waiting – one of the few things that went according to plan – and between them the four men dragged the boat to safety. Nicolle gave Martel and Mulholland information about the numbers and where-abouts of the Germans, the curfew hours, and so on; and then he and Leitch set off for the submarine.

They were almost clear of the breakers when the boat was again swamped and sank in four or five feet of water. Martel and Mulholland were already half-way up the cliff path but fortunately they saw what had happened and came back. Nicolle and Leitch could not have salvaged the boat on their own. They cleared the breakers at the second attempt but the Berthon had been damaged and was shipping water. Leitch rowed and Nicolle bailed. The wisdom of timing the trip during the turning of the tide now became apparent. Had they had to contend with the lop which would develop within a few minutes they would have sunk. As it was, they struggled back to the submarine with exactly a minute to spare.

Lieutenant Colvin, an innocent victim of the Prime Minister's impatience, again provided his assessment. The operation had been

Author's copyright

1. Operation 'Hardtack 28'; Petit Port, Trinity, Jersey, 25 December 1943 (pp. 244-5). This was the only raid on Jersey. Its leader, Capt. P. A. Ayton, was killed by a mine.

2. Elizabeth Castle, St Helier, Jersey. Heavily fortified by the Germans, and also used as a punishment camp by the Organisation Todt.

Author's copyright

3. Operation 'Anger': Le Jaonnet Bay, Guernsey, 7 July 1940 (pp. 80-5). Mr Hubert Nicolle, the first British agent to land in the occupied Channel Islands (from a submarine) surveys thirty four years later the climb he had to make.

Author's copyright

Author's copyright

4. *Petit Port, Guernsey. Second-Lieutenants Hubert Nicolle and James Symes landed here on 4 September 1940 to find out how Channel Islanders were faring under occupation. The M.T.B. which was to take them off failed to make the rendezvous, and after remaining in hiding for five weeks they had to give themselves up.*

Author's copyright

5. Operation 'Dryad': the Casquets Lighthouse, off Alderney, 2 September 1942 (pp. 228-40). The raiders removed the seven-man lighthouse crew, which led Hitler to order an immediate study of all German lighthouse defences.

A, Dog and Lion Rocks; B, Petit Port; C, Jerbourg Headland.

6. Operation 'Ambassador': against the south coast of Guernsey, 14 July 1940 (pp. 85-90). It was the largest and least successful of the commando raids on the Channel Islands. Three parties took part, but only one got ashore — on the Jerbourg peninsula.

Author's copyright

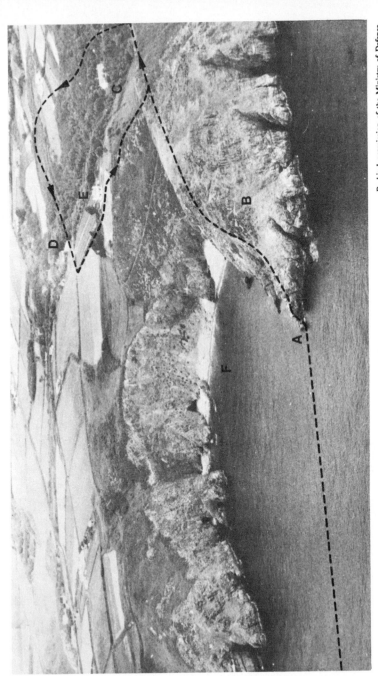

A, Point Chateau; B, Hogsback; C, Petit Dixcart; D, Dixcart Hotel; E, Jaspellerie; F, Dixcart Bay.

By kind permission of the Ministry of Defence

7. *Operation 'Basalt': Hogsback. Sark. 3 October 1942 (p. 240). This small raid removed a German prisoner for interrogation. It led to the shackling of allied prisoners of war captured at Dieppe. and to the second wave of deportation from the Channel Islands to Germany.*

By kind permission of the Ministry of Defence

A, Derrible Point; B, Petit Derrible Bay; C, Derrible Bay; D, Petit Dixcart.

8. *Operation 'Hardtack 7'; Derrible Point, Sark, 27 December 1943 (p. 243). A small party landed on Derrible Point but failed to reach the plateau. In a second attempt on the Hogsback two days later the party was trapped by a minefield and two men were killed.*

planned too hastily, which made improvisation necessary. Luckily the three agents chosen all had experience of boats. Otherwise a rehearsal would have been essential. A canoe was ideal for landing from a submarine, but only in calm weather and if no more than one agent was involved. The Berthon could carry three men at a pinch and was more seaworthy, although slower. It was vulnerable in breakers if the sea was at all rough. The commander repeated that such an enterprise was too much for a submarine, especially in the summer when it was necessary to remain submerged for long periods. The batteries had been heavily strained and were virtually exhausted when they got back to Devonport. He again stressed the navigational difficulties – the need to negotiate dangerous offshore rocks, to compensate for powerful and complex tidal streams, and to make a landfall with pinpoint accuracy after being submerged for many hours.

The way was now clear for the third and main element in the 'exploit' – 'Ambassador'. 140 men of No. 3 Commando and No. 11 Independent Company were to be taken by two destroyers, the *Saladin* and the *Saracen*, to the south coast of Guernsey and transferred there to seven air-sea rescue launches. They were to make three separate landings, while two Ansons droned overhead to drown the noise of the launches. One party was to head for the airport from Point de la Moye and destroy planes on the ground, petrol stores and the aerodrome installations. The second was to land further east at Petit Port on the Jerbourg peninsula to attack a machine gun post and German billets which Nicolle had reported at Telegraph Bay.[1] The third was to go in at Le Jaonnet Bay midway between the other two to intercept any German troops sent from St. Peter Port or Fort George. It was hoped to capture prisoners to establish the size and nature of the occupying force.

So far the weather had been on the side of 'Anger/Ambassador' but this luck could hardly last. The third leg of the operation had been planned to catch the most favourable tide. Full use had been made of the experience gained on 'Anger', but because of sudden bad weather 'Ambassador' had to be postponed for 48 hours. This meant that on the night finally chosen the tide was less than perfect. Moreover, there was no way of warning Martel and Mulholland, hidden away on Guernsey, that the operation had been held up, although they had been briefed that there might be a delay. They were to lie low until the launches carrying the Commandos moved inshore, and then signal from Le

[1] ADM 199/278.

D

Jaonnet beach by flashing the letter 'D' in Morse code if it was safe to come in; and groups of short flashes if they had spotted enemy troops near the chosen beaches.[1]

As the tiny fleet set off it was found that two of the launches (which were intended to land 20 men each) were unserviceable – further evidence of the impromptu nature of the whole affair. Their stores were transferred to the others and the convoy left Dartmouth on time, but two launches short, early on the evening of 14 July. The two destroyers sailed in line ahead with three launches to port, and four to starboard. Landfall was made at the appointed time (in spite of having to wait for a slow launch) and they approached to within 5 miles of the shore. The moon was hidden by mist, and visibility was poor. The outline of the lofty cliffs on the Torteval peninsula could just be seen, but it was virtually impossible to identify individual bays. Nevertheless it was decided to go ahead. The Commandos climbed down the scaling ladders into the launches 'with reasonable speed and silence' although none of them had ever before embarked into boats from a ship.

There was now only one launch available for the landing at Le Jaonnet, instead of two; and there were only two instead of three for La Moye. For the latter landing the *Saladin*'s whaler was pressed into service and towed by one of the launches. The full complement would be carried, but at a reduced speed. Only the landing on the Jerbourg peninsula could go ahead according to plan, with two launches and 40 men of No. 3 Commando under Lieutenant-Colonel J. F. Durnford-Slater.

Stress was laid on the importance of making simultaneous landings – at precisely 50 minutes past midnight – to maximize surprise and minimize the danger that the parties would be picked off one by one. The launches were to anchor close to the beaches to cover the withdrawal. Re-embarkation had to be completed by 2.30 a.m. at the latest, which gave the raiders an hour and forty minutes on shore.

The single launch destined for Le Jaonnet drew away from the *Saladin* at 40 minutes past midnight. It was immediately seen to take a course too far to the east; but there was nothing the destroyer could do about it. What went wrong was never satisfactorily explained. One theory was that the launch's compass was affected by the destroyer's degaussing equipment. Another, more likely, that the landing party's guns had been stowed too near to it.[2] Whatever the truth the launch

[1] AIR 20/2068; WO 106/2958.

[2] Sir Bernard Fergusson has suggested that the compasses were affected by the launches' own degaussing; but they were of wood and not degaussed. *The Watery Maze* (London, 1961), p. 49.

made a fruitless journey to an Island which one of the Commandos (a Channel Islander) believed to be Sark, but which was more probably Herm, although it could equally well have been Jethou, off Herm, or Brecqhou, off Sark. Whichever it was the party made no attempt to go ashore and successfully returned to the *Saladin* after an hour and three quarters in which they had accomplished precisely nothing.

The second party left the *Saladin* for La Moye five minutes later in two launches and the towed whaler. The latter at once started to leak and ship water. Bailing and pumping were of no avail and the men transferred to the launches, one of which kept the whaler in tow, and fell behind. A close watch was kept for the prearranged signals from the shore, but nothing was seen. This was hardly surprising since under the final plan Martel and Mulholland were not at La Moye but a mile and a half away at Le Jaonnet. They had duly taken up their position – as they had done on the two previous nights – but the party which should have seen their signal at Le Jaonnet was making an unscheduled trip to a distant and unidentified Island.

Neither launch found a suitable beach. The one towing the near-submerged whaler gave up the search at 5 minutes past three, and 20 minutes later was safely back at the destroyer. There was no sign of the other, which, having failed to rendezvous with the *Saladin*, headed for home, arriving at Dartmouth at 6 a.m.

The party under Durnford-Slater reached their destination – Petit Port on the Jerbourg peninsula. At first they found that they could not get right in to the beach because of the rocks and the swell. They had to wade through three or four feet of water carrying their equipment and weapons, but all managed to reach the shore. Patrols were sent out, a road block set up, and the Jerbourg peninsula searched. Nothing was found. There was no machine gun post in Telegraph Bay. Not a single German was to be seen. The men were therefore ordered to re-embark. As they scrambled down the cliff path a searchlight was switched on briefly, apparently looking for the Ansons which were providing noise cover, but fortunately it missed the launches and destroyers. There was a solitary burst of machine gun fire, then silence, broken only by a shot from Durnford-Slater's revolver, which went off accidentally when he slipped.

Re-embarkation was unexpectedly difficult. One launch was badly damaged and neither could get close in. A naval rating made several trips in a dinghy, ferrying men three at a time. On his fifth trip, when carrying all the guns and one soldier, the dinghy overturned in unusually heavy breakers. The soldier was swept away and presumed lost.[1] The men still on the beach were ordered to swim, but three who had already tried to wade out could not make it. They were given some French money and told to be at Creux Mahie between moonset and sunrise on the night of 16/17 July, when an attempt would be made to rescue them. Meanwhile they were to hide, or find shelter in friendly households. Later, Commander-in-Chief, Plymouth vetoed 'for naval reasons' the proposal to take the men off – a wise decision.

The others reached the launches with the help of the naval officers and ratings. The damaged launch was taken in tow by the other, and sunk when they reached the *Saracen*. The destroyer then headed for home. 'Anger/Ambassador' had been a resounding failure.

It had, however, provided experience for future Commando raids. The summing-up made it clear that air-sea rescue launches were unsuitable for this sort of enterprise. The morale of the men had been high throughout, in spite of their being soaked to the skin. In future every effort must be made to land men dry. The Commandos needed much more training. They had shown 'regrettable hesitation in entering deep water – even to avoid the risk of capture or death' during the withdrawal. All must learn to swim and have confidence in their lifebelts. The navy also came in for criticism, despite their help in getting the soldiers back into the launches. They had been less expert than the military force commander expected, and showed signs, in his opinion, of lack of experience.[2]

The main trouble was inadequate planning. One operational plan assumed that 'all landing parties will be accompanied by reliable local guides'. Another said that it was 'hoped that guides will be waiting at Le Jaonnet Bay'. A pilot well acquainted with the waters round Guernsey was supposed to join the leading destroyer, but he never materialized. The most remarkable thing about 'Ambassador' was that it cost no more than four men captured.

The operation caused much excitement on Guernsey. The Germans ordered Sherwill to make a thorough search in case some of the raiders were still at large. In passing this on to the police he observed: 'I can foresee all sorts of trouble if people land here clandestinely . . . however

[1] This was Gunner J. McGoldrick, who in fact struggled back to the shore and was taken prisoner. He returned to the United Kingdom with other prisoners of war in 1945. The others left behind were Privates F. T. Drain and A. Ross and Corporal D. Dumper. DEFE 2/66, 18 July 1945.
[2] WO 106/2958

detestable the duty of reporting the presence in our midst of such strangers may be, in the present circumstances I can see no way of avoiding it.' The police found more abandoned equipment[1] and someone reported sighting a waterlogged boat drifting out to sea (which suggests that the attempt to sink the damaged launch had failed), but no more men were found.

On 18 July Sherwill drafted a letter to Markbreiter at the Home Office saying: 'I do not know what the object of the landing was but to us it seems senseless.' Military activities of this kind were most unwelcome and could result in loss of life among the civilian population. He begged that the Islands should be left in peace, now that they were demilitarized. 'The Bailiff was amazed when he learned of the landing and in writing you thus I know I am expressing his view and that of many prominent people here.'[2] He hoped that the Germans would contrive to get this letter into the hands of the British authorities, but they refused to co-operate.

The Germans conducted a careful investigation into the raid as much to inform themselves about the nature of British Commando operations as to establish where their defences needed strengthening. The picture they built up from the evidence of the four prisoners, statements from the Islanders, the tracks of the raiding party, and abandoned equipment was limited to the landing on the Jerbourg peninsula.[3] They did not realize that there had been two other parties, and they were not enlightened by the prisoners. Had they been aware of the full extent of 'Ambassador' they would have formed an even lower opinion of the enemy's efficiency.

They concluded that the objective had been to take prisoners, preferably officers. Between 25 and 30 'long service volunteers' under the command of a lieutenant had been given some special training. The reconstruction of the voyage and landing is accurate, except that the Germans could not find out the names of the destroyers. The party climbed the cliff steps in single file, and when they reached the road leading to the Jerbourg peninsula split into three groups, after erecting a road block with stones from a nearby rock garden. One group went towards the centre of the Island to intercept any German patrols. The second attempted to destroy telephone wires, but failed because they had no climbing irons. They did, however, find one mast fitted with steps and cut sixteen wires leading from it. The third group went in search of the strong points in the peninsula, and were surprised to find

[1] Report of 15 July 1940.   [2] GF 7/1/3.   [3] MOD 588/306–7.

none. They threatened the occupants of a house and asked where the Germans were. Finally, after an hour and a half on shore, they returned to the beach, where they abandoned their equipment.

Having thus established the facts the Germans made a dispassionate appraisal of the operation. The raiding party had only two hours to do the job if they were to get away under the cover of darkness, which meant that detailed preparations were essential. In fact the preparations had been quite inadequate. The party had been hastily drawn from many different units; they had practised landing on a flat coast without any opposition; they were told the purpose of the mission only after they had sailed from England; they did not have the necessary equipment, for example, irons to climb telephone poles; and they had been mad to include non-swimmers in the party.

On the other hand the enemy had shown some good judgement. It was sensible to land near the narrowest point of the Jerbourg peninsula, as it seemed likely that there would be an observation post there. The landing place was well chosen, which showed good knowledge of the terrain. The road block was erected at a strategic point and if guarded by machine guns it would have been difficult to pass. It was also right to seek to destroy the communications with the centre of the Island and to carry barbed wire to cover the retreat.

The main lesson to be learned by the German garrison was that outposts on promontories were vulnerable, especially at night. They must be supported by detachments of troops which could help in their defence until reinforcements arrived. For some stretches of coast, however, motorized patrols would be enough. All posts should be protected at night by obstacles, and they should be connected to the nearest supporting troops by hidden telephone cable. The public telephone lines must not be used.

Admiral Lindau referred to 'Ambassador' in an assessment of the possibility of enemy landings in Northern France. He thought that it was on the cards that there would be landings of little military importance on beaches and in river mouths with the object of destroying harbour installations, railways, and communications, and taking prisoners. Such an attempt had taken place in Guernsey without success. There was also a danger that agents would be landed, and great vigilance was necessary.[1]

Meanwhile Martel and Mulholland were still on Guernsey. They

[1] T 314 445/578.

evaded capture – Martel stayed for a time with his sister and Mulholland with his mother – but after making several attempts to escape they gave themselves up. They got in touch with Sherwill, who provided them with uniforms of the Royal Guernsey Militia suitably doctored to look like British battle dress (they had landed in civilian clothes and were technically spies), and arranged for them to be handed over to the German authorities. They were lucky enough to be sent to France as prisoners of war. Martel's sister and Mulholland's mother were also lucky. It became known that they had given them shelter and they could properly have been convicted of helping spies, which carried a penalty of 15 years' penal servitude; but they were merely transferred to a place on the mainland of France at least 15 kilometres from the coast, where they were required to report daily to the German authorities. They were kept there until January 1941, when they were sent home. The Germans announced that they had been deported to stop any support by the civilian population of further English reconnaissance attempts on the occupied British Channel Islands.

The Wehrmacht wanted to learn as much as possible about their mission. They concluded that they had landed from a submarine on 10 July and that for part of the time they had been in civilian clothes. One of them, their inquisitors thought, had been told off to find out the whereabouts of German officers and men whom it was hoped to capture later; and the other to carry out a reconnaissance of the airfield. It was correctly presumed that they were the advance guard of the more powerful raid carried out on 14/15 July and that they were supposed to be picked up between 12 and 15 July; but this failed because of poor briefing. The rendezvous was too vague and the bays on the south coast looked very much alike. After an abortive attempt to sail to England they gave themselves up on 28 July. This, the *Armeeoberkommando* 6 version of the episode, was near the truth.

The lessons which the Germans decided they had learned were that a more alert coastal watch must be kept, especially by night; that there must be stricter control of all boats, including even the smallest; and that the movement of civilians near the coast must be carefully policed.[1]

The Prime Minister was personally responsible for setting in motion 'Anger/Ambassador'; but he did not mince his words about the failure of the enterprise. He had seen the folly of launching attacks on the

[1] MOD 583/310.

coasts of the occupied territories, which would simply encourage the enemy to strengthen their fortifications there. He minuted the Secretary of State for War on 23 July:

It would be most unwise to disturb the coasts of any of these countries by the kind of silly fiascos which were perpetrated at Boulogne and Guernsey. The idea of working all these coasts up against us by pin-prick raids and fulsome communiques is one strictly to be avoided.[1]

He was still anxious, however, to get the maximum amount of information about the occupied territories and said in the same minute:

It is of course urgent and indispensable that every effort should be made to obtain secretly the best possible information about the German forces in the various countries overrun, and to establish intimate contacts with local people and to plant agents. This I hope is being done on the largest scale, as opportunity serves . . .

It was probably because of this directive that special arrangements were made, too late as it turned out, to rescue Martel and Mulholland from Guernsey, in the hope that they had gleaned useful information during their enforced stay.

Sergeant Stanley Ferbrache, a Guernseyman serving with the Hampshire Regiment, was landed at Le Jaonnet Bay in the early hours of Saturday 3 August to collect and bring them back. The use of a motor torpedo boat showed that one of the lessons of 'Anger/Ambassador' had been learnt. Ferbrache found that they had surrendered a few days earlier. He therefore himself set about collecting information about the occupying forces so that his hazardous trip would show some profit. He was due to be picked up on either the following Monday or Tuesday. He waited in vain on the first night, but made a successful rendezvous on the second (6 August) and returned safely to England with the intelligence he had gathered. He was awarded the Distinguished Conduct Medal.

The next attempt to comply with the Prime Minister's directive was a return visit by Hubert Nicolle, who was on this occasion accompanied by Second Lieutenant James Symes, another Guernseyman serving with the Hampshire Regiment, and Robert Le Masurier[2] who was destined for Jersey. On 4 September Nicolle and Symes were landed at Petit Port from a motor torpedo boat which was to take Le Masurier on to Jersey; but they were three hours late in reaching Guernsey. It was after

[1] Churchill, op. cit. vol. ii. p. 572.
[2] Later Sir Robert Le Masurier, Bailiff of Jersey from 1962.

3 a.m., too near dawn to risk the trip to Jersey, and Le Masurier was therefore taken back to Portland. This time the agents, who wore civilian clothes from which all identification marks had been removed, were briefed to gather information about the situation generally on the eve of the first winter of occupation. How were the Islands off for fuel, food and medical supplies? Had any of the Islanders been removed to Germany? What was happening about employment? Were communications with France open? Was there trade with France and Germany? Nicolle and Symes were also to try to get in touch with Sherwill in Guernsey and Coutanche in Jersey.

Even in the dark they had no difficulty in scrambling up the 300-foot cliff path which they both knew well from boyhood and which they chose in preference to the winding steps provided for the less agile visitor. They found sanctuary that night – Nicolle with his uncle, the assistant harbour master, and Symes with Mr. Wilfred Bird – at his home in St. Peter-in-the-Wood. They had three days in which to carry out their mission, which was made the easier since Nicolle's uncle gave them an account of the state of affairs in the harbour, and his father, who was an official of the States, was well placed to tell them about the military government. One of the Island butchers provided an estimate of the size of the garrison, using his knowledge of the rationing arrangements and the amount of meat being supplied to the Wehrmacht.

They were thus well informed when they left their sanctuaries in the middle of the night of 5/6 September and made their way to the beach at Petit Port where they were to be picked up; but there was no sign of a boat, nor did it appear on the second or third nights. The weather had worsened and it had proved impossible for a motor torpedo boat to make the trip. They realized that they were marooned, for as the days passed the waxing moon would make it too dangerous for a boat to come inshore. During the next five weeks they lay low with friends and relatives, with some misgiving because of the heavy penalty for harbouring spies. They met regularly and worked out escape plans which for one reason or another came to nothing.

Nicolle, Martel, Mulholland, Ferbrache, Nicolle again, and Symes had all landed in Guernsey at great risk to themselves and to the exasperation of the population, who believed that their visits could only lead to greater oppression by the Germans; and in fact they had done little to further the Allied cause. When was the procession of unwanted, and on the whole unsuccessful agents, whose arrival was due to the Prime Minister's directive, to end? There was one more to come – Captain John Parker of the South Lancashire Fusiliers, who was sent to Guernsey to gather information for the purposes of Operation 'Tomato', the biggest assault on the Islands so far contemplated. It was planned in September 1940 as a follow-up to 'Anger/Ambassador'. The preparatory study says that 'the object given to us by the Prime Minister was to destroy or make prisoner all the enemy in the Channel Islands'. This was now much too ambitious; and indeed the Prime Minister's directive had been issued at a time when the German garrison was reasonably assumed to be small. It was now recommended simply that the aerodromes in Jersey and Guernsey should be captured and put out of action; and that as much damage as possible should be inflicted on the German military and civilian population in the Islands. Two forces, each 750-strong, were to attack Jersey and Guernsey, and 250 men were to be divided between Sark and Alderney. It was argued in favour of 'Tomato' – which was really four separate operations – that it would greatly benefit morale in Britain, and that it would shake some of the complacency out of the all-conquering Germans; but if the Islands were occupied for 24 hours, which was the intention at first, it was believed that the local population 'who were abandoned in the first instance' would feel that they were abandoned all over again. Therefore it would be better to have a 'tip-and-run' raid.

The provision of landing craft was a major problem. Air-sea rescue launches, which had been used in 'Ambassador' without much success, were now badly needed for their real job – picking up airmen from the sea. Possible alternatives were water taxis and Scottish salmon fishing 'cobles'. The latter could carry 30 men each at a speed of 6 knots, and it was suggested that they could be brought to the Islands slung from the davits of half a dozen small merchant ships.

At this time Nicolle, Symes, Martel, and Mulholland were all presumed to be in Guernsey, although their actual fate was, of course, not known. Sir Roger Keyes, the Director of Combined Operations, asked that yet another agent should be landed in Guernsey in the middle of September and that he should be brought back two or three days later to provide the latest possible information for 'Tomato'. He also noted that an attempt to land an agent – presumably Le Masurier – on the north coast of Jersey on 4 September had failed.

The new agent – Parker – had been brought up on Guernsey, where his father still lived. He was put ashore at the wrong place, and shortly afterwards fell noisily into a ditch. This alerted a sergeant in charge of an anti-aircraft gun, who shone a torch on him as he lay there, and made him prisoner.[1]

The intention had been to attack Guernsey at two different points between Point de la Moye and the Jerbourg peninsula. A small advance party would land from a submarine to create a diversion in the rear of the Germans defending the beaches. Much the same was to be done in Jersey, where there were also to be two landings – one on the north coast at Grève de Lecq, and the other on the west coast. Once again a small party was to be smuggled ashore from a submarine before the main attack began. The final decision as to which beaches would be used was to be made only when the agents had returned from Guernsey with the latest information about the dispositions of the Germans and the state of the defences. When no one returned, Operation 'Tomato' was called off.[2] On 21 September Sir Roger Keyes minuted the Prime Minister: 'I understand from my conversation with you today that in present circumstances you do not wish me to proceed with the project against the Channel Islands, especially in view of the lack of guns required if the Islands are to be held for a period.' He went on to say that he was still trying to get information about the German garrison through agents, but that their withdrawal had been delayed by bad weather. Churchill replied: 'Hold up the project for the present.'[3]

The records of Parker's interrogation still survive.[4] The points which most concerned his captors were how he had entered the Island; how long he had been there; whether he was an enemy agent; and what his objective was.

He was flown to Cherbourg on the day of his capture. He gave his name, rank, and regiment, and admitted that he had come by sea, but refused to give details. The Germans thought he might have landed by parachute but found no harness marks on his body. Several pieces of his equipment were wrapped in waterproof covers, which seemed to confirm that he had come by sea.

His interrogators badly wanted to establish how long he had been in the Island. The longer he had been there the better the chance of organizing sabotage. All the evidence, however, pointed to a recent arrival. The bread in his knapsack was white, and white bread was no longer available in Guernsey. Moreover, it was fresh. Parker referred to an article in the London *Evening Standard* of 26 September about the

---

[1] MOD 650/158.   [2] DEFE 2/613.
[3] PREM 3/87.   [4] T 315 1639/343-8, 666.

export of French goods to Guernsey, and another in the *Daily Sketch* of 27 September which he could not have seen had he been in Guernsey on those dates. Therefore he had probably arrived when he said he did. He had had no chance of organizing any resistance, or indeed of doing anything at all before his capture.

It was more difficult to determine his status. Was he, as he claimed, a captain in the South Lancashire Regiment carrying out a military task in Guernsey – a one-man invasion – or was he a spy? He wore a captain's battle dress with three pips adorned with thistles; but his uniform did not necessarily absolve him from being a spy. (The Germans knew that his predecessors had been given uniforms locally before they surrendered.) It was strange that he had no beret – he claimed he left it on the boat – and that he wore tennis shoes. His only papers were photographs of his three-year old daughter. He had no identity disc and although he said he had forgotten to wear it, this was considered suspicious. Nor had he a paybook, but then a British officer would not carry a paybook. There was nothing sinister in his equipment – an army pistol, electric torch, collar stud with built-in compass, silk handkerchief escape map of Europe, and a small file sewn in his pullover. He also had a thermos flask of coffee, some concentrated meat to go with his bread, and a bottle of whisky. His interrogators decided that none of this made him a spy.

It remained to guess his real objective. The Germans were unconvinced by his tale that he had come to make a reconnaissance of the airport. A captain would not be sent for that. More likely he was preparing the way for a raid, or setting up some means of communication with England, or finding out German plans for invading Britain. Whatever he was there for, it was not to reconnoitre the airport. But Parker stuck to his version and nothing would make him change it.

The Germans told him that he would be regarded as an enemy agent until he proved that he was not. The simplest thing, they said hopefully, was to make a full statement as to how and why he had come. He was not to be drawn. Then they said that other British raiders had been captured, and promised not to report him as an agent until he had met these men who might recognize him and establish that he was not a spy. This, according to the German report, made him hesitate. He must have wondered if the other captives were Nicolle and Symes, in which case there was little point in maintaining his fiction about visiting the airport. He admitted that the others might be connected with his own mission; but when they were brought before him next day they turned out to be the four men left behind in 'Ambassador', and they could not identify him.

All his statements were meticulously tested. His father's house in Guernsey was searched but nothing incriminating was found. There were, however, photographs which proved beyond all doubt that Parker was Parker. When his father, who had not seen him since 1938, was questioned, he corroborated the details of his son's career and family background. They checked the Army List. Parker passed all the tests with flying colours.

It was decided that he was no spy. He had refused (as was his right) to give military information, but he had been anxious to dispel doubts about his being an officer. He did not seem like a spy. Indeed it was clear from his bearing that he was an example of the younger, decent, and upright British officer. So after an interrogation spread over many days Parker found himself not before a firing squad but a prisoner of war.[1]

One result of his mission was that Admiral Schuster issued orders for increased precautions against the landing of enemy agents.[2]

During the time that Parker was steadfastly refusing to implicate them Nicolle and Symes were still at liberty; but they were becoming increasingly anxious about the trouble they might be storing up for those who were helping them. In the middle of October, when they had been in the Island for more than six weeks, they received a warning from a member of the staff of the *Guernsey Star*, who saw German announcements before they were published. He informed them that all British soldiers who had stayed behind at the time of demilitarization and were still at large, or who had since come to Guernsey would be required to report to the police by 21 October, as would people helping them. They would be regarded as prisoners of war and no action would be taken against their friends. Symes wanted to lie low and try to escape later on, but Nicolle thought they were endangering too many people. They consulted Major-General Williams, a retired officer of their own regiment, who advised them to give themselves up. Sherwill took the same line when approached by Nicolle's father.

Before they could safely surrender they had to find uniforms, which Nicolle's uncle helped them to do. Suitably attired, they presented themselves at St. Peter Port police station five minutes before the amnesty expired at 6 p.m. on 21 October. They believed that the

[1] He was repatriated on health grounds in 1943 and died in 1971.
[2] MOD 581/398.

Germans would honour their pledge, and had been so assured by Sherwill. But they were wrong. The entry in 216 Infantry Division's War Diary for 21 October records that the English officers Nicolle and Symes surrendered 'following an announcement by the Inselkommandant that servicemen who gave themselves up would be treated as prisoners of war'; and adds that they had been sent to obtain military information on behalf of the English secret service. Their case would be dealt with first by the *Kriegsgericht* of *Feldkommandantur* 515, and thereafter by the military administration on the mainland. There was no question of allowing the amnesty to apply to them. Thus from the first they were seen by the Germans for what they were – British spies, and not soldiers.[1]

They were thrown into the civilian prison, transferred to Fort George, where they were separately interrogated for many days, and finally brought before a court martial – at which one of the judges proudly informed them that he had been a Rhodes scholar. They were found guilty but Oberst von Schmettow, the *Befehlshaber*, refused to confirm the court's finding and referred the verdict to his superiors in France. In the meantime Nicolle and Symes languished in the condemned cells, believing that it was only a matter of time before the death sentence was carried out.

Thirteen of their relatives and friends with whom they had been in touch were also arrested and after questioning sent to prison in France. The Germans discovered that Sherwill had concealed the fact that Nicolle and Symes were on the Island. He too was arrested and sent to France. In a letter to Sir Alexander Maxwell at the Home Office written in July 1944 from the internment camp at Laufen[2] he gave his version of the affair:

As, from the German point of view, we were undoubtedly guilty things looked black. The then German Kommandant in Guernsey, a man of great charm and humanity, took a very chivalrous view of the matter and largely through his efforts Berlin ordered our release on 30th December 1940; and we returned to Guernsey, the sentences we had attracted

---

[1] T 315 1639/667. Nicolle and Symes both gained the impression that the Germans at first regarded them as soldiers but that halfway through their interrogation someone informed them that they were enemy agents, whereupon the interrogators' attitude suddenly changed and they became very hostile. The War Diary entry, however, makes it clear that they were regarded as spies right from the start; and the sudden change in attitude was probably part of the interrogators' technique to break down their resistance.

[2] Sherwill had been interned at Laufen since the beginning of 1943 as a former British officer. See Chapter 10.

(some very grim) being washed out. Knowing all the facts and appreciating the implications I was very impressed (and relieved) at the German decision.

Von Schmettow had the reputation of favouring the Channel Islanders whenever he could. Sherwill knew him well for more than two years and his judgement must be respected. It is possible, however, that von Schmettow's intervention in the Nicolle/Symes case was based less on his wish that no harm should come to the two young men (who were clearly guilty of espionage) than on his fear that if they were shot, which is what their judges wanted, the Islanders, who had accepted German rule with comforting docility, would become very difficult.

In an announcement on 24 December Oberst Schumacher, the *Feldkommandant*, said that it was established that Symes and Nicolle were guilty of espionage. Those who had helped them were guilty of high treason. Sherwill knew that there were spies on the Island and was also guilty. Nevertheless the German authorities, bearing in mind the amnesty which they had offered, had decided to be merciful. Nicolle and Symes would be treated as prisoners of war. The others, including Sherwill, would be brought back to Guernsey. Sherwill, however, could no longer be trusted. He would be released from his duties as President of the Controlling Committee and Attorney General. One of the prisoners did not return. Symes' father died in the Cherche Midi prison in Paris. The others were received with great sympathy by their fellow Islanders.[1]

The final decisions were transmitted to the Bailiff on 18 January 1941. Sherwill could hold no public office, nor could Nicolle's father and uncle, and Wilfred Bird. It was pointed out that the last three were not being punished for sheltering the agents – the amnesty saved them from that – but because they had tried to mislead the German authorities after the spies had given themselves up. It was of course necessary to make this clear in the interests of the honour of the occupying power. There was nothing against the rest of the thirteen, but the formal dismissal of the Nicolles and Bird had to be made effective right away.[2]

As a reprisal for the help given to Nicolle and Symes civilian radios had been confiscated; but when the prisoners came back from France the radios were returned. According to 216 Infantry Division's War Diary 'great gratitude was expressed by the Islanders for the generosity of the German military administration'.[3] Von Schmettow had been instrumental in saving the lives of the two agents – whatever his motive – and

[1] GF 8/1/5.   [2] GF 7/1/3.   [3] T 315 1639/658, 669.

the War Diary had to demonstrate that his plea for clemency had paid a dividend from the German point of view. It was still the German policy to establish a benevolent image and if the terms of the amnesty had been dishonoured, or had seemed to be dishonoured, it would not have helped. Honour still meant something to some German soldiers, and there were occasions when they were prepared to fight to see it maintained.

While the British were landing a series of agents in the Channel Islands, German Intelligence in France were planning to return the compliment. On 9 October 1940 they informed Admiral Schuster that it was proposed to send 'a specially qualified agent' from Jersey to England in a fishing boat at the end of the month. It would have to be made to look like an ordinary escape, and to facilitate this the coastguard must not be let into the secret – the implication being that if the agent was killed or captured by his own side, it would be just too bad. There had, however, been discussion with the *Inselkommandant* about how to post the guard on the chosen night to give the agent the best chance of getting away unobserved. His boat, which was being used as an 'auxiliary harbour patrol boat', would have to be anchored where it could easily be reached. Intelligence were under the impression that there had been some trouble about the theft of boats in Jersey, which had led to the restriction of fishing; they asked to be briefed on this, lest it had some bearing on the story with which their man would have to be armed.

Schuster arranged for the *Hafenkommandant* in Jersey to be consulted and in due course reported that there was no objection to the plan. The only other reference to the mission which has survived is a memorandum of 10 November from German Intelligence, France, informing Schuster that on 10, 11 or 12 November 'a boat will sail for England between 19.30 and 20.00 hours'. The fact that this information was passed to the Admiral on the first of the three days selected for the enterprise, and the fact that it was stated so definitely, leaves no doubt that German Intelligence had already selected someone for the job, and that he was fully briefed and ready to go.[1]

Who was he, this specially qualified agent, what was his background, and what was he going to do in England? We can only guess. He may have been a Channel Islander, most likely a Jerseyman, who would have no difficulty in substantiating an escape story; he may have been a

[1] MOD 583/416, 438.

Frenchman, who had ostensibly escaped to Jersey, where he had stolen a fishing boat to complete his escape from German occupation; or, and this seems to be the most likely, he may have been one of the Irishmen living in the Channel Islands who had no love for Britain and were assiduously cultivated by the Germans – perhaps one of the men with whom the German agent rubbed shoulders in 1938.[1] The authorities in Britain were so careful in their examinations that they would have little difficulty in exposing anyone not in one of these categories, particularly as there were now so many Channel Islanders in Britain who could be called in to test the escaped man's story. The mystery remains unsolved.

The German documents disclose nothing more on the subject. There is no record of an escape on any of the three days mentioned, and indeed if anyone had ventured single-handed from St. Helier harbour at that time he would have had a very difficult passage. Gales raged during the whole of November and on 13 November gusts of 100 miles an hour were recorded.[2] If the agent did set off for England on the evening of 12 November it is unlikely that he reached his destination.

A survey of the early operations during the occupation of the Channel Islands would be incomplete without reference to the part played by the R.A.F. A number of bombing raids were carried out, with some misgiving, since it was impossible to ensure that only military targets were hit. Moreover, it was probable that if the attacks were successful the Germans would organize reprisals against the people. In fact the raids achieved little, and they were carried out for propaganda purposes more than anything else. The newspaper reports, which were no doubt read with great trepidation by the thousands of Channel Islanders evacuated to Britain, made the most of them. In the middle of August 1940 there were raids on Guernsey aerodrome on three successive days. On the evening of Friday 9 August the raiders counted between 40 and 50 German planes – fighters, twin-engined bombers and transports – and claimed direct hits on one of the transport planes and the hangars. The official German report said that there were five English planes, that one soldier was killed and four civilians wounded. A barracks near the aerodrome and petrol stores were destroyed by fire.[3]

When a second raid was made the following day all the planes had disappeared, but there were hits on the hangars. There was a night attack when three waves of Coastal Command aircraft went in at short

[1] Chapter 4, p. 61.   [2] Sinel, p. 25.   [3] MOD 581/175.

intervals. On the third day there was 'accurate bombing from high altitude' by medium bombers, and smoke from the fires they started was seen seven miles away.[1]

A *Times* correspondent suggested on 29 July that the Channel Islanders could be kept in touch with the affairs of the outside world if the R.A.F. were to drop leaflets from time to time summarizing the more important events; and this idea was developed by the Political Intelligence Department of the Foreign Office. It was proposed to drop a news-sheet once a fortnight. Two were prepared, the first, dated September 1940, being dropped during the night of 23/24 September. The second, dated 30 September, was dropped in the middle of October.[2] At this time a member of parliament wrote to the Home Office suggesting that leaflets should be dropped in the Islands, and was told that it had already been done. The Home Secretary added: 'I am most anxious that nothing should be said in public on this subject ... there is obviously a danger that the enemy may take steps to penalise persons picking up such leaflets.' It is difficult to see what difference the fact that it was known in Britain that leaflets were being dropped would have made.

Shortly afterwards it was decided to stop the leaflets. For the time being at least the Islanders could get the B.B.C. news on their radios; and there was the danger that the continued dropping of leaflets might induce the Germans to take a tougher line. There is some evidence in diaries kept by Islanders that leaflets did help morale; but except for the text of the Archbishop of York's sermon at St. Martin-in-the-Fields in 1943[3] no more were dropped until 1944, when a new campaign was started – this time not to boost the morale of the people, but to hasten the collapse of the garrison.[4]

[1] *The Times*, 12–13 August 1940.   [2] GF 7/1/3.
[3] See below p. 316.   [4] See Chapter 11.

Note: Captain John Parker carried in his head a code to be passed to his fellow prisoners of war, should he be captured. This code, one of the first recipients of which was Lieut. the Hon. Terence Prittie M.B.E. (who subsequently escaped) was widely dispersed among prisoners of war. It was used to send much valuable information back to Britain, and to facilitate escapes.

6

Occupation Government

(a) The theory

THE right of the German government to rule the British Channel Islands derived from the fact of military occupation; but the Islanders submitted to the will of the occupying authority by registering German orders in the Royal Courts. On the other hand neither bailiwick signed an instrument of surrender; both owed allegiance to the British Crown, which was not a party to the surrender. But whatever the constitutional theory, whatever the implications of international law, whatever the attitude of the British government, whatever the intention of the Island authorities, all were swept aside by force of arms.

At first the troops, under Major Lanz in Guernsey (where the Wehrmacht had its headquarters) and Hauptmann Gussek in Jersey, were responsible for civil government. The most important early measure was published in Guernsey on 2 July and in Jersey six days later. It provided the basis of a constitution which changed little throughout the occupation. The Island administrations were to carry on as usual, except that new laws would be submitted to the German *Kommandant*. Legislation which would have needed the sanction of the King in Council must be approved by the *Kommandant* and the Bailiff. German orders must be registered so that no one could plead ignorance of them. The Island courts would continue, but offences against German military law would be tried by German courts.[1]

Divine worship was permitted, so long as church services were not used for propaganda 'or utterances against . . . the German government or forces'. Prayers for the British Royal Family and the welfare of the British Empire were allowed. The National Anthem, however, could not be sung without permission, although it might be listened to on the

[1] It was later laid down that no German could appear before an Island court. NG Ia/1.

radio. Public entertainments were permitted so long as there was no propaganda against the Reich. For the rest, prices were to be controlled, publicans were adjured to keep their clients sober, and civilian passenger traffic between Jersey and Guernsey was prohibited. Finally, a warning note was sounded. The privileges accorded to the people would depend on their good behaviour.[1]

At this time relations were remarkably cordial. Anyone could write direct to the Island *Kommandanten*; and as a rule replies were prompt and helpful. Someone who reported that a German soldier had stolen his bicycle was assured that every effort would be made to trace it. A proposal to export melons and grapes from Guernsey to Jersey was welcomed. 'We shall be only too pleased to see normal trading re-established between the two Islands.'[2] When the answer had to be no, it was given with exemplary courtesy. A lady seeking permission to write to her bank in London was told: 'Unfortunately at the present moment we can see no possibility of communication such as you mention in your letter.'[3] It was announced that the *Kommandant* of the German forces, or one of his staff officers, would be available for interviews between 11 a.m. and 1 p.m. on weekdays.[4] The officer in charge of Castle Cornet appealed for football boots, books, and cigarettes for the prisoners of war there; and he welcomed offers to arrange sporting fixtures for them.[5]

According to Lord Coutanche, writing many years later, Gussek took little interest in civil administration, and was perfectly happy that the existing government should carry on as usual.[6] No doubt he and his fellows were more concerned with the next move in the Blitzkrieg – the conquest of Britain.

The initial phase of the occupation ended in August 1940. The German military government organization took over the administration from the troops. The Channel Islanders were considered to be part of the *Département de la Manche*, and thus found themselves in one of the sub-districts in military government Area A, which was centred on St. Germain. *Feldkommandantur 515*[7] was established in Jersey with

[1] NG 01/3.
[2] Ibid.
[3] NG Bundle D.
[4] 5 July 1940.
[5] NG Bundle D.
[6] Coutanche, p. 37.
[7] *Feldkommandantur 515* (Field Command 515) was assembled in Munich in September 1939. The unit served in Luxembourg before being transferred to the Channel Islands. Orders of the day on 10 September 1942 conveyed third birthday greetings to all the staff. NG 01/31.

responsibility for all the Islands. The *Feldkommandant,* Oberst Schumacher, arrived on 9 August. He set up three subordinate posts – a *Nebenstelle* (branch) on Guernsey; an *Aussenstelle* (outpost) on Alderney; and a *Zufuhrstelle* (stores assembly point) at Granville in France. Sark, which had few administrative problems, was managed from Guernsey.

It was logical for the Germans to regard the Islands as part of France for administrative purposes, particularly since Hitler believed that they were unwilling British colonies. The more they were deemed to be French the more willingly they would accept the regime that had liberated them from the colonial yoke. A lawyer sent from Germany to study the constitution in July 1940, however, reported that the Islanders were 'very good English patriots. It would be a mistake to assume otherwise, even though according to us they are of Norman origin.' His other findings were less near the truth. Jersey and Guernsey, in which there had been repeated attempts to increase Whitehall's authority, were classic cases of 'Home Rule'. 'The inhabitants therefore watch jealously over their rights and privileges.' The British parliament had great influence in the Islands, whose interests took second place to those of the United Kingdom. The lawyer admitted, however, that it was difficult to understand the constitution. The usual German concepts of 'democracy and authoritarian state' did not fit. 'Representation and government are scarcely to be differentiated . . . one must go back to the conditions of the middle ages, the concepts of fief, court leet, feudal lord, feudal tenant, in order to understand the constitutional position in Guernsey, which even now in the twentieth century is feudal.'[1]

Oberst Schmundt, Hitler's Wehrmacht adjutant, touched on the same point in October 1941. He observed that the Islands had had their own constitutions since 1204, when they were separated from Normandy. 'They look on themselves as neither French nor English, but as British subjects of the Duke of Normandy, the King of Britain, and a part of the Empire.' In his opinion the military government needed to be specially briefed as to how they should handle the constitution and the people.[2]

The headquarters of the military government in Paris was divided

[1] NG 01/3.
[2] T 78 317/6271803. German propaganda consistently stressed that the Islands were oppressed by Britain. An article in a German newspaper published in Zagreb said that they were independent only on paper. Wherever the English went all freedom was lost – there was plenty of evidence of this in world history. *Neue Ordnung,* 16 August 1942.

into the *Verwaltungsstab* (administration staff), which was concerned with civil affairs; and the *Kommandostab* (military staff), which dealt with the armed forces. This division was repeated in the area head-quarters, and the subordinate units. FK 515 had a military branch (*Militärische Führung*) and a separate branch responsible for the administration of the civil government of the Islands. The former was headed in Jersey by a major who kept in close touch with the military commander. Three captains and two lieutenants looked after quarters, victuals, recreation, transport, weapons, defence against air raids and gas attack, the *Geheime Feldpolizei* (secret military police), complaints from the men, and so on. There was a court martial branch, a paymaster, a medical officer, and a veterinary officer. There was a smaller parallel branch in the *Nebenstelle* in Guernsey.

FK 515's administration branch was in the charge of an *Ober-kriegsverwaltungsrat* (senior war administrator), who supervised the civil government. He had four subordinate branches covering between them general administration, occupation costs, war damage, price control and financial matters, police, education, health, justice, propaganda, postal services, and the control of essential supplies and services. Again, the *Nebenstelle* in Guernsey had smaller parallel branches. The *Aussenstelle* in Alderney had virtually no civilian responsibilities since at no time was there more than a handful of civilians there. The stores assembly point at Granville was managed by a *Sonderführer*.[1]

The civilians on the staff of the *Feldkommandantur* were liable to military service until the end of the war, but did not wear the uniform of serving officers. They were, however, issued with pistols and ammunition. They trained with the troops for half a day each week, and they also had a week's training every six months. In 1943 it was asked whether this training represented 'military duty'. What happened if a man was killed or wounded? There could be complications, for example about life insurance. It was ruled that civil affairs personnel must be regarded as combatants.[2]

When Oberst Schumacher took up office as *Feldkommandant* he announced that he had assumed command 'so far as there are no military objects concerned'. The military commanders were still fully responsible for military affairs. (This was for the benefit of the civilian population and was not strictly accurate since the *Feldkommandantur* was in fact concerned with military supplies.) He would honour the undertakings already given about preserving the lives and property of

[1] NG 01/34.   [2] NG II; 01/1.

the inhabitants. In return he expected that the people would continue to be loyal to the occupying power.[1]

FK 515 was in effect a secretariat responsible for ensuring that the government of the Islands was carried on efficiently. This followed the pattern set for occupied France, where the Germans contented themselves with controlling the French administration. It was strictly forbidden for civilians to deal direct with the troops. All transactions must go through the *Feldkommandantur*.

The relationship between the military government and the troops was at times strained. After the first month or two of occupation the Wehrmacht was concerned only with the military security of the Islands, a matter which increased in importance with Hitler's increasingly exaggerated idea of their value. Its strength was built up to an enormous level, in spite of the fact that a relatively small force would have been enough to keep both bailiwicks under control, to give the military government all the support they needed, and to defend the Islands against any likely attack.

When they were appointed the officials of the *Feldkommandantur* had no doubt assumed that they would follow in the wake of the victorious Wehrmacht, and that before long they would come into their own as the true governors of the Islands. That this did not happen was partly due to the prolongation of the war, and to Hitler's insistence that the Islands must become a permanent German fortress. FK 515 had to continue to deal with huge numbers of troops, long after they had expected to be rid of most of them. They resented this, particularly those of them who were civilians in uniform who bore no great love for combat troops. The Wehrmacht for their part made no secret of the fact that they despised the military government officials. Since they had little to do other than fire the anti-aircraft and coastal guns from time to time there was plenty of opportunity for mutual resentment to build up.

This feeling was not peculiar to the Channel Islands but it was more marked there because the two organizations were thrown closer together. In October 1940 the Wehrmacht and the civil affairs units had to be formally reminded about their respective roles. This had been done three months earlier, but it seemed that the position was not understood – or was not being accepted. The military government was responsible

[1] NG 01/30. Schumacher remained in office until August 1941 when his health failed. He was replaced on 18 September by Oberst Knackfuss from FK 735.

for supervising the administration of the occupied territories, and for the maintenance of order. The Wehrmacht was permitted to arrest suspicious characters and offenders caught in the act; but threats to security were to be dealt with by the *Feldkommandantur*. The Wehrmacht had been shorn of the wide powers it enjoyed in the early days of the war in the west; although commanders of Army Groups shared with the military government certain rights in the field of civil affairs, they could exercise them only when required by unforeseen and immediate military expediency, and after the *Feldkommandant* had asked for their help. No military commander could give orders to the *Feldkommandant*.

The order concludes by exhorting both organizations to co-operate: 'This is a duty. The troops must support the work of the military administration. The military administration must have regard to the interests of the troops.' There must be comradeship between officers of the Wehrmacht and those of the civil affairs units; if there was any more friction it had to be reported to the *Oberbefehlshaber des Heeres* (Commander-in-Chief of the Army) in person.[1]

A few months later an order was issued jointly by the *Inselkommandant* (von Schmettow) and the *Feldkommandant* (Schumacher) defining the relationship between the troops and the civil affairs units in the Channel Islands, which suggests that the earlier exhortations had not had much effect.[2] In October 1941 the new *Feldkommandant* (Knackfuss) had once again to warn off the military. They had no right to interfere in the agricultural and economic life of the Islands.[3]

The Island administrations were the third element in the occupation government of the Channel Islands. They had already, before invasion, been tailored to meet the circumstances of occupation, in so far as they could be foreseen. The most important change was the severance of the link with the King in Council; but this had been partly compensated for when the Islands were given the right to make their own defence regulations. The Assembly of the States in Jersey and the States of Deliberation in Guernsey were not designed to produce the swift decisions which might be needed under occupation, and they created subordinate bodies which effectively exercised most of their powers for the duration. In both Islands, however, the States continued to meet to deal with the annual financial estimates, the Budget, and so on.

The main burden was carried by the Superior Council in Jersey, and

[1] Order of 9 October 1940.   [2] NG 01/3.   [3] Ibid. 01/1.

by the Controlling Committee in Guernsey. The latter was set up by the States of Deliberation on 21 June 1940, with Sherwill, the Attorney General, as President.[1] He was chosen rather than Victor Carey, the Bailiff, because he was a younger and more energetic man. The Controlling Committee was given virtually all the powers of the States. It had a minimum of three members including the President, who had the right to nominate further members. At first there was a total of eight.

The Committee held its first meeting on 25 June and met roughly once a week for the whole of the occupation. The frequency of its meetings depended on the ruling situation. It had ten meetings in July 1940 when no one knew what occupation was going to mean; but only two in October 1943 when things had settled down. It became more active again during the siege which followed the invasion of the continent by the Allies, and met nine times in November 1944. It transacted business like any other committee. Papers were prepared for discussion, and officials concerned with particular problems were called in and examined. When its conclusions called for action they were transmitted to the department concerned. Its proceedings were admirably recorded and typed on paper the diminishing quality of which reflects the increasing stringency of the times.

In Jersey the functions of the large number of existing Committees were concentrated in eight Departments, each under the Presidency of a member of the States.[2] The Presidents, together with the Crown Officers, were formed into a Superior Council under the Presidency of the Bailiff. The Council first met on 24 June and thereafter at least once a week. On 27 June the States formally transferred to the newly-constituted Departments the powers which previously had been vested in the Lieutenant-Governor and the Committees of the States.[3] According to the Bailiff: 'The Council became the emergency administration subject to the over-riding authority of the States, which continued to meet from time to time as required. It became the duty of the Superior Council and the Presidents of the Departments to act as a buffer between the civil population and the army of occupation.'

Thus each bailiwick had a small 'cabinet' which could manage the affairs of the Islands more efficiently in the circumstances of the occupation than could the elaborate machinery of normal times. The

[1] *Billet d'État* No. X, 1940.

[2] Finance and Economics; Transport and Communications; Public Instruction; Public Health; Agriculture; Labour; Essential Services; and Essential Commodities.

[3] Through the Defence (Transfer of Powers) (Jersey) Regulation, 1940.

Controlling Committee in Guernsey, however, was more of a cabinet in the true sense than the Superior Council in Jersey. The Guernsey Committees, over which the members of the Controlling Committee presided, met infrequently as compared with the corresponding bodies in Jersey. The members of the Controlling Committee acted more as Ministers in charge of a Department of State than did their opposite numbers on the Superior Council. Since the two bodies met in private it was easier to frame policies which favoured the inhabitants against the occupying authorities than in the public sittings of the States; and if the States had met in secret session it would have aroused suspicion. If we are to understand the Islanders' contribution to the government of the occupied bailiwicks it is to the performance of the Superior Council and the Controlling Committee that we must look. Probably, in the event, the somewhat different systems of administration were best suited to the needs of each Island and the personalities involved.

Finally, the Hague Convention had some bearing on the relationship between the Islanders and the occupying authorities. In September 1940 the civil affairs headquarters of Area A at St. Germain made a study of the legal procedures to be followed in the Channel Islands, and gave a ruling about the application of the Convention. The Islands belonged to the British Empire, with which the Reich had not concluded an armistice. Therefore the Hague Convention was not directly relevant. Nevertheless, since the Island administrations were subordinate to the occupying power the German authorities should conduct themselves according to the Convention. This was laid down on the assumption that the Islanders would obey laws made by the occupying power and that there would be no serious friction between occupier and occupied.[1] When there was an argument about jurisdiction in Guernsey in 1942 the *Feldkommandant* agreed that the Convention allowed the Island courts to deal with offences by civilians which did not affect security; but he ruled in the case in point that German interests were at stake, and that the *Feldkommandantur* court must therefore try it. In fact, throughout the occupation the Germans cited the Convention when it suited them, and ignored it when it did not; but they did at least take it into consideration in making their own calculations. For example, in October 1944 they decided that 'dire need' for the purposes of the Convention had not been established, since the garrison's supplies were not exhausted.[2]

[1] NG 01/3.   [2] T 77 787/5515370; see also below p. 131.

(b) The practice

The Island authorities' objectives were to remain on reasonable terms with the occupying power, to maintain law and order, and to keep the people as well fed and in as good health as possible. The Germans for their part had to keep on good terms with the Islanders, for without their co-operation it would have been difficult to run the bailiwicks.

The Islanders could have caused trouble had they opted for a trial of strength. They were superficially in a much stronger position than they realized. General Jodl said that if many were evacuated it would leave a desert – the Wehrmacht simply could not do without them.[1] It was estimated that three-quarters were working directly or indirectly for the troops. Had they sought to deviate from the line mutually convenient to occupier and occupied the *Feldkommandantur* would either have had to bring in specialists to keep essential services going, and many thousands of other helpers, which was virtually impossible; or they would have had to compel the people to do their bidding. Although at first they wanted to maintain a benevolent image, in view of their pending occupation of Britain, they would have had no hesitation in showing themselves in their true colours if it became necessary to put pressure on the Islanders.

Secondly, the Germans were just as much concerned as the Islanders about the maintenance of law and order. If they seemed to be indifferent about the innumerable robberies at the end of the occupation when hunger drove many – Islanders and troops alike – to crime, it was simply because they did not have the resources to stop them.

Thirdly, so long as there was enough food, the civilians had their fair share; and although there were attempts to discriminate in favour of the troops, the condition of the Islanders was a good deal better than that of the Wehrmacht in May 1945. The Islanders had to be kept in good health. Epidemics are no respecters of persons and if disease became rampant among the civilians it was bound to spread to the forces.

In June 1941 the *Nebenstelle* raised the general question of security with the *Inselkommandant* in Guernsey. Three months earlier *Geheime Feldpolizei* Group 131, which was assigned to the troops, and Group 312, which had been watching the civil population, had been withdrawn. This was dangerous since the people might grow hostile as food became scarcer and the war bore more heavily on them. It was agreed at a

[1] T 77 788/5517288.

meeting at area headquarters in St. Germain that the *Geheime Feld-polizei* should again be assigned to FK 515. The *Feldkommandantur* must at all costs be enabled to be the dominant partner in the government of the Islands. The people must not be shown 'unnecessary mildness' nor should the military government be lulled into a sense of false security by friendly relations with the local administrations. If necessary the full rigour of the law must be applied against them. This makes it clear (if there was ever any doubt) that while the Islanders could for a time have undermined the occupying power, for example, by withholding their labour, it would have swiftly led to their destruction.[1]

During the occupation the States continued to pass 'statutes', although in a smaller volume than in normal times. The Superior Council and Controlling Committee issued orders which were blessed by the military government. The office of the military governor in Paris poured out *Verordnungsblätter* (VOBIFs for short).[2] These sometimes contained one or two clauses relating to the Channel Islands in particular and on rare occasions a whole issue was devoted to them. Finally, the Wehrmacht issued for its own purposes orders which applied to the civil population, their justification being military necessity, and their legal basis the armed might of the Wehrmacht.

When the Islanders initiated legislation the Department concerned drafted an order which was approved by the *Feldkommandantur*. At first these measures were endorsed 'by Monsieur le Commandant of the German forces'. In Jersey they were sanctioned by 'Monsieur le Bailiff in his capacity of Lieutenant-Governor and Bailiff'; and in Guernsey the Bailiff signed as 'British Civil Lieutenant-Governor', or 'His Majesty's Lieutenant-Governor'. The *Feldkommandant* objected to these forms at the end of 1941 on the ground that the local administrations now derived their authority from the occupying power. After this the Lieutenant-Governors signed simply as 'Bailiff'.

The *Feldkommandantur* required most of the orders originating from the military government in Paris to be registered and published; but there were exceptions. An order of 1940 about miniature films had to be registered but not published. Another, also concerning films, had to be neither registered nor published. One about hunting game had to be registered and published in both German and English; but since there

[1] NG If/1; Ic.
[2] The full title of this publication was *Verordnungsblatt des Militärbefehls-habers in Frankreich* (Official Gazette of the Military Governor in France). It was published in German and French.

were no gamekeepers in the Islands a paragraph dealing with them had to be omitted. Only the preamble and signature of the second order concerning anti-Jewish measures (which required Jewish undertakings to declare their shareholdings) had to be published.

The Island authorities could have turned the anti-Jewish laws into a test case. There were few Jews left in the Islands, and little was at stake, except a principle. If the Islanders had refused to register the legislation it would have been promulgated by decree, but at least they would have made a stand. At what cost we cannot tell.

In his unpublished memoirs Sherwill has left an account of the Royal Court's discussion of the first anti-Jewish measures. He says that he had satisfied himself that the few Jews had all gone – although in fact at this time there were still four Jewesses resident in Guernsey.[1] The order disgusted him, but he felt that there was no point in opposing it. He wrote:

Nevertheless, I still feel ashamed that I did not do something by way of protest to the Germans: a vital principle was at stake even if no human being in Guernsey was actually affected. The honour of refusing to concur in its registration fell to Sir Abraham Lainé who, when called on as a Jurat to vote on the matter, openly and categorically refused his assent and stated his grave objections to such a measure . . . this courageous act of his should never be forgotten.

Sherwill himself deserves credit for recording so frankly that Lainé was right and he was wrong. He later made the point that he was anxious at this time – October 1940 – to avoid a collision with the Germans while his manoeuvre to save Nicolle and Symes from being shot as spies was still in progress.[2]

Two Channel Islanders may have been saved. The laws against the Jews may have seemed unimportant at the time. They assumed a new significance, however, when Jewish Organisation Todt workers began to pour in. The newcomers – no less human than Nicolle and Symes – were deemed by the law of these British Islands to be just as far beyond the pale as the most despicable German Jew-baiter would have them. But the Island authorities were not omniprescient. They could hardly

[1] GF 1/1/2.
[2] Sir Abraham Lainé had had a distinguished career in the Indian Civil Service before retiring to his native Guernsey. He was President of the Committee for the Control of Essential Commodities from its inception in 1938; and he was a member of the Controlling Committee also from its inception. His wisdom and experience proved invaluable in both capacities and he was regarded by the German authorities as a man to be reckoned with.

foresee that a matter of academic principle might suddenly become a matter of hard and shameful practice.

In Jersey 12 Jews were registered, and in both bailiwicks shops which had been owned by Jews were placarded 'Jewish Undertaking'. Some, managed by administrators, were allowed to display a notice stating that they were 'under an Aryan administrator'. One or two small businesses which were too small to justify the appointment of an administrator were closed.

The courts continued to function much as usual, and tried the great majority of civil and criminal civilian cases. For most of the occupation there were four other courts with overlapping jurisdictions before which the Islanders might have to appear.

The *Feldkommandant*'s court, which was mainly concerned with the civil population, was serviced by the *Feldgendarmerie* and the *Geheime Feldpolizei*. If a traffic offence was spotted by the *Feldgendarmerie* the offender would appear in the *Feldkommandant*'s court. If the same offence was reported by the Island police the case would be heard in the magistrate's court.

All three sections of the Wehrmacht had their own courts under the *Befehlshaber*, who was the chief military judge. The *Feldgericht der Luftwaffe* was responsible for trying all 'Luftwaffe cases'. It had jurisdiction over Luftwaffe personnel, members of specialist organizations (e.g. the Organisation Todt) working for the Luftwaffe, and foreigners accused of crimes on Luftwaffe property, directed against Luftwaffe property or personnel, or in aid of enemy air forces. The other elements of the Wehrmacht – the army and the navy – had comparable courts. It was thus technically possible for a Channel Islander to appear before any one of five courts depending on who employed him, the nature of his offence, and who arrested him.

Sometimes offenders would appear before both an Island court and a German court for related offences. In 1942 four Guernseymen were accused in the *Feldkommandant*'s court of buying and reselling livestock without authority. They were found guilty under German penal law (VOBIF of 9 April 1941) but this did not cover their other offences, which included illegal slaughtering. The *Feldkommandant*'s court ordered that they should be tried on the other charges; and they were duly found guilty in the police court.[1] On another occasion a group of Guernseymen were accused of offences against both the military

[1] GF 5/1/8.

government and the civil codes. They were first tried and sentenced by the *Feldkommandant*'s court, and were then handed over to the civil authorities to be tried and sentenced for their other offences. The Bailiff ruled that the sentences must be consecutive, since the Royal Court was not concerned with the findings of the German courts. This ruling may have had the merit of purity so far as the Royal Court was concerned, but it did substantially increase the sentences which the men had to serve.[1]

The three Wehrmacht courts were relatively independent of each other and of the *Befehlshaber* who was their nominal head. 'Only in the event of an enemy landing does the *Festungskommandant* [i.e. the *Befehlshaber*] of an isolated fortress in the battle area have unrestricted judicial authority.' Otherwise his powers were limited to offences affecting the safety of the fortress or involving more than one element of the Wehrmacht. When the fortress was under attack or cut off from the main German forces the *Befehlshaber*, in his capacity as chief judge, was deemed to have judicial powers, and indeed the power of life and death over the whole of the Wehrmacht and civil population in the fortress area.

Comprehensive prison rules, based on instructions to the French Ministry of Justice from the military governor in Paris, were issued to the Bailiffs in October 1941. It was laid down that 'sentences of imprisonment inflicted on inhabitants of the country by German courts martial are, even in the native institutions, to be executed according to German principles'. The prison governor was responsible for applying the rules, but a German office, which, in the case of the Channel Islands, was FK 515, had to satisfy itself that German principles were in fact being followed.[2]

Early measures to ensure stable government included orders to surrender all weapons within 24 hours. The Island authorities had taken the same step before the invasion but the Germans could take no risks. A single firearm in the hands of a hot-headed patriot could remove the *Inselkommandant*, or even the *Führer* if he deigned to visit his latest conquest. The Germans agreed, however, that souvenirs might be retained. Licences were solemnly issued for spears, assegais, tulwars, krises, and kukris, reflecting the imperial careers of many residents; for

[1] Some of these men appealed to the Judicial Committee of the Privy Council in 1952.
[2] FK Ia.

cutlasses inherited from the Island's piratical past; for pikes, also from an earlier age; for starting pistols, evoking memories of sports days in happier times; and even for a tomahawk and a pop-gun. A colonel, 'late Royal Siamese Gendarmerie', was allowed to retain a sporting gun given him by the King of Siam.[1] At first people were allowed to keep air guns, but later even these were called in.[2]

When a Guernsey doctor who was not well-regarded by the *Geheime Feldpolizei* belatedly handed in a pistol found in his attic he came under suspicion. Although the weapon was useless the *Inselkommandant* was tempted to make an example of him, but in the end did nothing.[3] About the same time (March 1941) the discovery of a light aeroplane in a garage in St. Peter Port caused excitement. It was damaged and the owner claimed that he had already reported it. The *Inselkommandant* summoned the Bailiff, who, according to the German account, was reduced to 'a rather nervous state' and disclaimed all knowledge of the matter. It was proposed that if the Island authorities did in fact know about the plane the official concerned should be arrested; but it was finally agreed that the Controlling Committee should be responsible for its safe custody.[4]

This episode gave rise to a new Island-wide search for arms in government establishments and unoccupied premises, which caused much work and produced massive nil returns. The Harbour Master did, however, report two Russian guns dating from 1856, and two ancient swordsticks formerly used by customs officers for pricking bales when looking for contraband.[5] The Bailiff warned the public to obey the order to search every nook and corner for weapons and implements of war. Householders were told that it covered any aeroplane they happened to have on their premises. The lesson of the plane in the garage had been learned![6]

There were parallel searches in Jersey. The *Feldkommandant* wrote to the Bailiff saying that he presumed that all weapons had been handed in in July 1940; but that a further examination, especially of abandoned houses, must now be carried out. At the end of 1941 there was yet another search. When it was completed the *Feldkommandant* handed over to the States a selection of 'curios, antiques, hunting weapons of savage races from overseas, and museum pieces' to form the nucleus of a collection.[7] The chosen items – which included blunderbusses, flintlock

---

[1] NG Bundle D.   [2] GF 1/1/8; NG Ia/3.   [3] NG Ia/3.
[4] GF 7/1/3.   [5] NG Ia/3.   [6] Ibid.
[7] JFW 57/2.

guns, halberds and pikes – were deposited with the *Société Jersiaise* in January 1942.[1]

One of the major tasks of government was to replace the supplies from Britain on which the Islands had depended before occupation. Much of their food was imported, as were feeding-stuffs for the dairy herds, fertilizers for the glasshouses and fields, and petrol for the tractors. Evacuation had reduced the number of civilians to be fed, especially in Guernsey, but the troops looked to the Islands for milk, butter, vegetables, and potatoes, so that maximum production was essential.

Jersey normally grew successive crops of potatoes and tomatoes outdoors; because her arable land sloped conveniently towards the south she was less dependent on greenhouses than Guernsey with her northern aspect. The latter produced mainly greenhouse tomatoes and flowers for the British market in which activities about two-thirds of the working population were engaged. Growers had to switch from profitable cash crops for export to a wartime agricultural economy designed to feed the people, which was not easy, particularly since at least in Guernsey horticulture had in recent years become more remunerative than agriculture. The greatest impediment, however, was the constant interference by the Germans in the highly-skilled business of farming, which the Islanders had carried on successfully for many generations. Hardly less important was the knowledge among the farmers that the Germans' misguided pressures were intended to produce more food for the Wehrmacht rather than for the civilians.

In Jersey the Department of Agriculture was given power to control agricultural land. Inspectors were appointed to advise as to its best use. Seed was provided at reasonable prices and workers were made available by the Department of Labour.[2]

Sherwill announced in Guernsey soon after the occupation that it would be necessary to conserve food stocks and to take special measures to ensure fair shares for all. 'We are living under siege conditions and must behave accordingly.'[3] Three control boards were set up – Farm Produce, Potato, and Glasshouse Utilization. The first two did a good job; but the last – an excursion into nationalization forced on the authorities by the very large numbers thrown out of work by the drastic fall in the demand for tomatoes and flowers – was less successful. The glasshouses were over-staffed and over-managed, simply because jobs had to be found; and the Board was also hampered by too close

---

[1] JFW 57/3.   [2] JFW 31/2/39.   [3] GF 1/1/8.

E

control by the Germans. They 'wanted us to regard glasshouses as vegetable factories in which crops could be grown at any time at the will of the producer . . . to produce crops was wholly a matter of organization . . . we had to listen to a nauseating amount of cant about nothing being impossible.'

At the end of 1941, when the task of converting the glasshouses from tomatoes and flowers to vegetables had been completed, it was decided to offer them back to their owners. The Board would now do no more than control planting, and buy crops at subsidized prices. From January 1942 the acreage managed by the Board dropped steadily, as did the numbers of men it employed.[1]

Interference by the officials of the *Feldkommandantur* persisted throughout the occupation. In both Islands the military commanders were given detailed information about the food situation immediately after the invasion; but as soon as the civil affairs unit arrived an elaborate new investigation was set in motion. Particulars of stocks and storage facilities were called for; also the acreage of cultivated and uncultivated land, the yield of the normal harvests, milk production, the animal population, the number of farmers and the size of their holdings. A German official admitted that it might all seem to be a waste of time, but claimed that the *Feldkommandantur* could not make its plans without the information.

This sort of thing was repeated again and again. The farmers had to contend with endless demands for statistics; and they had to be patient while the amateurs of the military government told them how to do their job. For example, the Germans laid down the law about the correct moment to harvest grain – 'barley should be harvested when the ears have become an even yellow and are still standing upright'.[2] They controlled gleaning, organized the loan of horses from the Wehrmacht, issued permits for the supply of stable manure, checked the yield of cows to see if farmers were selling milk on the black market, and appointed 'agricultural commandos' to police affairs on the farms generally. It would have been much better to leave all this to the farmers and the Island authorities.[3]

Surplus potatoes and tomatoes had to be sent to France. It was optimistically announced that, in return, the Islands would be able to obtain from that country all the things they had imported 'from England and her colonies'. Even more optimistically it was promised that 'if this is found to be impossible, the reserves of the German

[1] GF 1/1/18, 19.   [2] JFW 31/2/94.   [3] JFW 31/2/159.

Reich can be kept in sight'. A stream of orders was issued, apparently on the assumption that nature could not ignore the orders of the *Feldkommandant*. Wheat production must be increased. The number of cattle, pigs, sheep, and poultry must not fall below a certain level. The public must be warned through the press about the difficulties of the food situation and asked 'to use disciplined restraint'. The Germans had no doubt that the Islanders would co-operate in all the necessary measures.[1]

The agricultural officer in the *Feldkommandantur* told the Bailiff of Jersey in 1941 that he had received orders to increase the potato crop in the following year, so that the troops might have at least 400 tons a month. In 1942 two 'respected and capable inspectors' were to be appointed in every parish to ensure that cultivation orders were implemented. The Director of Agriculture was required to initiate a press service for farmers; but, believing perhaps that the farmers were better able to get the maximum yield from the soil than the military government, he turned a blind eye, and was severely criticized. He had failed to carry out the letter or the spirit of the order, although it was essential to issue directions about production methods, the more so since the farmers did not 'show signs of having attended an agricultural school'.[2]

In the winter of 1944-5 the Germans made their final effort to increase agricultural production, and to ensure that as little as possible went into the black market. The Islands were, of course, now cut off from France, and there was a real danger that the Wehrmacht and civilians alike would face starvation. The *Feldkommandant* established a corps of *Hilfspolizei* (auxiliary police) who had had some experience of agriculture in civil life. There were about forty of them in Guernsey, six of whom were able to act as interpreters. After a short course of instruction in the Islands' agricultural legislation they were ordered to 'supervise intensively' all glasshouses and outdoor cultivation, and milk production and distribution. They were armed with passes in German and English explaining their functions, and also with revolvers. They took their orders not from the military government but from the *Festungskommandant*. They were in a strong position at a time when everybody was desperately hungry, and no doubt exploited it to the full. One was caught with a washbag full of grapes which he had picked up on his rounds. He was promptly dismissed and sent to prison – a mild punishment in the light of the death sentences meted out to some members of the Wehrmacht for stealing food.[3]

[1] JFW 31/2/9.   [2] JFW 31/2/31.   [3] Loose Guernsey paper.

Milk is essential in any wartime diet. The Islands were fortunate in possessing fine herds of Jersey and Guernsey cattle – ready-made sources of best quality milk. Rationing was not necessary before the invasion, but it had to be introduced in October 1940 and remained in force for the whole occupation. The adult ration in Guernsey was half a pint daily of skimmed milk for everyone over 14; and in Jersey half a pint of whole milk for everyone over 16. There were more generous rations for children, nursing mothers, and invalids, which were of whole milk in both Islands.

It was difficult to strike the right balance between meat and milk production. Was it better to keep the meat ration high and face up to tapering off the milk supply over the years; or to reduce the meat ration in the interest of keeping up milk output? Further, was there a case for retaining calves for post-war export, the immediate slaughter of which would make more milk available? The Guernsey doctors felt strongly about this. One of them, Dr. Sutcliffe, wrote in April 1944:

To sacrifice the general public in order to maintain a high standard of Island cattle for presumed post-war sale is nothing short of criminal . . . Desirable as it may be to maintain a good Island stock, I consider it more desirable to maintain the Island population, and I am sure that this view would be shared by the many people who have been evacuated. They would rather come back to be greeted by a healthy relative than by a large and healthy herd of Guernsey cows.

Admiral Hüffmeier, who succeeded von Schmettow as Commander-in-Chief of the Islands in February 1945, saw the dairy herds as the saviours of the Wehrmacht. He had no doubt that the garrison could hold out longer if the production of milk, butter, and cheese was kept up; and he was therefore against the slaughter of cattle to provide even the troops with a meat ration. He proposed in the interests of the garrison that the civilian milk ration in Jersey should be converted from full to skimmed milk; but Coutanche successfully resisted this move.

The Germans received a good deal of help from a Dutch national who grew vegetables for them under contract. He made a large fortune although there were frequent complaints about poor quality and short deliveries. In 1941 he was given numerous greenhouses in Guernsey which he cultivated expressly for the Germans. They provided seeds, fertilizers, transport, and diesel oil for driving the water pumps; and the States were required to maintain the houses, supply tools and so on.[1]

[1] NG 15/5; GF 1/1/19.

This man incurred the cordial hatred of the Islanders; but at least they had the satisfaction that he was stripped of his ill-gotten gains by the war profits legislation.

The special circumstances of the occupation greatly changed the nature of the Islands' agriculture. In Guernsey the main change was the conversion of glasshouses from tomatoes and flowers to vegetables. In Jersey it was different. The changes there have been summed up by Lord Coutanche as follows:

The face of Jersey, as the inhabitants had so long known it, was transformed. Wheat, oats and barley largely displaced the potato. The old water mills were repaired and brought again into use, and it was indeed fortunate that some of the old millers were still alive. They were recalled from their retirement and operated the mills and taught many younger men the art of milling. From the harvest of 1941 onwards Jersey produced almost enough flour to supply to the civilian population a minimum weekly bread ration of about four and a quarter pounds per head for all adults, in addition to breakfast food (mostly oat flour) for adults and baby food (made mostly of oats) . . .[1]

It is a moot point whether agricultural production would have been higher had the Island farmers been left in peace by the military government. It was in their interest to grow as much as possible for their own sakes and the sake of their fellow Islanders; but the knowledge that the more they produced the better the occupying troops would eat had an inhibiting effect. Further, no farmer in any country likes to be told how to do his job. When the unwanted instructor is a hated enemy with little or no experience the resentment is inevitably intensified. The Island governments, however, were just as much in the hands of the *Feldkommandantur* as were the farmers and there was little they could do to help them to resist the irksome demands of the occupying authorities, which were generally counter-productive.

The fishermen had to contend with even greater difficulties than the farmers. Even before the war, fishing had been declining. Boats had to go further afield to find the fish, except for occasional shoals of mackerel, and many fishermen had taken shore jobs. The problem during the occupation, however, was security. The Germans would not allow the fishing boats to visit distant and more productive waters because of the danger of escapes. Immediately after the invasion fishing was allowed up to a mile from shore unescorted, and up to two miles with escort. Then, in September 1940, all fishing was banned because of a successful

[1] Coutanche, p. 40.

escape. In Guernsey boats of every description had to be taken to St. Peter Port harbour by 1 October. This was a typically foolish all-embracing order. Some boats had been laid up and were unseaworthy. Others had their engines dismantled and could not be got ready in time. The Water Board found that they were required to deliver to St. Peter Port the rowing boats which they used to service the pumping machinery at the reservoir. The octogenarian Sir Havilland de Sausmarez, a former Bailiff of Guernsey, enquired, perhaps with tongue in cheek, if it was necessary for him to despatch to St. Peter Port the punt which he kept on the pond at Sausmarez Manor to trim the banks.[1]

When the ban was removed fishing was allowed only out of St. Helier and St. Peter Port. All through the occupation there were restrictions which made it more difficult to bring home satisfactory catches. It was forbidden to go out in fog or rain, and if the weather turned bad boats had to come in at once. Permits were issued only to professional fishermen 'who for family reasons are unlikely to flee' and certainly not to anyone who had near-relatives in Britain. As a result of three escapes in August 1943 fishing was once again banned pending the tightening up of the security arrangements. Substantial bonds were required – up to RM 1,000 (about £100) for a boat, and RM 500 for the fisherman. Fishing was allowed only in groups under escort, and permission was given for only one trip at a time. Petrol was also restricted to a single trip, and to prevent boats from taking on provisions or passengers in isolated coves they were allowed to land only at stated destinations. The *Geheime Feldpolizei* were made responsible for supervising these arrangements.[2]

The Germans seriously considered whether fishing should be completely banned for the duration to prevent the leakage of information about the fortifications. They also debated whether all fishing should be taken over by the navy, perhaps having in mind the precedent of the vegetable-growing soldiers;[3] but decided against this step. Instead the closest possible supervision would be exercised. The fishermen naturally hated this, and their incentive was further diminished by the fact that – like the farmers – they had to hand over a substantial part of their meagre harvest to the Wehrmacht. The result was that fish contributed much less to the general diet than it would have done under a more liberal regime. But, once again, there was little the governments could do about it.[4]

It was, however, quite impossible for the Islands to become self-supporting even if agriculture and fishing had been allowed to make their maximum contribution. In July 1940 Sherwill wrote to Jersey pointing out that unless flour and a host of other things were imported the Islands would be reduced to desperate straits before the winter was over. The Germans had said that France would help but he thought that there would not be enough ships. It was unlikely that the two Islands could exchange much to their mutual benefit, but he asked for ideas. In the event there was some exchange of surplus produce, but the total output of the two bailiwicks fell far short of their total requirements.

The Germans had an interest in making good the deficiencies. Apart from their need to keep the Wehrmacht fed they were responsible under the Hague Convention for the Islanders; and they might therefore have been expected to take the lead in bringing in imports of food for the civilians. They had a network of *Feldkommandanturen* in north-west France which was well-informed about the availability of goods and maintained close liaison with the French. Yet immediately after the invasion the Islands were encouraged to send their own people to France to buy what they could. This is yet another illustration of the fact that the military government were so few in number that they could not undertake any but the smallest executive task.

At first the Islands' representatives went to France *ad hoc*, but before long a permanent purchasing commission was established with head-quarters in Granville. There was a triumvirate in charge – a German official and someone from each of Jersey and Guernsey. Mr. Raymond Falla, who blazed the trail for Guernsey, described the sort of men needed. They must speak French, put up with many disappointments, and keep their temper. They must be prepared to work hard from dawn to dusk, and to travel great distances seven days a week. Mr. George Vaudin became Guernsey's permanent agent in Granville, and Mr. J. L. Jouault represented Jersey.

By the end of August Falla reported that he had bought all the seeds needed for 1941 (to which he had given the highest priority) plus substantial quantities of wheat, barley, flour, and chemicals for the waterworks. Three weeks later he had added 1,000 tons more of flour, 125 tons of sugar, 15 tons of butter, and 400 cases of tinned pork – an almost miraculous feat in a land of general scarcity where the suppliers had no traditional loyalty to the Channel Islands.

It was one thing to buy the goods, quite another to get them shipped.

Falla said that it was essential to be able to swear effectively in French and German if any progress was to be made on the quayside. '*They* tell you to get everything on the quay at a certain time, then some superior officer comes along and countermands the orders, and the whole lot has to be moved somewhere else.' Eventually Falla found it necessary to have 'a good old row' with the Germans. 'I told them I was fed up with their shipping arrangements and unless they stuck to their promises and gave me better facilities I was returning to Guernsey and leaving them to sort out the job.' After this, shipping was easier, although military stores and troops inevitably had priority. Falla had some misgivings about his success in buying scarce foodstuffs since he believed that the Islanders were much better off than many of the people he had seen in French cities. Nevertheless he found the French suppliers very co-operative.

The multifarious activities of the purchasing agents may be gathered from the lists of goods they bought. They included, in addition to foodstuffs, insulin, yeast, hand tools, sole-leather (some for the German troops), wax for bees, willows for crab-pots, sewing cotton, underpants ('winter weight, ankle length'), G-strings ('6 dozen, for violins'), bill-hooks, putty, X-ray films, and 'gasogenes' to convert cars and lorries to producer gas. The agents became expert in a dozen fields, and there was no limit to the demands put on them.

Their activities were observed with some anxiety by the French authorities since every pound they bought meant one pound less for the French consumer. To prohibit exports from France would seriously undermine the garrisons in Hitler's prize possession, which could not be contemplated; but the *Intendant* of the *Département de la Manche* very reasonably insisted that if the Islands continued to draw supplies from his area, at least their rations must be kept at the same level as in France. The Islands produced a third of the meat they needed to maintain the ration. Therefore no more than the balance of two-thirds should be bought in France. In return the Islands were to send what they could spare from their own produce, and in fact many thousands of tons of potatoes and tomatoes were exported to France, for both civilian and military consumption. Smaller quantities of hides, which came from live cattle imported from France, were also sent.

A proposal that the Islands should import from neutral Portugal was put to the Superior Council in Jersey at the end of 1941 by a private individual (who was confident that the United Kingdom would bear the cost). It was turned down very sensibly on the ground that any quantities thus imported would simply be deducted from supplies from France.[1]

The Granville purchasing commission continued to function until the Allied invasion of France. When Granville was threatened the commission moved on to St. Malo. After the capture of St. Malo the staff kicked their heels there until the liberation of the Islands made it possible for them to return. In the meantime two Guernseymen had contrived to escape to England.[2]

The military government took over control of civilian transport. In October 1940 the *Feldkommandantur* limited the use of motor cars to essential purposes, including agriculture and milk distribution. Shortage of petrol was the primary reason, but there was also a security point. The less mobile the people were, the smaller the risk of sabotage.

The number of cars and lorries in the Islands was reduced by a German purchasing commission, which between September 1940 and August 1941 requisitioned all vehicles up to five years old. They also requisitioned tyres. This made it necessary to set up special transport services. In Jersey the *Feldkommandantur* established a civil transport organization, for which buses, private cars, lorries, and tractors were earmarked. The service was intended primarily for carrying labourers, Island produce, and goods from the harbours.[3] The Superior Council was ordered to set up a car service for the troops, which could be used only on a warrant from FK 515. Twelve drivers stood by during the day, and four at night.[4] A similar arrangement was made in Guernsey, where buses were held in readiness 24 hours a day for the use of the troops in various parts of the Island.[5]

The petrol shortage became acute at the beginning of 1941. Cars of more than 14 horsepower were banned, and the strictest economy was enjoined on all road users. Shortly afterwards the *Feldkommandant* announced that supplies of motor fuel were coming to an end and that the number of civilian cars must be still further reduced. Next year all cars of more than 12 horsepower were taken off the roads.

The military government requisitioned bicycles under Article 53 of the Hague Convention in spite of protests by the Island authorities. When Guernsey failed to supply the quantity demanded the *Nebenstelle* accused the authorities of 'intolerable sabotage', and threatened to hold the President of the Controlling Committee personally responsible. This quickly produced the requisite number and set a pattern for future

[1] GF 16/3/1; JF W 61/4.   [2] SHAEF/501/1.
[3] JF W 31/4/7.   [4] JF W 31/ 4/6.
[5] CCM 20 July 1940.

demands. The *Feldkommandantur* sent out an order for so many cycles and they were duly supplied.

Virtually everyone whose cycle was requisitioned appealed. A journalist could not travel round the Island to collect news. A greengrocer could not make his deliveries. The managing director of a drapery firm had to call on customers in outlying districts. A 75-year-old man had to visit his 81-year-old sister. A laundry employee had to cycle to work to light the boiler at 6 a.m. A victim of muscular rheumatism found cycling easier than walking. An Islander who worked for the OT and whose appeal was supported by his employer had to travel five kilometres to work. An observer at the meteorological station had to take observations at 10 p.m. and without a cycle he could not get home before curfew. A boy had to cycle six miles to school. The *Feldkommandantur* turned a deaf ear to most of these appeals.

Although wood was scarce it was more plentiful than petrol. It could be used to make charcoal to generate gas to drive internal combustion engines. This was done by providing what was in effect a portable gas works attached to the vehicle. The complexity of the device as compared with the ordinary car may be gathered from the instructions. To start it all doors in the apparatus had to be closed, firebox filled with charcoal, cover replaced, locking-screw fastened, and decanters and dust filters cleaned out. The charcoal was lit by opening the extractor-tube shutter, switching on the extractor-fan motor, closing the air inlet, and inserting a torch soaked in petrol to light the charcoal. It was also a noisy process. 'We jumped into our taxi and sat there for about four minutes while a fan like an air raid siren shrieked in its efforts to generate enough gas to allow us to move off.'[1] When the gas burned blue the extractor-fan was stopped, the engine started by the self-starter, and the air lever adjusted to get the best mixture of gas. If everything had gone according to plan, the vehicle would now actually move.

Guernsey was quicker to see the possibilities than the sister bailiwick. The *Feldkommandantur* wrote to the Bailiff of Jersey in June 1942 complaining that Guernsey already had 17 producer-gas vehicles in operation, and was preparing to convert another 54, whereas at the same date only four buses and one taxi had been converted in Jersey. 'I request that you will take every means to catch up with Guernsey's lead.'[2] In Guernsey in September 1943 the *Nebenstelle* was still calling for lorries suitable for conversion to gas.[3]

[1] Mr. Louis Guillemette's unpublished *Diary*.
[2] JFW 32/8/3.   [3] Sinel, p. 155.

The *Feldkommandantur* devoted much attention to traffic control, perhaps because of the many accidents in which the troops were involved. In June 1941 – after a year of occupation – the rule of the road was changed. All traffic now drove on the right, until 14 June 1945. The order said: 'Drivers should drive on the right-hand side of the road . . . anyone wishing to turn to the left should keep to the extreme left.' If they had been faithfully observed, these instructions would have led to numerous head-on collisions at cross-roads, and they had to be hastily modified. It was announced a week later: 'The order says that those wishing to turn to the left shall first drive their vehicles as far as possible to the left. This refers only to the right-hand side of the road-way.'

At first the existing system of traffic signs was carried on. When the *Feldkommandantur* arrived they asked that missing signs and those which had been obliterated as a security measure should be restored 'in order that circulation may take place without friction'. Their letter, which is polite and in great contrast to later peremptory orders, points out that traffic notices in English are not understood by many of the troops. 'A German translation would be appreciated.' In 1942 all traffic signs were replaced by a type which had been introduced in France.[1]

In an attempt to reduce the accident rate in Jersey, 'Stop' signs were erected at busy junctions. They were unpopular with the civilians, who objected to dismounting from their bicycles, and they pulled many of them down. The *Feldkommandantur* ordered that they should be replaced immediately, and warned that if this sabotage was repeated a civilian guard would have to be posted – the favourite punishment for presumed sabotage.[2]

At the end of 1942, as part of the process of gentle Germanization, alternative German names were provided for all places of any importance; but for the time being it was permitted to put the original name in brackets after the German version. Bec du Nez became *Nasenfelsen*, Castle Cornet *Hafenschloss*, Petit Bot Bay *Grüne Bucht*, Pleinmont *Westberg*, Torteval *Spitzkirchen*, and so on. One or two names – Albert Pier, for example – were already German enough to be allowed to stand.[3]

The banks carried on much as usual for the first 18 months of occupation, after which an official of the Reichsbank was appointed to

[1] JF W 30/46.   [2] JF W 50/133.   [3] Loose Guernsey paper.

administer them from Paris. The rate of exchange varied and was finally fixed at 9.36 Reichsmarks to the pound, where it remained until the liberation. Although German currency was principally used the banks continued to maintain all accounts in sterling. This meant extra work, but it was one way of hinting that the occupation would not last for ever. Before long, small change became scarce, partly because of hoarding and partly because the troops sent coins home as souvenirs; and in both bailiwicks it became necessary to print notes of small denominations. Their value was expressed in sterling, another example of the Germans' reluctance to carry out a thorough-going Germanization of the Islands. In Jersey the notes were designed by the distinguished artist Edmund Blampied.

In 1943 the banks were told that all items held in safe custody were to be examined. In the few days that elapsed before the inspectors arrived virtually everything deposited by customers temporarily disappeared from the bank vaults. To the managers' surprise – and relief, for they were running a serious risk – the Germans accepted without comment the fact that the banks held little of value. Later, however, all sterling currency was confiscated, in spite of claims that this was a breach of the Hague Convention.[1]

Before the war Jersey and Guernsey used United Kingdom postage stamps. Indeed the postal and telegraphic services on both bailiwicks were manned by the United Kingdom Post Office. Stocks of stamps ran out within a few months of occupation. It was necessary in Guernsey to bridge the gap until locally-printed penny stamps became available by bisecting twopenny ones, thus creating a philatelic curiosity. The first Jersey stamps were designed by Major N. V. L. Rybot. When he was approached he refused the job on the ground that it helped the enemy; but it then occurred to him that he could insult the Germans in the design – 'hence the insertion of four minute "A"s in the corners of the design, which were intended to stand for "Ad Avernum, Adolfé Atrox": that is to say "To Hell with you, Atrocious Adolf" '.[2] Edmund Blampied who designed a set of pictorial stamps, contrived to introduce the Royal cipher G R in the scroll-work. All Guernsey's stamps were produced in the Island, but the later Jersey issues were printed in France.

There was regular sparring between the Island authorities and the

[1] There is a detailed study of the banking arrangements during occupation in John Wadsworth, *Counter Defensive* (London, 1946), pp. 39–58.
[2] N. V. L. Rybot, Jersey postage stamps issued during the German occupation 1940–1945, *Bulletin of the Société Jersiaise*, vol. xvi (1953–6), pp. 97–9.

Feldkommandantur about liability for the costs of occupation. It was, however, accepted by the Germans that the Islands could not be expected to support the heavy concentration of troops with which they were burdened. They agreed in April 1941 that the Islands need not meet new costs, except for the supply of milk to the troops. They later said that to keep costs at a bearable level the Islanders would be held liable only for billeting. In August 1941 the *Feldkommandantur* took over the payment of civilian drivers used by the troops and the military government, who until then had been paid by the States. In 1942 three-quarters of the sums paid by the States towards the cost of occupation were waived. When the Dame of Sark heard about this she suggested to the *Feldkommandant* that Sark should also have a refund; she was told that since her Island had paid nothing there could be no question of giving anything back. The *Feldkommandantur*, disregarding the constitutional position, ruled that the cost of billets in Alderney must be shared between Guernsey and Jersey.

The financial position was summed up by the *Feldkommandant* in March 1944. Up to that date Guernsey had paid RM 1,410,000 and Jersey RM 1,000,000 as their contribution towards occupation costs. They were excused, however, from paying compensation on top of that, unlike France. About 10 per cent of the available land had been taken over by the troops, for which no compensation was being paid to the owners. The annual cost of land and dwellings occupied by the troops was RM 2,230,000 in Guernsey and RM 1,500,000 in Jersey. The States were bearing the whole cost of maids, charwomen, gardeners and the like, and also the cost of lighting, heating, and water, which amounted in the case of Jersey to RM 2,000,000 a year and of Guernsey to RM 2,500,000.

These liabilities were reckoned to be well beyond the means of the Islands, which were surviving thanks to the credit afforded by the French government and the local banks. When the attention of the Reich Minister of Finance was drawn to this situation he said that the occupation costs must be regarded as the liability of the British Empire as a whole, and not just of the Channel Islands.[1]

Finally, the management of labour posed difficult problems. Essential jobs which had been left vacant by the evacuation had to be filled, and at the same time employment had to be found for the large number of people without a job and whose particular skills were no longer

[1] NG 03/7; 03/7a.

required. On 25 June 1940 – a week before the Germans arrived – it was announced at a meeting of the Controlling Committee in Guernsey that many estates had been abandoned by their owners and that the labourers on others had gone to the United Kingdom. The Constables were asked to find out where the shortages were and to reallocate as best they could the men who were still available. All who registered as unemployed were immediately sent out to work, as it was essential to avoid interruption in the horticultural and farming industries at that time of year. Labourers who were penniless because their employers had left the Island without paying their wages were given public assistance. The Controlling Committee decided to institute a register of reserves of labour, and asked the States Insurance Authority to make the necessary arrangements.[1]

In Jersey at the end of 1940 there were 2,300 men looking for work, and the Department of Labour embarked on a programme of road-widening and road-building to absorb the surplus labour. A factory which had been closed was re-opened to provide work for 350 women and girls making clothing and footwear, which could no longer be readily imported. The Department was also entrusted with the task of rehabilitating buildings damaged in the German air raid on the eve of occupation; and providing wood fuel for the whole of the bailiwick. Its other activities included repairing sea-walls; operating a salt-making plant; preparing charcoal for producer-gas vehicles; cutting peat; collecting and drying seaweed; and putting into working order the water mills which had been in disuse for many years – which meant removing thousands of tons of mud from old mill streams and digging miles of new streams. In this way a great deal was accomplished that was necessary, or at least desirable, and unemployment, which added to the general depression caused by the occupation, was kept as low as possible.

In fact nearly the whole of the able-bodied population could have got work with the German forces had they wanted it – the men on the construction sites or the railways, or as casual labourers generally, and the women as domestic servants, cleaners, or helpers in the *Soldatenheime* and *Soldatenkaufhäuser*. But there were two impediments. Article 52 of the Hague Convention gave the occupying power the right to requisition labour only for work of a non-military character. Moreover, people were unwilling to do work of any sort for the Germans.

The Island authorities were naturally reluctant to encourage men to

[1] CCM 25 June 1940. See above pp. 117–18 for the problem of finding employment for Guernsey's glasshouse workers.

take jobs with the Germans even if it was the only way to find work for them, and even if the jobs were arguably non-military. The Germans accepted, certainly in the early years, that they were bound by the Hague Convention and that they could not require the Islanders to work on military installations, especially if these were to be used against their fellow-countrymen. The Germans could, however, get round the Convention by tempting people to work for them, even on projects which were clearly military, by offering very high wages and – in the early years – better rations than were available to ordinary civilians. This attracted a considerable number of volunteers, especially from the Irish community, which decided that it owed no loyalty to the Islands (despite the fact that its members earned their living there). Numbers of Irishmen even volunteered to go to Germany to help with the war effort there.

At the beginning of 1943 German demands for local labour increased. The *Feldkommandant* announced that whereas hitherto they had called only on the unemployed, from now on they would have to ask for the transfer of men who were in employment. He repeated earlier under-takings that these men would not be required 'to take part in military work against the mother country'. The authorities in both Islands took the sensible line that it was better to encourage employers to meet the German demands, however distasteful it might be, since the only alternative would be direct conscription of labour. They pointed out that if there was co-operation in this field it would be easier to persuade the occupying authorities to keep their demands at a reasonable level.

There was much argument as to what constituted war work, and when 180 men in Guernsey were required to clean ammunition and dig trenches the President of the Controlling Committee, John Leale, demanded to see the German Commentary on the Hague Convention. This revealed that the German government had accepted that the civilian population in an occupied territory could not be required to undertake any activity which 'even indirectly is of assistance to operations of war and is of a nature to harm the fatherland of the person concerned'. Leale at once drew the *Feldkommandant*'s attention to this (having in mind the German intention to use civilian labour to dig trenches) and was told months later that 'Islanders will not be com-pelled to perform fortification and entrenchment work'. Further, they were being asked to sign a declaration that they agreed to work for the Germans, it being understood that they would not be required to do anything against their own country.

The Island authorities were of course quite right to hold the Germans to the Convention, although the whole of the argument was academic. The Germans could, and did, get round the restrictions in the Convention by inducing people to work for them on military projects through offers of high wages, better rations, and other benefits. But what really made the argument academic was the impossibility of drawing a clear dividing line between military and non-military work. The Germans themselves reckoned that up to three-quarters of the civilian population were working directly or indirectly for them; and this is undoubtedly true. Every unit of electricity, every gallon of water, every pint of milk produced was of benefit to the garrison. Nearly all the Islanders were working for the enemy, although few of them realized the fact.[1]

[1] NG 18/6.

7

Daily Life: Islanders

No two Islanders were affected in exactly the same way by the occupation. Most resented the presence of the Germans right to the end. Some, after they had recovered from the shock of seeing field-grey uniforms in the narrow streets of St. Peter Port and St. Helier, decided to follow the advice of the Island authorities and patiently wait for liberation. Some found themselves pleasantly surprised by the impeccable behaviour of the troops, which belied tales of atrocities in other countries, and they allowed themselves to believe that the Germans were human after all. Some – happily few – thought that Hitler would win the war and were prepared to help the invaders on the assumption that after the final victory they would be rewarded. Some believed – wrongly, as it turned out – that they could have their cake and eat it: that when the Germans were expelled from the Islands their collaboration would pass unnoticed in the relief and excitement of liberation. Some young women, moved by a natural desire for male company, or by an equally natural desire to enjoy the fruits of fraternization – cigarettes, liquor, and scarce foodstuffs, rather than the occasional child – were prepared to receive the occupying troops with open arms.

It was, however, not only the personal qualities of the individual Islanders that made them react in an infinite variety of ways to the occupation. Their place in society, and their wealth, or lack of it, were equally relevant. A poor man – labourer, clerk, or shop assistant – faced years in which most of the necessities of life would become scarcer and more costly with less equanimity than a man of ample means. The latter could buy in the black market and raise his standard of living to something like the peacetime level; and even when food became seriously short towards the end of the occupation richer people continued to be relatively better off.

It was more difficult for the town dweller to grow vegetables than it was for the countryman with the large garden. Some people kept their gardens all through the occupation; others lost them when their houses were taken over for billets. The farmer, at the risk of heavy fines or imprisonment, could so manage things that some of his produce found its way into his private storehouse in greater quantities than the regulations allowed. It was hardly likely that the fisherman would go without fish. The single person who had been living on a pension from England, now cut off, found life much more difficult than someone who took a job with the occupying forces with the good pay and the extra rations that went with it. The very old, perhaps with no one to fend for them, were particularly vulnerable to the shortage of food and the cold winters, and were worse off than the very young, who were well-provided for under the rationing schemes and better able to resist disease. In short, no two people had exactly the same experience. This must be borne in mind when generalizations are made about life during the occupation.

The evacuation of a large part of the population meant that immediately after invasion food stocks were relatively high. In Jersey in September 1940 there was, for example, 4 months' supply of canned fruit and vegetables and nearly a year's supply of sugar.[1] But stocks ran down before imports from France could arrive in any quantity, and special economy measures were needed. It was proposed in Guernsey to produce a wartime cookery book with attractive dishes based on the limited selection of ingredients available, and to provide recipes which could be cooked in bakers' ovens to save fuel. Communal meals for children were started in Jersey in September 1940. Two meatless days a week were ordered, but this could not be policed and was soon forgotten. Eggs became scarce because of the lack of feeding stuffs; and in October 1941 poultry keepers were advised to kill off all birds over 2 years old. Nevertheless, people made the best of things. At Christmas 1940 'the general provision of festive cheer was nothing short of wonderful . . . for some time now there had been a lot of secret pig killing . . . if the Germans had seen some of the tables laden with good things still produced after six months of occupation, no doubt many new Orders would have been issued to "adjust" the situation.'[2]

In Guernsey food began to run short in 1941. There were few

[1] JF W 31/1/17.   [2] Sinel, p. 29.

potatoes. There had been a poor crop and the Germans had comman-
deered a large part of it. Other vegetables were also scarce at this time.
According to the Health Services Officer the worst period in the whole
occupation (except for the last six months) was the winter of 1941–2.
Most people had exhausted their stocks, which had supplemented the
official rations, but had not yet adjusted themselves to the new food
pattern nor learned where and how to procure extras.

The first consignments of food – flour, eggs, cheese, and onions –
began to arrive from France towards the end of 1940. The Germans
required in return that potatoes and tomatoes should be sent to France,
in spite of objections by the Island authorities; it was sense to show that
the French were getting something for the goods they sent to the
Islands – which included coal, clothing, shoes, medicines, fertilizers,
and agricultural machinery. There was less scope in Guernsey than in
Jersey for growing wheat; and for most of the occupation Guernsey had
to depend on French flour. In July 1940 the Controlling Committee
sampled bread made from wheat flour mixed with 50 per cent potato
flour, and with 50 per cent potato mash, and voted for the latter
mixture. After the stocks of ordinary flour were exhausted, bread was
made from high-extraction flour, which the bakers found difficult to use.
At first the loaves were moist and heavy but eventually the occupation
loaf improved and became popular with most people. There was even
some regret when the white loaf returned after the liberation. Bread
rationing began in 1941, when the ration was $4\frac{1}{2}$ pounds per adult per
week. By 1945 it was reduced to a pound, but for some weeks in Guernsey there was no bread at all.

Potatoes were rationed in 1941 – 7 pounds a week for adults at first,
dropping to 5 pounds. Except for seasonal scarcity other vegetables
were plentiful and were not rationed; and without them the situation
would have been parlous. In the early days the meat ration was 12
ounces a head but it fell quickly and finished up at a theoretical 1 ounce a
week in 1945. The milk ration was half a pint of whole milk daily for
adults in Jersey. In Guernsey the same amount was allowed, but it was
skimmed.

The Medical Officer of Health in Jersey estimated that until July 1943
the average diet fluctuated between 2,100 and 2,500 calories per head
daily; but towards the end of 1944 it had fallen to less than 2,000. In a
working class family it was as low as 1,700. His opposite number in
Guernsey reckoned that the average diet did not fall below 2,300
calories daily; but in the opinion of the medical team which visited the

Islands immediately after the liberation the diet in Guernsey was lower than in Jersey for two reasons. Jersey had more arable land; and the Jersey relief schemes – for example, communal feeding – were better developed.

Although the basic rations were enough to support life, many of the things which help to make a diet interesting were missing; and much ingenuity was exercised in providing tolerable substitutes. Ersatz tea was made from pea pods, carrots, and bramble leaves. 'The flavour of bramble leaf tea can best be described by saying that if one could contrive to think of something else while drinking it one might forget that one was not drinking the genuine article.'[1] Other things pressed into service were seaweed to make jellies, and mangel-wurzel to make jam, which looked like molasses. In Jersey in 1943 tanks of sea-water were set up at strategic points for use in cooking, to compensate for the scarcity of salt; in both Islands sea-water was the only source of salt during the siege.[2]

Some people contrived to fare better than others. In 1942 in Guernsey a retired officer objected to the requisitioning of his garden. He wrote to the *Feldkommandantur* pointing out that there had been many cases of starvation and some cases of death due to malnutrition. Supplies from France might fail and people without gardens would suffer. He added that the produce of his garden, which was adjacent to a house where troops were billetted, would be a bonus to them. International law forbade an occupying army to take produce from civilians whose life might depend on it.

The *Nebenstelle* replied that there were good military reasons for requisitioning gardens adjoining billets. Civilians were not allowed into quarters – not even to read the electricity meter – and it would be a security risk if people pottered about in gardens near billets. They ordered the retired officer to appear before them. Sensing that he had a tiger by the tail, he obtained a letter from the Health Services Officer countersigned by the other doctors confirming that his allegations were true; but this cut no ice. He was required to provide concrete evidence within 24 hours.

Next day he submitted a list of five deaths allegedly due to malnutrition; and ten cases of people whose inadequate diet had led to chilblains and loss of weight. Dr. Brosch of the *Nebenstelle* found that the death certificates related to a man of 59 who had died of heart

[1] Durand, p. 99.
[2] For substitution generally see Durand, Chapter XIII.

failure, and four others aged 66, 67, 68, and 74 whose primary cause of death had been something other than malnutrition, though it did appear in some cases as a secondary cause.

The *Nebenstelle*'s medical advisers commented at length on the evidence. Rations were ample for the whole civilian population except perhaps children between 6 and 14, whose needs were disproportionately high.[1] The Health Services Officer, who was under instructions to notify all cases of serious malnutrition, had reported only one. Patients supposed to be suffering from malnutrition were invariably discharged from hospital before they could be examined by German doctors. Finally, it was natural that people in the retired officer's age group should lose weight.

The doctors then made some pointed suggestions. The Guernsey authorities must again be ordered to report cases of undernourishment. The occupying power was under no obligation to maintain the civilian diet at peacetime levels; but much more food could be produced if only the people would put their backs into it. President Leale, who pushed responsibility on to others in time-honoured English fashion, should be ensuring that the unemployed were forced into work gangs to engage in agriculture. Idle fields and glasshouses must be brought into cultivation. Supplies should be spread more evenly to guarantee the poor a better diet. Sports fields should be closed from Monday to Saturday to save the starving English from themselves. Otherwise they would continue to use up their precious calories, for example, in arduous games of tennis. Finally, they recommended a house-to-house search among well-to-do citizens and the distribution among the poor of any food hoards brought to light.[2]

After consulting the *Feldkommandant* in Jersey, Brosch ruled that the retired officer's allegations were without foundation. No action would be taken against him – although he should face a military tribunal – but he must be reminded that the food shortage was caused by the English blockade. The Controlling Committee was told that food production could be increased if people would work harder and adopt the German spirit of self-help. The occupying authority had done its best to see that the Islanders were well fed. Oil had been provided for their greenhouses. The petrol which had been made available had been used for tractors bringing in the hay at a time when the fishing fleet was going short. In

---

[1] This is interesting since it was precisely this age group whose development was retarded (see p. 140).

[2] NG 01/3.

brief, there was no doubt that the food situation could be improved if the Controlling Committee really tried.

It was proposed that the houses of the retired officer, his brother, and the doctors should be searched; but in the event the list was reduced to the two brothers and the Health Services Officer. The quantities of food brought to light included tinned ham, tongue, turkey, sardines, soup, jam, honey, marmalade, syrup, tea, coffee, powdered chocolate, canned milk, pudding mixtures, and so on. The retired officer had 266 items in his own store cupboard, including 19 cans of condensed milk (a useful supplement to the 2 pints of milk which he was allowed to retain daily from the output of his own cow), 27 tins of meat, and 50 jars of marmalade. It was first mooted that these should be distributed among the poor. Then the *Nebenstelle* suggested that they should go to Channel Islanders working for the Wehrmacht. But in the end, surprisingly, nothing was confiscated.[1]

The scarcity of food was matched by the shortage of fuel. The Islands had depended on coal from Newcastle and South Wales, and on petrol and oil from Southampton. When these were cut off, transport, gas, electricity, water for the glasshouses and the domestic supply, and cooking were all put at risk. In Guernsey in July 1940 there was only enough coal and kerosene to keep the gas works and electricity generators going for another three months. Emergency measures were necessary. Steam rollers, which burned coke, were taken off the roads. Gas and electric heaters were disconnected from baths. Houses with ranges were discouraged from using electric or gas cookers. The sale of coal was restricted. A proposal to keep the gas supply going as long as possible by using house coal was turned down by the Germans on the ground that there should be no difficulty in getting coal from France. Other Guernsey proposals included the early closing of shops, a ban on the use of pumps in quarries, and the manufacture of briquettes from sawdust and tar.

In Jersey fuel rationing began in October 1941, when only wood was available; but later a small amount of coal was allowed in the ration. Next year the gas was cut off at 8 p.m. which meant that many had to spend the rest of the night in the dark. In 1942 Sinel records:

A notice issued by the Fuel Control today is not very cheering. As the coal issued in the spring was for October, November and December, there will be no more issued this year, and unless further supplies of

[1] NG 01/3.

house coal can be obtained it is possible there will be no allocation until next January, February or March.

At this time the average family was receiving a hundredweight of wood each month. Householders with hot-water boilers or slow combustion stoves were entitled to a small amount of anthracite dust which they could mix with coal tar obtainable at the gas works, in the proportion of two gallons of tar to a hundredweight of anthracite dust. The electricity ration was reduced from 5 to 4 units per household.[1]

There was a steady decline throughout the occupation in the amount of domestic fuel available, and therefore in the general standard of living of the people. This is reflected in the diary of a Guernsey resident, who noted in August 1940: 'It is now a crime to waste gas, electricity, and water, and we are only allowed two baths a week with a depth of two inches of water.' In May of the following year the gas works almost ceased production because a cargo of coal on which it had been relying turned out to be unsuitable for gas: 'Hundreds of families depended on gas for cooking, so we all hoped that gas, at least, would continue as long as possible.' There was a slight improvement in October 1941 when the Guernsey gas ration was increased to the same level as in Jersey. 'We were delighted as it made things much easier for us and gave us a chance to light up a little in the evenings instead of going to bed when it got dark or sitting up with a candle . . . candles were not plentiful and our stock would not last all the winter if we had to burn them every evening.' Many people, who had neither gas nor electricity were allowed to buy one candle a week per household, later the allowance was increased to two a week. Paraffin was unobtainable after the middle of September. In May 1944 'we have heard that the gas has been entirely cut off in Jersey. This is very serious as no doubt the same thing will happen here before long. We shall have to do all our cooking with wood.'[2] In fact the gas did not stop finally in Jersey until September 1944, but it was heavily reduced in May.

The Bailiff of Jersey recorded that it was obvious from the first that coal from France would be insufficient and that local timber would be necessary. The Department of Labour employed large gangs to fell trees, but they were always hampered by the German authorities, who feared that if too many trees were felled near military installations they would be more readily spotted from the air. The Fuel Controller did his best to share the available supplies fairly over the whole population, but there was nevertheless a great deal of illicit trading in wood.

[1] Sinel, p. 157.   [2] Miss A. Le M. Lainé, unpublished diary.

Everything possible was done to stamp it out, but 'a cold and hungry population cannot easily be dissuaded from finding the means of cooking its scanty rations and of keeping itself as warm as possible'.

It is surprising that the health of the Islanders remained as good as it did, given the shortage of food and fuel. It is true that the abrupt change in the balance of their diet, which had to include a disproportionate amount of vegetables (in terms of calories nearly twice as much as the wartime diet in the United Kingdom), affected virtually everybody. Looseness of the bowels was universal, and it was so serious in some cases that it was considered to be dysentery. There was hunger oedema, which, though not as a rule serious in itself, lowered resistance to disease. The poor diet adversely affected the physical development of children. Measurements made by the Medical Officer of Health in Jersey in 1940 and 1943 revealed that all age groups between 6 and 14 were on the average several pounds lighter in 1943. More significant, height was similarly retarded. The 14-year-olds averaged 5 feet 1 inch in 1940, and only 4 feet 10·7 inches in 1943.

The effects of the scarcity of food were not all bad, however. Although the children's development was retarded they survived the occupation well, in spite of serious loss of weight towards the end of 1944, when conditions were particularly bad. The International Red Cross parcels arrived in the nick of time, and by the liberation most of the children were back to normal. On the credit side their teeth were in excellent condition. There were benefits for the adults as well. Many fat people were forced to keep their weight at a healthier level than they would otherwise have done. Some lost all traces of the heart and lung troubles from which they had suffered. The Health Services Officer in Guernsey commented: 'Many people lost weight . . . if a man felt weaker from insufficient food he had a great advantage if he had half a hundredweight less to carry about all day.' But the loss of weight could go too far, especially among those whose jobs called for a great deal of physical effort. For example, between June 1940 and June 1943 the eleven men of the outdoor telephone staff in Guernsey lost an average of 22 pounds a man. There were fewer colds and sore throats and also fewer cases of appendicitis. Infectious disease was kept to a low level, although there was an outbreak of diphtheria in Jersey in 1944, when an unusually large number of adults were affected.

Shortage of water was always a potential danger to health. In November 1944 the *Nebenstelle* in Guernsey ruled that to conserve stocks of diesel oil needed for pumping water, water closets could no longer be used. 'The population is therefore advised in a suitable manner to create installations independent of water.' Nicely put, but anathema to the doctors. They agreed that water might be cut off for part of the day but

to cut off water from the closets entirely would be an act of the greatest cruelty . . . to expect old men and young to go into their gardens in winter, perhaps at night, like cats and dogs, can hardly be considered humane . . . If the use of buckets is suggested, where are the buckets? Who is going to cleanse them, especially without water?

This powerful protest was signed by the Health Services Officer, Dr. Symons, who was unpopular with the Germans. They demanded his resignation, partly because he had accused them of cruelty. After much wrangling he was allowed to retain his position, and it was agreed that water should be available for all purposes, at least for part of the day.[1]

By and large the health pluses and minuses balanced out during the greater part of the occupation, but in the two or three months before the Red Cross supplies began to arrive there was a real threat of general starvation.

The black market flourished almost from the beginning of the occupation, as it did in every occupied country. Indeed, there were two black markets. The crews of vessels plying between the French ports and the Islands smuggled in considerable quantities of easily-carried foodstuffs, including butter and eggs, and saccharin, which they sold for Reichsmarks. This was more of a grey market since it increased stocks of food at the expense of the French consumer rather than at the expense of fellow Islanders; but the extra food did of course go to those who could afford to pay for it, and not to the community as a whole.

The main black market was run by greedy and unscrupulous Islanders for their own profit and the benefit of other greedy and unscrupulous Islanders at the expense of those who were prepared to abide by the rationing rules. According to one authority, however, only a few hundred people did not participate in it, either because they could not afford black market prices, or because they were too old or infirm to fetch the goods. If this is true the discriminatory effect of the black market may have been less. Except for the small number who could not or would not join in, most households obtained their supplies

[1] GF 8/1/2.

partly through the official rationing schemes and partly through the black market.

A member of the Superior Council in Jersey makes fun of the black market in his memoirs and leaves the impression that those who could pay high prices survived the occupation much more comfortably than the poor, and also that their consciences were not greatly troubled. A Guernsey doctor commented: 'It was interesting to watch certain people who lost weight at the early part of the occupation gradually put it on again as they overcame their scruples.' A colleague in Jersey confirmed that life was easy enough for those who could afford to buy butter, milk, and meat in the black market. Although it was illegal to slaughter animals without a licence, many calves and pigs were slaughtered on the farms. The man who slaughtered the animal was paid for his efforts – and his silence – with some of the spoils. Thus the farmer had something for his own larder, as did his well-to-do customer and the slaughterer, so that black market food from this sort of source was spread three ways. For the first eighteen months or so many households had sufficient stocks to enable them to survive without too much hardship; but from 1942 onwards, when things began to get very difficult, the black market spread rapidly. In 1942 there were 40 successful prosecutions in Guernsey, about 50 in 1943, and over 100 in 1944; but these were only a handful when compared with the undetected offences. Typical cases were breaches of price control, for example on strawberries and raspberries, which were not subject to rationing; illegal sale of controlled foodstuffs, in particular meat and potatoes; the illegal slaughter of animals; the failure of farmers to deliver to the central depot all the milk they produced, except for the amount they were permitted by law to retain for their own use; the acquisition of rationed food in excessive amounts; and the sale of food to individual members of the German forces.

Sometimes the treatment meted out to convicted offenders seems harsh; but the Island courts were aware of the importance of ensuring that the limited supplies of food were fairly shared, and they had to make an example of the black marketeers brought before them. A Guernsey widow found herself in serious trouble in 1942. For being in possession of a pig, which was over six weeks old and whose existence had not been notified to the Farm Produce Board, she was fined £5, with the alternative of five weeks in prison; for permitting the pig to be slaughtered contrary to the regulations she was fined £10 or ten weeks; for being in charge of a pig more than six weeks old, which was slaughtered or died from some other cause, and failing to give notice of the pig's decease, another £5 or five weeks was added to the bill. Her son, who received the carcass, was fined £10 and sentenced to two weeks' hard labour; and the earthly remains of the pig were awarded to the Farm Produce Board so that they might find their way into the legal ration stream.[1]

Perhaps the widow was luckier than she realized. In December 1944 a farmer was sent to prison for six months and fined £100 for removing a cow without permission from the place where it was usually kept; for obtaining meat for household consumption without authority he was sentenced to two more months in prison (to run consecutively) and fined another £25. Shortly afterwards someone else was fined £50 (with the alternative of three months' hard labour) simply for owning a pig above the age of six weeks without informing the Farm Produce Board.[2]

As the occupation dragged on, the price of black market food went steadily up. In Jersey the price of meat went up from 11s. a pound to 15s. between July 1942 and July 1943. In the same period sugar went up from 12s. 6d. to 16s., and a year later it was 20s. Between July 1943 and July 1944 butter went up from 25s. a pound to 30s., and to 50s. at the end of the occupation. In 1945 tea was fetching between £20 and £30 a pound; and a pound of tobacco went for £112. At an auction in Guernsey in September 1944 an assortment of goods worth 10s. before the war fetched £30. This, of course, was not a black market transaction, but it does show what people were prepared to pay.

After a year of occupation, goods had become so scarce that many retailers virtually ceased to carry on their normal businesses and devoted themselves simply to providing an exchange service. Their shops were stocked with goods deposited by owners who, as a rule, still had a use for them, but needed something else more urgently. The price of the goods on offer was designated not in currency but in terms of the goods wanted in exchange, and the shopkeeper was paid in cash a percentage of the theoretical value of the articles 'sold'.

At first rationed goods, which careful housewives had accumulated over a period, or which they had laid in before invasion, as the authorities had encouraged them to do, were offered for exchange. A great deal of business was also done in the advertisement columns of the newspapers. The legality and indeed the wisdom of these arrangements was questioned, and in October 1941 in Jersey many articles were banned

[1] GF 5/1/8.   [2] Ibid.

from exchange in the barter shops and through the newspapers. Auction sales had also become an important feature of daily life, and prices bid for goods auctioned, which included all sorts of things not usually sent to auction, steadily increased with the passage of time.

At the beginning of 1942 the Attorney General in Guernsey was told by Wolff, the head of the small group of Gestapo, that the Island should come into line with Jersey, where barter had already been curtailed by order. This was a departure from the normal administrative link between the occupying authorities and the Controlling Committee, and it is interesting to speculate why the Gestapo should choose on this one occasion to meddle in affairs which were the responsibility of the *Feldkommandantur* and its *Nebenstelle*. The approach was informal. The Gestapo's ostensible reason for intervening was the fact that barter enabled the well-endowed to obtain scarce commodities to the disadvantage of the poor. They also feared that sooner or later the people who were offering goods, which were largely bought with cigarettes by the troops, would be in difficulty when they found that they really needed the articles they had offered for exchange. This, coming from the senior member of the Gestapo in the Islands, may seem to be surprisingly solicitous. It seems likely that Wolff was seeking to conserve the troops' tobacco ration, and perhaps even more likely that he hoped further to reduce the morale of the people by denying them the comfort of tobacco, which they could now get only from the troops. If the latter guess is right it may mean that he was dabbling in the game of psychological warfare contemplated by a mission which visited the Islands in 1941 to see what they could learn for the purposes of the German occupation of Britain.[1]

The President of the Controlling Committee saw no reason to stop barter as a means of exchange and suggested that it would be simpler if the still generous German cigarette ration was reduced. However, the occupying authorities had their way, and rationed goods were banned both from the barter shops and from newspaper advertisements.

Auction sales were also controlled, at first by designating goods which could be sold at no more than the controlled price. This made sales by auction unattractive to those whose sole objective was to cash in on the very high prices which could be obtained. Later a wide range of goods was completely banned from auction, including all rationed foodstuffs, most clothing and footwear, soap, tobacco, leather suitable for shoes, cycles, twine (essential on the farms and in the glasshouses), and pigs,

[1] See Chapter 14.

goats, poultry, and rabbits. Towards the end of 1944, when the effects of the siege were becoming serious, auctions were completely banned. The growing shortage of goods and the complete cessation of imports had raised prices astronomically, and the Controlling Committee decided that 'it is in the general interest to remove altogether the undesirable encouragement to high prices which the auction sale offers'. The ban, which did not apply to cattle or real estate, would of course be removed at the earliest possible moment.[1]

The barter shops caught the eye of one German soldier. He wrote that since there was no industry in the Islands – apart from agriculture – the few goods that existed 'are bandied back and forth. The shop windows are filled with goods that are not to be sold but exchanged for other goods. Tobacco is much sought after as supplies have run out. Anyone who doesn't smoke can do good business – even soldiers take part in this. They are after pure silk of which there is still some.'[2]

There was no attempt to use the educational system for political purposes, except for the introduction of the teaching of German. There were probably two reasons. A campaign to capture the minds of the children would have called for teachers from Germany, since it was unlikely that those who remained in the Islands would willingly co-operate in such an exercise; but the Germans could no more spare teachers for the Channel Islands than they could spare administrators. Secondly, although there is little evidence to support this conclusion, it seems likely that the policy was to make as few changes as possible in the Islands in the hope that when Britain was conquered the people there would be the more willing to accept occupation because their Norman brothers had survived and possibly even benefited from a peaceful and benevolent occupation.

Although the numbers of school children had been reduced by evacuation – especially in Guernsey, where only 1,100 remained out of 7,000 – there were accommodation difficulties, since many school buildings were taken over by the Wehrmacht. There was also the problem of keeping classrooms heated, which became more acute as time went on. Special arrangements had to be made to help those pupils who, in the ordinary course of events, would have taken the Oxford and Cambridge Joint Board examinations, papers for which could no longer

---

[1] GF 5/1/8; 5/1/23.
[2] Gerhard Nebel, *Bei den Nördlichen Hesperiden* (Wuppertal, 1948), p. 50. Dr. Nebel is now one of Germany's leading literary figures.

be sent to the Islands. In Jersey papers were set at the appropriate level, duly marked, and retained until the liberation. They were then submitted to the Joint Board and certificates were issued to the successful candidates. In Guernsey there was an examination for a special Guernsey School Leaving Certificate; these certificates were also recognized in England after the Islands had been freed. On the whole, thanks to a good deal of improvisation and ingenuity on the part of the education authorities and the teaching staffs, the schools were able to carry on very much as in normal times – except for the addition of German to the curriculum.

Early in 1941 the *Feldkommandantur* asked how many children wanted to volunteer to study German, and there was quite a good response. It was difficult to find teachers and text books, but enough of each were found to start up voluntary classes. This was not enough, however, and the question of compulsory German was broached by the *Feldkommandantur* in 1942. Their memorandum on the subject, the main purpose of which was to determine whether it was feasible to make German compulsory, reveals something of German thinking in this field. It begins by noting that relatively few children remained in the Islands, and that standards had fallen 'since the intelligent ones went to England'. In general the pre-occupation arrangements were still in force. It was considered that given the make-up of the population, and also on political grounds, French instruction should not be cut out. A strengthening of the Norman and Breton elements as a basic movement was desirable. Further, there were historic grounds for retaining French.

It was nevertheless considered possible to introduce German, which had hitherto been taught three hours a week, on a voluntary basis. Ideally there would be compulsory German for all pupils over 10 but it would be difficult to find teachers outside the main centres, so the country schools would have to be excluded from any scheme. The memorandum concluded: 'Opposition to the German language naturally exists in large measure. People do not want to learn the language of the enemy.'

The proposals were approved by the *Feldkommandant*, Oberst Knackfuss, who in signifying his agreement added 'but not at the expense of French'.[1] English instruction was to be reduced to allow for the introduction of five 45-minute periods of German a week.

At the beginning of 1943 the *Feldkommandantur* tried to push things

[1] NG 05/1.

rather further. In Guernsey Sonderführer Bleul addressed the Education Council and issued what they took to be an order that there must be compulsory German in all schools. They felt that they had to accept this, but told the Controlling Committee that they had done so with great misgiving. It was nonsense to burden the average children who were already studying English and French with a third language. As the Council interpreted international law, the occupying authority had no right to interfere in the domestic affairs of the occupied territory, including education, except in so far as security was concerned 'and we cannot see how the introduction of compulsory German into our elementary schools can affect the security of the army of occupation one way or the other'. This letter was addressed to the President of the Controlling Committee and sent on by him to the *Nebenstelle* without comment. He made no attempt to back up the Education Council's protest and the Germans had their way.

A year later Oberst Knackfuss attended a prize-giving where book prizes were presented to teachers and pupils who had shown aptitude in teaching or acquiring knowledge of the German language. (The books were bought with money raised at German military band concerts.) Knackfuss said that knowledge of German had much improved in the last twelve months. Bleul also spoke, stressing the importance of German, which was the most important language on the continent of Europe. It was spoken by 100,000,000 people and understood by 50,000,000 more.[1]

German also found its way into the curriculum in Sark. The Dame told the *Nebenstelle* that there were 22 children there willing to learn German and that classes would shortly begin. Books were a problem, and she appealed for help. She had tried all the bookshops in Guernsey in vain. She hoped that Sonderführer Bleul, to whom she addressed her appeal, would help. She added: 'We shall be very pleased to welcome you here any day you are free to come and have lunch with us.' Later in the same year, when writing about the difficulty of heating the school, the Dame said that she was prepared to have the school children in the Seigneurie to encourage the learning of German.[2]

In 1942 she reported that German classes had begun in October 1941. Some children had dropped out because they were not up to it, and others had too much to do at home to make it possible for them to study. Nevertheless 'we are well satisfied with the instruction book, and the children study with enthusiasm and tell stories and sing a few songs'.

[1] NG 01/1. [2] GF 1/1/5.

It was very difficult in winter because the schoolroom was badly heated and the children could not concentrate when they were cold. 'Won't you come over yourself or with a few of your gentlemen and hear the children?'[1]

The problem of how to occupy leisure time was difficult at first, but towards the end of the occupation it gave place to the more serious problem of how to survive. In the early months life was more or less normal, but the effect of the blackout, the curfew, the closure of beaches because of mines, the banning of the use of coastal roads after dark, the restriction in the supply of electricity and gas, and frequent shooting practices, which made it unsafe to go out of doors, imposed progressive limitations on the usual forms of recreation.

The stock of English-language films was soon used up, although an exchange between Guernsey and Jersey put off for a short time the evil day when all the Islanders who went to the cinema had seen all there was to see. German films were provided to replace the products of Hollywood and Elstree, and the people were encouraged by the Germans to go and see them. Some made the most of the opportunity. One sent his thanks for the chance to see these magnificent films. 'We have to rush home from work, bolt our food, so as to be in time, but it's worth it. Please let us have some more.'[2] The cinemas continued to function by showing old films from time to time, and German films and newsreels mainly intended for the troops. Civilians and Wehrmacht were segregated by order. That the Islands were under an authoritarian regime was made clear by an announcement in 1941 that it was permissible to applaud comedians and heroes; although the announcement did not spell it out, presumably villains might be hissed.

As the cinema lost its attraction amateur dramatics took over. In both Jersey and Guernsey companies put on shows which were well patronized, but, given the curfew hours and the difficulty of transport, these were mainly of benefit to the people in the towns. Permission had to be obtained for each performance, and programmes had to be submitted to the *Feldkommandantur* for approval. The Germans also put on variety shows with professional entertainers from Germany, and there were numerous military band concerts.

Sport could still be enjoyed, in particular football, which continued to be something of a spectator sport. Matches were played against German teams, but the main interest was in domestic competition. In 1944, for example, the final of the Occupation Cup in Jersey attracted between 4,000 and 5,000 spectators. On Derby Day, 1941, sweepstakes were organized and a number of enterprising citizens set up as bookmakers for the occasion – the results being received on radios, which were still permitted at this time.

Dances, which were not very popular in the early days, and which at one time were forbidden by the Germans on the ground that the troops attending them might indulge in careless talk, began to come back, and round about Christmas 1942 there were several public and private dances. Sinel records: 'There is much more entertainment than there was during the first two years; one always expected the Germans would attend these functions but they are prohibited from doing so. Some of the dances held during the Christmas period have been more boisterous than they should have been and drink, mostly of inferior quality, has been consumed in greater quantity than was desirable.'[1] In the circumstances, this was perhaps rather a harsh judgement. When dances were banned 'on medical grounds' in 1943 a Jersey hotel hopefully substituted dancing classes. The device was quickly spotted by the Germans and stopped.[2]

The Germans did make some attempt to allow the Islanders to enjoy their normal recreations. The Island *Kommandant* graciously gave permission for excursions from Guernsey to Sark on Easter Sunday and Monday, 1941. 'As far as space will permit, the population will have a chance of an excursion to Sark.' Tickets would be 4s. return, and the journey would be at the traveller's own risk. But on the whole the attitude of the occupying authorities was negative. Photography was banned for all Islanders (although it was still permitted to the German troops) mainly because of the danger that people might escape to England taking with them photographs of military installations – as indeed some of them did. In any case supplies of films and photographic chemicals soon dried up, and had to be reserved for photographs for identity cards. Although the cameras that were called in were supposed to be carefully stored by the Germans, it was discovered that they were rusting and becoming mouldy; and the *Feldkommandantur* decided that the responsibility for their safe custody should be transferred to the States.[3]

When a Guernsey amateur theatrical company, anxious to provide entertainment for the sister Island of Jersey and perhaps to enjoy a change of scene themselves, proposed that they should take one of their

[1] Sinel, p. 112. [2] JFW 50/96. [3] GF 7/1/25.

F

productions to St. Helier, the *Feldkommandantur* refused permission. The generally oppressive nature of the regime is reflected by a German order – aimed primarily at France, but nevertheless effective in the Channel Islands – which banned all societies except those 'founded on public law'. No new associations were to be formed. 'The population is forbidden to beflag property and to display streamers, standards and other emblems on vehicles, unless these be official badges.' Freemasonry was made illegal. Even the Salvation Army was forbidden to hold meetings in the open air.

Individuals trying to enjoy themselves could sometimes get into trouble. In May 1944 the *Feldgendarmerie* were summoned to a private dance which was being held without permission and which had become rather noisy. The blackout had been removed from some of the windows and when the police arrived the guests were walking about in the street (despite the fact that it was after curfew) and were making a great deal of drunken noise. They were taken back into the house and kept there until morning. They duly appeared in the *Feldkommandantur* court and were fined.

Reading was one pastime that continued, although the stock of English books was not increased during the occupation. Indeed, if anything, it was diminished, not only by natural wastage but by occasional purges of books which were considered to be anti-German. In December the *Feldkommandantur* complained that anti-German books were still in circulation. The lending library of a Jersey shop had recently issued to a member of the German forces a book called *Some Other Beauty* by I. A. R. Wyllie, which contained a number of violently anti-German passages 'amounting to an outrageous hate propaganda'. The book had been seized. All libraries were again required to check whether they held any anti-German books and to hand any found to the *Feldkommandantur*. If subsequent searches brought to light such books those holding them would be called to account and punished.[1] The opportunities for reading became more limited towards the end of the occupation because of the restriction in the use of gas and electricity.

Radio was even more important than books, for it helped to temper the feeling of isolation which troubled most Islanders. It was virtually impossible to move from one Island to another and quite impossible (except for a few officials) to visit France. Red Cross messages provided a link with relatives in the United Kingdom, but they were slow, brief,

[1] NG 01/1.

and infrequent. Radio, however, kept people in touch with the outside world and kept alive hope that the nightmare of occupation would not last for ever. At first, radios were freely allowed, but towards the end of 1940 they were called in in all the Islands as a reprisal for the help given to Nicolle and Symes in Guernsey. In December 1940 they were surprisingly returned to their owners but were again confiscated in June 1942, ostensibly for military reasons and not as a punishment. The B.B.C. had been broadcasting that an Allied invasion of the continent was imminent and asking listeners to help the invaders when they arrived. It was therefore reasonable for the Germans to interrupt communications with potential insurgents. This led the Islanders to make crystal receivers (the B.B.C. explained how this should be done), which enabled many to listen clandestinely. It also led to the establishment of groups disseminating news from Britain, including, for example, the Guernsey Underground News Service ('GUNS'), the sponsors of which – Charles Machon, Cecil Duquemin, Ernest Legg, Francis Falla, and Joseph Gillingham – were informed against, and sent to prison in Germany, where Machon died.[1] The circulation of these underground news sheets was probably the most intelligent and effective form of resistance open to the Islanders. They did a great deal for the morale of the people, and correspondingly undermined the morale of the garrison.

A final attempt to secure the return of the radios was made in Jersey in September 1944. The Bailiff pointed out to von Schmettow and his Chief of Staff, von Helldorf, that since they were completely cut off from the continent there was no reason why people should not listen, particularly as crystal sets did not use electricity. The Germans replied that the order about radios had come from Berlin and could not be changed. Von Helldorf confessed that it had never been popular with the occupying authorities and the Bailiff quickly suggested that they should therefore ask Berlin to rescind it. He was told, however, that Wehrmacht headquarters had more important problems on their plate at this time and must not be troubled with anything so trivial.[2]

Perhaps the greatest single strain on the people was the fear of thieves. Theft was widespread, and everyone knew that an attempt to defend his property might be rewarded with a shot from a German revolver, or a blow from whatever weapon a foreign worker could lay his

[1] For an interesting account of 'GUNS' see Frank W. Falla, *The Silent War* (London, 1967).
[2] GF 7/1/36.

hands on. The troops were the worst menace. They could move freely
during curfew hours, and probably felt that they were entitled to help
themselves to anything they wanted, whatever the niceties of international law. The foreign workers did not carry firearms, but they were
more desperate because of their lower standard of living. In the winter
of 1941-2 nearly 60 thefts a week were reported to the police in Guernsey, but this was only a fraction of the total. Most people realized the
futility of trying to bring the culprits to book and to recover food which
was probably eaten as soon as it was stolen.

Even the milk in the cows was at risk. The Controlling Committee
asked that farmers should be allowed to stand guard over their herds at
night to stop people from milking them. There were many complaints
about the theft of growing crops, but the main objectives of the thieves
were chickens, goats, rabbits, pigs, cows, food-stuffs generally, and soap.
It was not only at night that there was trouble. A consignment of
apples from France was openly pilfered by foreign workers at the docks
in St. Peter Port, in spite of all efforts to prevent it.

The situation was no better in Jersey. In the autumn of 1942 robberies were increasing daily, and German troops and foreign workers
were blamed. Next year things became worse. There was much violence,
especially in the country districts. Farmers took on the intruders,
arming themselves with farm implements, and there were casualties,
sometimes fatal, on both sides. The Germans were especially severe with
foreign workers who were caught, perhaps to distract attention from the
crimes of the soldiers. Sinel records in March 1943 that 'practically all
the residents in certain country districts take their rations with them
when they go to bed'. However Germans and foreign workers were not
the only offenders. Islanders were also guilty of theft, sometimes from
the enemy, which could be regarded as sabotage; but they also stole
from each other.

The Islanders cannot be criticized for not starting a resistance
movement. They are rather to be congratulated on their good sense.
But the actions of a small minority who set out to collaborate right
from the beginning of the occupation cannot be too strongly condemned.
Almost before the victims of the air raids were buried some members of
the community in Guernsey accepted the Germans with the greatest
cordiality. The vicar who invited the troops to attend his services ('we
are not at all high') was perhaps in a privileged position. Not so the
market gardeners who sent flowers to the invaders and received this

acknowledgement: 'The Commandant has asked me to inform you how much he appreciates the gift of flowers which you are making to him for the adornment of our residence.'

Another firm was heartily thanked 'for your gift of those marvellous grapes', which had been much enjoyed at Government House, where the commander of the invading forces then was. Someone else volunteered to find badly-needed maps of the Island; he was at pains to conclude his letter forwarding them with the words 'no charge, gratis, and with compliments' to make quite sure that the Germans understood that he wanted them to be a free gift. The elegant replies to the donors of these things were couched in faultless English – even *Kommandant* was rendered with an English 'C' – which would have done credit to the Lieutenant-Governor's private secretary. It must have seemed to the Germans that they had got off to a flying start and that it was only a matter of time before the whole population came into line.[1]

A German soldier who spent some time in Jersey, Guernsey, and Alderney was struck by the friendliness of the people as a whole, especially when they were compared with the French 'who always show resistance to the German occupation'. In France German officers and officials were being murdered and the Germans were retaliating by shooting innocent hostages. In the Channel Islands, on the other hand, 'we are greeted spontaneously, and eagerly shown the way when we ask'. He reckoned that this was all the more remarkable as the people were forced to live a frugal existence, with vegetables as the main item in their diet. Perhaps there was an element of wishful thinking in this assessment of the friendly attitude of the Islanders, but there is no doubt that the atmosphere was very different from France.[2]

It was one thing to show ordinary courtesy to the Germans in the street, but numbers of people went a good deal further, no doubt hoping that they would reap some reward. Some girls formed friendships with German soldiers, for which they incurred the contempt of most people. According to a businessman who made a dispassionate report on the occupation to his principals in England after the liberation, it was not the fault of the troops, who were well behaved and kept under strict discipline, but rather of the girls themselves. This was confirmed by a man who escaped towards the end of 1941 who reported that there was no molesting of women. More illegitimate children were produced than usual, and in view of the reduced numbers of Island men it is a possible inference that the German troops must have been partly responsible.

[1] NC Bundle D.   [2] Nebel, p. 68.

A father wrote to a certain *Unteroffizier* who had left the Islands, starting his letter: 'I expect you know why I am writing. It came [as] rather a shock to her mother and myself when we knew of her condition.' He pleaded with him as a gentleman for the sake of his daughter and the child to suggest some arrangement – it is not clear if this was to be financial or matrimonial – but his letter was buried in the files of the *Feldkommandantur*, who probably never troubled to inform the *Unteroffizier* that he had left a liability in the Islands.[1] One girl was alleged to have had a daughter by a member of the Gestapo, and another to have lived with the Gestapo chief in Havre des Pas in St. Helier. They were openly criticized during the occupation. Sinel records that at the funeral of two R.A.F. sergeants, whose bodies had been washed ashore, 'a couple of ugly incidents were narrowly averted outside the cemetery during the day when some young men gave expression to their feelings to some women there who were known to be friendly with the enemy'. About the same time a Jerseyman was sent to prison for telling a woman whose husband was in the British army that she should not go out with Germans.[2]

The most despicable form of collaboration – if indeed it merits the name – was informing the Germans about the activities of Islanders simply to get them into trouble. It must have been assumed by those that played this game – anonymously – that they could work off personal grudges. They were moved, not by a desire to help the occupying power, but by spite. One offence in which the Germans took a particular interest was the illegal possession of radios, but it seems likely that most people broke some law sooner or later and therefore nearly everybody was vulnerable to the informer. Probably the worst example was in Jersey in 1942 when a father and son were arrested on the strength of a report that they had a radio in their house; they were taken off to concentration camps in Germany where they died. But there were many other cases, including one of a sister who informed on her brother.

The Germans were selective in their handling of the information they received anonymously. They were well aware that people might seek revenge for real or imagined grievances, and they were reluctant to be used as the tools of such people. They therefore made a thorough investigation before they made an arrest. There was a case in 1943 involving two Hungarian women. The *Feldgendarmerie* were warned in an anonymous letter to keep an eye on them, since one of them was known all over the Island as a black market queen. She was said to be dealing in butter, sugar, marmalade, and tobacco which she kept in her friend's house because it was safer. It was added, for good measure, that she was Jewish, that she spread radio news among the Islanders, and that she was always criticizing the Germans behind their backs.

The *Feldgendarmerie* went into action and searched the houses of the two women. They found rather more rationed goods than they expected; but they admitted that they could have been saved up over a period. Nor could they find proof that the alleged black market queen was Jewish, and they believed her when she said that she was not. They concluded that the writer of the anonymous letter – who was assumed to be a third Hungarian – was prompted by hatred and envy. It was then discovered that a German soldier had supplied her with rationed goods – he claimed that this was done out of sheer kindness. Although the amounts were not great the *Feldkommandantur* court decided to prosecute. In his preliminary consideration of the case, which was based on a study of the papers, Dr. Casper decided to ignore the allegations in the anonymous letter, and to judge the women on the evidence the *Feldgendarmerie* had collected.

Then something happened to make him change his mind. He recorded that the offender had been known as a grasping black marketeer for some time, and that although her main stock of black market goods had never been discovered, there was no doubt about the extent of her operations. He had originally had in mind a fine of 100 marks, but he now changed this to 200 marks and two weeks' imprisonment, with a six months' suspended sentence. He noted that it was only by imposing severe sentences that the black market could be stamped out. Justice may have been done in this case although there was not enough evidence to justify the sentence dictated by Casper before the trial was held.[1]

The Germans were very careful in their assessment of people who claimed to be well disposed, fearing no doubt that they might invite an enemy into the camp. A certain Guernseyman asked permission in 1944 to move to Jersey to work for the Germans, and it was argued in his favour that he 'had betrayed owners of radio sets'. The *Feldkommandantur* were not satisfied with this however. They wanted positive proof that he was friendly and the *Geheime Feldpolizei* were instructed to investigate him to establish whether he really favoured the German cause. In the event he was refused permission to move as he was not considered a good risk, in spite of the help he had given.[2]

---

[1] Loose Guernsey paper.   [2] NG Ic.

It is manifestly impossible that there should have been in the Channel Islands anything like the resistance movements which developed in the larger countries occupied by the Germans. There were plenty of military installations to attack, and their destruction would have contributed something to the Allied cause. Hitler was so insistent that the Islands must be strongly fortified that any damage by saboteurs would have had to be made good, with a small resultant drain on total German resources. But the Islands were so tiny, and so densely filled with German troops that saboteurs had little chance of escape. The Islanders were so few that if the occupying authorities had seen fit to take punitive measures they could have been directed individually against almost the whole population. Indeed, every man, woman, and child could have been gassed and incinerated in a single day in one of the larger and more efficient German concentration camps.

Early in the occupation the Germans threatened to shoot twenty leading citizens in Guernsey unless they could be satisfied that no one was harbouring members of the British armed forces. Although this may have been an idle threat (given the benevolent line which was as a rule followed for the Channel Islands in the early days of the occupation) there is no doubt that massive sabotage would have brought forth massive retaliation.[1]

This was wisely recognized by the two bailiwicks right from the start. In Jersey the States charged the inhabitants to keep calm and to offer no resistance whatsoever to the occupation of the Island. In Guernsey the Controlling Committee announced that 'the public are notified that no resistance whatever is to be offered to those in military occupation of this Island. The public are asked to be calm and to obey the orders of the German commandant.'[2] This line, which followed logically on the demilitarization of the Islands and the attitude implied by the United Kingdom government's few pronouncements on the subject, was simply plain commonsense.

[1] A proclamation by the *Feldkommandant* in July 1942 said that since August 1941 all inhabitants of the Channel Islands held in custody were liable to the death penalty in the event of sabotage against the occupying power. 'In addition I declare that henceforth I reserve to myself the right to nominate certain members of any parish who will be liable to the death penalty in the event of any attacks against communications as for instance harbours, cranes, bridges, cables, and wires, if these are made with the assistance or the knowledge of the inhabitants of the parish concerned. In their own interest I call upon the population for increased activity and watchfulness in combating all suspicious elements, and to co-operate in the discovery of the guilty persons.'

[2] See Chapter 4.

The only possible criticism of the Island authorities is that sometimes they may have seemed to go beyond the bounds of passive co-operation; but this depends on where the line is drawn. There is a broad spectrum stretching from active resistance to active collaboration; and the intermediate bands – passive resistance, reluctant co-operation, and so on – shade into one another with all the delicacy of the colours of the rainbow. There is no doubt that according to their own standards the Island administrations never went beyond passive co-operation; but sometimes they give a false impression of willingness to co-operate. The agreement of the President of the Controlling Committee in Guernsey to record a message for German radio was one example.[1] Perhaps another was the anxiety of a Guernsey newspaper to include German lessons in its columns, which was discussed in the Controlling Committee and then blessed by the German authorities.[2] In 1941 the Controlling Committee agreed that the States should, as a memento of the occupation, bear the cost of publishing a small booklet on the Island of Guernsey written by a German officer. But on the whole the official attitude was correct and unforthcoming; if the Island administrations seem occasionally to have leaned too far in the direction of collaboration it was their judgement that was at fault and not their loyalty. There were many occasions when they dug their toes in – for example when the Superior Council in Jersey refused in August 1941 to repair a road on the ground that it led to an ammunition dump, and they were not prepared to undertake work of a military character.[3]

The policy of steering a course of passive co-operation was endangered from time to time by bold spirits who felt that it was wrong not to resist actively and who did not see the harm it could do to their fellow Islanders. Those who put them most at risk were probably the considerable number who contrived to escape from Jersey and Guernsey, at great danger to themselves. Escapes were naturally deprecated by the Germans, who saw in them a security risk, especially as the building of the fortifications became more advanced. There was always the chance that vital information about the state of the defences would be carried to England to be used to brief an invading force, or the R.A.F. There were occasional attempts to discipline the populations as a whole after an escape, in the hope that further attempts would be discouraged; but those who wanted to get away from the Islands were not inhibited by the knowledge that they might be causing trouble for those they left behind. The motives of the escapers varied. Some went to join the

[1] CCM 4 July 1940.   [2] GF 7/1/3.   [3] JFW 31/5/6.

forces. Others simply wanted to escape from the harsh life in the occupied Islands, on the assumption that life in Britain was less disagreeable.

Such acts of sabotage as occurred were unspectacular and from the military point of view worthless. In March 1941 a cable at an antiaircraft gun site in Guernsey was cut in two places. As a punishment the curfew was lengthened by an hour and 60 men between 18 and 45 were required to do night guard duty at various places for 18 days.[1] This episode earned a rebuke from the head of the military government in Paris. General von Stülpnagel issued a special proclamation in Guernsey warning the public against any further acts of sabotage: suspects would be tried in the military court and, on conviction, sentenced to death. The proclamation, which was aimed only at Guernsey, no acts of sabotage having so far taken place in Jersey, concluded dramatically: 'People of the Island! Your destiny and welfare are in your own hands. Your home interests demand that you should refrain from, and to the best of your power prevent, all such actions, which must inevitably be followed by disastrous consequences.'[2] The *Feldkommandant* considered whether the whole population should be punished, but after discussion with von Schmettow and the *Geheime Feldpolizei* it was decided that this was not necessary, although there was no doubt that the cutting of the cable was a deliberate act of sabotage.

From time to time there were other acts which could come under the general head of resistance. In 1941 two 16-year-old girls were arrested in Guernsey for alleged spying, but nothing more came of this.[3] A member of the crew of a ship plying between the Islands and the mainland of France – an Islander – was suspected of carrying information to enemy agents in France; but again the records do not show that he was found guilty.[4] The Germans took even the smallest matter seriously. When some schoolboys stuck on a wall a sheet of cardboard inscribed 'Come on Guernsey. Britain will win. To Hell with the Germans!' it was reported by the *Feldgendarmerie* to the *Feldkommandantur*. The Controlling Committee was warned that anti-German propaganda could not be tolerated and would have serious consequences. The Island police must ensure that nothing like this ever happened again.[5] In October 1942 more cables were cut in Guernsey and the *Feldkommandant* announced that this could lead to reprisals against the

[1] T 315 1639/610; NG Security file.   [2] NG Security file.
[3] Ibid.   [4] T 315 1639/672.
[5] NG Security file.

whole population.[1] It was admitted, however, that damage to cables could be caused by cows or storms, and the German police were ordered to check this possibility before reporting cases of sabotage.[2]

Although most of the sabotage was in Guernsey, there was an attempt to set up a resistance movement in Jersey in 1944. A group of young men asked several retired officers for advice as to how they should set about it, but were given no encouragement. Eight of them, fired by the news from France, and satisfied that there was no point in trying to organize resistance in Jersey, decided that they must escape to Britain to join the forces. They set off in the afternoon of 20 September from a stretch of coast which they had observed was not closely guarded. One of their three canoes was damaged on the way to the beach, and it shipped water and had to turn back. It was last seen by the others heading for a rock not yet fully submerged by the rising tide. After six hours' paddling the other two canoes reached the coast of France – now in Allied hands – and the young men made their way to England except for one who found the trip too much for him and had to go to hospital. The three who failed to get away were rescued and imprisoned. Two of them escaped, however, and lay low with friends for the rest of the occupation.

Right from the beginning there were attempts to escape. Some of them were successful, in spite of the enormous hazards. Escapers were compelled to use the smallest of boats, and to navigate some of the most dangerous waters in the world, and it is a miracle that as many of them got away as did. Inevitably there were casualties. In May 1943 three young men left Jersey. Their boat capsized a short distance from the beach. One was drowned and the others taken prisoner. They were trying to do something for the Allied cause, for they had in their possession photographs of gun positions which they were unable to destroy before they were captured. Their exploit brought forth a warning that there would be serious trouble if anything like this happened again. Parents and guardians would be held responsible for the actions of their sons, and as a reprisal men of military age would be taken to the continent for internment.

Although escapes took place all through the occupation the rate increased after the invasion of France, partly because there was a greater incentive to get away from the siege conditions which prevailed after June 1944, and partly because young men wanted to play their part in the liberation of Europe. In July 1944 an enterprising Jersey boy, who had taken part in demonstrations at the time of the deportations, mingled with OT workers embarking for France, and eventually made his way to England. He was thought to be a marked man, which seems to be confirmed by the fact that his absence from the Island was quickly spotted by the Germans. About the same time a Dutchman and a girl were caught attempting to escape and were given prison sentences. In November three men and a woman left Jersey, but their boat struck rocks off Saline Bay and all were drowned.

At the beginning of July 1941 Islanders responded to the radio appeal from Britain to put up 'V for Victory' signs as part of the general resistance campaign in Europe. The appeal was not directed at the Islands. Indeed the British authorities deliberately excluded the Channel Islands from their resistance broadcasts on the ground that organized resistance was not feasible there, after a cryptic Red Cross message from Guernsey had asked 'to hear more of Ogilvy' – Lord Ogilvy then being Chairman of the Board of Governors of the B.B.C. A special service would have had to take the same line about resistance and sabotage with the Islanders as with Europe – otherwise the Germans would have exploited the fact that the British were asking Europeans to fight for the common cause, but not their fellow countrymen. The alternative – to provide a special service and to make the same demands of the Islanders – was seen to be inciting them to commit suicide, since there was not the slightest hope of meaningful active resistance in the Islands.[1]

Nevertheless, reports of the success of the resistance campaign in Europe were broadcast in the ordinary services of the B.B.C. and picked up by the Islanders. A few bold spirits decided to do what others in occupied Europe were being asked to do, and 'V' signs began to appear. There was naturally a strong reaction from the Germans. Under pressure from them the Bailiff of Guernsey announced that if the culprits were not discovered the whole population might be punished. He warned against 'committing these foolish acts which accomplish nothing, but merely bring grave consequences in their train'. Three weeks later the *Feldkommandantur* added its warning. People had drawn 'V' signs at various places in St. Martin. A German street sign had been besmeared. This was 'damage to a contrivance of the German forces' and therefore ranked as sabotage. Since the Island police had been unable to lay their hands on the offenders all the people in the neighbourhood must suffer. All radios within a thousand metres of the

[1] Information provided by Mr. Cecil de Sausmarez who was at this time Deputy Regional Director at the Political Warfare Executive.

Beaulieu Hotel would be confiscated; and two men of St. Martin parish must stand sentry from 10 p.m. to 6 a.m. by the besmeared signboard.

In Jersey 'V' signs were painted on houses and walls in the Rouge Bouillon district. This was also considered to be sabotage. The Germans threatened that if those responsible did not give themselves up all radio sets in the district would be confiscated, the local population fined, and a civilian guard posted nightly. The first and last of these punishments were inflicted. At the end of July the Germans began to put up their own 'V' signs to minimize the effect of the Islanders' demonstration; and before long both bailiwicks returned to the sensible role of patient, passive co-operation.

Shortly after the invasion of Europe began two Jersey half-sisters, no doubt thinking that the end was in sight, began to type messages inciting the troops to surrender. They were caught, tried by a military court, and sentenced to six years in prison for listening to the radio, and to death for distributing the messages. When one of them asked which sentence would be served first, the judge said the death penalty. The Bailiff made a special plea for mercy, however, and in the event they escaped execution.[1]

One final example of resistance must be mentioned: the help given to a number of Russian prisoners who escaped from the Germans. The Soviet government later recognized this by the presentation of gold watches to those who had risked their lives by looking after the escaped men.

The Islanders were sorely tried throughout the occupation by the administrative incompetence of the Germans. The fact that the Channel Islands were governed by orders issued by the head of the military government in Paris meant that much legislation was aimed primarily at France. There would have been no problem if FK 515 had had the nous to turn a blind eye on edicts which had no real application in the Channel Islands. There were occasional attempts to legislate selectively, but as a rule so inflexible was the military government that when a VOBIF became law they deemed it necessary to implement every clause down to the last comma, so that not even the Führer himself would be able to point to an error of omission. This passion for blind over-administration is seen at its best in the handling of the orders banning 'unions, societies and associations'.

[1] JFW 50.

It was obviously reasonable from the German point of view to keep a careful watch on activities in France, where there was scope for genuine resistance. Societies could there foster the will to resist and provide facilities for organizing resistance. It was predictable that even in the Islands bodies like the Freemasons would be dissolved, although it was unnecessary on security grounds. The Bailiff of Guernsey did his best for the Freemasons, pointing out that they were non-political, unlike Freemasons in France. He suggested that the orders against them must have been transmitted in error; but to no avail. The activities of Rotary, the Freemasons, and the Oddfellows must cease. The assets of the two last were taken over by the States in both Islands as a result of tripartite agreements between the bodies concerned, the States, and the *Feldkommandant*. Some of the masonic treasures were seized and sent to Germany in the early days of the occupation.

In addition a host of societies, large and small, were prohibited except under licence by an order of the military governor in France of 28 August 1940. The military administration districts were authorized to delegate their powers to subordinate commanders, and a general exemption could easily have been provided for societies and clubs in the Islands. This was not done, however. Every single organization had to be dealt with separately, which imposed completely unnecessary burdens on the *Feldkommandantur*, the Island authorities, and the unfortunate societies. In Jersey these included bodies incorporated by act of the States, ranging from the Jersey Chamber of Commerce to the Royal Jersey Golf Club; charitable and welfare societies, for example, the St. John Ambulance Brigade and the Girls' Friendly Society; sports and games clubs of every nature, church organizations, social clubs, and professional and trade associations, none of which really threatened the German regime.

Voluminous correspondence erupted from dozens of club secretaries, the Bailiff, and the Germans. On 24 October 1940 the secretary of the Contract Bridge Circle drew the Bailiff's attention to his recent letters and asked him to try to expedite a decision about the Circle's application for permission to play bridge. He assumed that contract bridge must be specially licensed by the German authorities before the cards were cut for another rubber. The Bailiff's secretary replied that the decision was up to the *Feldkommandant* and that he had no idea when it would come. The Circle decided to take a chance and go on playing – thereby adding the knock of the Gestapo to the normal hazards in making their contracts.

The societies which were given permission to continue their activities were required to get authority from the *Feldkommandantur* every time they met; but after a year the Germans realized that they were granting permission in every case. They then decided that it would be enough to require eight days' notice of meetings – perhaps to enable the Gestapo to organize surveillance, for example, of the members of the Jersey Maternity and Infant Welfare Centre, as they went to and from their meeting-place.

This close control was maintained right to the end of the occupation, but only once was it found necessary to take action against a group. In November 1944 the Germans ordered the dissolution of the Jersey School of Physical Culture because at a meeting of the club, at which approximately 40 members were present, the possibilities of escaping from the Island were discussed. How this information reached the *Platzkommandantur*, and how seriously escape was discussed is not recorded; but the German authorities must have been delighted at catching someone out, however flimsy the evidence, after four years of intensive effort in this subversive field.[1]

[1] JF W 30/13.

8

Daily Life: Germans

However uncomfortable life may have been for the civilians, the Wehrmacht before long were much worse off, although knowledge of the fact would have been cold comfort to the Islanders. At first the soldiers were on top of the world. They had fought a great campaign. They had captured a land flowing with milk and honey – or so it seemed after the austerity to which they were accustomed in Germany. The shops were full of exciting things – woollens and silks and perfumes – and with the aid of Reichsmarks they were raided for presents to send back to wives and sweethearts. So much was sent that in September 1940 the field postal services lodged a complaint and asked that the number of parcels should be restricted.[1] There was plenty of food and drink, plenty to do settling into the new way of life, which it was assumed would be temporary, plenty of places to photograph – to prove that the occupation of Britain had already begun – and to write home about. Communications were good. Letters, always an important element in morale, did not take too long. There was the invasion of England to speculate about; and perhaps the more ambitious wondered what part they would individually be called on to play when Germany had finally mastered Britain and the world.

All this vanished. The shops were gradually emptied. After only a few days of occupation limitations were imposed on the quantities of goods which the troops could buy, including cigarettes, wine, beer, and clothes, although fruit and vegetables continued to be freely available to them.[2] As soon as the military government was established the *Feldkommandant*, Oberst Schumacher, issued a formal proclamation in German and English requiring all German officials to make their purchases through the *Feldkommandantur*. Articles in everyday use, in

[1] NG 01/34.   [2] JFW 31/1/7; NG 01/34.

particular textiles, soap, footwear and foodstuffs (though not fresh fruit and vegetables) could be bought by members of the Wehrmacht only on the production of a warrant from the head of their unit countersigned by the *Inselkommandant*.

These provisions immediately turned out to be unworkable, as anyone with administrative experience would have spotted when they were being drafted. Less than a week later Schumacher had to explain what he really meant. He attempted to save face – for this was his first major edict – by attributing the confusion to 'misunderstandings on the part of the local people' rather than to their correct interpretation of a singularly stupid order. Bulk purchases for the Wehrmacht, for example of paint for army vehicles, could be made only through the *Feldkommandantur*, and indeed this presented no problem. But in the second part of the order the *Feldkommandant* had unwittingly made it necessary for the *Inselkommandant* to issue a licence to every single member of the Wehrmacht every time he wanted to buy anything at all – even a box of matches, or a bar of chocolate.

In his explanation of the order Schumacher said that it was undesirable that any member of the Wehrmacht should buy more than his immediate needs; and it was for this reason that the system of warrants had been introduced. It would, however, impose too great a burden on the military administration if warrants were needed for all goods – which was precisely what his order *had* required. 'One cannot, for example, demand a warrant for shoelaces, blacking brushes, nail brushes, toothbrushes, razor blades and the like.' It was up to the shopkeeper to prevent excessive purchases of this type of article by refusing to sell 'more than what his practical experience tells him is necessary for the immediate needs of one person'. Thus it followed that warrants were required only for foodstuffs (except fruit and vegetables), textiles, soap, and leather footwear. If, however, the Island authorities thought that other goods should be controlled it was up to them to say so. In explaining away his first major mistake the *Feldkommandant* put on the Island shopkeepers the responsibility for deciding what individual members of the Wehrmacht might reasonably buy, and enforcing their own decisions.

The need for a licensing system was explained to the troops on the ground that 'the small size of the Islands makes unlimited purchases a danger to production and economic distribution'. At first the permitted quantities were very generous. A man could buy a suit, coat, and pullover. In addition he could buy every six months a pair of trousers, two shirts, two sets of underwear, three pairs of socks, six handkerchiefs, and a pair of pyjamas. But the possession of a warrant did not guarantee supply, and the Island shopkeepers discriminated against the Wehrmacht, as far as they dared, in favour of their regular customers. As time went on the licensing system became less important. There was no point in issuing warrants for goods which were unobtainable.

The quantities of food available to the troops declined steadily as communications with France, to which they looked for most of their supplies, became more difficult. By May 1942 things were already becoming tight, especially in Alderney. Gerhard Nebel, who was there at this time, records: 'For the first time since I became a soldier I have difficulty in making do with the bread ration. Half our daily ration is lost through being mouldy.' When his company was weighed it was found that everybody had lost a great deal. Nebel himself had lost over two stones. The food generally was miserable – only the *Oberfeldwebel* (sergeant major) and the kitchen staff had full stomachs. The former spent much of his day in the kitchen sampling titbits.[1]

Alderney, however, was the least agreeable of the three main Islands so far as the Germans were concerned. Compared with Guernsey where Nebel had spent some time 'it makes a bleak impression. There are lacking the villas, the gardens, the greenhouses and the fields'. Instead, there was the ugliness of 'a technical landscape' – barracks, iron scaffolding, cement mixers, mountains of cement, sand heaps, bunkers, tank traps, piles of timber, field railways, locomotives, and lorries. 'The whole place was overrun with Frenchmen, Berbers, and Spanish Reds. The remains of civilian life which the conditions on the neighbouring Islands alleviate are here lacking. One is in a war and work camp where there are no women and no children.' Nevertheless, Alderney pointed to the shape of things to come in all the Islands, especially after the middle of 1944.

The decline in the troops' standard of living is illustrated by the reduction in their tobacco ration. When they first arrived, their purchases from Island shops, which were additional to what they were entitled to buy from their own canteens, were limited to 50 cigarettes at any one time. In November 1940 the amount was reduced to 20 a day (or the equivalent in pipe tobacco or cigars). Tradesmen who were unwilling to supply the troops were threatened with punishment and the closure of their shops. They were also instructed that in the event of scarcity the military forces must have preference over the civilian population. In

[1] Nebel, p. 186.

March 1941 the daily ration was reduced to six cigarettes, and four months later it was down to three. Originally the troops had been instructed not to buy more than one day's ration at a time; they were now ordered to buy five days' at once, for the sake of the tradesmen's convenience. After September 1941 the troops no longer had access to civilian tobacco supplies, but had to make do with the ever-diminishing forces' issue, which finally disappeared completely.[1]

Soldatenkaufhäuser (soldiers' shops) were opened in Jersey and Guernsey in 1942. Their purpose was to give the German garrisons the same chance to buy luxuries as their comrades enjoyed in France. They were the responsibility of the *Feldkommandantur*, although they were managed and staffed by Channel Islanders. The assistants were mostly young girls. Some of the goods they stocked were intended for the troops – toothpaste, razor blades, and shaving brushes, for example; but they mainly sold gifts for their womenfolk in Germany – handbags, silk stockings, perfume, underwear, and so on. They were open to men of the Wehrmacht in uniform and to German members of the Organisation Todt. They were extremely popular when they were still offering goods that were scarce in Germany – so popular that the troops were asked to keep their purchases as low as possible. In Guernsey there were 400 customers a day soon after the shop was opened, and there were complaints from units in the more distant parts of the Island that they could not get into St. Peter Port during the hours the shop was open.

Later there were also complaints about prices, to which the *Feldkommandantur* replied that the troops must not assume that the *Soldatenkaufhaus* was intended to be just another Wehrmacht shop. It was supposed to carry luxury goods which would inevitably be expensive; but the practice was to discontinue the sale of things which were considered to be much too expensive. Cognac had been banned from the shops for just this reason. In any case, the prices charged were exactly the same as on the mainland. The *Feldkommandantur* area headquarters were sensitive about complaints of this nature, and they toyed with the idea of closing the shops on the ground that they were more trouble than they were worth; but it was concluded that since they were doing brisk business in spite of the complaints, they must be serving a useful purpose.

Their success depended, of course, on the volume of goods they could bring in from France, through the agency of the *Soldatenkaufhaus* in

[1] NG 01/34.

Granville. With the passage of time it became more and more difficult to keep them adequately stocked. Nevertheless, they continued in business. In the Guernsey shop, business fell away by nearly half after the first six months, simply because goods were not available; but it was not until the end of 1944 that the shops finally closed.[1]

The *Soldatenheime* (soldiers' homes) were clubs where the men could relax during off-duty hours. *The Feldkommandantur* was responsible for staffing them and running them. They were managed by Red Cross sisters, who had to conform to a strict code of conduct. Lipstick and nail varnish were banned, and hair had to be worn short. A formal 'Heil Hitler' was the only permissible greeting – certainly not 'Good morning' or the like. The *Soldatenheime* were governed by regulations drawn up by OKH. Food and drink were provided, and guests could be invited. There were separate rooms for the officers, who had to be treated with proper respect. If, however, a superior entered one of the ordinary rooms, subordinates need not rise unless he approached their table, in which case they must leap to their feet and 'maintain a military posture'. When a general came in everyone had to rise and give the German greeting. The manageress was encouraged to keep a good lending library ('to satisfy the reading hunger of the troops'), which was to be kept stocked out of the profits of the *Soldatenheim*.[2]

In Guernsey the first home was opened in 1940 at Old Government House; the troops were told to use it as carefully as if it was their own home. When Gerhard Nebel visited it in 1942 he complained:

'The nearer to the front, the more the Soldatenheim lacks. In Paris, where it was not needed there was a superfluity. Here in a land of shortage we get in the morning a cup of homely tea and two thin slices of black bread thinly spread with jam. At lunchtime and in the evening there is mostly nothing, for the rations don't stretch to such numbers as pour in all at once. You can see people gazing hungrily at the food and driven crazy when the waiter with his tray, perhaps the last, turns to another table. The meals are meagre and it is difficult to believe that people can be hungry enough to come a long distance and wait hours for them. We were told to stand by for this evening and promised a special treat . . . After the usual wait we were served with a plate of potatoes with watery broth in which a few noodles floated. The worst thing, though, is that here we are given no wine.'[3]

The *Soldatenheime* were supposed to play their part in keeping morale high, but if they could offer no more than watery noodle soup they were hardly likely to succeed. In spite of all efforts morale steadily

[1] NG 10/7.   [2] NG I d 1.   [3] Nebel, p. 47.

sank. In Guernsey in 1940 the *Inselkommandant* said that he was alarmed by the amount of drunkenness, and that if it did not stop men would have to be back in their quarters at 9 p.m. instead of 10. Next year things were no better. Far too many men were drinking themselves silly, allegedly because they were unaccustomed to the strength of liquor sold in the Islands; and it was threatened that if the troops did not pull themselves together alcohol would be banned.[1] In the middle of 1941 there were four or five suicides a week in north-western France, including the Channel Islands. When the problem of morale was discussed at a meeting of the *Feldkommandanturen* in the region it was decided that the officers must do more to help their men to keep in good heart. Indeed one of the reasons why officers and men used the same *Soldatenheim* was 'so that the soldier can talk to the officers off the record' about the problems he faced.

Given the inactivity forced by circumstances on the Wehrmacht it was important to make the maximum provision for recreation. In the very early days, which some Channel Islanders were prepared to regard as a honeymoon period, the troops were invited to watch cricket at the Guernsey cricket club and even to join the club and take part in matches; but there is no evidence that the English national game was the answer to the Wehrmacht's problems of morale. At first the cinemas were a great stand-by, as they were for the civilian population. In December 1941 in Guernsey it was calculated that every member of the Wehrmacht there – 15,000 in all – could go once a week to the Regal Cinema, where there were 1,100 seats. The troops were admitted free to the Regal, but they had to pay at the other cinemas, which were shared between soldiers and civilians. The forces sat on the left-hand side of the mixed cinemas and the civilians on the right. 'Anyone looking for adventure sits at the end of the rows.'[2]

There were numerous band concerts for the troops, and variety shows given by visiting performers including 'Strength through Joy' groups.[3] Swimming was possible in the summer, but here there was an element of regimentation. The men had to bathe in groups so that it would be easier to round them up in the event of an alarm. Further, lifeguards or lifeboats had to be available.[4] The troops, unlike the civilian population, were allowed to shoot game, and on at least one occasion there was an organized hunt, followed by horse racing. They were also allowed to take photographs, but this was a diminishing asset

[1] NG 01/34.   [2] Nebel, p. 327.
[3] T 314 1604/867.   [4] NG 01/34.

since the necessary materials soon ceased to be available. A small number of photographic shops were allowed to process films handed in by the troops. The men could also read, provided that they were prepared to stick to the books officially approved by the *Feldkommandantur*, which ranged from Clausewitz's *On War* to a number of volumes by Edgar Wallace, who was apparently above suspicion. There was a constant watch for unsuitable books. *Soldatenheim I* in Guernsey was found to have a copy of *Der 9 November* by Bernhard Kellermann, which was considered to be much too pacifist for soldiers, and it was ceremonially thrown in the fire. *Soldatenheim III* stocked *Der Abenteurer* by Rudolf Herzog until it was decided that pages 152 and 153 deviated from the gospel about the Jews, and after consultation with FK 515 it was destroyed.

There was a strenuous campaign to boost morale in the winter of 1943. The military government in Paris offered prizes for numerous competitions. Who could compose the best marching song? What was the best way to shorten the long winter evenings? There were also literary competitons, and one, devised perhaps by a *Kriegsverwaltungsrat* with an un-Teutonic sense of humour, for the best model of a war grave. There were some local competitions – for the best occupation painting, for example – athletics meetings, tennis tournaments, and so on. Games of all sorts were encouraged – football, volley-ball, and ping-pong were specified in the official guidance on this subject. After a strenuous afternoon on the playing fields there were lectures on fascinating subjects like The British Commonwealth.[1] The need for self-entertainment became all the greater at this time since Ob. West had to reduce the number of entertainers visiting the Islands because of transport difficulties.[2]

Some of the young women of the Islands may have bestowed their favours on the German troops, but the demand in this field was greater than the supply, and official brothels were established both in St. Helier and St. Peter Port. The queues of customers waiting in the gardens of the chosen houses afforded a certain amount of innocent amusement to the inhabitants of both towns, although in Guernsey the authorities were upset by the management of the institutions.

The first Guernsey brothel, which was opened in February 1942, had an establishment of two men, who were in charge, and thirteen women, all of whom were brought over from France. By order of the *Feld-*

[1] NG I d 1; T 314 1604/784–9, 1250.   [2] T 314 1604/867.

kommandantur they were provided with civilian ration books, although it was arguable that they should have been regarded as part of the military establishment. Later more women were imported, and two more brothels opened. The *Feldkommandantur* issued verbal instructions that the inmates should be given heavy workers' rations, which were substantially more generous than the ordinary ration. This was considered by the Essential Commodities Committee (which perhaps did not have proper regard to the facts of the case) to be an injustice. Sir Abraham Lainé, the President of the Committee, protested violently, but to no avail. The *Feldkommandantur* refused to give written orders, 'thus clearly showing how ashamed they were of the baseness of the whole matter'.

Since the workers in question were French citizens the Essential Commodities Committee was entitled to recoup from France the heavy workers' rations issued to them; but their application was rejected by the French authorities on the ground that the women could not reasonably be classed as heavy workers. This was reported by the Committee to the *Feldkommandantur*, no doubt with satisfaction, whereupon they were ordered to lump the inmates of the brothels with the heavy workers in the quarterly returns submitted to the French authorities, so that they would not be able to detect the precise nature of their profession. Although the quantity of food involved was small, it did not prevent the Essential Commodities Committee from waxing eloquent about the iniquity of being compelled to submit false returns in such a cause as this.[1]

The Guernsey brothels caused other trouble. The *Feldkommandantur* demanded the services of a local doctor to carry out routine medical examinations. The doctor selected, who was in charge of the States Venereal Diseases Clinic, objected on the grounds that it was up to the German army doctors to do the job. At a stormy meeting Rittmeister von Oettingen explained that the work was done by civilian doctors in all the occupied territiories, including Jersey where there seemed to be no problem. The doctor said that it would take a direct order to make him carry out the examinations, to which von Oettingen replied that the Health Services Officer could issue the necessary order. It was pointed out, however, that the Health Services Officer had no power to order his colleagues to do anything. A slanging match developed, at the end of which the Rittmeister said that the conversation which had taken place must be regarded as an order; and that was that. The President of the

[1] *Report on Essential Supplies and Services*, p. 39.

Controlling Committee ruled that the Germans had formally ordered the doctor to provide the necessary services.[1]

So that there could be no misunderstanding von Oettingen wrote to the Controlling Committee instructing that the examination of the women should be carried out twice weekly, payment being made by the keepers of the brothels. Further, there was to be a once-for-all examination of the women employed in the kitchens of the Organisation Todt. The *Geheime Feldpolizei* were made responsible for the surveillance of the personnel of the brothels and had to provide the *Inselkommandantur* with detailed information about their comings and goings.[2]

In October 1942, in an attempt to control venereal disease, the chief German medical officer ordered that all women who had been under treatment should be handed a notice reading:

Sexual relations, whether with German soldiers or civilians, are strictly forbidden during the next three months. In case of non-compliance with the order severe punishment by the occupying authorities is to be expected, even if no infection takes place.

This notice was transmitted to Sark, but without the intended qualification that it was to be handed only to women who had been under treatment. When it was presented to the Dame of Sark by the *Inselkommandant* she was highly indignant. 'Looking the Commandant squarely in the face, with no attempt to hide my disgust, I said . . . "I will not publish anything so insulting to my people".' Her husband's reaction was more light-hearted. He observed: 'They must be having a lot of fun and games in Guernsey, which is more than can be said of Sark.'[3]

After theft (which increased all through the occupation and reached a climax when the Islands were cut off from the mainland) and drunkenness, the most common offence was careless driving. An order of August 1940 deprecated the amount of wild driving, and threatened severe punishment in the event of an accident. In an attempt to control things it was ruled that an officer's approval must be obtained before any journey was undertaken. Next month a more powerful order was issued. There was more reckless driving than ever. Speed limits were being ignored. Drivers were not driving on the left (the rule of the road had not yet been changed). Severe punishment was again threatened, along with the withdrawal of driving licences. Fatal accidents continued, and in December von Schmettow issued an order of the day saying that

[1] GF 8/1/4.   [2] NG Security file.
[3] Sibyl Hathaway, *Dame of Sark* (London, 1961), pp. 147–8; GF 8/1/4.

his patience was at an end. His orders had been repeatedly flouted. It was a shameful indication of the lack of discipline among the troops. But in spite of orders and exhortation dangerous driving continued, and there was further loss of life among both the Wehrmacht and the civilian population. Indeed, this was a general problem. In June 1942 Hitler himself signed a circular letter to all troops ordering that driving errors, excessive speed, and unauthorized journeys should be cut out.[1]

To begin with, the amount of theft and petty crime was no more than one would expect from any army of occupation. The day after the troops arrived in Guernsey some of them helped themselves to 15 cases of spirits from the bonded store at the Jetty, in spite of protests, and this sort of thing inevitably continued.[2] An order at the end of August 1940 drew attention to the fact that the Island authorities were reporting more offences by the troops, and unit commanders were instructed to carry out a careful investigation in every case. It was important that the number of incidents affecting the good name of the Wehrmacht should be kept to the absolute minimum. The men must be left in no doubt that discipline would be maintained, even if the most severe punishment was necessary. In January 1941 a sergeant was convicted of stealing two clocks and given a prison sentence – which fact was notified to all units. The warning had little effect, however.

In March yet another order was necessary. Plundering and looting were continuing at an unreasonable level. The men were reminded that the Islands had been occupied without a fight, and that they therefore had not been conquered. The Island governments had themselves arranged for the abdication of the former occupying power – Britain. They had done everything they possibly could for the troops – far more than they were required to do under the Hague Convention. They had done their best to supply the army of occupation, and the least the troops could do now was to abstain from theft.[3] Little attention was paid to this plea. At the end of 1941 about 30 thefts allegedly by the forces were being reported monthly. The figure for the first quarter of 1942 was 65 a month, and for the last quarter over 200 a month. In the middle of 1943 it had soared to over 330 a month – this before the seige had reduced the Wehrmacht to a really serious position.[4]

Theft was by far the commonest, but by no means the only offence. Some Wehrmacht court records have survived, including those of the

[1] NG Bundle C.
[3] NG 01/34.

[2] GF 7/1/3.
[4] GF 1/1/6.

Feldkriegsgericht des Kommandeurs der 13 Flakdivision, and the *Gericht des Festungskommandanten, Abteilung Luftwaffe*. They show that the troops were guilty of the usual military offences – failure to keep proper watch, insubordination, absence without leave, desertion, and so on. The records of the trials reveal that they were often conducted with surprising leniency. A soldier who deserted his post for five minutes during which an alarm was telephoned in vain to his strong point was sentenced to only six weeks in prison. Another heard about the unsuccessful attempt on Hitler's life and was reported to have said 'Pity! Otherwise we could all be home by Christmas'. He was acquitted on the ground that the witness was unreliable. In April 1943 four sailors stole a pig, which they hid in the roof of their strong point. Next day one of them who left his post to fetch it was spotted by the *Geheime Feldpolizei*. The offence was only a minor one in the eyes of the court but since it involved food the sentence must be relatively harsh. 'In the existing food situation the sabotaging of the whole cannot be tolerated.' Yet in spite of deserting his post and stealing food the man got only eight months. Things did, however, become tougher towards the end of the siege. A man was given six months for milking a cow in the fields. And in one or two cases of food theft the death penalty was inflicted.

It was not only the increasing shortage of goods, especially food, drink, and tobacco, that lowered morale. The loss of the Battle of Britain raised doubts about the possibility of ever invading Britain. There was little or nothing for the men to do, beyond training for no obvious purpose. The anti-aircraft and coastal batteries were in action from time to time, but for most of the troops there was nothing but unalleviated boredom. The majority were accustomed to a more sophisticated way of life than the Islands offered in wartime, and their peculiar charm was lost on them. Letters from home became more and more infrequent, and when the Allied bombing of Germany began in earnest there was always the fear that womenfolk and relatives might have suffered. The casualty lists printed in those of the German newspapers that reached the Islands made depressing reading. A page from a Nuremberg paper of 18 August 1943 is preserved in the records of the *Feldkommandantur*. It lists in bold type the names of 407 civilians who were killed in the British 'terror' air raid on Nuremberg on the night of 10/11 August. No doubt many other similar announcements had their effect on morale.

The miserable life of the private soldier may be gathered from Gerhard Nebel's account. It is true that he was sent with a construction unit to Alderney as a punishment, and that conditions were worse than average; but many of the things he experienced were common form. Moreover, he was writing in 1942, when things were infinitely better than they were a year or two later.

He went to the Islands in a steamer carrying ammunition which lay off St. Peter Port for a whole day as air raids made it too risky to go into the harbour. The men were herded together in the hold with nothing to eat or drink; nor could they go to the toilets, which were locked and reserved for the officers. Eventually the construction unit reached Alderney where, before long, they were submerged 'in a hopeless existence of duty, exercise, building up the terrain, insupportable misery . . . Our Prussian masters make a religion out of watch and guard duties . . . Everything is made into a torment, the system is founded on terror, punishment, menaces . . .'. To make matters worse, the company commander was a Nazi who took every order literally 'not so much out of cruelty as of a pedantic pettiness born out of stupidity and fear of superiors'. He forced men 'who can hardly remember the *Paternoster*' to learn by heart long sections of the regulations; held exercises for the corporals, the sole purpose of which was to belittle them; and for trifling reasons cancelled the leave of married men with large families who had not been home for years.[1]

This sort of treatment was hard enough to take in 1942. At the end of the occupation it was accompanied by a desperate struggle for existence in which the men's misery was intensified by the feeling of isolation. Shortly after D-Day an Islander who escaped reported that morale visibly lifted for a day or two after the arrival of the weekly mail plane; but there were not enough planes to keep up this service, and for three months in the autumn of 1944 not a single mail plane got through to Jersey. There was great excitement when one finally arrived in October, and took back with it letters complaining bitterly about the long delay between posts. It was shot down, however, and its load fell into Allied hands. One of the letters said that there were going to be serious difficulties in the Islands over heating, lighting, and water; and that the people, who had thought in June that the war was over, had become more and more troublesome. 'But they will calm down again when they feel that the war is not won just yet. What is finally going to happen to us, that is written in the stars.' The troops were told that the mail plane had been shot down and that another would be due shortly. As on the previous occasion, each man would be allowed to send only one letter, written on airmail paper. Even at the beginning of 1943 the postal

[1] Nebel, p. 81.

services were liable to serious interruption. In February there was a period of 12 days when there was no service to Guernsey and Alderney.[1]

The shortage of shipping also had its effect. In July 1943 it became necessary to order that all but the most serious surgical cases should be treated in the Islands to reduce the number of men carried to and from the mainland, which meant a lower standard of surgery for most of the garrison. It was also laid down that duty and leave journeys should be combined as far as possible; and the troops were now required to travel on cargo ships.[2]

Things got much worse at the beginning of 1945. The cinemas which had provided a welcome escape, closed because there was no electricity. They were replaced by 'cultural presentations' by the troops, including performances by the Luftwaffe and Wehrmacht orchestras, which were probably better than nothing, but not much. It was still the irregular postal services that caused most complaint. A reasonable amount of mail came from some regions, Silesia, for example; but there was very little from Berlin and west Germany. There must be something wrong with the internal services. Further, a lot of unnecessary printed material was being sent – it was considered that the troops would be much happier with magazines. A plea from the Islands said that while soap was the thing most missed, and medicines of all kinds were badly needed, it would be good for morale if space could be found for 'pictures of home' to brighten barracks' walls. It would also help if news bulletins made much of the importance of holding on to the western fortresses. At the beginning of February the men were rationed to four letters at a time, but the real limiting factor was the paucity of mail planes. It was more important to use the available transports to carry food, but not all of these got through. Some were shot down, but many more were lost because of difficult flying conditions.[3] Shortly after the invasion of Europe began there was a general order to stop all compassionate leave, except in the case of the death of the man's wife or one of his parents. A marginal note on this order by someone in the *Feldkommandantur* demanded 'What about our children?' The order was of course meaningless in the Channel Islands since no one could go on leave, compassionate or otherwise. The best that could be done for them was the establishment of an enquiry centre where men were told how to find out if relatives were still alive and where they had gone.[4]

[1] T 314 1604/233.   [2] T 314 1604/739–40.
[3] MOD 509/271; T 77 787/5515353; NG 01/33.   [4] NG I d.

There were in the Islands some *Reichsdeutsche* (native Germans) – about 50 (including children) in Jersey, and about a dozen in Guernsey. There were also one or two *Volksdeutsche* (people of German origin). They were entitled by an order of the military government in Paris to the same quantities of rationed food as were the civilian population in Germany. This meant, for example, that they had 7 ounces of fat a week compared with the 4 ounces drawn by the Islanders. The *Feldkommandant* accepted that because of the supply position in the Islands it was undesirable that they should have the full amounts theoretically current in Germany; but nevertheless they were considerably better off than the Islanders, and although the amount of food involved was negligible the discrimination rankled with the people.

The authorities in Jersey did make an attempt to mitigate the discrimination by assuming for the purposes of rationing that while the children of *Reichsdeutsche* were entitled to the full 'native' ration, they were not also entitled to the supplementary rations which Channel Islands children drew. The *Feldkommandant* soon got wind of this and sent a stern note to the authorities ordering them to give the 'native' children both the 'native' rations and the children's supplement. The extra rations for *Reichsdeutsche* continued to the end of the occupation, but they were considerably reduced. From the middle of 1943 *Volksdeutsche* were also given extra rations, but on a less generous scale than the native Germans.[1]

[1] JF W 31/1/37. Both *Reichsdeutsche* and *Volksdeutsche* were given the opportunity of going to Germany in November 1940.

9

The Fortress

HITLER at first saw the capture of the Channel Islands as a triumph out of all proportion to its true military significance, although if Operation 'Sealion' (the invasion of England) had gone ahead the Islands would have played a part in supporting the invading troops.

Within eight months they were no longer a useful propaganda item, nor were they to be a base for combined operations against south-west England. Rather they had become territory that must be defended, whatever the cost – at least in Hitler's view. He feared in the spring of 1941 that Britain would undertake relieving operations in areas hitherto unthreatened, including the Channel Islands. They must therefore be made so strong that no force could land there, even if the Luftwaffe could not help the defenders. The necessary measures, for which guns were available thanks to the abandonment of Operation 'Felix' (the invasion of Gibraltar), were to be completed by mid-April; and the enemy were to be given the impression that these moves were all part of the build-up for 'Sealion'.[1]

On 2 June 1941 Hitler asked for maps of the Islands' defences, which reached him next day.[2] Von Rundstedt, *Oberbefehlshaber West* and commander of Army Group D, noting the Führer's sudden renewed interest, on 4 June ordered measures to strengthen the defences, including reconnaissance planes and more men for the guns already in position.[3] General Jodl recorded that the Führer assumed that the British would be impelled by Operation 'Marita' (the German invasion of Greece) to launch an attack on the Channel Islands or Norway as soon as Operation 'Barbarossa' (the invasion of Russia, which began on 22 June) was under way. It worried him a great deal and he asked for

---

[1] MOD 583/307; T 78 317/6271925.   [2] T 78 317/6271907, 920.
[3] T 78 317/6271905.

assurances that the Islands' garrisons were strong enough, that they had plenty of ammunition, and that it was safely stored.[1]

Having studied the defences, he decided that they were inadequate. The infantry were too few. Defence against naval attack was weak. Why were there no captured French tanks? All this must be remedied at once in view of the danger of attack during the Russian campaign. Keitel, in passing these points on to von Rundstedt, said that the Führer was impatiently awaiting new proposals, and wanted to be kept constantly informed about the state of the Islands' defences. Von Rundstedt ventured to demur about the tanks. The Islands were unsuitable for landings from planes, or by parachute. Nor were tanks much use, even if deployed singly. Nevertheless, perhaps as a sop, he agreed to provide two French tanks for the harbour area in Guernsey.[2]

Hitler issued a consolidated order about the defences on 13 June. There must be a reinforced regiment on each of Jersey and Guernsey. Heavier coastal batteries must be installed. More tanks must be sent. There must be protection against bombardment from the sea. In view of the large number of troops, special emphasis must be placed on active and passive protection against aerial attack. Supplies must be made secure by means of generous provisioning. Machine Gun Battalion 16 would remain permanently in the Islands. No army construction troops could be spared and therefore the Organisation Todt must be used. Progress reports were needed twice a week. The *Inspekteur der Westbefestigungen* (Inspector of Western Fortresses) was given the general oversight of the building programme; when all this had been put in hand plans for the long-term fortification of the Islands must be worked out.[3]

It was agreed that 42 guns would be made available on 1 July, 12 of them with a range of 25 kilometres. If longer-range guns were needed, those destined for 'Barbarossa' would be drawn on; but, not surprisingly, OKH was against this.[4]

On 19 July Hitler again expressed his fear that Britain would take advantage of German preoccupation on the eastern front: 'In the west and north all three elements of the Wehrmacht must be prepared to withstand possible English attacks against the Channel Islands and the Norwegian coast.'[5] Throughout August and September everything possible was done to implement his orders – for example, armour plating was brought from the Maginot Line[6] – and detailed progress

[1] T 78 317/6271897.   [2] T 78 317/6271895, 898, 899.
[3] T 78 317/6271874, 875, 884; MOD 583/376.   [4] T 78 317/6271882, 887.
[5] Directive No. 33.   [6] T 78 317/6271852.

reports were duly prepared. Yet it was not enough for the Führer. He saw in the landing of small parties on the French coast a positive signal that Britain was about to attack the Islands to pin down German forces in the west and demonstrate her willingness to help the Russians. 'We must be prepared for skilful handling on the enemy's part. Moonless nights and bad weather can favour such undertakings.' If Britain recaptured the Islands she would win great prestige, and it would be very difficult for the Wehrmacht to get them back. Von Rundstedt must check the defences again, and press on with mining the beaches.[1] Later in the year he was still obsessed with the security of the Islands, which he deemed vital for the protection and escort of German shipping. They must be made impregnable, their fortifications being modelled on the West Wall.[2]

The navy entered into the spirit of the thing. They pointed out that the existing coastal guns could not deal effectively with enemy ships passing between the Islands and the mainland of France. There must be three new batteries on the mainland with a range of 25 kilometres so that ships would be caught between two fires.[3]

On 8 October yet another appraisal was made. The infantry must be brought up to full divisional strength. Female workers and construction labourers must be armed. More of everything was needed – more searchlights, more long-range guns, more anti-aircraft guns, more ammunition, more squadrons of the Luftwaffe on the mainland to cover the Islands, a new cable link, more escort vessels, more ships to carry building materials. When Jodl put this to Hitler he agreed and added a few points of his own. Flame-throwers must be sent; there must be extensive minefields; and the air defences must be equipped to last out a 14-day battle.[4]

Ten days later the Führer again expounded his view that Britain must launch an offensive as a result of Russian pressure. The mood in Britain would force the British government to try to restore lost prestige. Their objective could be the Channel Islands, possession of which would be useful in the air offensive against the Atlantic strong points. There might be an attempt against all three main Islands. The British had barges ready to land tanks and heavy weapons. He saw them first trying to subdue the defences by aerial bombardment and naval artillery, and then landing under cover of a smoke screen. If they took the Islands neither the navy nor the Luftwaffe would be able to dislodge them. He reminded his audience of the behaviour of the British in

[1] T 78 317/6271843; MOD 591/329.   [2] IWM MI 14/49.
[3] T 78 317/6271829.   [4] T 78 317/6271798; MOD 95/990, 37/1099, 1103.

Malta, where, in spite of thousands of bombs, they still held on. Therefore full preparations must be made to withstand combined sea and air operations. There must be more, and yet heavier guns, including batteries with a range of 40 to 50 kilometres, on Cap de la Hague, at St. Malo and on Guernsey to give absolute mastery of the seas between these places.[1]

Hitler suggested that there should be between 200 and 250 strong points on the larger Islands. The walls were to be 2 metres thick, except in places of particular importance (for example, observation posts), where $3\frac{1}{2}$ metres of reinforced concrete would be needed. He had no objection to the use of foreign workers, and indeed recommended that Spanish communists should be employed. 'Educated workers' among the Russian prisoners of war could also be used, and if necessary the civilian population could be conscripted. Having in mind the experience of the eastern campaign the Führer said that it was essential that bunkers should be used only as a protection against very heavy artillery fire. In all other circumstances men must stay outside and fight. He added, it may be thought prophetically: 'Whoever disappears into a bunker . . . is lost!'[2]

There were in addition to the main short-term defences a number of supplementary devices which came into play when an invading force landed. In many fields anti-paratroop 'spiders' were installed. These consisted of captured 300-pound French shells standing in the middle of the field. Numerous wires led from the detonator through an overhead ring to posts round the perimeter of the field, so that if a parachutist landed on any part of the 'spider's web' he would pull the wire and detonate the shell. The wires were supported about 9 feet from the ground so that people and cattle could walk safely beneath. There were also 'roll bombs' suspended from the cliffs by wire, their detonators being attached to the cliff by a second wire. When the supporting wire was cut the 'bombs' (also 300-pound French shells) fell and exploded at beach level when the second wire pulled out the detonator. Shells, attached to the pillars supporting the main piers in the harbours, could be detonated electrically. Finally, shells fixed to anti-tank girders set into the beaches were detonated on impact, and made explosive *chevaux de frise*.

The effort which Hitler devoted to making the Islands secure in the short term, disproportionate though it may have been, made sense in

---

[1] MOD 37/1103; T 77 788/5517308.   [2] T 77 788/5517310.

G

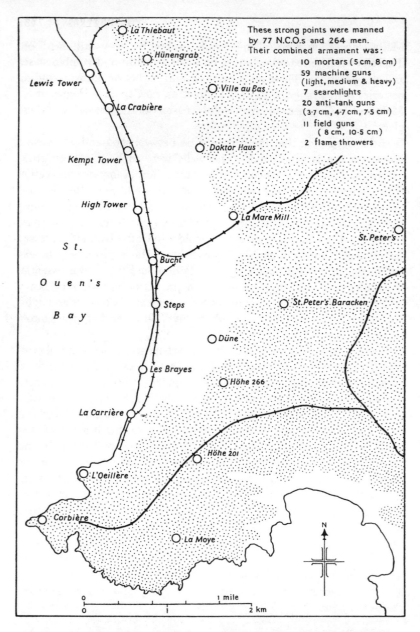

These strong points were manned
by 77 N.C.O.s and 264 men.
Their combined armament was:

10 mortars (5 cm, 8 cm)
59 machine guns
    (light, medium & heavy)
7 searchlights
20 anti-tank guns
    (3·7 cm, 4·7 cm, 7·5 cm)
11 field guns
    (8 cm, 10·5 cm)
2 flame throwers

La Thiebaut

Hünengrab

Lewis Tower

Ville au Bas

La Crabière

Kempt Tower

Doktor Haus

High Tower

La Mare Mill

St. Peter's

S t.

O u e n ' s

Bucht

B a y

Steps

St. Peter's Baracken

Düne

Les Brayes

Höhe 266

La Carrière

Höhe 201

L'Oeillère

Corbière

La Moye

N

0   1 mile

0   2 km

4. *In addition to the heavy batteries shown in the maps of the individual
islands the German defences of the Channel Islands included many coastal
strong points, each with its own battle plan and battle orders. St. Ouen's
Bay, Jersey, had 21 guarding a four-mile stretch of coast.*

terms of German prestige, and perhaps also in terms of strategy. The much greater effort devoted to making them for all time an impregnable German fortress – before the war had been won – made no sense at all.

Hitler was not the first to see the Channel Islands as a long-term naval base. After Admiral Lindau (who had wrongly guessed that the British were lying in wait for the German invasion)[1] visited them in 1940, he reported that these 'beautiful and efficiently-administered Islands' could become a base for U-boats and S-boats; but it would have to be done quickly as there was a move to make them 'Strength through Joy' recuperation centres. They had good harbours, with room for arsenals, workshops, and so on, a secure food supply ('both Islands have a super-fluity of agricultural produce'), it hardly ever froze, there were excellent recreational facilities for any number of troops, and both main Islands had airfields beneath which bomb-proof underground hangars could be built.

The Führer made up his mind that the Islands would never be returned to Britain. They would remain in German occupation, to guard the western approaches to the English Channel.[2] Therefore a long-term constructional programme must run in parallel with the short-term plan. Preliminary surveys for the long-term fortifications began in June 1941, and the first plans were ready in October.[3] There would be strong permanent fortifications with special attention paid to the areas where tanks might be landed.

The two plans inevitably overlapped; and Hitler was far from certain what he wanted in the long term. Kapitän Voss, representing OKM, tried to disentangle them in a Führer conference. He agreed that if the Islands were to remain German for all time they must be fortified on the lines of the West Wall; but surely anything done with the future in view must be reconciled with the needs of the moment. This meant that first priority must be given to the new very heavy battery on Guernsey. Further, the sister batteries at Cap de la Hague and St. Malo must also be made operational as soon as possible.[4]

Hitler, perhaps taking his cue from Lindau's earlier fulsome report, said that St. Peter Port should be built up into a base for light naval forces; but the OKM representative presumed to reply that this was pointless. There were better bases on the occupied mainland; in any case after the war the harbours of France would be more important to the

[1] See Chapter 4.
[3] T 78 317/6271852, 817.
[2] MOD 37/1103.
[4] MOD 37/1106.

German navy. Hitler insisted that even if this was true St. Peter Port should be regarded as a base for motor torpedo boats and small U-boats; but Kapitän Voss would still not be persuaded and pointed out that this would duplicate installations at Lorient, Cherbourg, and elsewhere. Then, perhaps feeling that he had gone too far, he conceded a case for minor bases, since the mainland would be returned to France after the war. Germany would thus lose the coastal batteries, and with them absolute control over the gulf of St. Malo. Nevertheless he could not refrain from adding that if there had to be bases they should not be built until after the war. The matter seems to have been left there, but Hitler did go on to say that building in the Islands during the war must have regard to the navy's post-war needs. All plans must be fully discussed with the navy to avoid later modifications to meet their requirements. Von Rundstedt was also unhappy that the future of the Islands should loom so large in Hitler's mind when that future was still uncertain. Dr. Todt stressed the importance of keeping possession after the war of these great feats of German engineering, which he perhaps saw as a memorial to himself.[1]

There was much discussion as to which service the commander of the Islands should be drawn from. The first commanders were Major Lanz in Guernsey and Hauptmann Gussek in Jersey, who held their positions as the senior officers with the invading troops. Major Bandelow of Machine Gun Battalion 16 (part of the occupying force) replaced them both on 18 September 1940, and was in turn replaced a fortnight later by Oberst Graf von Schmettow, who had his headquarters in St. Helier and used Government House as his official residence. Von Schmettow was a nephew of von Rundstedt. To begin with, Alderney was commanded from Cherbourg.[2]

Marinegruppe West wanted a naval man as commander-in-chief and proposed that his seconds in command should be the battalion commanders in Jersey and Guernsey. OKW ruled that the army should continue to have overall command, and OKM, in spite of *Marinegruppe West*'s plea, agreed that the navy had no real interest. They did not want to be saddled with the defence of the Islands.[3] In June 1941, in response to Hitler's decree that the Islands must be manned by a full division, 319 Infantry Division took over in Jersey and Guernsey from the units of 216 Infantry Division which had been there for most of the

---

[1] MOD 37/1096; IWM AL 1685.   [2] NG 01/34; NG Bundle C.
[3] MOD 583/307–8.

time since the invasion; and the commanding officer, Generalmajor Müller, took over from von Schmettow as *Befehlshaber* of the British Channel Islands. Shortly afterwards von Schmettow replaced Müller as commander of 319 Infantry Division, and again became commander-in-chief of the Channel Islands. Alderney was held by part of 83 Infantry Division until December 1941 when it was transferred to the commander of 319 Infantry Division, which in 1942 became recognized as the permanent occupation force.

In the middle of 1942 Oberst Lamey was sent to study the chain of command in the Islands. He concluded that fundamental changes were needed. The *Befehlshaber*, Channel Islands, was on Jersey, and the Divisional Command on Guernsey. Lamey thought that the latter should be on Jersey, which he regarded as being the strongest element in the whole of the Islands' defences. He simply could not understand how this point had been missed. Further, personality problems were causing trouble in both Islands. There was rivalry between them, which was not bad in itself but which, nevertheless, had unfortunate effects on the two staffs. Alongside the Wehrmacht stood the military government, which was quite superfluous in Lamey's opinion. Its duties could readily be handled by the military commands. There were also supply problems. The main organization was on Guernsey with the Divisional staff, but the Divisional supply officer was in Granville; and there was need for the rationalization of the movement of supplies from St. Malo, Granville, and Cherbourg.

The Division's influence on the conduct of the war could only be slight, because of the distance between the Islands, and their poor communications. The troops were aware of this, and their morale was suffering because of the general feeling that they were unlikely to be relieved. Lamey wrote: 'A young officer and leader of a strong point told me quite openly that it is sickening to be always stuck in the same post without any hope of ever being moved.' The senior officers felt much the same way. They saw themselves commanding a field division which was being required to perform a role for which it had not been trained. In particular von Schmettow disliked having to remain in one place. He was devoting great energy to the completion of the fortifications in the hope that when they were complete he would be posted elsewhere.

Lamey proposed that there should be a new and improved supply organization. Units should be pulled out and freshened from time to time. In general he found that the commands were cumbersome and needed to be streamlined. There were too many men with no useful task at a time when troops were urgently needed elsewhere. Alderney and Sark were too small to matter; but he advised that the command of the former should go back to the mainland.

These proposals were not well received by Army Group D. 319 Infantry Division must not become a fortress division. It was proud of its name and number and must retain them. Otherwise the men would feel second class. (In fact, although the Division did not change its name or status it became for all practical purposes a fortress division, since it remained in the Islands for the remainder of the war.) The *Befehlshaber* must remain on Jersey, and the Divisional staff on Guernsey. Ob. West did not agree that Jersey was the more important Island strategically. OKW did not agree that Alderney should come under the command of a different division. Except that it was agreed that the supply arrangements should be rationalized no significant change was accepted. Not for the first time did an organization expert see his recommendations cast aside.[1]

Whatever his motives, von Schmettow devoted a great deal of energy to the fortification programme and to ensuring that the long-term and short-term plans dovetailed. It was only after a Führer conference of 18 October 1941 that the short-term programme – which was to be completed in 14 months – got properly under way. Before then little had been done, partly because of transport difficulties. *Marinegruppe West* commented that escort services were inadequate, and indeed this was a perennial problem.[2] Enemy mining of the harbours at Cherbourg and St. Malo hindered the movement of supplies, and more minesweepers were needed. Defensive minefields, more aerial reconnaissance, and light naval forces were also necessary. More searchlights, especially if the fact of their existence was leaked to the enemy, would be a cheap way of strengthening the defences.

The strong points round the coasts were tackled first by the troops, and later by military construction units. Full use was made of the existing forts, especially on Alderney. They had massive granite walls – some more than 20 feet thick – and were sited in the most strategic positions. Old granite towers and mills were pressed into service as observation posts. Some Martello Towers were, alas, demolished because they restricted fields of fire. The front-line strong points were

[1] T 78 317/6271731–7.
[2] See, for example, MOD 753, which deals with the escort services.

hidden from the sea and sited to help each other with flanking fire. This was simplified by the succession of cliffs and bays which make up the coastline of the Islands. There were also pairs of heavily-armoured machine gun turrets, which could turn through 360 degrees to provide cover where the main strong points were further apart than usual.

Stretches of open beach were protected by anti-tank walls 10 feet high and up to 6 feet thick, with foundations sunk deep into the sand. Tanks surviving the crossfire during landing could make no progress until these walls had been breached. The strong points and command posts were connected by a telephone network 'sunk deep in earth and cliff'; and the three main Islands were linked by submarine cable.

Of the many coastal defence guns by far the biggest were the four 30·5-centimetre guns of the 'Mirus' battery at Le Frie Baton in the heart of Guernsey. The barrels had a remarkable history. They began life on a Russian battleship, which was taken over by the Germans in 1918, returned to the Russians, and broken up in 1935, when the guns were removed and stored in Bizerta. In 1939 they were sent to Finland to be used in the Russo-Finnish War by the Finns, captured en route by the Germans, returned to Germany for reconditioning, and sent to Guernsey.[1] It took a year and a half to build the emplacements, which absorbed 45,000 cubic metres of concrete. There was an underground barracks for the guncrews, with room for 400 men. The first gun was fired on 13 April 1942;[2] and the battery as a whole was handed over to OKM in November of the same year.[3] It had a range of 50 kilometres and controlled the gulf of St. Malo.

The drain on the German resources caused by the fortifications is illustrated by the progress records. By June 1942 – after nearly two years of occupation – 18,000 mines had been laid on the main Islands, which, in the eyes of the professional soldiers, was just about all they needed.[4] But it was only the beginning and by April 1944 the total had increased to 114,000 – 54,000 on Guernsey, 39,000 on Jersey, and 4,500 on Sark, where, originally, fewer than 1,000 had been considered to be enough. Nor did the pace slacken in 1944. In Alderney the final total of mines laid was 37,000. In Jersey it exceeded 67,000.

The mines are only a part of the total picture. At the end of January 1944 the fortifications had taken 484,000 cubic metres of reinforced concrete, compared with 6,100,000 cubic metres for the whole of the

[1] Carel Toms, *Hitler's Fortress Islands* (London, 1967), pp. 67–73.
[2] IWM AL 1846.   [3] T 78 317/6271623.
[4] IWM AL 1864; T 78 317/6271637–86.

rest of the Atlantic Wall. The Wehrmacht, obeying Hitler's orders, but with misgiving, had devoted one-twelfth of the resources in question to the protection of the Channel Islands, which, in strategic terms, were only a tiny fraction of their total responsibility. Had the materials and labour thus squandered been devoted instead to strengthening the Atlantic Wall, it would have been about ten per cent stronger over the whole of its length; and it is conceivable that this would have made some difference to the progress of the Allies in 1944.

When excavation work is brought into the account the balance becomes more remarkable. At the beginning of 1944 the Atlantic Wall had involved the excavation of 255,000 cubic metres; at the same date 244,000 cubic metres had been excavated in the Channel Islands. The Atlantic Wall could have been doubled in strength, so far as excavated works are concerned, had the resources devoted to the Islands been retained on the mainland. Furthermore the effort in the Islands was disproportionately costly in men and materials because many ships carrying them were sunk on the hazardous passage from France.[1]

The building of the fortifications depended on transport within the Islands just as much as on shipping from France. Imported building materials had to be carried to the gun sites and strong points, as had great quantities of granite quarried locally. This meant setting up light railways, since the Island railways had given place to motor transport some years earlier. In Jersey the Germans built a one-metre gauge line from St. Helier, skirting St. Aubin's Bay and running across St. Brelade to Corbière at the south-west corner of the Island. A second line connected this to Ronez Quarry on the north coast, which was the main source of stone for the fortifications. A 60-centimetre line went from St. Helier round the coast to Gorey in the east of the Island and another ran down the west coast from Western Quarries to La Pulente. This system made it possible to carry building materials to about two-thirds of the coast, leaving only the precipitous north, where less fortification was needed, uncatered for. The first railway was opened with great ceremony in July 1942 to the amusement of those Jerseymen who were present, and who were later reprimanded for their frivolous behaviour when the German national anthem was played.

[1] Had all the plans been carried out to the letter the fortifications would have been much greater. A report in January 1943 said that since May 1942 only 28,000 cubic metres of concrete a month had been laid compared with the target of 50,000. Excavation had fallen even further short of the target. This was due to scarcity on the mainland and not to interruption to shipping. T 314 1604/46.

KAMPFANLAGE BEL ROYAL
4,7 cm Pak (t) und 6-Schartenturm

ANSICHT

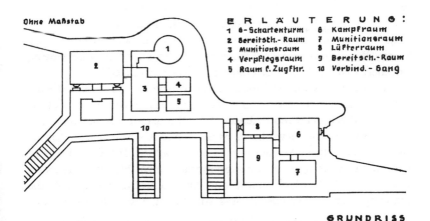

Ohne Maßstab

E R L Ä U T E R U N G :

1 6-Schartenturm   6 Kampfraum
2 Bereitsch.- Raum   7 Munitionsraum
3 Munitionsraum   8 Lüfterraum
4 Verpflegsraum   9 Bereitsch.-Raum
5 Raum f. Zugfhr.   10 Verbind.- Gang

GRUNDRISS

Sketch and plan of a typical strong point, at Bel Royal, Jersey

The legend reads: 1 Gun tower (6-loopholes); 2 and 9 Alert stations; 3 and 7 Ammunition stores; 4 Supplies; 5 Command post; 6 Operations room; 8 Ventilation plant; 10 Passage. (The armament included a 4.7 cm anti-tank gun coupled with a machine gun (in 6); two heavy machine guns (in 1); and two light machine guns.)

The railway in Guernsey started at St. Peter Port and ran north-east along the coast to St. Sampson's, thence to L'Ancresse Bay and down the west coast to L'Erée. The main line was 90-centimetre gauge, but there were spurs of 60-centimetre. As in the case of Jersey, the railway gave access to about two-thirds of the coastline; but there was no attempt to carry it to the high ground in the south.[1] Given the nature of the terrain in Alderney and the size of the Island there was less scope for railway transport, but by November 1942 2·7 kilometres had been laid to carry stone from the quarry to the nearer strong points.[2]

The German high command was disturbed by the imbalance between the fortification of the Islands and of the mainland. The relative figures were gratuitously emphasized in one of the progress reports, perhaps to hint to the Führer that he had his priorities wrong. In October 1941 OKH and OKM concluded that it was essential to get a ruling from OKW 'on the tasks finally to be aimed at in the fortifications of the Channel Islands'. Perhaps what they really meant was, how could the build-up be kept within reasonable limits.[3] Shortly afterwards von Rundstedt asked that men should be brought back to the mainland since 'the garrison strength of the Islands is no longer justifiable having regard to the needs of coastal defence generally'. He hoped for speedy agreement, but none was forthcoming.[4] When he was ordered to make proposals for increasing the infantry strength in the Islands even further, he said that they had enough troops. They already faced grave supply difficulties, and so many men were being sent there that the defence of France had been prejudiced.[5]

A conference at Führer headquarters in August 1942, when Keitel, Jodl, and Schmundt were present, examined the relative strengths of the Islands and the mainland defences. Von Rundstedt was not there but note was taken of his view, shared by the Island *Kommandanten*, that the garrisons were strong enough to take on any attack. It followed that an increase in the Islands' building programme must hinder progress on the Atlantic Wall, which should now have priority.[6] In April of the following year von Rundstedt was still saying the same thing. The

---

[1] For a detailed description of the German railways in Guernsey see Frank E. Wilson, *Railways in Guernsey* (Guernsey, 1970) and N. R. P. Bonsor, *The Jersey Eastern Railway and the German Occupation Lines in Jersey* (Lingfield, 1965).

[2] T 78 317/6271623.   [3] T 78 317/6271808.
[4] T 78 317/6271757.   [5] T 78 317/6271786, 795.
[6] T 78 317/6271599.

Islands were more heavily fortified than any other coastal area held by Germany. Moreover, they were manned 'in a manner which no other sector can match'. But Allied aerial attacks on railways were seriously impeding the movement of supplies in France generally, and more anti-aircraft guns were badly needed there. 'If those on the Channel Islands become available, so much the better.' Given the Führer's well-known views, however, even the Feldmarschall dared not say that the guns *should* be transferred.[1]

The Allied air attacks which affected movement in France were no less effective in the gulf of St. Malo. It became increasingly difficult to transport materials to the Islands. From April to September 1943 shipments, mainly of cement and constructional steel, averaged 20,000 a month – an annual rate of nearly a quarter of a million tons; but from October onwards they dropped to a mere 3,700 tons a month, well below the rate needed to complete the fortifications. The decline in the supply of materials was matched by the reduction in the labour force. In September 1943 it had fallen to 9,500. By January 1944 it was down to 4,500 and by April it was 3,800.[2]

In November 1943 Vizeadmiral Friedrich Rieve, *Kommandierender Admiral Kanalküste* (Admiral Commanding, Channel Coast), inspected the defences, and found them in good order. He saw the guns in action in earnest when half a dozen Allied bombers successfully attacked shipping in St. Peter Port; and then visited the 'Mirus' battery, where good progress was being made with the camouflage, consisting of mock farm buildings. The 'Elsass' battery on Alderney, and 'Strassburg' on Guernsey were short of equipment. 'Steinbruch' on Guernsey needed camouflage; and it was proposed that hedges should be planted and dummy greenhouses erected round it. More surprising, the Doyle Monument column, about a hundred yards from 'Strassburg' and a perfect landmark for attacking aircraft, had been left intact. It must come down immediately. Other batteries needed better protection. The 'Lothringen' battery in Jersey was badly camouflaged and its ammunition store was virtually unprotected.[3]

[1] T 78/317/6271530–1.
[2] MOD 653/47.
[3] MOD 588/597. In 1944 the memorial to Guernsey's most distinguished sailor, Admiral Lord de Saumarez (1757–1836), a 90-foot Guernsey granite obelisk on Delancey Hill near St. Sampson's was demolished because it interrupted the field of view of neighbouring batteries. Unlike the Doyle Monument, it was not rebuilt.

Although the Admiral was satisfied with the troops as a whole he was unimpressed by the recent arrivals. The younger men were bad enough, but the older – in the 47–49 age group – 'had broken bodies and little enthusiasm'. Only a few would be of any use, and most would do no more than fill the hospitals. 'They seem to be the last reserves of the Wehrmacht.' They would have a bad effect on morale and the garrison had been weakened by their arrival.

The Admiral was also dissatisfied with the transport arrangements between the Islands and the mainland. Bad weather and difficult navigation were one thing, but there were too few transports. Even in good weather the trip from St. Malo to Guernsey took five or six hours and 250–300 soldiers had to stand on deck. Two fast troop transports were absolutely essential. The postal service was too slow. Letters from Germany took up to 12 days, which worried the older men, especially now that Allied bombing of the homeland had been intensified. The only plane making regular trips to the mainland belonged to the OT. The harbour protection flotilla was in a sorry state – ninety per cent unusable. No repairs had been carried out for years, and requests for replacements had been turned down over and over again. The Casquets could be supplied only in daylight and in good weather. The fastest possible boats were needed to minimize the danger of aerial attacks, which were getting heavier every day. Indeed it was doubtful if supplies could continue to go to the Casquets unless faster boats were available. The relief boats would have to sail at night, which would be very dangerous.[1]

At least the war correspondents were untroubled by misgivings of this sort. One of them made the most of the fortifications in an article for German consumption:

An army of OT workmen has been for years working along with the soldiers of the Wehrmacht and is still busy building fortifications . . . Hundreds of thousands of cubic metres of concrete now protect the coasts, many more will follow . . . Dense minefields and mile-long anti-tank walls hermetically seal the beaches. German soldiers, tried in battle, man our best weapons and form a ring of steel around these former British possessions, which lie like anchored fortresses in front of the Atlantic Wall.

Fighting words, but by 1943 doubts about the impregnability of the fortresses were beginning to arise. Orders from OKW said that it was expected that the enemy would now have air superiority, and that all

[1] MOD 588/599; 653/45.

coastal batteries which did not have adequate protection from the air must be covered with concrete. Ideally, they would be given armoured turrets, but none were available.[1] Hitler may have been satisfied that he would never lose the Islands; but his generals must now have had their doubts.

As the strength of the fortifications increased, so did the number of troops in the garrison. In Jersey, for example, there were only about 1,750 in December 1940, mostly army. Twelve months later the number had swollen to 11,500; and it remained roughly at this level to the end of the occupation, except that in December 1943 it fell to just under 10,000.[2] The overall strength of the garrison followed much the same pattern. In June 1941 – a year after the invasion – there were about 13,000 men;[3] in October 1941, 15,500;[4] and in November 1941, 21,000, including 15,000 army, 5,000 Luftwaffe, and 1,000 navy. At this time there were about 600 horses.[5]

In August 1942 the approved establishment for the whole of the Islands was nearly 37,000; but it is doubtful if as many as this were ever posted there. The breakdown of the establishment was:

Army	18,460
Luftwaffe	9,500
Navy	4,100
Supply troops	3,500
Construction troops	1,400
Total	36,960[6]

[1] T 78 317/6271627.

[2] These figures are taken from two volumes in the Library of the Bailiff of Guernsey, which contain a detailed description of all the strong points in the Island, including their establishment, weapons, battle task and battle plan. There is an incomplete set of the same material in the Priaulx Library; and in the Library of the Société Jersiaise there is an incomplete set of comparable material for Jersey.

[3] T 312 500/94416.   [4] T 312 512/8109903.   [5] T 312 512/8109861.

[6] The army figure comprised: Staff, 500; garrison troops, 7,500; field troops, 5,000; and artillery, 5,460. The figures for the navy were: Staff, 150; heavy batteries, 1,200; medium batteries, 2,500; harbour defence, 100; other harbour personnel, 150. Of the Luftwaffe troops, 7,000 were engaged in anti-aircraft defence – guns and searchlights – and 2,500 were air crew with their ground support. The 3,500 supply troops included 825 in two medical companies, 130 in two field hospitals, two workshop companies (230 men) and smaller numbers concerned with catering, bakery, fuel supply, slaughtering, and the field postal service. There were also 70 men in Cherbourg, Granville and St. Malo dealing with the shipment of supplies from these ports. IWM AL 1864.

At the beginning of May 1943 the total strength of the Wehrmacht was 26,800 (Guernsey, 13,000; Jersey, 10,000; Alderney, 3,800). Six months later it had fallen to 23,700 (Guernsey, 12,000; Jersey, 8,850; Alderney, 2,850); and it was much the same in July 1944, after the invasion of the Continent had begun – 23,578 (Guernsey, 11,266; Jersey, 8,869; Alderney, 3,443). When the strength of the Organisation Todt is taken into account it seems that the heaviest concentration of enemy personnel was in the first half of 1943, when the total number, including 16,000 OT workers was 42,800. This was equivalent to more than two-thirds of the men, women, and children remaining in the Islands.

In November 1941 there were 2,426 men on Alderney – 1,104 army, 1,100 Luftwaffe, 179 navy, and 43 civilians, plus 31 horses. The numbers were expected to increase to 3,171. The army and Luftwaffe would stay the same, but the navy would go up to 429, the civilians to 83, and 455 prisoners were due.[1] There was some apprehension about feeding the increased numbers. There were supposed to be sufficient reserves to feed 3,000 men for 60 days, but because of shipping difficulties there was less than half that amount in stock. Most of the supplies, including live cattle, were shipped from Cherbourg in small Dutch and German coasters; they were often held up by bad weather, which made it difficult to ensure the steady replenishment of stocks.[2]

There was sometimes bad management as well. Some supplies came from Guernsey in HS boats, two of which turned up in Alderney with nothing for the troops, although they were laden with goods for the small number of Guernsey civilians there. The *Kommandant* in Alderney sent an angry radio message to the *Nebenstelle* in Guernsey ('Orange' to 'Tomato', to give them their code names) asking why not even the troops' mail had been sent. Von Oettingen replied swiftly. The *Kommandant* knew quite well that the HS boats were under orders not to report their movements; and it was therefore a matter of luck if supplies were ready on the quayside when an HS boat was due to leave. It was outrageous to suspect that rations destined for Alderney were being eaten by the troops in Guernsey. He accepted that the garrison must be upset when their mail failed to arrive, but he criticized the *Kommandant* for his lack of 'comradely spirit'. If such indignation was expressed again he would certainly report the matter to higher authority.[3]

[1] T 312 500/94515.   [2] T 312 512/8109863.
[3] NG Ia/1.

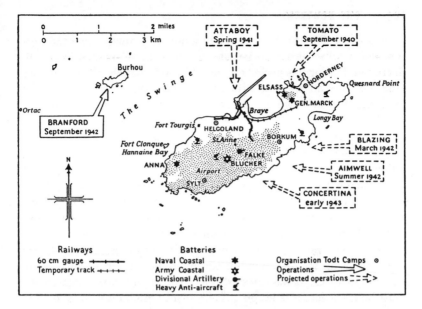

5. *Alderney and Burhou*

Alderney was for all practical purposes completely evacuated before the Germans arrived,[1] and for an account of conditions there we are largely dependent on surviving *Feldkommandantur* papers. A few people did remain, however, including George Pope and Frank Oselton, letters from whom were broadcast by German radio on 10 and 11 October 1940. Pope wanted to deny a B.B.C. statement that not a living soul remained on Alderney. 'We have been and are being treated with the greatest respect and kindness by the forces occupying the Channel Islands.' He was grateful to the German authorities for allowing him to say so. Oselton said much the same. 'We are all in good health, being treated with every consideration by the local German commandant.'

There were three phases in the occupation of Alderney. At first, as in the other Islands, fortification was not tackled on a great scale. The existing forts were reinforced and some new strong points were built. During this period the Island was regarded as much as a source of food as part of the fortress. The second phase came at the end of 1941 with the arrival of the Organisation Todt and the beginning of the feverish building activity generated by Hitler's orders to make the Islands

[1] See Chapter 3.

impregnable. The third phase lasted from early 1943, when the construction workers began to be withdrawn to the Continent, until the
liberation. During this period the idea that Alderney should help to feed
Guernsey was abandoned, although the Germans continued to grow
food there for their own use, and the Island became a fortress pure and
simple.

In February 1941 an agricultural expert from the *Feldkommandantur*
in Jersey and a member of the Controlling Committee in Guernsey
visited Alderney to examine the possibility of growing more food there.
There was not much agricultural land, but every little would help. It
was decided that first priority must be given to cleaning up the Island
generally, as it was feared that insanitary conditions might lead to an
epidemic. A squad of about 50 civilians came from Guernsey to clean
the abandoned houses, remove their furniture to a central depot, and
board them up for the duration. Clothing and household goods were
sent to Guernsey. It was stressed that chalices and 'priestly garments'
must be taken into safe keeping. Particular attention was to be paid to
maintaining a pure water supply and an efficient drainage system.
Equipment abandoned by the British troops, which was still lying
about on all sides, was to be collected in one place; and anything that
was scarce in Guernsey was to be sent there.

It was agreed that it was essential to get agriculture back on its feet
again as soon as possible to augment the food supply in Guernsey.
Rabbits had multiplied enormously since the evacuation and if any
crop was to survive it was necessary to reduce their numbers. Shooting
was permitted only to members of the Wehrmacht who had hunting
licences; but civilians were encouraged to hunt the rabbits with nets and
snares – so long as they did not stray into the areas where the Wehrmacht were established. Agricultural machinery was to be carefully
looked after, since spare parts would no longer be readily available.
Cultivation was to be left to the few civilians still on the Island and those
sent from Guernsey, and not undertaken by the troops. Cows which had
been imported from France were also handed over to the civilians,
on condition that their milk would be available to the Wehrmacht under
arrangements to be worked out by the *Aussenstelle*. The *Inselkommandant* was reminded that the maximum amount of food must be produced.

In September 1941 there were four working parties on Alderney.
The biggest was an agricultural working party, with 31 men. There was
a second agricultural party, with seven, and a central party for the
maintenance of property, with eight. There was a breakwater party with

26 men, of whom 17 came from Sark, engaged on the improvement of the breakwater. A working party of 30, which went to Alderney from Guernsey in the following year at the request of the Germans, was billeted in huts on the farms, where there were also French, Russian, and Spanish workers. They were all treated much better than the Jews and the men from the enforced labour camp and the concentration camp. The guards on the farms were 'quite decent and very helpful', unlike the OT guards in charge of the forced labourers and the SS men in charge of the Jews and the concentration camp prisoners, who were regularly guilty of shocking brutality.[1]

The Germans felt some misgiving about allowing even a small number of civilians the relative freedom of Alderney; and indeed from time to time people escaped from there to England. Special precautions were taken to see that they did not get up to mischief. The *Feldpolizei* were instructed to keep them under surveillance, especially when they were entering or leaving the Island, which they were required to do through a special customs point. They were under the charge of an overseer – a Guernseyman – who at first had the title of 'civil commandant', which the Germans did not like, and which he had to give up. In general the *Feldkommandantur* regulations were applied in Alderney through the *Aussenstelle*.

Reports from Alderney to the *Nebenstelle* in Guernsey illustrate the day-to-day problems. At the beginning of September 1941 Rittmeister von Oettingen visited Alderney accompanied by representatives of the German Red Cross to discuss among other things the establishment of a *Soldatenheim*. They examined two possible buildings – the Grand Hotel, and the convent – and decided in favour of the latter. They surveyed the crops, which were being harvested in excellent weather. Threshing machines were still awaited, however. One was due from Herm, and a second from France. Repairs to the roof of Fort Tourgis were being held up through lack of pitch. The reinforcement of the breakwater was going well – 6,000 tons of stone had been sunk. A week later another 800 tons had been added. Someone had had the temerity to name one of the streets in St. Anne 'Adolf Hitler Platz'. The offending sign must come down immediately.[2]

A grave had been opened in the churchyard, but the *Feldgendarmerie* decided that there was no question of robbery, since the body had been buried in 1875. The grave was restored to its former state, and it was

[1] Note provided by Mr. W. J. Allez, who worked in Alderney in 1942.
[2] NG Ia/1.

hoped that this would 'close the unhappy event'. The church was being used as a wine cellar – a second case of sacrilege. Excellent progress was being made with the harvest, but there was still no sign of the threshing machines. Two civilians had been sent to Guernsey to hurry them up.[1]

The Controlling Committee in Guernsey came to hear about the cases of sacrilege and weighed in with some pointed comments about the barbarity of German soldiers. When the *Inselkommandant* was asked for observations, he replied that these events had occurred during his absence on leave, and that he could not therefore be held responsible. When the guilty men were caught he would come down on them with all the authority at his command, and mete out the maximum permitted punishment – the *Nebenstelle* could rest assured about that. He agreed that it was wrong to store wine in the church, but there was nowhere else. The wine spoiled if it was left in the open, and it was wrong to waste valuable material just because there had been some trouble in the churchyard and a complaint about the barbarity of German soldiers. The English, who shamefully waged war against helpless sailors and clearly-marked hospitals, were the real criminals. So let the gentlemen of the Controlling Committee put aside their haloes.

Von Oettingen agreed with the *Inselkommandant*'s assessment of British soldiers: 'Simply because we judge such behaviour to be wrong we must ourselves show that we do not stoop to such levels.' As to the wine, if it could be stored elsewhere, so much the better; but if it had to stay in the church he had no objection, so long as only the Wehrmacht were allowed access to the building.[2]

The Germans at this time were understandably sensitive about their reputation. The occupation of the Channel Islands was a test case. The better it went the better the prospect of a trouble-free take-over of Britain as a whole. Conversely, if the Germans were seen to be just as beastly as British propaganda made them out to be, it would be a defeat. It was for this reason that the German authorities went out of their way to make a *cause célèbre* of the trial of a number of men who were supposed to have looted in Alderney when serving with working parties sent from Guernsey before the Germans arrived. Little was at stake – except the reputation of the Wehrmacht. The German high command was aware of allegations that there had been looting in Alderney, and on 3 September 1940 the *Feldkommandant* received orders from OKH and the military governor in Paris that it must be established at all costs that

[1] NG Ia/3. [2] NG Ia/1.

the culprits were 'the refugees' and not the troops. Evidence must be obtained in writing.

This set in motion a vast enquiry, and some of the reports cannot have been to the liking of the German authorities. The *Inselkommandant* in Alderney, with an unpleasant regard for the truth, pointed out that anyone could have plundered the Island between the time the British left and the Germans arrived – for example, French fisherman who knew what was going on and who had an eye for the main chance. Worse still, he said that the units of the Luftwaffe who first came to Alderney did not hesitate to take for their canteens furniture from the unoccupied houses. Three days after he made this report, however, George Pope came to the rescue. He said that there was no doubt that the pillaging was done by the men from Guernsey. They had broken into houses, taken what they wanted, and left chaos behind them. They were to blame, and nobody else. Pope's wife confirmed his evidence. The German troops were blameless. They had been much too busy to have time for looting.

The Germans hoped that the Royal Court in Guernsey would try the case, since a verdict of guilty from the Islanders' own court would have much more propaganda value; but the Guernsey authorities were not prepared to co-operate and the Germans had to fall back on their own court. Of the thirteen accused, six were acquitted, including two who gave King's evidence.

In the course of 1942 the management of agriculture in Alderney was transferred from the Controlling Committee working through the German authorities there to the Organisation Todt, which was not particularly well qualified for the task. Yields were poor, but this was attributed to the neglect of the soil for many years. In 1943 60 hectares were planted with potatoes, but 8 hectares produced nothing at all. The other 52 hectares yielded 250 tons, which were supplied to the troops, along with a small number of sheep and cattle. At the beginning of 1944 it was decided that the OT's performance was unsatisfactory, and the management was taken over by the *Aussenstelle*, which decided to concentrate on milk production at the expense of the supply of meat – thereby anticipating the plan which the high command thought would save the garrison in 1945.[1] Butter-making equipment was brought in from the other Islands.

It quickly became clear that the *Aussenstelle* was fighting a losing battle. Ample quantities of seed potatoes were promised, but nearly

[1] See Chapter 12.

half were lost en route in France, and only 40 hectares could be planted. 200,000 vegetable plants did arrive, but they had been held up so long 'owing to military traffic difficulties' that they were all dead when they reached the Island. Ten precious hectares were withdrawn from agriculture to be used for minefields and new fortifications – last-minute defences prompted by the invasion of Europe. The threat of invasion was also responsible for the withdrawal of the last Guernsey agricultural labourers at the most critical point in the agricultural cycle; it was impossible to replace them with troops because of the urgent building programme. Eventually a squad of 20 soldiers was released for agricultural work, but by this time it was too late. For good measure an Allied bomb hit a potato store and substantial quantities were destroyed.

The Organisation Todt was, of course, concerned with building rather than agriculture. It had become obvious soon after the decision to fortify the Islands that the Wehrmacht could not do the job on their own. It is possible that army construction troops could have carried out the short-term programme; but the gigantic plan for posterity was well beyond their capacity. This meant calling in the OT, which first arrived in the Islands in November 1941. Dr. Todt himself came at this time to see what was needed.[1]

The OT had been developed by Todt before the war. Its function was to put German and foreign labour at the disposal of German contractors for military construction work. The foreign workers retained their civilian status and wore civilian clothing. The German personnel (workers, foremen, camp administration staff, and officials) wore the OT uniform. Although the OT was purely civilian it had a chain of command on the lines of the army, with headquarters in Berlin. The subordinate groups corresponded to army formations. Thus the *Einsatzgruppe* was the equivalent of an army group, and the *Einsatz* of an army. Beneath that came the *Oberbauleitung*, the *Bauleitung* or *Abschnitt*, and finally the *Baustelle*, which was a single construction site. For the purposes of the OT, Jersey, Guernsey, and Alderney were *Abschnitte*, with code names 'Jakob', 'Gustav', and 'Adolf' – the initial letters of which corresponded to the initials of the Islands. They were all part of *Einsatzgruppe West*. Alderney came under *Oberbauleitung* St. Malo until February 1943, and after that under *Oberbauleitung* Cherbourg until June 1944, when the OT was withdrawn.

[1] T 78 317/6271761.

The OT workers were in theory non-combatants, but in so far as they were German citizens they could be armed – as the military government officials were – and they occasionally supported troops which had been cut off, as, for example at St. Nazaire and Lorient. They were then used to dig trenches, lay minefields, carry out demolition work, and so on. There were at least ten German firms represented in the Organisation Todt in the Channel Islands.

The nature of the OT changed when political prisoners and prisoners of war were drafted in. They received very different treatment from the ordinary workers. There is no doubt that they were treated little better than animals by their German masters. The evidence in the case of the Channel Islands is overwhelming.[1] It is impossible, however, to substantiate claims that thousands died and were either buried in mass secret graves, or thrown into the sea. These claims are as a rule made about Alderney, where there were few Channel Island witnesses; conditions were certainly much harder there, especially for the prisoners.

The arrival of the OT in Jersey is noted by Sinel:

Germans are absolutely pouring in, including civilians; stores are arriving galore, and there were over forty different steamers and barges in the harbours today, all unloading. German building firms are trying to get labour, and more 'builders' are springing up, the labour consisting of the camouflaging of gun emplacements etc with the Island becoming more and more of a German armed camp.[2]

At the end of the year he records:

Thousands of foreign workers are being poured into the Island; these are of all nationalities and include Spaniards who during the Civil War were interned in France; the majority of these workers are very poor specimens – badly clad and shod, and all of them terribly hungry; some were seen on Christmas day eating raw limpets and acorns, while if they got a chance they are always ready to beg for a bit of bread; the Germans keep strict supervision over them and they have an early curfew.[3]

Some of their slave workers have left accounts of their existence in the OT, but even so it is difficult to arrive at the whole truth. Most of the documents dealing with the OT in the Channel Islands have been destroyed, which perhaps fortifies the view of those who suggest that many thousands of workers died.

[1] Cf. Alan and Mary Wood, *Islands in Danger* (London, 1965), pp. 157–63; Toms, pp. 93–7.
[2] Sinel, p. 58.   [3] Ibid., p. 64.

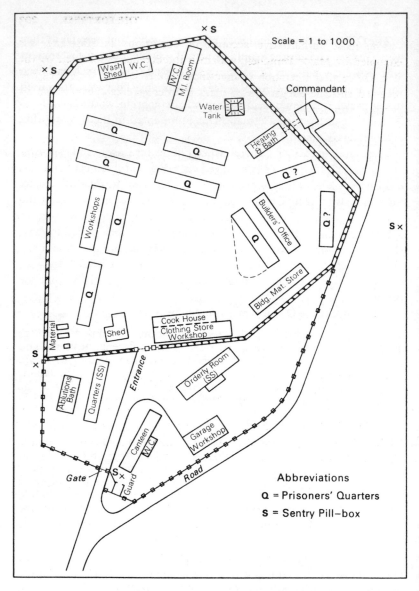

Scale = 1 to 1000

Wash Shed
W.C.
W.C.
M.I. Room
Water Tank
Commandant
Heating & Bath
Q
Q
Q
Q
Q ?
Q
Q ?
Workshops
Builders' Office
Q
Bldg. Mat. Store
Q
Material
Shed
Cook House
Clothing Store
Workshop
Orderly Room (SS)
Ablutions Bath
Quarters (SS)
Entrance
Canteen
W.C.
Garage Workshop
Gate
Guard
Road

S
S
S ×
S ×
S ×

Abbreviations

Q = Prisoners' Quarters

S = Sentry Pill-box

Plan of 'Sylt': the SS Baubrigade I concentration camp on Alderney

The most authoritative account of conditions in Alderney was compiled by Major Pantcheff, a British intelligence officer sent by the War Office after liberation to investigate the treatment the slaves had received and the allegations of mass murder. He calculated that the average number of workers on Alderney from September 1942 to October 1943 was about 2,500 to 3,000.[1] They were accommodated in four camps, Helgoland, Norderney, Borkum, and Sylt. The Russian and European slave workers were in Helgoland and Norderney respectively. There were specialist German workers in Borkum. In March 1943 Sylt was taken over by *SS Baubrigade I* – a mobile concentration camp whose prisoners were used for constructional work. Pantcheff could find no evidence of mass graves or wholesale slaughter; but there was ample evidence of sickening inhumanity by a large number of individuals against the OT workers and the concentration camp prisoners.

Arbitrary beatings were a daily occurrence in Norderney camp, where in September 1943 there were 300 French Jews, and in Helgoland, where there were 700 Russians.[2] Workers were beaten for trivial offences against the regulations, such as looking for food in garbage buckets; and sometimes for no reason at all. Rations were wholly inadequate for men engaged in heavy construction work. In the winter of 1942 breakfast was half a litre of coffee without milk or sugar; lunch half a litre of thin vegetable soup; and supper the same amount of soup plus a kilo loaf between five or six men. No clothing was issued. The workers had to make do with whatever they wore when they were conscripted. The only exception was that they were given wooden sabots when their shoes wore out. No one was allowed to report sick unless he was so ill that he could not work. The decision as to who should see the doctor rested with the *Lagerführer* in charge of the camp who would 'beat up the sick parade if he considered it too large'. The men worked at least 12 hours a day with a break of 10–30 minutes at midday, 7 days a week. One Sunday a month they worked only half a day. Pantcheff reckoned that the probable number of foreign workers buried in Alderney was

---

[1] The German records (Bailiff's Library, Guernsey, volumes 63 and 64) show the following:

	Guernsey	Jersey	Alderney	Total
May 1943	6700	5300	4000	16,000
November 1943	2890	3746	2233	8959
July 1944	489	83	245	817

[2] There is ample evidence of the abominable treatment of the OT workers in the other Islands. In Guernsey, for example, Mr. Ronald Mauger saw a German kill a worker with a spade in a fit of temper. This was by no means an isolated incident.

337, of whom 104 died in November and December 1942 – during which period not one of the 3,000-strong garrison died.

Moreover his conclusions are independently confirmed by the scanty records of the deaths of OT workers which have survived – those for the last quarter of 1942. At their face value they suggest that the Germans in Alderney were less callous than has been believed. The original death certificates were meticulously made out and signed by one of three doctors. They contained the name, birthplace, and home of the dead man; the day and hour of his death; his basic illness, accompanying illnesses, resultant illnesses, and the immediate cause of death. Was there any evidence that the man might have died from unnatural causes? If so, what was it? Was an autopsy needed? No doubt those who believe that many more died than the Germans admitted will claim that the records should not be taken at their face value; but it is difficult to believe that the certificates are not honest records.

Why, at a time when the Germans were so fully in command of the situation, when they still saw themselves as potential masters of the world, should they trouble to engage in a deception which they thought would never be revealed? It seems likely that even if ten times as many OT workers had died they would have produced death certificates for them, secure in the belief that they would never have to answer to the world for their deaths.

After the certificate had been made out the death was reported by the OT to its immediate headquarters at St. Malo, to the *Inselkommandantur* in Alderney, and to the *Aussenstelle*, which passed the information on to the *Nebenstelle* in Guernsey. This notification amplified the death certificate. It gave, for example, the name of the firm for which the man had worked, and it included three sentences which were almost common form: 'The dead man was brought from the Norderney camp to the cemetery at St. Anne in a lorry and was carried by his comrades to his grave. A cross prepared by his firm was set up. The dead man left no personal effects.' This document was signed by the *Sozialbeauftragter* (welfare officer).[1]

Although the total of 158 deaths in the three months must be on the low side, since the certificates for the first week in November are missing, the sample is big enough to give a picture of the ages of the men and the recorded causes of death. The date of birth is shown on 133

[1] *Der Verstorbene wurde vom Lager Norderney mit einem LKW zum Stadtfriedhof St. Anne gefahren und von seinen Kameraden zu Grabe getragen. Ein Grabkreuz wurde von der Firma angefertigt und aufgestellt. Nachlass wurde beim Verstorbenen keiner vorgefunden.* Loose Guernsey paper.

certificates in respect of 2 Dutchmen, 17 Poles, and 114 Russians. No
fewer than 64 of them were 21 or younger, including 10 17-year-olds,
and 8 who were only 16. There were 27 between 22 and 31; 30 between
32 and 41; and only 12 over 41. The oldest man was 57. It is perhaps
surprising that so many were so young, but without knowing the
composition of the whole of the working population it is impossible to
deduce much from the figures. It may be that most were young men,
although it seems unlikely; or it may be that young men were left an
easier prey to disease than their older comrades.

The recorded causes of death are what one would expect to find in the
circumstances of the OT camps, where the rations were barely enough
to support life and where superhuman physical effort was required over
long periods. The most common cause is simply exhaustion or exhaustion followed by heart failure. A variant is cachexy, which also
appears frequently. Next come dysentery and tuberculosis, which are
respectively half, and a quarter of the 'exhaustion' rate. A remarkable
feature is the large number of cases of fatal poisoning, usually caused by
eating the tempting berries of deadly nightshade.

A German soldier who was stationed on Alderney has left a description of the Russian workers:

The mixture of people on the Island has been increased with the
arrival of Russian civilian workers, smelling sour, dressed in rags, often
barefoot, and wearing peaked caps. We see their rigid and melancholy
silhouettes everywhere. I attribute their condition partly to insufficient
food, and partly to their wooden-soled shoes. The most pitiful Frenchman is a cut above them. An Arab, about to leave the Island hoping to
join the Foreign Legion,[1] said he could liquidate 400 of these types in an
hour . . . The Russians beg for cigarettes when one meets them. They
follow us home waiting to pounce on stubs.[2]

Von Schmettow puts the peak strength of the OT in the Islands at
about 15,000: 7,000 on Guernsey, 5,000–6,000 on Jersey, and 2,000 on
Alderney – the last figure must exclude the political prisoners and the
Jews. A memorandum of June 1942 says that the OT labour force
amounted to 11,800, 'the decline being due to the call-up of German
workers who were not replaced because of the fuel position in the
Islands'.[3] In the course of 1943 many of the construction firms were
pulled out to work on the Atlantic Wall on the mainland, and by the
middle of 1944 virtually all had gone.

[1] To fight against the Russians.
[2] Nebel, pp. 302–3.
[3] IWM AL 1864.

10

Deportation

IN THE autumn of 1941 the German Foreign Ministry became aware
that Britain had asked that German citizens working in Iran against the
Allied cause should be handed over. Hitler was incensed and ordered
the Foreign Ministry to consider reprisals. They therefore assessed the
value of the captive population of the Channel Islands as a bargaining
counter. How many residents were United Kingdom citizens, were they
interned, could the measures against them be intensified, were any
officials from the motherland still there?[1] The answer came that all were
interned in that they could not leave without permission, but normal
activities were not curtailed. The Islands were not colonies, as the
Foreign Ministry seemed to think, but had extensive self-government.
True, there were officials from England and her colonies, but they had
come simply to spend the evening of their life, attracted by the favourable climate and taxation. The number of United Kingdom residents
would be checked immediately. Their life could be made more difficult
in many ways, for example by manipulating the curfew.[2]

Estimates of the make-up of the population were supplied on 7
September. Accurate figures could not be given since there were
no police registers; but of the 66,000 remaining in Jersey and Guernsey about 6,000 had been born in Britain. 2,000 of them were
'prominent citizens'. There were 12 British-born officials who were
indispensable. Later on the same day the *Feldkommandantur* estimated
that there were 1,000–2,000 United Kingdom citizens available for
internment; and this was passed on to Berlin by the German Embassy
in Paris.[3]

Estimates were not enough, however, when the Führer was personally

---

[1] GFM 1808/411655.　　　　[2] GFM 280/180089/90–1; 1808/411656–7.
[3] GFM 98/108904; 1808/411658–9.

interested. The Bailiff of Jersey was ordered to provide by 16 September a list of men over 15 living in the bailiwick who had been born in Britain. More information was then demanded in a flurry of telegrams. On 15 September the number of English nationals in Jersey (already asked for), of English officials living there on pension, and the total population were required immediately. The Island authorities, correctly interpreting 'English' as 'United Kingdom citizen', replied that there were 180 pensioned officials, that the total population was 41,101 and that they had no idea how many British nationals there were. Three days later lists of Britons between the ages of 15 and 56, and 56 and 68 were asked for. On 23 September there was a new request, the significance of which was lost on the Island authorities. A list of 'all the Iranian nationals at present in Jersey' had to be compiled. Surprisingly enough one was found – a 69-year-old man born in Smyrna, who hardly balanced the hundreds of Iran Germans about to be interned, and who mercifully never learned what hung over his head.[1]

On 22 October the *Feldkommandantur* asked that United Kingdom-born women and children should be added to the lists. Finally, on 3 November, after much confusion and near-panic on the part of the Germans, the tabulations were completed to the satisfaction of the *Feldkommandant*. The Controlling Committee in Guernsey received the same questions, each letter from the *Nebenstelle* being marked more urgent than the one before; and the lists were duly submitted on 10 November.[2] There is no evidence that the Germans in Guernsey tried to track down Iranians, but since they began their enquiries later than Jersey and were under great pressure the Iranian point may have been overlooked. At any rate, no Guernsey Iranian was brought to light.[3]

While the scope for reprisals was being established the Foreign Ministry was busy trying to save the Germans in Iran by diplomatic means. The German Embassy in Ankara was instructed to let it be known to the British Ambassador through the Turkish Foreign Minister that if the Iran Germans were interned British citizens in the Channel Islands would also be interned. The Embassy was also to offer the return of British subjects who had fought for Finland in the Russo-

[1] JF W 60/4; 60/5/2.

[2] The figures were: men 18 to 45, 1305; 46 to 60, 700; over 60, 728; women over 18, 2391; boys under 18, 213; and girls under 18, 189 (Jersey); men 18 to 45, 432; men 46 to 60, 359; men over 60, 444; women over 18, 1525; children 5 to 18, 70 (Guernsey). JF W 60/5/2, 60/7; GF 1/1/10.

[3] GF 1/1/10.

Finnish war and who were marooned in Sweden. The Ambassador was to be reminded that in a recent exchange of severely-wounded prisoners of war Britain had received 1,000 more than she had handed over. The Foreign Minister passed all this on to the Ambassador, who telegraphed it to London.[1]

Two days later the German government made a more formal approach through the Swiss Legation in London. They claimed that German subjects in Iran were detained because of British intervention, and said that if they were interned they were ready to deport and intern an equal number of United Kingdom citizens living in the Channel Islands, who had so far remained 'at liberty'. These people would receive the same treatment as the Iran Germans; but if the latter were given a safe-conduct the matter would be forgotten.[2]

Hitler continued to be deeply interested in saving his agents in Iran by using the British in the Channel Islands as hostages; but when he spoke on 12 September to a member of Ribbentrop's personal staff he was thinking more in terms of a punitive operation. He said that for every German deported ten 'selected Englishmen' must be deported from the Jersey Islands to the Pripet Marshes. They should include prominent British civilians, and in particular 'Churchill's nephew'.[3] The reason for their deportation must be made clear to the world and their property must be redistributed among Jerseymen who were of French descent.[4] On the same day the Foreign Ministry calculated that there were about 900 Germans at risk in Iran, and assumed that only an equal number of Channel Islanders would be interned. Then the news of Hitler's edict reached them, and they accepted that 'a tenfold number of Englishmen' should be arrested. They stressed, however, that while everybody must be ready to carry out the Führer's order at a moment's notice, it was still provisional. They also proposed that the Iranian Ambassador in Berlin should be 'sharply reprimanded' for the outrageous behaviour of his government towards the German Embassy in Teheran, which had been surrounded by troops.[5]

It was assumed that the factor of ten to one meant deporting 5,000 United Kingdom-born Islanders (the estimate of the number of Iran Germans having been reduced), and the *Feldkommandantur* was

[1] FO 371/27212.
[2] FO 371/27213.
[3] There was a Churchill living in the Channel Islands at this time who was in fact deported, but he was not related to the Prime Minister.
[4] *Documents on German Foreign Policy (1918–1945)*, vol. xiii, no. 306, pp. 482–3.
[5] GFM 98/108911; 1808/411660.

ordered to make plans to remove this number. The proposal to re-distribute the deportees' property caused misgiving, and the Foreign Ministry consulted their lawyers. They produced a balance sheet which showed that Britain held 18,000 Germans 'of interest to us', whereas Germany held only 3,500 British excluding, of course, the population of the Channel Islands. The protecting power had free access to the internment camps of both sides, and if the Channel Islanders were subjected to unduly harsh treatment it would soon be spotted. The treatment of German internees would worsen, especially in Britain's overseas territories, where it was more difficult for the protecting power to keep an eye on things. Further, the funds which German internees had in Britain were retained in controlled accounts. If the Channel Islanders' property was confiscated – it would be the first time that Germany had ever done such a thing – Britain would take the same line with German internees. Therefore the Channel Islanders' assets should be held as enemy property in the usual way.[1]

The Wehrmacht was also unhappy about Hitler's proposals. The internees should not be sent to the Pripet Marshes, which were in an operational area. It was undesirable that United States officials, representing the protecting power, should go there, and the receipt and despatch of mail would also raise difficulties. If the Islanders had to be interned, they should be sent to the east only if there were well-founded complaints about the treatment of the Iran Germans.[2]

While the Foreign Ministry studied the implications of carrying out Hitler's order the British Foreign Office took their time in replying to the note suggesting that a deal should be arranged. On 15 September the Germans asked the Swiss Minister to inform the British that if they did not agree to leave the Iran Germans unmolested the Channel Island deportations would be carried out immediately. The Minister learned that the matter was still under consideration by the Foreign Office, but gained the impression that the British might give way. This was enough to restrain the Germans, and they asked the Minister to continue to press their case.[3]

The Foreign Office sent a formal reply next day. There was no parallel between the Iran Germans and the Channel Islanders. Britain had been forced to take action against German specialists in Iran who were furthering the war aims of Germany. She would not intern women and children, or men over military age, unless they were enemy

[1] GFM 1808/411661; 1808/411662–4; 98/108913–5.
[2] GFM 1808/411662–4; 98/108913–5.   [3] GFM 281/180254.

agents. The deportation of non-combatant British subjects from their permanent homes in the Channel Islands was quite different, and was expressly forbidden by the Hague Convention. It would be one more example of the illegal and inhumane treatment of the inhabitants of territories occupied by the German military forces.[1]

Meanwhile the Foreign Ministry pressed on with their contingency planning. They thought that if the order to deport the Channel Islanders was acted on before the Iran Germans' families were safely on their way to Germany the British would assume that they too were entitled to intern women and children. Therefore nothing must be done against the Channel Islanders before 20 September, when the German families were due to leave Iran.[2] The next few days were spent working out how many Islanders would have to be deported, given the Führer's ratio of ten to one. On 16 September the Foreign Ministry believed that only 300 Iran Germans had been seized, which would involve 3,000 Channel Islanders.[3] Two days later it was reported that up to 400 Iran Germans had fallen into British hands and that the final figure might be as high as 500. It was also confirmed that when Hitler had demanded ten for one he really meant what he said.[4]

It was one thing to calculate how many British-born Channel Islanders had to be deported and quite another to find the required number of bodies. The *Feldkommandantur*'s original estimate that there would be 1,000–2,000 suitable for deportation proved near the mark. It was agreed that since the British had interned Germans between 18 and 45, reprisals should be restricted to this age group; but when allowance had been made for essential workers and the sick only 1,200 could be found.[5] This raised an awkward question. Should the native-born Islanders also have to suffer for the misdeeds of the United Kingdom government? If the Führer continued to insist on ten to one, nearly 4,000 of them would be involved. OKH asked for a straight answer to this question, but none was forthcoming.[6]

This did not interrupt the contingency planning. It was suggested that the first to be deported should be the intelligentsia and 'naval people'. Camps should be earmarked in France until the internees could be moved to Germany.[7] The provision of ships was a problem. Several vessels had been withdrawn from their normal runs, but OKH

[1] FO 371/27213; GFM 281/180247–9.   [2] GFM 1808/411666–7.
[3] Ibid.   [4] GFM 1808/411669–70: 281/180245.
[5] GFM 1808/411665; 1808/411668.   [6] GFM 1808/411665.
[7] GFM 1808/411666–7.

proposed that they should be released.[1] The Foreign Ministry, however, asked on 23 September that the ships should be held for a few days longer in the hope that a positive decision would be forthcoming.[2] The military government in France was also worried about transport. When they said that ships could not be held indefinitely, they were told that the Führer was still discussing the next move with the Foreign Minister. In the meantime on no account were the ships to be released. The Foreign Ministry added that the military government and OKH both seemed to be at cross-purposes with the agreed policy and the sooner the misunderstandings were cleared up the better.[3] This hint of confusion is interesting in the light of later developments.

It was now mooted that reprisals should also be taken against the Russians, who had been associated in the action against the Iran Germans. The internment of prominent Soviet citizens would be announced to the world along with the news of the Channel Islanders' deportation. Although the Foreign Ministry considered that 'truly effective measures are scarcely available to us' against the Russians, it was necessary on propaganda grounds to treat them in the same way as the British.[4]

By the middle of October the Foreign Ministry saw that if the reprisals were to be on the scale demanded by Hitler the net would have to be cast wider. They therefore ordered a more comprehensive survey of the British-born Islanders. The results reached Berlin on 11 November and showed a grand total of 8,166 for all the Islands.[5]

Hitler again referred to the possibility of deporting the Islanders at a meeting on 18 October. He was pontificating about the importance of fortifying the Islands, on the ground that the British were likely to attack them, and suggested that Russian prisoners of war might be used on the construction work. He added that the Channel Islanders could also be used, and went on to say: 'In the event of any difficulty with the civilian population, I shall not shrink from deporting those of the inhabitants who were born in Britain.'[6] An order about the fortifications mentioned briefly that instructions about deportation would follow.[7]

The British note of 16 September still awaited a reply. This reached the Foreign Office in the middle of November and claimed that the British government had distorted the truth and deployed false legal

[1] GFM 281/180232.   [2] GFM 1808/411672.   [3] GFM 98/108932-3.
[4] GFM 281/180223.   [5] GFM 1808/411678.   [6] T 77 788/5517308.
[7] T 77 788/5517313; MOD 95/993-4.

arguments. By their action in Iran they had forfeited the right to appeal to international law, while the German government's authority to carry out reprisals derived from the natural right of every state to requite wrongs perpetrated by another state against its nationals. Britain's disregard of the warning about interning Germans in Iran justified the immediate internment of an appropriate number of British subjects in the Channel Islands. The Ministry did not add that the Führer's idea of an appropriate number was ten to one.[1] They concluded by saying that they had decided to postpone retaliatory measures in the hope that Britain would agree to a general exchange of interned civilians, in which it seems likely that several thousand Channel Islanders would have been thrown into the balance.[2]

From this time until September 1942 the records are silent about the proposed deportation, except for one or two references in January 1942. The Wehrmacht were still holding a camp for the deportees near Cologne. The prisoner of war branch of OKW asked the Foreign Ministry if the deportation of 'the 6,000 Channel Islanders' was still under discussion and when it was likely to happen. Unless there was an early decision the camp reserved for them would have to be used for prisoners of war. The Foreign Ministry consulted the military government about the need for the deportation, but the only answer was that the Wehrmacht saw no reason for it on military grounds.[3]

A passionate and unequivocal order from the Führer was plainly on the record, but it had not been carried out. The statistical information about British-born Channel Islanders, so painstakingly collected by the *Feldkommandantur* and its *Nebenstelle*, which was to be the basis of the deportation, lay undisturbed in their files. The Islanders had no idea what they had just escaped.

Hitler's order might never have been carried out had it not been for proposals about an exchange of seriously-wounded prisoners of war in 1942. The Swiss government, with the best of intentions, suggested that the deal should include Channel Island residents who wanted to go to Britain. A memorandum of 2 September 1942 examined the proposal from the Wehrmacht's point of view. It was desirable to bring home the prisoners of war, and OKM badly wanted over 5,000 merchant seamen who were in British hands. But Ob. West pointed out that if the Channel Islanders went to Britain they would pass on information

[1] FO 371/27224.   [2] Ibid.; T 77 788/5517318.
[3] GFM 1808/411679.

about the Islands' defences. It was admitted, however, that the British must already know a good deal from aerial reconnaissance, and OKM accepted that they must be well informed about the marine defences, which were visible from the air. They had no objection to including Islanders in the proposed exchange. It was in any case suggested that the danger would be mitigated because many of those who went would be called up. They would spend several months in training camps, during which the Island defences would be changed.[1]

The Swiss proposal was important enough to come before Hitler. He immediately guessed that the Channel Islanders whom he had ordered to the Pripet Marshes a year earlier had never been deported. A marginal note in Field Marshal Keitel's hand says that the Führer wants to know why, contrary to his order, the evacuation of 'these English people' did not take place. Alternatively, if the order *had* been carried out, how many Islanders were involved and where were they now held? Keitel added that there was no longer any question of including the Islanders in the proposed exchange. If they had not been deported, it must be done forthwith. General Jodl scribbled his marginal comments, including the observation that the 'permanent residents' of the Channel Islands must be allowed to remain there. Without them the German troops would have a desert on their hands.[2]

An inquest was at once carried out by General Warlimont. He reported on 21 September 1942 that the deportation had been first considered at a meeting with the Führer in the *Wolfsschanze*[3] map-room on 18 October to discuss the fortification of the Channel Islands. The record showed that Hitler had said: 'If difficulties arise, I shall not hesitate to evacuate the purely English civilians.' The resultant order about the fortifications promised a further order about deportation. Warlimont judged that the deportation had first been seen as a reprisal for the action against the Iran Germans, but there had also been a security element. Some had thought it unwise to leave British-born residents at liberty in Hitler's new fortress, since they would be more likely to engage in sabotage than native Channel Islanders. In any case, Hitler had made it clear that the British would not be allowed to remain permanently, and that Britain would have to get used to the idea that the

---

[1] T 77 788/5517288.

[2] *Die ständigen Bewohner der Kanalinseln müssen bleiben. Ohne sie bekommen wir eine Wüste.* T 77 788/5517289.

[3] The *Wolfsschanze* (Wolf's lair) was Hitler's secret headquarters at Rastenburg in East Prussia.

H

Islands had passed into German possession.[1] Against this it had been argued that there might be some advantages in not deporting the British-born at that stage. Many would be needed to help to build the fortifications and to provide services for the German troops. Further, their mere presence meant that the Islands were less likely to be attacked by the British.

This was the only record of what the Führer had said, presumably, suggested Warlimont, because the fire in the *Wolfsschanze* map-room had destroyed everything else. But an officer recollected a telephone call from the Foreign Ministry asking that deportation should be held up while the Iran German business was settled, which would take at least six weeks. This suggested that the deportation of the Channel Islanders had been regarded as a measure of great political significance and that the Foreign Ministry wanted to proceed with great caution. If, however, it became necessary to evacuate the civilians on military grounds – a possibility which Hitler had envisaged – the position would be changed.

Warlimont traced the history of the deportation order as far as the surviving documents allowed. Headquarters, West France, had wrongly assumed that the deportation was to go ahead only if the British Channel Islanders were causing trouble. They were at first unaware of the connection with the Iran Germans. The Foreign Ministry added to the confusion when they said on 8 October that the deportation was already under way, when they really meant that the preparatory work was under way. When OKH asked what was happening, after waiting for the political implications to be clarified, they were told by the Foreign Ministry that no measures against the British-born Channel Islanders were contemplated. They took this as being conclusive, and suspended the preparation of camps for the internees. They released the ships which were still standing by. Headquarters, France, also gained the impression that the deportation had been cancelled, but Warlimont was unable to discover how this came about since all their records on the subject had been destroyed by fire.[2]

His verdict was that the Foreign Ministry had mistakenly believed

[1] T 77 788/5517298–307. In fact the deportation was being considered as early as 2 September 1941, and Hitler himself was involved as early as 12 September.

[2] The fire in the *Wolfsschanze* map-room may or may not have been accidental, but it seems strange that documents elsewhere which would have enabled Warlimont to apportion the blame should have been conveniently destroyed by fire. It is just possible that someone in Headquarters, West France, became aware of the mistake in the course of 1942 and attempted to cover it up.

that the military authorities were carrying out the deportation according to plan, whereas the military authorities were under the impression that the Foreign Ministry wanted it to be postponed on political grounds. This seemed to make sense to them because they considered that there were neither political nor military reasons for the deportation. How this extraordinary state of affairs came about Warlimont could not demonstrate from the records at his disposal.

He concluded his review by rather boldly observing that there had been no need to arrest or intern anybody in the Channel Islands. On the contrary, the population, including the British residents, had been thoroughly loyal. There had been no sabotage, no passive resistance. German orders had been carried out quickly and without opposition. Furthermore, and this looks like a direct protest against the line taken by Hitler, there was no reason to suppose that if the British-born remained in the Islands there would be any damage to German interests.[1]

It is remarkable that the German administrative and military machines could allow a Führer order to fall between them in this way; but the mistake was not repeated. The order was issued again, as a matter of principle, since the Iran Germans had long been forgotten, regardless of political, military, or humanitarian considerations. It was carried out immediately, ruthlessly, and unquestioningly.

It was transmitted to the military governor in France on 9 September 1942. The Führer had given instructions for 'the immediate evacuation of British subjects on the Channel Islands who do not belong to the indigenous population'. They were to be brought to Germany, where the Wehrmacht would have the job of guarding them. The military governor was to organize the deportation and to report its successful conclusion as soon as possible.[2] Warlimont, however, was doubtful about the wisdom of making the Wehrmacht responsible for the deportees. He thought it would be more sensible to hand them over to the police.[3]

The Bailiff of Jersey was summoned by the *Feldkommandant* on 15 September. He was to bring the Constables with him to discuss 'the evacuation from Jersey to Germany of the English-born members of the population'. At the meeting an order was read out which required the immediate evacuation of British subjects who did not have their permanent residence on the Channel Islands, and of all males from 16 to 70 who had not been born in the Islands, together with their families. The *Feldkommandant* said that 1,200 would have to leave the following

[1] T 77 788/5517307.   [2] T 77 788/5517269, 275.   [3] T 77 778/5517278.

day. The evacuation notices would be served by the Constables, who would be consulted as to who should go.

At this point the *Feldkommandant* agreed to see the Bailiff privately. Coutanche said he was shocked by the order and formally protested against it. Knackfuss pointed out that it came from the Führer himself and must be carried out to the letter. Coutanche replied that in that case he and his colleagues would have to consider resigning. In any case the Constables must not select the deportees. Knackfuss conceded this and when the Constables objected even to serving the notices he said it would be done by the troops. It seems that he would have been prepared to agree to almost anything so long as 1,200 British-born Jersey men were on their way to Germany the following day.

The Superior Council met that afternoon and again next morning. Should they resign? They sensibly decided that it would serve no useful purpose. In office they could ensure that justice was done, or rather, since the whole operation was manifestly unjust, ensure that individuals with the strongest cases were not deported. There was precious little time to help the first batch, who left on the evening of 16 September, but they did what they could. A second shipload left next day. A third was reprieved for a week when their ship was taken out of service because of inadequate sanitation.

The Council met again on 21 September to consider a request from the *Feldkommandant* for lists of British subjects remaining in Jersey. It was decided to ask him to withdraw it, which he agreed to do, at least for the moment. Some members said that it was wrong that only British-born Islanders should be deported, but it was felt that argument on this line would merely widen the field in which the Germans could select their victims, and perhaps encourage them to take more. The Council had, of course, no idea why the order had been issued in the first place, or of its curious history.

A resolution was passed drawing attention to the German ultimatum of 1 July 1940, which included the promise that: 'In case of peaceful surrender the lives, property and liberty of peaceful inhabitants are solemnly guaranteed.' In Jersey the Germans were unhappy when they were reminded about this undertaking. The inhabitants had been peaceful. Indeed it must have been on the advice of the *Feldkommandant* that Warlimont gave the Islanders full credit for their good behaviour when he was inquiring into the fate of Hitler's original order. They recognized that they were in honour bound to act in the spirit of the surrender agreement, but they had received a clear order from the

Führer which forced them into a shameful breach of faith. Many Germans still held their honour in high esteem, but on this occasion there was nothing they could do about it. On 22 September, when it was too late to help, the Superior Council sent their resolution to the *Feldkommandant* and hopefully asked him to submit it to his government.[1]

In Guernsey the Bailiff, Sherwill, and Leale met Dr. Brosch of the *Nebenstelle* and expressed horror at what was proposed. Brosch, always neurotic, was more excited than usual and said that nothing could be done about it. A series of questions was put to him. Could the maximum age of the deportees be reduced? Would they be sent to Germany? Would they be billeted in towns likely to be bombed? Would they be treated as hostages? Why were they being deported? Brosch merely replied that those selected must be ready to travel on 20 September at the latest. He asked the Controlling Committee to prepare lists of those eligible, by parish, before noon on 18 September.

The newspapers carried announcements describing the categories to be deported, with coupons to be completed and returned to the authorities. The Controlling Committee thought that if the arrangements were left to Brosch in his highly excited state the deportees might suffer unnecessarily. They decided to help by providing clothes, food for the journey, transport to the harbour, and a hot meal before the ships sailed.[2] They succeeded in getting some exempted on compassionate grounds or because their services were essential, but the number that finally went was still large: 825 men, women, and children. They were given a medical examination, ostensibly to establish that they could stand the journey. The Germans assured them that once they were in an internment camp they would be well looked after.

The transports – the *Robert Müller* and *La France* – were supposed to leave on 21 September, but the Controlling Committee objected to the use of the former, a cargo boat which was quite unsuitable for passengers. The only seats were loose forms in the hold. Had the Committee been dealing with Brosch they would probably have got short shrift; but Knackfuss, who by now had despatched the Jersey contingent, came over to Guernsey. He was easier to deal with, and agreed that the *Robert Müller* should not be used if it was rough. The deportees embarked on 21 September but the weather was so bad that they were taken off again. Eventually they left on 26 and 28 September on the *Minotaur*.

[1] SCM, p. 279.   [2] GF 1/116.

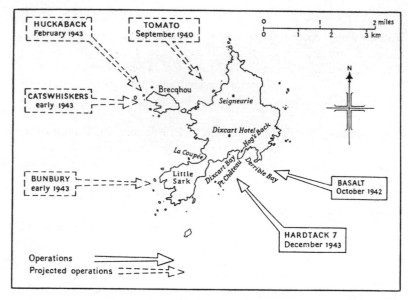

6. *Sark and Brecqhou*

Even before they had sailed Brosch was badgering the Controlling Committee with further deportations in mind. His own records listed 2,400 British-born Guernseymen, yet only 1,846 had been reported. Where were the missing 554? He was reminded that the deportation order did not cover males below 16 and over 70, single women, widows, and women married to Guernseymen. Brosch also ordered the preparation of a card index of those who had been selected for deportation but had been exempted for one reason or another; and an index of 'all persons who were born outside Guernsey as British subjects and who have not yet been listed for the evacuation'.[1] He at least would be well prepared to carry out any further orders in this field.

Sark had to supply its quota of deportees. Eleven were told off to join the transports in Guernsey. The Dame ensured that all had food and warm clothing. Two of the eleven – a Major Skelton and his wife – failed to report. Later Skelton was found dead with his wrists slashed. His wife was seriously wounded, but alive. They had left farewell letters with the Dame, which she had assumed were simply to tell friends that they were being deported. The Germans heard about the letters, and suspected that Skelton might have been a British agent. They cross-

[1] GF 1/1/16.

examined the Dame but could not find the letters, which she had hidden in a rabbit hutch. Mrs. Skelton was taken to hospital in Guernsey, where she recovered.[1]

The deportation came as a great shock to the Islanders. They had lived peaceably under German rule for more than two years, and had no idea why large numbers should suddenly be removed. 'No logical reason can be thought of for this distressing order, except that it is out of pure spite for the bombing of Germany by the R.A.F. . . . words fail to describe the wretched state of the Island at the moment, for those not affected have scores of friends who are; everyone is distressed and there is scarcely a dry eye to-night'.[2] 'Nobody so much as tried to assign a motive for the forcible carrying off of a number of people. The most plausible theory suggested was that for some unfathomable reason Germany intended to hold them as hostages and that the German authorities supposed that the British Government set a higher value on English-born, than on Guernsey-born, British subjects'.[3] The deportees were given an emotional send-off in both Jersey and Guernsey. They 'were magnificent, and England can be proud of them; they sang and joked on their way to the quay, and for all the world seemed to be going on a great picnic'.[4]

There were further deportations in January 1943 in reprisal for a Commando raid on Sark. The categories to be deported were to include people who had offended against the German regime; communists and others politically suspect; work-shy people; young men without important work in the German sense; former officers and reserve officers; Jews and high-ranking Freemasons;[5] people prominent in public life; rich men who were considered to be anti-German; and finally people on Sark not engaged in agriculture, and those living in the centre of the Island. About 1,000 would be involved altogether, and their families would be deported with them.[6]

Further investigations suggested that there would be only about 500 in the chosen categories. Since many would be excluded on medical grounds, perhaps no more than 250 would have to be taken. OKW

---

[1] GF 1/1/16; Hathaway, op. cit. pp. 140–2; Michael Marshall, *Hitler invaded Sark* (Guernsey, 1963), pp. 34–5.

[2] Sinel, pp. 95–6.   [3] Durand, p. 87.

[4] Sinel, p. 96.

[5] The Freemasons' lodges in the Islands were 'liquidated' in 1941 by virtue of an order from the military governor in France.

[6] T 77 788/5517255; see also pp. 242–3 below.

agreed to the proposals on 29 December and asked that the deportation should be carried out as quickly as possible.[1] This was greeted with little enthusiasm in Germany. The Wehrmacht was reluctant to be saddled with more women and children, and asked that the new batch should be taken over by the civilian authorities. The Foreign Ministry, however, being well aware of the difficulties, said that it was up to OKW to make the arrangements. OKW let it be known that all camps were full, but five days later they agreed that the deportation should proceed 'as ordered'. Lists of the deportees must be sent at once, and, weather permitting, they would be taken to France at the end of January. By 30 January 1943, 115 men, and 86 women and children had left the Islands.[2]

Sinel records that on 11 January many retired army officers were required to report for a medical examination, but only five were found to be fit. They were told to hold themselves in readiness for deportation. Next day many other people were interviewed, including some who had been sentenced by the Royal Court for offences as long as 15 years ago. Others had been before the German courts, or were suspect for one reason or another. On 15 January more were examined 'but the number picked out to be sent to Germany is very small'. A fortnight later there was another round of medical examinations, but 'almost everyone got off again, and it seems that the local German authorities are not anxious to put the order into effect'.[3] The *Feldkommandantur*'s attempt to keep the number of deportees low suggests that the Wehrmacht's reluctance to be saddled with more women and children had been communicated to them.

On 11 February the *Reichsführer SS* told the Foreign Ministry that he was worried about the proposed further deportations, since he was the civilian authority who would have to cope with the Channel Islanders if OKW washed their hands of them. Camps must be available before the deportees left the Islands but it was difficult to see where they would be found.[4] The Foreign Ministry was equally unhappy. They asked at the beginning of March just how many Islanders Ob. West was proposing to bring out. They stressed again the problem of accommodation, especially for women with small children and old people; and they asked that these categories should be excluded from future plans, unless there was some overriding reason for including them.

Both the Wehrmacht and the Foreign Ministry were becoming heartily sick of the Channel Islands deportations, and it was recorded on

[1] T 77 788/5517249, 253.   [2] GFM 1808/411823, 834; T 77 788/5517264, 248.
[3] Sinel, pp. 118–24.   [4] GFM 1808/411861.

8 March 1943, apparently with relief, that 'as far as can be judged, the evacuation is over'. If, contrary to expectations, further deportations became necessary there must be discussion between the Foreign Ministry and OKW in which all the objections would be fully ventilated.[1]

Many appealed for exemption from the deportation orders. There were some unfortunates whose United Kingdom nationality was even more accidental than nationality usually is. Perhaps the extreme case was a man illegitimately born in England of a Channel Island mother (who had briefly left the Islands to have her child) who was himself now married with three children. Although they were English on the flimsiest of technicalities, their appeal was turned down. Another married man with two children had been brought to the Islands when he was an infant. His appeal was also rejected, although even the Führer himself could hardly have argued that he was materially tarred with the English brush. Others who failed included a hairdresser carrying on a 'business which is patronised extensively by the German forces and, as I believe, doing a useful service'; one who bottled beer for the occupying troops; the sole proprietor of a jewellery and watch repair business; an Englishwoman by marriage running a grocery store single-handed; and a man who submitted that 'for many years I have preached against war against Germany both of the 1914 war and this war also and have been ostracated [sic] for it. I have lived among the German people in Canada, USA, and Australia and have formed the finest friendships among them.' In rejecting the last appeal the *Feldkommandant* may have considered that by enabling the appellant to live among the German people in Germany and make new friendships he was doing him a positive kindness.[2]

The Island authorities did what they could to get people released. The Jersey Prison Board lodged a successful appeal on behalf of four warders, whose profession was rated more essential than beer bottling or hairdressing. The managers of the electricity works and water works in Guernsey were also released, as a result of powerful pleas by the subordinate branches of the *Nebenstelle*, which were well aware of the importance of keeping the essential services going – for the benefit of the troops rather than for the civilian population. Another who had the strong support of the *Nebenstelle* was less fortunate. He had 'put himself at the service of the Wehrmacht right from the beginning of the

[1] T 77 788/5517246-7.　　　[2] GF 1/1/16.

occupation'. He was at all times happy to collaborate with the occupying troops, which had earned him special merit in the eyes of the Wehrmacht and corresponding displeasure from the Island authorities. This time the *Nebenstelle's* impassioned plea failed. The man had to pack his bags and go with the rest.[1]

There were more appeals when the second deportation was being organized. Again, some of these were supported by the *Nebenstelle*, the most important being Sherwill, who had been in the wilderness ever since the Nicolle/Symes affair, although he had been reinstated as Attorney General in July 1942. The *Feldkommandant* decided that Sherwill must go – for the second time. He was eligible on two grounds: because he had helped Nicolle and Symes, and because he was a former British officer. The *Nebenstelle* also appealed on behalf of the German-born wife of an Englishman, who was considered to be essential for the teaching of German; a clergyman who was in favour of German in the schools and whose 'remaining here could only be beneficial'; and a business man whose services had been of great importance. The last had been nominated for the first deportation, but he was one of a number of people whom the *Geheime Feldpolizei* had recommended should remain free 'as he was used in various ways as an informer'. It was reckoned that it was in the German interest that he should stay behind on the present occasion, and this was accepted by the *Feldkommandant*. The cleric was allowed to remain to further the spread of the German language, but the German-born woman who had opted out of the Reich had to go with her husband.[2]

The Dame of Sark asked that her husband should be released.[3] He was an American by birth, but had adopted British citizenship, and would in any case have found himself on the deportation list because he had served with the Royal Flying Corps in the First World War. Her appeal was turned down, after a good deal of heart-searching by the Germans. One of their legal experts who had visited the Channel Islands had expressed the view that the Seigneurie of Sark was unique, being 'based on old German law' and that it was therefore in the interests of the Reich that 'this historical rarity' should be maintained undisturbed; but this was not enough to win Robert Hathaway's release.[4]

The German agent who had spent some time in Guernsey in 1938 was gratified to find the Irish community well disposed towards his

[1] Loose Guernsey paper.   [2] Loose Guernsey paper.
[3] GF 1/1/16.   [4] Loose Guernsey paper.

country. Ireland remained neutral (although many of her sons did not) and some Islanders might have derived comfort from the knowledge that Hitler's order accidentally caught one Irishman and swept him off to internment in Germany. The Irish Chargé d'Affaires in Berlin was assured by the Foreign Ministry on 12 October 1942 that there was no question of removing Irish subjects from the Channel Islands – even to friendly Germany; but in the same breath, fearing that something might have gone wrong, the Foreign Ministry asked OKW how many Irish citizens had been spirited away into the internment camps. If there were any, they must be released at once.[1]

Strangely enough one was found – a bartender by profession. OKW told the Foreign Ministry on 21 October that the military governor in France had been instructed to arrange his release.[2] The Foreign Ministry then informed the Chargé d'Affaires that a number of British subjects had been interned on military grounds (which was not true), and that there was no question of their being forced to work, as had been reported. The Irish community was exempt from the deportation but, regrettably, it had been discovered that there was one Irish citizen among the internees. He had now been sent back to the Channel Islands.[3]

This was also untrue. The administrative machine found it impossible to disgorge the bartender and he was still interned at the end of December. OKW ordered that he should be transferred to *Frontstalag 133* at Rennes, and immediately released from there. It is not clear what then happened, but two months later the Foreign Ministry issued a formal denial that they had deported any Irish citizens – having apparently decided to forget about the unfortunate bartender.[4]

As a result of this episode the Foreign Ministry was asked by the Irish community in the Islands, which numbered about 650, to appoint someone to look after their interests. Some had British nationality, but, believing that there were at least temporary advantages in not being British, 'they feel themselves belonging to the Irish race'. The Irish had already selected their representative, and the *Feldkommandant*, who approved of the individual chosen, asked the German Embassy in Paris about his title. The Embassy put the point to the Foreign Ministry, which properly said that this request must come from the Irish government; but they did not favour the appointment since 'we are striving to

[1] GFM 1808/411684–7.   [2] GFM 1808/411690.
[3] GFM 1808/411692.   [4] GFM 1808/411741.

keep down foreign representation in occupied territories, or at least to strip it to the narrowest limits'. There would be no objection, however, to an unofficial representative, in which case the Irish government need not be brought in.[1]

The net also caught a German living in Jersey. His parents were interned in the Isle of Man, a minor guarantee of his reliability from the German point of view, but he and his wife and child were rounded up and sent from Jersey along with the British deportees.[2] When his problem was put to OKW they disclaimed all responsibility. He was not a prisoner of war and therefore could not be released by the Wehrmacht. They suggested that the matter should be taken up with the *Reichsführer SS*. On 6 December he was still interned at Biberach, and the Foreign Ministry plaintively demanded a decision. The German Red Cross also made representations on his behalf. On 8 January 1943 there was an enquiry into his nationality. Was he German, or English? Four days later the verdict came that he was German. A month passed and he was still interned. The Foreign Ministry sent a stronger demand to the military governor to sort out the muddle, pointing out that the internment was 'contrary to orders'. On 16 February the German Red Cross again joined in the chorus. The unfortunate man was still interned. When was he going to be freed? At this point the records stop and it must be left to the imagination how long this German family remained victims of their Führer's policy.[3]

Because of the suddenness of the deportation there was no time to prepare suitable camps. The first allocated were Biberach and Dorsten, which had been barracks, and Laufen, which was a well-known *Schloss*. All three belonged to the Wehrmacht and were certainly not designed for women and children. The Wehrmacht, which did not take kindly to the role of nursemaid, said that 'the raw military atmosphere' was much in evidence, and asked that the women and children should go elsewhere.[4]

Much effort was devoted to searching for suitable accommodation. The department of the *Reichsführer SS* tried to find a camp where the women and children could be on their own. The police school in Geislingen was ruled out because it could not be properly heated in winter.[5] Reutlingen, used by the Hitler Youth, was suggested. It was

---

[1] GFM 1808/411829–30.   [2] GFM 1808/411746–7.
[3] GFM 1808/411767–8; 411780; 411783; 411827.
[4] GFM 1808/411704.   [5] GFM 1808/411698.

four miles from the nearest railway station, extremely cold, with un-heated washrooms and food delivered twice a week. Happily the Hitler Youth refused to surrender the place.

Events moved too quickly for the Wehrmacht, and in spite of all their objections they found themselves looking after the women and children. They deprecated having to supply milk for 'countless babies', to say nothing of having to provide the services of a midwife. The women and children must be handed over to the Foreign Ministry 'which is basically responsible and has the necessary organization'. Hopefully, and it might seem with great humanity, were it not for the ulterior motive, they suggested that if it was agreed that they could not properly look after children, and they had to be sent elsewhere, it would mean breaking up families. The kindest thing would be to hand all the deportees – men, women, and children – over to the care of the Foreign Ministry.[1]

The Foreign Ministry was still trying to find a solution in the middle of October. At a meeting on 23 October a compromise was reached. Dorsten was no longer to be used, and the Islanders would be housed in Biberach, Würzach, and Laufen. These camps would be guarded by the department of the *Reichsführer SS* and administered by staffs supplied by the Wehrmacht. This meant that the Wehrmacht would no longer be acting as a nursemaid in its own right.[2] Even so, it was being suggested in December 1942 that the internment of the Channel Islanders was more trouble than it was worth. The Foreign Ministry pointed out that there was no security case for interning women – especially pregnant women – and children, and suggested that they should be sent back to the Islands.[3]

The reports of the protecting power and the International Red Cross afford a detailed and dispassionate picture of conditions in the camps. A Red Cross representative who visited Biberach shortly after the deportees arrived gave a gloomy account which elicited a protest from the British Foreign Office. The camp was infested with vermin, food was short, sanitation was primitive, and there were 28 people in hospital because of the cold. The camp was on an exposed plateau and on the day when it was visited by the Red Cross it was bitterly cold, in spite of brilliant sunshine. The buildings were rough and ready, and it was very difficult to heat them.[4]

[1] T 77 788/5517282.   [2] GFM 1808/411715–6.
[3] T 77 788/5517266.   [4] GFM 1808/411788.

The Foreign Office asked the Swiss government to do everything they could to help, and were told in due course that the Germans had explained that adequate accommodation could not be provided because of the heavy demands for new hospitals, prisoner of war camps, and homes for air raid victims. The camp was visited again in the middle of January. There were 1,011 internees – 429 men, 437 women, and 145 children – all except 20 of whom came from the Channel Islands. The recreation hall was unheated and unusable, but even if stoves were installed there would be no fuel for them. When the visitors said the hall should be heated, if only for religious services, they were told that German churches were not heated. Toilet facilities were reasonable. There was a good shower-room, and hot baths were regularly available. The kitchen stoves were in poor order, to which it was replied that they had been all right when the internees arrived. Food was plentiful, but the quality was unsatisfactory.

There was no hot water in the infirmary. Drugs and medical equipment were seriously short. A German doctor was in charge and was assisted by one of the interned doctors. Biberach had a sports ground, but it could not be used in winter. The only exercise was to walk round the extensive camp grounds, but the internees wanted to go further afield. This had been refused because of the danger of escape; but the Swiss representatives pointed out that it would be good for morale if the internees were allowed outside the barbed wire from time to time. This was supported by a Foreign Ministry official.

By June 1943 there were signs of improvement. There were new buildings with well-heated rooms taking from four to ten internees. The kitchen was well-equipped and the food much better cooked. A canteen where beer and soft drinks could be bought had been added. A school had been organized. An amateur dramatic society gave weekly perfomances. There was a small orchestra, handicapped by the scarcity of instruments. Outdoor games were possible in the better weather and football and volley-ball were popular. Camp discipline had improved enough for the internees to be allowed country walks three times a week, with only a small escort.

The Red Cross representatives were puzzled by the Islanders' attitude to work. 'We gained the impression that the internees were loth to undertake work of any kind whatever.' Only one was employed – by an optician in a neighbouring town. The camp leader and the Foreign Ministry deprecated the 'spirit of lassitude'. The main reason seemed to be 'indifference', but there was also reluctance to do anything that might help the enemy. 'Their idle condition must certainly be adverse to them. On the one hand they do not know how to keep themselves occupied. On the other hand, when they have to resume life in ordinary conditions they will have lost all taste for or habits of work.' Because of this it was hard to maintain order. The camp leader had asked to be allowed to suspend the distribution of Red Cross parcels when discipline was really bad. The Red Cross representatives agreed, particularly as the Germans did not impose severe discipline.

From this time on the internees in Biberach began to make the best of their lot. Reports by the protecting power and the Red Cross reveal a steady improvement in conditions; but the refusal of the internees to work still puzzled the inspectors. The point was referred to London by the camp leader in the hope that the British government would give some guidance. There was occasional domestic strife. 'Now and then petty frictions occur, mostly due to some ill-minded trouble-maker. The inspectors considered that the material conditions were satisfactory, but 'upon unprejudiced examination it must be recognized that these internees who originate mostly from the Channel Islands have a mentality which is clearly different from the usual English character. They are generally untidy and seem to take pleasure in upkeeping a quarrelsome spirit which leads to trivial petty gossiping the whole day long.' When they delivered this verdict the representatives of the protecting power seem to have forgotten that the internees were all British.

Successive inspectors praised the Biberach camp leader. 'He is at one and the same time very strict, but perfectly just. He enjoys the confidence of everyone.' 'The excellent British camp administration, headed by Mr. G. G. Garland as camp leader is foremost reponsible for the prevailing satisfactory state of affairs.' 'The camp leader appears in every respect to be suited to his task . . . The atmosphere of the whole camp is exceptional.' In September 1944 Garland had to tell the British Red Cross that the German censorship had shown him letters from internees 'grossly misrepresenting our conditions here' which would cause unnecessary anxiety at home. He went on to describe the activities of the camp in glowing terms – boot repairing, tailoring, sandal manufacture, brush-making, carpentry, watch repairing, book-binding, and so on. It is clear that the whole atmosphere of the camp had improved.

The last recorded report on Biberach – by the protecting power in February 1945 – shows that standards were declining again, partly because of the arrival of internees from other camps, and partly because of the deteriorating situation in Germany. Heating became very difficult, especially when the collection of wood outside the camp was forbidden because of local protests. There was no coal. Hot baths were cut down to one a fortnight, and then to one every three weeks. There was no toilet paper, the factory that made it having been bombed. Food was getting scarce. But at least the internees could derive some comfort from the knowledge that these difficulties were related to the impending defeat of the enemy. The worse they were, the sooner their freedom would come – always provided that they survived.

The pattern in the other camps – Würzach, where there were about 600 Channel Islanders, men, women, and children, and Laufen, where the number of Island internees (all men) varied from 460 to 500 – was much the same as in Biberach, except that morale in Würzach remained poor the whole time. There were a number of contributory factors. The Würzach buildings were unsatisfactory. The mosquitoes were particularly disagreeable. The cooks had to wage a never-ending war against rats. The women's infirmary was infested with mice. Bread, which was delivered once a week, was a problem. It was sometimes mouldy when it arrived and its condition was not improved after several days in a damp store. The mouldy parts which had to be thrown away were not replaced. Jam was no better: it was covered with a film of thick green mould, and uneatable because of its fermented taste.

As in Biberach in the early days there was reluctance to work. The internees claimed to be unwilling to help the Germans even indirectly, but the camp leader thought they were simply lazy. The Swiss inspectors also blamed the internees. They suggested that morale could be much improved if they were to approach the inevitable problems of camp life in a different spirit. In particular they should make a point of avoiding unnecessary quarrels.

Laufen was happier than Würzach, largely, in the opinion of Mr. F. E. Stroobant, the first camp leader, because only men were interned there, and the camp was subject to military discipline.[1] Mr. Stroobant told the British Red Cross at the beginning of 1943: 'We are settling down to camp life quite well, and the men seem to be taking their deportation with the usual philosophical outlook characteristic of Britishers.' He strongly resisted German suggestions that the internees

[1] Mr. Stroobant's book *One Man's War* (Guernsey, 1967) provides a detailed and objective account of life in the internment camp at Laufen. It also has an interesting account of his visit to the scene of the atrocities at Katyn, which was organized by the Germans for propaganda purposes.

should volunteer for farm work; and when Sherwill succeeded him in the middle of 1943 the new leader took the same line. He disapproved of any sort of outside work and even asked the Red Cross to authorize him to stop the food parcels of any men who undertook it. This was not agreed. The Red Cross inspectors said:

We upheld the point of view that it would be of great benefit to the internees from the point of view of both their health and spirits to undertake some regular employment. The internees themselves, however, are not entirely of this opinion, declaring that even the slightest effort made by them necessarily helps the war effort of the detaining power. They base their opinion more particularly on a statement made by the Chancellor of the Reich in one of his most recent speeches which – to put it briefly – said that anyone working in Germany should be considered as being a soldier of the Reich. The internees would like to have the opinion of their own government.

When the opinion came it was clear that there was no objection to their working so long as they did not directly help the German war effort. The hundred internees who had outside jobs – mainly in agriculture – could carry on with a clear conscience.

All the time the Channel Islanders were interned there were rumours that they were about to be repatriated. Most of them arose from discussions between the British and German governments, through the protecting power, about exchanging civilians and severely-wounded prisoners of war, which began in 1940 and continued on and off for most of the war. The Germans regarded the Channel Islanders as a special case. They must be excluded from any general agreement about an exchange, because their deportation had been personally ordered by the Führer.[1] Nevertheless, a number of old and infirm men were returned to the Islands.[2] In March 1943 the Foreign Office told the protecting power that letters were being received by relatives of the interned Islanders suggesting that the German government was willing to release them, subject to Britain's agreement. The Foreign Office suspected that this had been engineered by the Germans to create resentment; but the Swiss found that they were innocent. The rumour had started among the internees themselves.

In December 1943 the Foreign Office took the initiative about an exchange. 'There are large numbers who will certainly accept an offer to be repatriated. The largest group is from the Channel Islands, of whom more than 2,000 are in Germany.' It was suggested that as a first

[1] FO 916/6; T 77 788/5117285.   [2] GF 1/1/16.

step 600 should be exchanged. 'I think that our line as regards the Channel Islands is that provided they satisfy the conditions there should be no discrimination between them and persons from the United Kingdom.' At least one of the camp leaders was unhappy at the suggestion that the Islanders should be sent home. Most of their houses were occupied by German troops; many of them depended on remittances from Britain; and food and fuel were short. He thought that only a handful of internees should return to the Islands, for special family reasons. The rest should go to England.

When the first major exchange was organized in 1944 it was feared that the Germans would discriminate against the Channel Islanders, again because of the Führer's special interest in them; and this indeed proved to be the case. Whether by accident or design there were virtually none in the first groups to go to England. The British government asked the protecting power to find out why. The exchange agreement covered Channel Islanders just as much as other British citizens and so long as the United Kingdom was prepared to receive them there was no reason for discrimination. The Germans, influenced perhaps by the way the war was now going, finally accepted this, and in a later exchange 100 Channel Islanders were released from Biberach and Würzach on medical grounds.[1]

As the end of the war approached, and the Germans' difficulties increased, the idea of a wholesale exchange had to be dropped. For most of the internees it was simply a question of waiting until they were liberated by the victorious Allied armies.

[1] FO 916/168.

11

Later Operations

ALTHOUGH no major assault was launched against any of the Channel Islands during the occupation there were minor raids which had little bearing on the course of events.[1] Others were planned and abandoned for a variety of reasons. Major Sherwill may have deprecated those of 1940 which, in his view, put the liberty of the people at risk without furthering the Allied cause. How would he have reacted had he been aware of all the assaults, large and small, which were planned but happily never came off? For example, Operation 'Petrify' was to be an attack on enemy shipping at St. Peter Port, carried out by a Small Scale Raiding Force unit of four men. They were to enter the harbour in canoes under cover of darkness to sink with limpet mines any ships found. The four stood by during the non-moon periods in December 1942 and January and February 1943, but in all three months the weather was unsuitable and the operation was abandoned.[2] Had it been carried out successfully there would almost certainly have been heavy reprisals against the people in Guernsey, and perhaps in the other Islands as well.

The Prime Minister, who had been the moving spirit behind the raids in 1940, still insisted in 1941 that something must be done to inflict losses on the enemy; it was to accomplish this that Operation 'Attaboy', a large-scale raid on Alderney, was conceived. It was opposed by the Director of Combined Operations, Sir Roger Keyes, for weighty reasons. He thought that a surprise landing was out of the question judging by the rapidity with which agents recently landed had been captured and the reception given to boats which had ventured near the Islands' coasts. Fighter support would be inadequate; covering fire would cause casualties among the civilian population; the enemy

[1] See Chapter 5 for the earlier operations.   [2] DEFE 2/264.

batteries could not be completely silenced, so that when the force withdrew it would still be under fire; and finally the Germans would probably take retaliatory measures, as they had done in Norway, against the Islanders.

At first Churchill was reluctant to accept this advice. On 8 March he minuted General Ismay:

I thought it would have been possible to take it one night, hold it the next day under strong Air patrol, and leave the following night. I understood that the Air Force might be able to give the Air support during the single day, and that this would bring about many fruitful engagements with the Germans such as are now sought over the Pas de Calais.

I do not know why it should be supposed that the French coastline is not so well defended as ATTABOY. There is this difference also, whereas the numbers in ATTABOY can be outmatched by us, those available on the mainland have measureless superiority.[1]

Operation 'Blazing', planned at the beginning of 1942, contemplated an attack on one or more of the Islands. If Guernsey was the target, a daylight attack using 8,000 troops with substantial naval and air support would be necessary. Jersey would require a daylight attack with 7,500 men plus a parachute battalion and a light anti-aircraft regiment. Alderney, however, could be attacked by day with much smaller numbers, and therefore 'Blazing' was designed to occupy and hold Alderney.

This may seem surprising in the light of the Committee of Imperial Defence's view that the Channel Islands had no strategic value for the United Kingdom, and indeed that they might even be a liability. Some of the advantages of 'Blazing' were referred to by the Chief of Combined Operations, Vice-Admiral Lord Louis Mountbatten,[2] at a meeting of his staff on 6 March 1942. It would be good for morale and prestige, it could possibly turn out to be a propaganda triumph, and it would open a second front, even though only in a very small way.[3] He elaborated on this in a paper for the Chiefs of Staff Committee on 16 April. The occupation of Alderney would provide a small-craft base for cutting the Germans' convoy route between the Channel ports and the Bay of Biscay; it would be a site for an advanced station to extend Fighter Command's radar coverage; and it would make available an

[1] PREM 3/87.

[2] Mountbatten was in charge of Combined Operations Headquarters as Adviser from October 1941, and then as Chief from March 1942 to October 1943.

[3] DEFE 2/106.

emergency landing ground. There were also strategic advantages, at least in theory. It might draw off enemy air forces from other fronts, in particular, bombers from Norway; and it might attract German troops which were badly needed elsewhere. It could provide a springboard for future operations against the Cherbourg peninsula.

The first plan envisaged a very considerable force. It included six destroyers, five infantry assault ships, eighteen tank landing craft, and a total of 4,800 men, including paratroops. Ninety men were to land at the foot of the cliffs at the western end of the Island to be the spearhead of the attack. The main defences were to be heavily bombed for 65 minutes from 25 minutes before nautical twilight. This was to be followed by a low-level bombing attack with high explosive and smoke on Fort Albert, commanding the entrance to the harbour. Five minutes later the paratroops would drop to the rear of the harbour defences and immediately attack, while the destroyers shelled the defences to cover the approach of the main assault force east of Fort Albert. Smaller forces would land near Fort Albert and in the old harbour. Anti-aircraft batteries would come in with the second wave of assault troops; this done, the units not needed for the permanent garrison would withdraw. The operation would be completed by early afternoon. The garrison would remain until further notice, being supplied weekly with 400 tons of food, ammunition, and general supplies. All very simple, as seen by the Chief of Combined Operations.

Not so simple in the eyes of Bomber Command. Air Chief Marshal Sir Arthur Harris pointed out at a meeting on 1 May that at no time, except in one non-official conversation, had the bombing plan ever been discussed. He had no intention of allowing his aircraft to continue bombing after 40 minutes before nautical twilight, when they would be far too vulnerable. He poured scorn on a theoretical assessment by Professor Zuckerman of the number of bombs which would fall on the Island. It was possible because of drift that most would land in the sea. In an area so full of flak and enemy fighters losses would be serious and accurate bombing impossible. 'I consider that in the general design of this Operation the entire Bomber Force is being put at hazard for no sufficiently worthwhile purpose.' Thus Harris to Mountbatten on 5 May.[1]

Fighter Command also weighed in heavily against the plan. Air Marshal Sir Sholto Douglas recorded on 2 May that he was opposed to keeping a garrison on Alderney long-term. The enemy could mount

[1] AIR 8/868.

heavy attacks against it since they had two large aerodromes less than 20 miles away, whereas the nearest fighter aerodrome in England was 70 miles away. It was just conceivable that the assault plan would succeed, but there would be heavy losses of fighters and bombers. Aircrew losses might run into three figures. This might be justified to achieve something of great value, but there was no prospect of such a gain. The loss of 20–30 bombers and as many fighters was a very high price to pay for an experiment. Fighter Command should support raids where they had the advantage over the enemy, but the opposite would be the case in 'Blazing'.

On 3 May the commander of the new Airborne Division, Major-General F. A. M. Browning, added to the chorus of objection. It was his considered opinion that the use of paratroops proposed in 'Blazing' entailed risks which simply were not worth while. It would be too dark to use support aircraft, but light enough for the anti-aircraft defences. There would inevitably be heavy casualties. The dropping aircraft would be easy targets for enemy fighters, especially on the return journey. This would have a bad psychological effect on a growing but largely untried formation in one of its first engagements. Moreover, if there were heavy casualties, public opinion would decide that the painful lessons of Crete had not been learned.[1]

These powerful broadsides were not enough to sink Mountbatten without trace. He put a modified version of his proposals to the Chiefs of Staff Committee on 5 May in the hope that opposition might be withdrawn. Alderney would be taken by a smaller force – 3,000 men, none of them paratroops – which would withdraw within 24 hours. He said that he was still firmly of the opinion that the original plan (i.e. to capture and hold Alderney) was the correct one, in that it offered the prospect of results commensurate with the forces employed.

The Committee rejected even the modified version, partly because the midsummer nights were too short; but they agreed to recommend that 'Blazing' should be considered later in the year. In Sir Alan Brooke's view the essential weakness was that coastal defences could not be neutralized by night bombing, particularly when they were well sited and the ground was undulating. Other methods would have to be evolved to break down the defences if 'Blazing' was to be looked at again. The Prime Minister was warned that the Chiefs of Staff did not consider the game worth the candle. At a meeting with them and the Chief of Combined Operations on 11 May he decided that there could

[1] DEFE 2/137.

be no question of going ahead with the operation because of the losses which Bomber Command would suffer; but he agreed that it should be reconsidered later.

Mountbatten accepted defeat, and was given approval for Operation 'Lancing', a series of raids in the Boulogne–Le Touquet area, in which the troops training for 'Blazing' would be employed.[1]

'Blazing' was duly resurrected in the summer and rechristened 'Aimwell'. The preliminary studies show much of the optimism which characterized the earlier plan; and they repeat the promised benefits – cutting the convoy route, providing sites for a radar station and an emergency landing ground, and affording 'a stimulus to the morale of this country'. The possibility that it would fail, with consequent stimulus to the morale of the enemy, was properly left out of the balance sheet.

Alderney was again the chosen target because it was nearest to England, could be taken by a relatively small force, and had been evacuated by the inhabitants. Mountbatten acknowledged that it was not for him to appraise the chances of holding the Island after it had been captured, but nevertheless did so, and expressed the view that it would not seem to involve any considerable manning or supply difficulties. He recognized, however, that the assault would not be plain sailing. The enemy could operate 84 fighters from the two aerodromes at Cherbourg, and 24 from each of Jersey and Guernsey, which meant that bombing must be carried out in the dark. Only 1,600 men could be landed at once on the four chosen beaches, so that two waves would be needed; and there were only four days in every fourteen when the tides were suitable. Nevertheless, the Chief of Combined Operations concluded that 'Aimwell' had every chance of success; but it followed 'Blazing' into limbo.[2]

Three other operations devised by Mountbatten met the same fate. 'Concertina', 'Coverlet', and 'Condor' were intended to capture one or more of the Channel Islands, and were collectively known as 'Constellation'.[3] It was suggested that the capture of Alderney was a prerequisite to a landing on the north-west beaches of the Cherbourg peninsula; the capture of Guernsey was highly desirable; and the capture of Jersey was desirable, but by no means essential – and in any event impossible without the prior possession of Guernsey. Even if only two of the Islands were taken the Germans would guess that the

[1] PREM 3/87; CAB 79/21, 79/56; AIR 8/868.   [2] DEFE 2/157; 2/106.
[3] DEFE 2/137.

Allies intended to re-enter France through the Cherbourg peninsula. Island bases would strengthen the Royal Navy's hand in the campaign against the U-boats – a point not made when demilitarization was under consideration. It was concluded that an assault on some of the Channel Islands should take place as a diversionary measure in relation to the major operations pending in the Mediterranean theatre; and that it should be followed by a large-scale deceptive action against the mainland of France to prolong the air battle and increase the diversionary effect.[1] The Chief of Combined Operations was satisfied that at least one of the elements of 'Constellation' should go ahead.

'Concertina' – the assault on Alderney – was the favourite; but the conditions needed to ensure success were difficult. 48 hours of good weather, with no more than a low swell and a cloud ceiling of 8,000 feet, were essential. Longy and Saline Bays had the best beaches for landing infantry and motorized transport; but there could be landings also in Telegraph Bay and Hannaine Bay. The Island could be assaulted by sea, and with airborne troops, after a normal preparation; or airborne troops could be landed after an abnormally heavy aerial bombardment; or there could be an assault from the sea, also after an abnormally heavy bombardment from the air. The first would not succeed because of the very strong defences; the second was not feasible because the dust and the wreckage caused by the bombing would produce too many casualties among the airborne troops. Only the third alternative was left.

The plans show how massive the assault would have been. The whole of Alderney was to be so heavily bombed that the attack from the sea would meet little opposition. There were to be three aiming points. One, dead centre of the long axis of the Island; the second, a mile to the east of that point; and the third, a mile to the west. 1,500 medium and heavy bomber sorties spread over three nights would carry a total of 18,180 bombs weighing 4,600 tons. Professor Zuckerman estimated that 14,180 bombs (3,650 tons) would reach their mark. It was admitted that if an Allied garrison was established on Alderney it would be difficult to maintain it, but this liability was not evaluated. It was also admitted that the Germans would be encouraged to strengthen the defences of the Cherbourg peninsula, which might not be in the Allies' long-term interest.

'Condor', perhaps the most terrifying operation against the Channel Islands conceived while Mountbatten was Chief of Combined Operations, could have been a second Dieppe. It was to begin with aerial bombardment of the east and west coasts of Jersey, followed by paratroop and infantry landings, and by scramble landings by commandos in the south-west. The paratroops were to drop on the race-course, on the airfield, and at St. Peter's Mill from 192 aircraft. On the second day artillery would land and more infantry would extend the eastern beachhead to the high ground overlooking Grouville Bay. The troops on the west coast would link up with the commandos who had landed at Noirmont Point in the south-west.

Next day tanks would be landed on the east coast, the western beachhead extended to the high ground north of St. Aubin's Bay, and La Moye peninsula 'pinched out'. The climax, at least on paper, came on the fourth day, with a three-pronged attack on St. Helier. Infantry would close in from the east and west – the beachheads having been consolidated – and tanks would descend from the north. The fifth day was set aside for mopping up and the final reduction of the Island. 33 fighter squadrons and 39 bomber squadrons would be used. The plan gives no estimate of the invaders' losses, nor of civilian casualties, nor of destruction of property in St. Helier, where the final battle was programmed to take place.

Mountbatten contended that the capture of one of the Channel Islands was strategically desirable in relation to 'Husky' – the invasion of Sicily – but the Chiefs of Staff found his arguments very thin. At best the proposed operation would cause a minor redistribution of German forces. They agreed with him that it would lead to air battles, but they would be fought under unfavourable conditions. He had failed to substantiate his claim that the Allies would be unable to land on the north-west beaches of the Cherbourg peninsula unless they held Alderney. On the other hand, there were many serious disadvantages. It would take a great effort to hold the Island once it was won. Fighters could not use it, and it was even doubtful if the airstrip could be used for emergency landings. Alderney would be exposed to constant bombing from nearby enemy air bases and would also be a target for long-range gunfire. In spite of the single-minded enthusiasm of the Chief of Combined Operations, 'Concertina', 'Coverlet', and 'Condor' never got beyond the planning stage; but had the Islanders known even of the plans they would have had many sleepless nights.

Minor raids planned but never carried out were 'Cats-whiskers', against Brecqhou; 'Pussyfoot', against Herm; and 'Bunbury', to kill or capture the garrison of Sark – all in the early months of 1943. 'Cats-whiskers' was timed to follow 'Pussyfoot', but the weather was unsuitable for the latter and both were called off.[1]

At least the German army shared Mountbatten's belief that the Islands could be recaptured. In June 1942 AOK 7[2], commenting on a suggestion by the navy that the British dare not attack the west coast of France, agreed that until that date an enemy fleet could not survive in the Race of Alderney. Their bases were a hundred miles away, and a large naval force would inevitably be spotted, especially in the short summer nights. Large ships could not reach the beaches. Treacherous currents made it difficult for small boats to land troops. The batteries on Alderney controlled the Race, at least when visibility was good; the four huge guns of the 'Mirus' battery on Guernsey would play their part; and the guns on Jersey were effective to within five miles of the French coast.

The position, however, had recently become much less certain. The German naval forces in the Islands could not begin to match the Royal Navy. British air superiority was undoubted, and could neutralize the German coastal guns, especially on Alderney. The enemy now had swift, powerfully-armed landing craft which could make light of the currents, and could put an infantry division ashore on a wide front. There was no doubt that before long they would be able to recapture all the Islands, and it was conceivable that this would be done as part of a general move against the west coast of France.[3]

The operations which did take place in 1942 and 1943 were training exercises or reconnaissances rather than serious attempts against the Islands. Most were so small that they were unlikely to force the Germans into reprisals against the Islanders.

Operation 'Dryad' was directed against the Casquets lighthouse six miles to the west of Alderney, which had a seven-man crew to maintain the light and to watch Allied shipping and air movements. There was no

---

[1] DEFE 2/68, 2/142, 2/264; AIR 9/257. All available background information about the Islands was assembled in November 1942 under the codenames 'Concubine I' (Jersey) and 'Concubine II' (Guernsey). DEFE 2/158. It was part of the 'Constellation' plan that those Islanders who survived the Allied assault should ideally be evacuated: 'It is quite clear that the civilians will have to be evacuated, or they will have to accept for a period immediately following our operations a standard of living very little better than that which they at present enjoy under German rule.' It is difficult to see how an Allied garrison could have dispensed with the civilian support which the Germans found essential. AIR 9/257.

[2] *Armeeoberkommando* 7.   [3] T 314 1604/580–2.

question of permanently holding the rock on which the lighthouse stood – the German guns on Alderney made it untenable. The attack had no more than a nuisance or training value.

A party of ten officers and two men of the Small Scale Raiding Force under Major G. H. March-Phillips approached the Casquets from the north at 11.45 p.m. on 2 September 1942, and landed from dinghies at 1.25 a.m. on the 3rd. They climbed the face of the cliff, believing that the usual landing place might be mined, which in fact it was not, since the Germans thought that the cliff was all the protection needed.[1] The heaving of the sea in the chasms round the base of the rock effectively drowned the noise of the climbers, who had to cut through barbed wire near the top. They surprised two men, supposedly on watch, and five others in bed. The prisoners were escorted to the dinghies while the radio equipment and spares were destroyed. The party, which included the Dane, Anders Lassen, VC, MC and two bars, left at 2 a.m. taking the code books and diaries.[2]

The raid was accidentally well-timed. A routine signal had been transmitted at 1.20 a.m. only five minutes before the raiders landed, so that it was some time before Alderney realized that anything untoward had happened. Eventually, because of the continued silence, a boat was sent to investigate. It was reported that the entire crew had disappeared, that the transmitter was smashed, and that confidential papers had disappeared. The light, however, had not been damaged. The raid must have been carried out by men familiar with the dangerous tides. A new crew, eight men this time, occupied the rock on 5 September.[3]

When Hitler was told about the incident he asked for details of the defences and of the attack.[4] He suggested that the light should be abandoned, and its value was therefore hastily reassessed. Predictably the verdict agreed with the Führer's view. It was difficult to keep the post supplied. All drinking water had to be brought in, and in winter the rock might be isolated for weeks on end. Further, the lighthouse could not be adequately protected from aerial attack. The crew must be withdrawn.[5]

This was translated into a Führer order issued on 5 September, the day on which the replacement crew reached the Casquets. The rock was not to be reoccupied unless its defence was absolutely secure. *Admiral Frankreich*, however, simply reported that the appropriate measures had been taken. The navy could not do without the Casquets, which was an admirable observation post.[6] Hitler accepted this, with the rider that

[1] MOD 584/213, 216.   [2] DEFE 2/109.   [3] MOD 506/10.
[4] MOD 584/214.   [5] MOD 584/209.   [6] Ibid.

the post must be held as strongly as possible.[1] Alarmed perhaps by the ease with which the small garrison had been spirited away, he ordered a study of the lighthouse defences generally.[2] This led to recommendations that they should be protected with mines and barbed wire, that permanent ladders should be removed, and special alarm systems installed. Von Rundstedt had argued that the navy was responsible for the Casquets, whereas *Admiral Frankreich* claimed that it was 319 Infantry Division. It was finally decided that no commander was to blame for the failure to beat off the raid. There would, however, have been serious trouble if the Casquets had been technically a strong point, and not just an observation post.[3] Lighthouses used for purely shipping purposes were now to be the responsibility of the navy.[4]

Hitler may have had the Casquets in mind when, on 29 September, he made a three-hour speech to a conference including Göring, Speer, von Rundstedt, and others about the possibility that the Atlantic Wall might be broken. He said: 'Above all, I am grateful to the English for proving me right by their various landing attempts. It shows up those who think I am always seeing phantoms, who say "Well, when are the English coming? There is absolutely nothing happening on the coast – we swim every day, and we haven't seen a single Englishman!" '[5]

Operation 'Basalt', a small-scale raid on Sark, had unexpected consequences. The raiding party comprised twelve officers and men under Major J. G. Appleyard and again included the Dane, Anders Lassen. They landed by dinghy from a motor torpedo boat anchored close inshore between Dixcart Bay and Derrible Bay at 11.30 p.m. on 3 October 1942, and, helped by a good moon, climbed up the Hog's Back to the plateau. They were told by a widow that Germans were billeted in the Dixcart Hotel. They also learned that the garrison (a reinforced company) were poor physical specimens, that they were polite and respectful, and that the Islanders regretted that the King had not mentioned them in his last Christmas broadcast. More important, they were given a newspaper with an account of the recent deportations. They went on to the Hotel, where, according to their report, which proved to be inaccurate, they encountered five Germans, killed four and captured one. They re-embarked at 3.45 a.m. with their prisoner, having met no opposition.[6]

The German inquest revealed surprising slackness. The harbour guard had reported hearing a motor boat, but the duty officer did nothing

[1] MOD 96/35.   [2] MOD 506/85.   [3] MOD 506/22; 38/97, 102.
[4] MOD 584/209; 506/22.   [5] T 78 317/6271569.
[6] ADM 199/846; DEFE 2/109, 241; MOD 96/33.

about it, nor did he inform the *Inselkommandant*. The last, by leaving men in the Hotel, had neglected a recent order that all personnel must be billeted in strong points. Both he and the duty officer were court-martialled. Von Rundstedt pointed out angrily that the raid had succeeded only because orders had been disobeyed.[1]

Footprints showed that the party had landed at Point Château on the south-east coast where there was no defence post because of the steep cliffs and a minefield – through which the enemy had found a path. It was deduced that sixteen men had been involved, and that they had known the tides and terrain, otherwise they could never have landed there. An officer and four men of a pioneer unit working on the harbour defences had been overpowered as they slept, bound, and led away. They tried to escape outside their quarters, when the officer was shot and stabbed to death; two privates were wounded, but escaped – one died later; the third got away unharmed; and the fourth was presumed to have been taken to England. It was suggested that the raid had been planned with the use of carrier pigeons, which the R.A.F. had dropped in the Island.[2] The man who got away – Obergefreiter Klotz – was presented with a watch in February 1944 in recognition of his bravery in escaping after he had been 'cold-bloodedly tied up by the English'.[3]

The incident was serious enough to be reported to OKW. General Warlimont summarized the earlier findings. He endorsed the estimate of sixteen raiders and also the improbable suggestion that the enemy were in contact with agents on Sark by means of carrier pigeons. It followed that nowhere outside the strong points was safe, and it was essential that every man should be quartered inside. Defences must be strengthened, and there must be increased vigilance all round.[4]

Hitler read this summary and immediately spotted that the prisoners' hands had been tied. He linked this to the tying of some German prisoners' hands during the Dieppe raid; and on 8 October ordered the shackling of nearly 1,400 Allied prisoners captured at Dieppe. This impelled the British to put out their version of the Sark raid. They at first denied tying hands. The raid had revealed large-scale deportations from the Channel Islands to forced-labour camps in Germany – which had been confirmed by the prisoner taken on Sark. To underline this the Ministry of Information issued photographs of the German orders.[5] If the Allied prisoners were not freed an equal number of Germans would

[1] T 314 1603/443, 445, 456, 593.   [2] MOD 586/521–2.
[3] NG 01/33.   [4] MOD 96/33.   [5] GFM 1808/411723–36.

be shackled. The Germans replied that they would then shackle three times as many British prisoners.

On 10 October the Canadian government put in chains German prisoners held in Canada to the same number as the Allied prisoners chained by the Germans. Then the British authorities, with scrupulous regard for the truth, admitted the issue of an unauthorized order at Dieppe to tie the hands of prisoners to prevent them from destroying papers. The order had been countermanded, and in fact none of the Dieppe prisoners had had their hands tied. In Sark the prisoners had been bound merely so that their arms would be linked with those of their captors. When they escaped they had to be shot to prevent them from raising the alarm. The Geneva Convention said nothing about tying prisoners, but merely prescribed humane treatment. The Convention did forbid reprisals, however, and the German government was clearly guilty.[1]

This was an astonishing outcome for a small raid, but there was more to follow. 'Basalt' was also partly responsible for Hitler's notorious 'commando order' of 18 October: 'In future, all terror and sabotage troops of the British and their accomplices, who do not act like soldiers but rather like bandits, will be treated as such by the German troops and will be ruthlessly eliminated in battle, wherever they appear.' This led to the murder of many men.

Thirdly, the raid led to the second wave of deportations from the Channel Islands. It was first proposed to evacuate the whole of Sark, since the Germans still believed that there were British agents on the Island; but this plan was halted when 'a helpless and somewhat simple-minded woman' (the widow who had directed the raiders to the Dixcart Hotel) appeared at the Island headquarters and volunteered the information that she had been awakened by the commandos and had given them a map. When the Germans examined her – and gave her a rough time – they promised that she would not be deported to Germany for more detailed questioning.

Von Rundstedt decided on the strength of her evidence that there had been no communication between Sark and England, and that the raiders had relied only on what the woman told them. He requested a decision from OKH as to whether she should be taken to Germany, or whether the word of a German officer must be kept in all circumstances.[2] He also

---

[1] GFM 1808/411723–36. See also M. R. D. Foot, *SOE in France* (London, 1968), pp. 186–7.

[2] T 77 788/5517261, 263.

asked if total evacuation of Sark was still considered necessary. If so, was it feasible in view of the extent to which the troops relied on the civilian population?[1] This echoed Jodl's comment that without the Islanders the garrison would have a desert on their hands.[2]

OKH passed von Rundstedt's telegram to OKW, adding that in a similar case it had been decided that an officer's word must be kept at all costs. It was arguable that the whole population of Sark should be evacuated on military grounds, and if this happened the woman could be taken to Germany without damage to German honour.[3] In reply, OKW pointed out that the earlier deportations had not eliminated all the unreliable elements in the Islands – this was hardly surprising since the people removed were guilty of being United Kingdom-born rather than potential saboteurs. A new check was ordered with a view to further deportations, in which the simple-minded woman would happen to find herself.[4]

The stage was now set for the second wave of deportations.[5] Unlike the first, they were a straightforward security measure, sparked off by a widow who herself posed no security threat. So that she might be removed from Sark without appearing to be punished for her accidental part in 'Basalt', several hundred others had to go. No price was too high for the honour of a German officer.

The widow's action also nipped in the bud a proposal that the women and children who had been deported earlier should return to the Islands. In January 1943 the German Foreign Ministry suggested that they should be sent home because of the difficulty of looking after them in internment camps. They were promptly told by the military authorities that there could now be no question of sending anyone back 'because the behaviour of a woman in one of the Channel Islands has made necessary an extension of the evacuation on military grounds'.[6]

There was another raid on Sark about a year later – Operation 'Hardtack 7'. The 'Hardtacks' were a series of small-scale raids against the coast of France and the Channel Islands to take prisoners and gather intelligence in the winter of 1943/4. The first attempt at 'Hardtack 7' was on the night of 25/26 December, when five men led by Lieutenant A. J. McGonigal tried to climb the cliffs at Derrible Bay. The same party tried again two nights later. This time they reached the

[1] T 77 778/5517261, 263.   [2] See above p. 213.
[3] T 77 788/5517260.   [4] T 77 788/5517257; MOD 38/351.
[5] See Chapter 10.   [6] T 77 788/5517265.

top of the Hog's Back and went north through the gorse, which provided excellent cover. They did not know it, but they were walking through a minefield, and eventually triggered off two mines. They retraced their steps hoping that they had only just entered the field, when mines exploded all around. Four of the five were wounded and they decided to abandon the operation. As they made their way back more mines went off. Two of the raiders – both French – were killed, and their bodies were left behind. For two hours after the explosion of the mines the survivors saw flares in various parts of the Island, presumably to help search parties.

The Germans referred in their communiqué to the second attempt within three days to land commandos on Sark. Since they had made no attempt to oppose the first landing they presumably learned about it from traces left. Although the *Inselkommandant* correctly reported to his superiors that two Frenchmen in British uniforms had been killed, the communiqué said that the body of one British soldier had been left behind. The raid had failed because of the minefields defending the Island.[1]

'Hardtack 28' was aimed at Jersey to coincide with 'Hardtack 7', and it had the same objectives. Ten men, four of them French, were taken to Jersey on the night of 25/26 December by motor torpedo boat. The party, led by Captain P. A. Ayton, scrambled ashore at 10.45 p.m. at Petit Port on the north-east coast close to a minefield with warning notices in German and English. They moved inland to Egypt Farm, passing a well-camouflaged observation post, which they tried unsuccessfully to enter. They then followed a road, hoping to meet a German patrol. They came to a farmhouse where a woman who answered their knocking refused to tell them where they could find some Germans, and directed them to another farmhouse. There they found two brothers, who were at first too terrified to speak but were eventually prevailed upon to give some information. There was no resistance movement, and the people were not really hostile to the enemy. Egypt Farm had been sacked by the Germans because it was, paradoxically, owned by a Jew. The brothers gave their unwelcome guests a glass of milk and sent them on their way.

They reached Les Platons, where there was a strong point, also unmanned; and, without having seen a German soldier, they made their way back to Petit Port. There Ayton trod on a mine. His companions

[1] DEFE 2/241; 345.

got him back to the boat, but he was severely injured and died in hospital.[1]

'Hardtack 22' was a small-scale raid planned by No. 10 Commando against Herm in January 1944. Responsibility for the proposed raid was transferred to No. 2 U.S. Ranger Battalion, but the operation was not proceeded with.[2]

The Royal Navy kept a lookout for ships plying between Cherbourg and Alderney, and occasionally mounted special operations against them. Operation 'H.K.' was designed to intercept convoys from Cherbourg and Alderney, which were believed to cross each other off Cap de la Hague, thus presenting a double target. Two destroyers, one of them Polish, left Plymouth at dusk on 3 February 1943. When they saw that the Quesnard light at the north-east end of Alderney and the leading lights of Alderney harbour were lit, they concluded that ships were on the move. They started to patrol in conditions in which ships might be seen at many miles range, for the moon was full and the sky cloudless. When they were five miles off Cap de la Hague the Quesnard and Alderney harbour lights suddenly went out, and the destroyers thought they must have been spotted; but then the Cap de la Hague light came on, presumably because a convoy had now entered its area. A moment later two unescorted 500-ton Dutch coasters were seen.

The destroyers opened fire at 1,000 yards range with 4-inch shells, and having hit both ships closed in to finish them off with depth charges. As they withdrew, the shore batteries awoke to the fact that an action was taking place under their noses, and fired a few rounds at one of the sinking vessels. The commander of the destroyers expressed disappointment that the shipping intercepted was so trivial, but he nevertheless hoped that the action would demoralize German and Quisling shipping, and that a redisposition of escort vessels would be necessary.[3]

The action had a greater effect than the commander could have imagined. It gave rise to a major row and a reorganization of transport between the mainland and the Islands. The German reports show that the vessels lost were the *Hermann* and the *Schleswig-Holstein*. It was presumed that they had been attacked by destroyers, but it was uncertain whether they had been sunk or captured. (The batteries on Cap de la Hague could have thrown light on this.) They had no escorts because

[1] NG Ic; T 314 1604/1296; DEFE 2/345.   [2] DEFE 2/254; 345.
[3] ADM 199/448. Operation 'Cloak', an earlier sweep in the vicinity of Alderney in March 1942, did not meet any enemy shipping.

I

of an administrative muddle for which the escort services were not to blame. To make matters worse there had been many men on board going on leave – 42 soldiers, 43 anti-aircraft gunners, and 43 OT workers (German, Flemish, and French)[1] who had no right to be there. They had been ordered off at Alderney but had contrived to get on board again, no doubt anxious to make the most of their leave passes.[2] The Germans suspected that two minesweepers might have been sunk in the same action.[3]

In the following weeks *Admiral Frankreich* and the *Befehlshaber der Sicherung West* (Flag Officer, Sea Defences, West) (responsible for all escort services round France) set about improving the security arrangements for shipping. They considered court-martialling those responsible for sending off the coasters without escort, but decided against it. A more experienced *Hafenkommandant* was posted to Alderney, the previous *Kommandant* having gone down with one of the coasters.[4] Radio communications and escort services must be improved – the slow HS boats should no longer be used.

Since there was no hope of bringing more escort vessels into service, because of pressures elsewhere, and since traffic between the mainland and the Islands was increasing, the most efficient use must be made of the available craft. Ships were needed which could travel to Jersey and Guernsey one night, and return the next; and which could make the round trip from Cherbourg to Alderney in a single night. It would help if Longy Bay on the south-west coast of Alderney could be used, as it would make the route to Cherbourg safer. There was a flat, sheltered beach there, which needed only a landing stage. Ships for Jersey and Guernsey should be escorted only as far as Jersey, to reduce the number of escorts needed. Cargo boats could sail without escort, provided that two went in company and had anti-aircraft guns.

On the assumption that Wehrmacht personnel and the OT workers went on leave twice a year, it was estimated that 500 people would have to be carried each way every week. Recent experience suggested that there should be no difficulty about this. In January, 4,253 men had been carried to the mainland in a period of 19 days; and on 17 February 1,800 were taken to the Islands in a single transport.[5]

The Royal Navy had its failures, however, including Operation 'Tunnel'. On the night of 23/24 October 1943 six destroyers led by the

[1] MOD 752/89.
[2] MOD 752/69.
[3] MOD 752/50.
[4] Ibid.
[5] MOD 752/41, 50, 97, 104.

light cruiser H.M.S. *Charybdis* carried out a sweep west of the Channel Islands beyond the range of the coastal batteries there, hoping to surprise a German merchant ship bound from Brest for the English Channel. In the event it was the British force that was surprised. It ran into the path of the escorting E-boats, which had been warned of its presence by shore radar stations. The *Charybdis* spotted the E-boats on her radar at a range of 9,000 yards, but before she could open fire was struck by two torpedoes and sank. Out of a complement of 569, 30 officers and 432 ratings were lost. The destroyer H.M.S. *Limbourne* was disabled by a torpedo and had to be sunk later. One officer and 41 ratings lost their lives.

The operation was severely criticized in the subsequent enquiry. 'A mixed force with no collective training, no knowledge of what enemy forces were at sea, and with deliberately-accepted disadvantages of light, was about to encounter a highly-trained striking force which almost certainly knew the numbers, position, course and speed, and probably had a good idea of the composition of, our own force.' Further, '*Charybdis* was more of a handicap than an asset in a night action in narrow waters', and the whole force was 'ill-assorted, unwieldy, and untrained'.[1]

Forty-one bodies were washed up on the Islands' beaches – 21 in Guernsey, 29 in Jersey, and one in Sark – and over 100 in France.

The Germans decided that they should be buried with full military honours, and as the people of the island [Guernsey] heard this they decided spontaneously that here was their chance to show their loyalty to Britain and their respect for the men who had died . . . So it was that on a grey, November afternoon in 1943 the people of Guernsey, five thousand of them, made their way to the Foulon Cemetery . . . The Germans were completely taken by surprise. Only a small number of their officers and a firing-party were present, and they were almost lost in this great mass of passive demonstrators who were determined that they should be left in no doubt where our sympathies and true feelings lay.[2]

The Germans did what they could to play down the funerals in Jersey, but there too the opportunity was taken by the Islanders to make it plain that more than three years of occupation had not diminished their loyalty to Britain.[3] There is still an annual commemoration service in Guernsey for those who lost their lives, and 'Charybdis Day' has become a permanent link between the Island and the Royal Navy.

The efforts of the navy to wear down the shipping services were

[1] ADM 199/541, 1038, pt. 1.   [2] Falla, p. 89.   [3] Sinel, p. 161.

supplemented by the R.A.F. In a typical engagement on 18 July 1942 two HS boats and two VP boats were attacked by Spitfires. All four were badly damaged, and of the crews 9 were killed, one missing (having jumped overboard) and 33 wounded. A week later ships of the Royal Navy attacked another two VP boats, one of which was beached at Cap de la Hague; the other escaped to Cherbourg.[1] These attacks, coupled with the increased volume of shipping needed to carry men and materials for the fortifications, imposed an enormous strain on the escort services. In August *Marinegruppe West* asked Ob. West to keep traffic to the absolute minimum, a clear sign that the Wehrmacht was no longer in command of events.[2] There was a further deterioration in 1943. In January lack of shipping made it difficult for men to take leave when it was due. More day sailings were needed, but *Luftflotte* 3 could no longer provide the fighters to drive off Allied air attacks.[3] Shortly afterwards losses from Allied air attacks became so heavy that there was a complete ban on the movement of ships by day – yet another sign that the might of the Wehrmacht was on the wane.[4]

'Branford' and 'Huckaback' were a pair of operations which provide further evidence of Mountbatten's unshakeable belief that sooner or later a major assault must be mounted against one or other of the Channel Islands. The purpose of the former was to determine whether the Island of Burhou, about half a mile to the north-west of Alderney, was occupied, and whether it would be possible to set up a battery there to support a later assault on Alderney. The latter was to assess the suitability of Herm for a battery to support an assault on Guernsey, to take prisoners, and to obtain information from any Islanders who were encountered.

'Branford' was carried out on the night of 7/8 September 1942 by eleven men of the Small Scale Raiding Force (including five officers) under Major March-Phillips who were taken safely by motor torpedo boat past the islet of Ortac, the Danger and Dasher rocks and the Burhou reef. Eight of the party paddled 600 yards to the Island, which proved to be unoccupied, and spent an hour there. There were signs that the guns of Alderney had been using it for target practice. The Casquets light was in action away to the west – three white flashes every 12 seconds – and they also saw the call-up signal from the Casquets to Alderney, a series of four Morse 'As'. No lights were seen on Alderney.

It was concluded that it would be possible to land pack artillery

[1] NG Ia/1.   [2] MOD 752/238.   [3] MOD 506/530.   [4] MOD 506/835.

without difficulty, but not wheeled or tracked guns; the higher the tide the easier the operation would be. Mountbatten himself noted that the raid had been successful and had provided useful information.[1]

'Huckaback', 'Branford's' twin, was originally planned as a simultaneous raid on Herm, Jethou, and Brecqhou, to take prisoners and gain information about the situation in the Channel Islands generally. It was set for the night of 9/10 February 1943 and was to be carried out by a party 42 strong chosen from the Small Scale Raiding Force and No. 4 Commando, but was cancelled because of bad weather.

It was reinstated, still as 'Huckaback', but with Herm as the sole objective on the night of 27/28 February. Ten men of the Small Scale Raiding Force under Captain P. A. Porteous, VC, landed 200 yards to the north-west of Selle Rocque on a shingle beach and made three unsuccessful attempts to climb the steep, soft-clay cliff that confronted them. Then the leader climbed up the bed of a small stream, taking a rope with him, on which the rest of the party pulled themselves up. Belvoir House was broken into and found to be abandoned. They went on to the Old Tower of Herm and searched the Château and surrounding buildings without finding any sign of life. Their report concludes that the reconnaissance was successfully accomplished but that no Germans (who were supposed to be billeted near the harbour) were found, nor were any Islanders encountered.[2]

By far the most interesting and potentially significant operation against the Germans in the Channel Islands was an exercise in psychological warfare planned and executed in the autumn of 1944, when the Allies felt that the privation which the troops were supposed to be suffering, coupled with the truth about the military situation, might bring them to the brink of surrender. It was regarded as part of the 'Nestegg' liberation operation.

The three main Islands were to be saturated with propaganda from the series of *Nachrichten für die Truppe* which was being dropped to the German forces in Europe generally. This was to be scattered from 'bombs, special, air burst, leaflet' and would make it clear that there was no point in seeking to hold out any longer.

The leaflets were to be dropped in the proportion three Guernsey, two Jersey, and one Alderney to conform roughly with the estimated size of the individual garrisons. Then, when the whole garrison accepted that their number was up, two things were to happen. A captured

German general was to telephone to von Schmettow (using the Channel Islands–Pirou cable, the French end of which was now in Allied hands) to arrange a parley. If all went well the same general would be taken to meet the *Befehlshaber* at sea off Guernsey; there the finishing touches would be put to the operation. The captured general, who had already seen the writing on the wall, would, the psychological warfare experts hoped, contrive to push the commander-in-chief over the brink. The enterprise had the full backing of Supreme Headquarters, Allied Expeditionary Force, but it was accepted that the chances of success were slim. It was unlikely that the enemy would surrender 'without an excuse compatible with military honour', which really meant that they must be confronted with overwhelming force rather than a shower of leaflets telling them that the game was up.[1]

The plan, however, did have some teeth. If von Schmettow agreed to surrender on the telephone, the next step would have to be worked out in the light of the conversation; but if he turned out to be a 'last cartridge' man, the newsletters would be replaced by leaflets demanding surrender, backed up by bombing raids. When SHAEF approved the proposals generally three points were made: the surrender must be unconditional; if bombing became necessary it should be used only against Alderney; and there was to be no promise of an early return to Germany for the garrison, which the psychological experts had wanted to include in the plan.

The first leaflet raid was carried out on the night of 30/31 August, the targets being Fort Richmond in Guernsey, St. Ouen's Manor in Jersey, and St. Anne in Alderney, where troops were presumed to be concentrated. In Jersey the indefatigable Sinel faithfully logged the flights. His entry for 31 August notes that: 'Leaflets in German were dropped during the night by an allied plane. These were not especially for the Channel Islands, but were some of those meant for Germans everywhere. Sailors were busy early picking them up, but not before many had been found by the troops and local residents, the latter keeping them for souvenirs.'[2] There were more raids on the next twelve nights (except for the night of 4/5 September when the weather was unsuitable) the targets being varied, but always places where troops were known to be: St. Peter Port, Les Effards, Hotel Grandes Rocques, Fort Richmond, Fort Doyle, and Fort Le Marchant in Guernsey; St. Helier, St Ouen's Manor, Fort Henry, Fort William, and Elizabeth Castle in Jersey; and St. Anne in Alderney. In the whole of

[1] AIR 37/258; WO 106/2989; SHAEF 1232/1.   [2] Sinel, pp. 213–14.

the operation 218 'bombs' were dropped, scattering tens of thousands of leaflets.

On 1 September it was decided that the time was ripe to get in touch with von Schmettow. At 11 p.m. an aircraft dropped by parachute two copies of a letter on SHAEF notepaper addressed to him; by the light of flares the pilot saw both copies land. The letter asked von Schmettow to arrange for a telephone to be connected to the Channel Islands end of the cable, and wait for an important message. Next day Major Alan Chambers, a Canadian, escorted the German general ('John Black', for the purposes of the operation) to France, where from 12 to 15 September they awaited a call from Guernsey – in vain.

The operation, or at least that part of it which could be followed from the Islands, is well documented in the diary of Mr. L. A. Guillemette, who was at the time Secretary to the President of the Controlling Committee in Guernsey. He wrote: 'Last Tuesday night although an allied plane flew low over the Island no newspapers were delivered. The plane dropped flares, however, an unusual occurrence and in the light shed by them many people saw parachutes falling.' Guillemette, whose office brought him into close contact with the *Feldkommandantur*, was told by them next day that a secret letter, the seals of which had been broken, had been found that morning in the letterbox at the *Befehlshaber*'s headquarters. He was asked if it was a hoax. He truthfully said he knew nothing about the matter. Later, however, he located the man who had picked up the cylinder containing the letter, and who (having a smattering of German) had read it. It contained instructions to the *Befehlshaber* 'to get into telephonic communication with France at a certain date and time. The telephone line to be used was indicated'. It was later established that the second copy of the letter had been found by a German and that it had also been delivered to the *Befehlshaber*.

In France, after waiting for four days, Chambers had reluctantly to conclude that the fish had not taken the fly. Indeed, if there was any doubt on this point, it was dispelled by a radio announcement from Berlin that 'the Channel Islands had refused several demands for surrender and were still holding out'. This was a clear indication that all was not going according to plan. Although it had been intended to arrange a meeting with von Schmettow only if it seemed worthwhile after talking to him on the telephone (and it now looked as if he *was* a 'last cartridge' man and that there would have to be recourse to bombing) it was nevertheless decided to send a second letter, this time proposing a parley. It was dropped by parachute on the night of 21/22 September and said that it was desired to enter into communication with him. A representative of SHAEF would come to a point 4½ miles south of St. Martin's Point near St. Peter Port with two companions in an unarmed boat flying a white flag – in accordance with the Hague Convention. Von Schmettow – not his envoy as had been originally envisaged – was asked to rendezvous there. He too must come in an unarmed boat with a white flag.[1]

Guillemette records on 22 September that 'last night allied planes dropped flares over the south of the Island and in their light many people saw small parachutes descending'. He again got in touch with the German authorities and was told that the parachutes had dropped in the sea. This was confirmed by Islanders who had been watching.

Meanwhile Chambers and the German general were waiting to make the trip to Guernsey. They had been given an American civilian launch as it was considered inappropriate to use a naval vessel. In spite of the fact that they had been warned that the second letter had probably landed in the sea, they left Cap Carteret at 10.45 a.m. on 22 September. They took a risk by running along the north coast of Jersey, for the Germans there had no idea what they were up to. Visibility was poor and their white flag might not have been seen.

They reached the rendezvous two hours later and, as there was no German boat in sight, the launch moved in slowly towards the shore. A white Very light was fired, which they took to be an invitation to approach. The dinghy's motor would not start so Chambers decided to row; he made contact with a German patrol boat at 2 p.m. He explained that he had orders to get in touch with the *Befehlshaber*, and his authority was transmitted by signal lamp. The shore asked, 'Specifically what matter does Major Chambers want to discuss?' and were told 'the military situation'. Half an hour later came the message: 'Lieutenant General von Schmettow is fully informed as to the military situation and therefore declines any discussion.' Chambers asked the lieutenant in command if the full import of this reply was understood, to which he answered 'yes'. An army officer who heard the exchange was visibly shaken, thinking perhaps that there would now be a full-scale assault. The Major returned to the launch and they made for Cherbourg. They were fired on by a coastal battery on Alderney and were lucky to get off with one minor casualty.

This was the end of the operation. The idea that surrender leaflets and

[1] WO 106/2989.

bombs should be dropped was not pursued. In the post-mortem it was concluded that either von Schmettow had been ordered not to treat with the Allies, or that the messages had been intercepted by the SS, who had kept the *Befehlshaber* out of the picture. That he was simply a loyal soldier who was unlikely to surrender except when all was obviously lost does not seem to have occurred to those on the Allied side.

The operation probably had little chance of success even if it had been properly handled. It fell short of perfection in two respects. It was vital to ensure that von Schmettow had received the second letter before the SHAEF representatives went to Guernsey. To drop only two copies was asking for trouble. One night all the thousands of leaflets dropped over Jersey were blown out to sea, and there was every chance that the letter to Schmettow would meet the same fate. If several copies were dropped over a period of a week or so there was a chance that one would get through; but the evidence of the pilot who dropped the letter was that both copies had fallen in the sea. Chambers should never have left Cap Carteret until he had reason to believe that the letter was safely in von Schmettow's hands.

The other weakness was to insist that the general himself should make the rendezvous. The plan assumed that it would be dangerous to allow the captured German general to set foot on German-occupied territory, since he would almost certainly be taken prisoner by his fellow-countrymen. The SHAEF representatives should have realized that the garrison commanders would be equally reluctant to allow the *Befehlshaber* to board an Allied vessel. Had the dialogue been planned to start at a lower level (as was at first envisaged) von Schmettow might have eventually been drawn in. The odds against success were heavy, but the impatience with which Chambers acted doomed the operation to failure. The efforts of the R.A.F. were wasted. More important, the chance of saving the Islanders from six months of untold misery was carelessly thrown away.

The strange confrontation was witnessed by many on the shore. Surprisingly enough, the version which reached Jersey was near the truth, except that it brought Chambers to Guernsey in a destroyer, and it made the German general a member of the Canadian parliament. When those concerned in the R.A.F. asked if the operation had been successful they at first received no reply. A month later they sent a reminder, which prompted the Psychological Warfare Division of SHAEF to say that the missions had been highly successful, in that they had delivered the propaganda material to the chosen targets. The proof was seen in the report of Major Alan Chambers, who had contacted members of the enemy garrison off Jersey (*sic*) and had been thanked for 'the newspapers which were being received regularly by the troops'. The fact that the main objective of the operation had not been achieved was not mentioned, and the commander of the R.A.F. squadron observed for the benefit of his colleagues that the reply must be regarded as a 'strawberry'. That is to say, it was a form of congratulation.[1]

When it became apparent that the Allied invasion of Europe had bypassed the Islands the *Befehlshaber* turned his mind to helping his comrades retreating on the mainland. His first plan was to send a battalion to reinforce St. Malo, but this was rejected by OKW, presumably because it was still felt that in no circumstances should the strength of the Island garrisons be impaired. This disappointed von Schmettow, who was sure that his plan would have succeeded. He had to content himself with sending smaller raiding parties equipped for anti-tank fighting. They acquitted themselves well, especially in the neighbourhood of St. Malo, and as a rule got safely back to the Islands. Ammunition was also sent, mainly to the Cécembre battery, whose resistance was thereby prolonged, but at a heavy cost in losses of ships and men. Many hundreds of wounded Germans were brought back from the mainland to swell the numbers in the Islands.

Just before Christmas 1944 a Naval Assault Troop cadet and four paratroopers who had been captured at Brest escaped from an American prisoner of war camp at Granville. They attached themselves to a working party in the harbour area, passing themselves off as interpreters, and slipped away under cover of darkness to an American landing craft, which they contrived to take out on the evening tide. With only a pocket compass and a sketch map to guide them, they reached Maîtresse Île in the Minquiers group, where the German observation post first fired on them, and then, when their identity was established, directed them to St. Helier.[2]

They reported that the harbour at Granville was in full operation. There were usually about five ships there, most of them discharging coal. A battalion of the United States army was billeted on the hill overlooking the harbour, there was a signal station on the south pier, and a radar station on the coast a short distance to the north. Von Schmettow, no doubt urged on by his dedicated Nazi chief of staff

[1] AIR 37/258; SHAEF 1232/1; WO 106/2989; MOD 508/681-2.
[2] MOD 509/169. 176-7, 227.

Hüffmeier, decided to seize the chance of hitting back at the enemy, and incidentally raising the morale of his men, which was suffering almost as much from lack of action as from lack of food. The plan was to put Granville harbour out of action, to capture a coal ship to help the desperate fuel situation in the Channel Islands, and to destroy the rest of the shipping. It was calculated that all this could be achieved if the port was held for an hour.

The escaped prisoners of war were treated as heroes. They were sent back to Germany at the beginning of 1945, but their triumph was short-lived. Their plane was picked up by a night-fighter and shot down near Bastogne. Hüffmeier announced the fact to all units of the navy under his command, for the plane had also carried Kapitän Fritz Breithaupt 'whom the enemy never managed to touch in all his time at sea'. He ordered that all flags should fly at half-mast on 5 January in honour of these distinguished casualties.[1]

Admiral Krancke received on 13 January a private letter from Hüffmeier describing his plan to capture a coal steamer proceeding from England to Granville for which he would need certain ships. Krancke decided that the operation had a good chance of success, since the observation post on the Minquiers could keep close watch on traffic into Granville, and agreed that it should go ahead.[2]

The assault was planned for the night of 6/7 February, but the weather was rough and there was thick fog, and the convoy was recalled soon after it had left St. Helier. One tug and three patrol boats failed to receive the signal. The tug proceeded according to plan to the entrance to Granville harbour, and the patrol boats went so close inshore that they could hear music from the Hotel des Bains. But before the men could disembark they realized that the rest of the assault fleet was missing and hastily withdrew.

The next month was spent perfecting the plan. There was no dearth of volunteers. Anything was welcome after months of idleness and inadequate rations. Training exercises were carried out on Guernsey out of sight of the civilian population. When the volunteers returned to Jersey they were kept apart from the rest of the garrison and were not allowed to communicate with civilians. As a further security measure there were no joint exercises between the ships and the assault forces, from which people might have deduced what was in the wind.

[1] MOD 653/219. Breithaupt was in command of 24 *Minensuchflotille*, which was based at St. Helier.
[2] MOD 509/230.

Most of the ships had been laid up at St. Helier for some months. They included six minesweepers, the masts of which had been removed to present a smaller target to Allied radar, three artillery carriers, two converted landing craft, three motor torpedo boats, a large tug, and a number of smaller craft. They were manned by 600 men. In addition there were 70 infantry and engineers to destroy the port installations and, with the help of 7 Luftwaffe men armed with light anti-aircraft weapons, to hold back the Americans; 8 naval ratings to blow up the vessels in port; 12 to destroy the radar station; and another 12 to take any prizes back to Jersey. 25 infantrymen were to create a diversion by attacking the Hotel des Bains to the north of the harbour.

In March the weather became favourable, and at the end of the first week Maîtresse Île reported that a number of Allied ships were heading for Granville. Hüffmeier decided that the moment had come. The assault force set off from St. Helier after dark on the evening of 8 March. When they reached Granville at 1 a.m. they saw that the harbour lights were burning, which suggested that there was some activity there. The three artillery carriers had taken up position between the Île de Chausey and St. Malo to cut off any Allied patrols in that area; and two of the minesweepers stationed themselves between Jersey and the Cotentin peninsula for the same purpose.

Another two of the minesweepers were to be the spearhead of the attack. Their plan was to sail straight into the harbour, and when challenged by the signal station simply to flash back the same challenge in the hope that this would momentarily throw the defence off their guard and give them time to get safely in. This was precisely what happened. Before anyone in the harbour realized what was happening the two minesweepers were secured alongside the quays.

The third pair of minesweepers was left outside the harbour area to provide covering fire. The three motor torpedo boats made straight for the beach by the Hotel des Bains to land their party. The tug moved slowly towards the harbour entrance to give the leading minesweepers time to secure themselves. Before this was completed the assault parties were ashore and had established themselves in positions from which they could control the approaches to the dock area. For an hour and a half they remained in command of the situation in spite of fierce counter-attacks by the Americans.

It now appeared that the Germans had made a serious miscalculation. They had assumed that during their attack all the vessels in the harbour would be afloat – otherwise none of them could be towed away – but in fact the tide was so low that of the four ships in the harbour three were firmly aground and only the 1,200-ton *Eskwood* was afloat. Further, the tide was ebbing, so that time was against the assault force. The engines of the three grounded ships were severely damaged by explosive charges, and the port installations – cranes, locomotives, wagons, and fuel dumps – were systematically demolished while the Americans were kept at bay. It had been intended that the tug should tow away any vessel that was captured but in the event it was not needed. The *Eskwood* left the harbour under her own steam. According to the German account 'her crew took a sportsmanlike view of the proceedings and worked their ship', encouraged perhaps by German guns.

Meanwhile the artillery carriers off the Île de Chausey were doing the job assigned to them. An American submarine chaser was alerted by the noise of explosions at Granville and approached from the west to investigate. In the fight that developed the American ship was sunk by the superior fire power of the three artillery carriers, which themselves suffered no damage. Some of the Americans were taken prisoner. It was believed that another Allied ship was hit, and withdrew. The two minesweepers patrolling off the Cotentin coast sighted no ships.

The attack on the radar station failed because the boats covering this part of the operation found that the tide was so low that they could not get close enough in to provide adequate covering fire. In trying to get close in one of them ran aground and had to be blown up with depth charges, the crew having been transferred to another boat. The diversionary assault on the Hotel des Bains was completely successful. There was little resistance and nine Americans were taken prisoner.

On the return journey the lighthouse and signal station on Grande Île de Chausey were attacked and put out of action. All the German vessels, except the boat which had to be blown up, returned safely, taking with them 30 prisoners captured in the harbour area and 55 prisoners of war who had been released. The only German casualties were one officer presumed killed and five men wounded.

The Germans were highly delighted at the success of the operation. In the words of Admiral Ruge: 'Boldness, a sound plan, thorough preparation, and complete secrecy had enabled the Channel Islands to strike a shrewd blow. Compared with the battle in Germany it was no more than a pinprick, yet it was the best they could do for their suffering country.'

In the following month there was another attempt to strike a blow for the suffering Fatherland. In the account which von Schmettow was required to write while a prisoner of war he merely says that it was an attempt against the Cotentin peninsula mounted from Guernsey and launched from Alderney. 'It is known that only one soldier returned, and that it was unsuccessful.' Presumably this was an attempted landing, perhaps with the objective of establishing a beach-head which could be enlarged by reinforcements from the Channel Islands to an extent which it was hoped would seriously embarrass the Allies.[1]

[1] This narrative is based on Ruge's and von Schmettow's accounts.

12

Siege

PREPARATIONS for the last-ditch defence of Europe began in January 1944 when Hitler established combat zones, in which von Rundstedt was given supreme authority, and designated twelve *Festungen* (fortresses) covering the coastline from Ijmuiden in Holland to the Gironde estuary in south-west France. In February Guernsey, Jersey, and Alderney were added. The Führer laid down that they must in all circumstances be held to the last man and the last bullet, and personally approved the appointment of the fortress commanders. Von Schmettow was assigned to Guernsey, Oberst Heine to Jersey, and Major Schwalm to Alderney. They would have to make do with the men already there, since no additional troops could be spared. It was up to von Rundstedt to ensure that they had enough food, ammunition, fuel and equipment generally.[1]

The next development came on 19 May, when the increasing gravity of the threat to German-occupied Europe was recognized by the conversion of the *Feldkommandantur* into a *Platzkommandantur*. The military government originally set up to bridge the gap between conquest and peaceful co-existence was replaced by an organization which, in theory, had its eye principally on the resumption of hostilities. Yet the change was little more than academic. The *Platzkommandantur* had its headquarters in Jersey, where the *Feldkommandantur* had been. There was still a *Nebenstelle* in Guernsey, an *Aussenstelle* in Alderney, and a *Zufuhrstelle* in Granville. Business carried on as it had done under *Feldkommandantur* 515. All the powers and duties vested in FK 515 were transferred to *Platzkommandantur I*, its legal successor. All its orders, regulations, and notices continued in force. There was, however,

[1] T 77 789/5518189; MOD 38/720.

one difference: the court was not taken over by PK I but was made responsible to the *Festungskommandant*.[1]

The three Channel Island fortresses, thus stripped for action, waited for the Allied assault on Europe, in which it was conceivable that they would be used as stepping stones. All von Rundstedt's corps and divisional commanders were summoned to a conference at Rennes on 6 June – admirable timing, since it turned out to be D-Day for the Allied invasion. Von Schmettow left Guernsey for St. Malo on 4 June and travelled to Rennes via Granville. There was a preliminary conference at which General Marcks, who commanded LXXXIV Corps, said that the invasion was expected at the latest in the middle of the month. There was much speculation as to which sectors the Allies would attack. The west coast of the Cotentin peninsula seemed unlikely since the Channel Islands would have to be taken first.

After the conference von Schmettow inspected the Cotentin fortifications. He thought that they were not in the same class as his own. He was in Granville when news of the invasion came, and at once got in touch with the Islands. Everything was under control. There had been no attempt to land. Nevertheless, he had to get back quickly. In spite of constant air raids he reached Guernsey by boat in the early morning of 7 June.

From this moment the Islands became progressively more isolated. Many vessels which had served them were lost in the invasion battles, and the few that were left had little fuel. Rhine barges were chosen to supply the Islands because their low build made them difficult radar targets, but they could be used only in calm weather. When it was rough the *Robert Müller*, which had carried the deportees in 1942, was called in.[2] At first fortnightly transport planes were some help, but they became less frequent and finally stopped.[3] In October the German observation post on the Minquiers became untenable and an alternative had to be established on Maîtresse Île.[4] Next month it was decided that U-boats operating in the English Channel should use St. Peter Port, and a stock of torpedoes was built up there. It was mooted that the U-boats should bring in food for the garrison – 25 tons at a time. Von Schmettow listed goods which were 'well suited to delivery by U-boat' (10·5 tons of sugar, 11 tons of fat, 3 tons of soap, $\frac{1}{2}$ ton of razor blades, plus grape sugar, dextrose, and as much diesel oil as could be carried) but this scheme never came to anything.[5] In December the wisdom of retaining

[1] NG 01/2; JFW 43/17.   [2] MOD 653/195; 509/143.   [3] MOD 509/96.
[4] MOD 653/120.   [5] MOD 509/94, 111, 230.

the Casquets lighthouse was debated. There were 35 men there without any real defence against aerial attack. They had no doctor, and the wounded might have to wait several weeks before being taken off. Since Battery 'Anna' on Alderney covered the lighthouse the Allies could not take it over; but Krancke decided that the garrison must remain, despite the hardship, since it provided useful information about the movement of Allied ships and planes. In November five of the men were awarded the Iron Cross.[1]

It became obvious to the Germans soon after D-Day that the Allies intended to by-pass the Channel Islands and starve out the garrison. On 27 June Jodl said that the enemy would not attack the Islands but would try to bring about their downfall by cutting off supplies.[2] On 3 July – the day von Kluge took over from von Rundstedt as Ob. West – constant Allied air reconnaissance and the presence of the Royal Navy near the Islands were seen as evidence of the intention to isolate them.[3] While there was still time the Germans set about removing non-effectives. OT workers, for whom there would be no more cement or steel, were brought to the mainland. At the end of June Hitler himself ordered out the SS penal construction brigade, not in this instance to reduce the number of mouths to be fed, but 'because in no circumstances must they fall into enemy hands'.[4] The concentration camp prisoners were also to be removed.[5] 1,222 men and 46 women went from Alderney to St. Malo, and the construction brigade was put at the disposal of the LXV Army Corps.[6] Men were brought out, and munitions sent in. There had to be at least six months' stock of everything – this was an OKW order which von Schmettow was never told about – and shipping was provided to make good the deficiencies. But the losses in north-west France had been so heavy that the things needed, especially anti-aircraft shells, simply could not be found.[7]

In the middle of July *Marinegruppe West* considered that the garrison could not be kept supplied. The civil population, except those working on the land, should be evacuated. At least Jersey and Guernsey could keep the troops fed – so long as the unproductive civilians, for whom much of the meat, flour, and fuel imported from France was destined, were evacuated. 'Their removal by sea seems possible if the enemy is informed that English civilians are on vessels leaving the

[1] MOD 653/169–70; 157.   [2] MOD 110/241.
[3] T 311 16/16743.   [4] MOD 110/151.
[5] MOD 110/241.   [6] MOD 110/243, 508/5; T 311 16/16732.
[7] T 311 16/16794; T 77 787/5515417.

Channel Islands. We should also make sure that during the evacuation period Englishmen, preferably of the ruling class, are on board ships both coming and going.'[1] Ob. West agreed that at least a small number of civilians should go.[2] At the end of the month the additional supplies had still not been sent. No food had been available for shipment in the last seven weeks. In Guernsey the shortage of bread was serious: there was only 44 days' supply left. In the meantime the Führer reserved to himself the decision about evacuating civilians.[3]

On 31 July Hüffmeier pointed out that in spite of the Führer's order about strengthening the Islands, nothing had been done. Rations were down to three months' supply. 500 tons of flour were needed monthly, even if the civilians were left out of the account. Diesel oil was essential if the waterworks on Guernsey was to be kept going, and without water there would be disease. Everything was dangerously short, especially coal, sugar, and salt. These must be sent at once. Finally, there was still no decision about the evacuation of civilians, which would increase the amount of food available for the troops, and at the same time reduce crime.[4]

On the day of this *cri de coeur* over 500 tons of food went from St. Malo to Guernsey. It had now become apparent that, whatever the merit of the proposal to send away the civilians, Hitler was taking so long to make up his mind that it would soon be too late to do anything about it. Granville had fallen. St. Malo was about to fall. Even if ships could be found there was nowhere for the people to go. Some other means would have to be found to give the Wehrmacht the food it needed.[5]

It was estimated on 10 August that the troops had enough meat and vegetables to last three months, and other food two and a half months.[6] A message was sent to the commanders of the three Island fortresses that they should seek to guarantee their survival as long as possible by controlling their food supplies rigidly, and by ruthlessly cutting down civilian rations.[7] By the beginning of September virtually nothing was getting through by sea. Long-range planes were called in to supply 'the beleaguered Atlantic fortresses', but they too failed to make much of a contribution. The drop equipment which they needed (because they were too big to land on the Channel Islands' airfields) had been captured by the Allies at Rheims; but so long as planes were available at

[1] MOD 508/80.   [2] MOD 508/181.
[3] MOD 508/185.   [4] MOD 111/63.
[5] MOD 508/190, 198, 215, 181.   [6] T 77 787/5515262.
[7] T 77 787/5515260.

least one a week was to try to visit the Islands.[1] On 8 September *Luftflotte* 3 reported that they were still waiting for drop equipment.[2] A week later the estimate of the overall food supply was down to 45 days – on the assumption that stocks were shared by all three Islands and that rations, both to the Wehrmacht and to the Islanders, were cut to the absolute minimum.[3]

It now became abundantly clear that something drastic must be done if the garrison was to survive. The plan was still to remove the civilians, but Hitler's procrastination had made it much more difficult. The whole of the population could have been removed while the shipping routes were still open, but this was no longer possible, at least in German ships. Britain should be asked to do the job. All civilians not needed for the war effort in the Islands would be allowed to leave; and Britain would have to find the ships to carry them. Alternatively, the Islanders' rations should be stopped. The British would have to send food and find the ships.[4] This was put to Hitler in the *Wolfsschanze* by Jodl on 18 September. He agreed, almost certainly with reluctance, for it was an admission of defeat, that the British government should be approached.[5] Keitel told Ob. West that in spite of the reduction in civilian and Wehrmacht rations the civilian population, less men capable of bearing arms, must be handed over to the enemy, who were to be informed that civilian food stocks were exhausted. In the meantime the civilian rations must be reduced to the 'minimum existence level'.[6] It was suggested that Ob. West should broadcast the proposal to 'the Anglo-Americans' but, in the event, the more conventional channel was used.

On 19 September the German Foreign Ministry asked the protecting power to inform Britain that 'on the former British Channel Islands supplies for the civilian population are exhausted'. The German government was willing that all except men fit to bear arms should be evacuated; or to allow food to be sent in. If the British government agreed they should make proposals at once.[7]

There were immediate consultations in Whitehall. The Ministry of Economic Warfare, which had resisted proposals to send food in the early days of the occupation, saw no objection. The Chiefs of Staff said that the Islands now had no military importance, and advised acceptance of the German offer. Of the alternatives they preferred to send food,

---

[1] MOD 508/500.   [2] MOD 508/514.   [3] T 77 787/5515246.
[4] T 77 787/5515245.   [5] T 77 787/5515403.   [6] MOD 490/12.
[7] MOD 47/757. Admiral Krancke noted in his War Diary that he knew the English character and that they would not accept the proposals. MOD 508/642.

since evacuation would need ships earmarked for the build-up in Europe. The Home Office also wanted to send food on the ground that many Islanders would refuse to leave. To transplant them forcibly after years of occupation 'would be most discouraging'. The Germans might be exaggerating the food shortage, and it would have great propaganda value for them to say that the British government were indifferent to the privations of the Islanders and would uproot them rather than send the necessities of life. The Home Secretary agreed.

The Prime Minister did not. He demanded in a minute of 4 August to the First Sea Lord: 'What are the Navy doing on the western flank of the armies? I should have thought that they would be very lively all along the Atlantic shores of the Brest peninsula, driving off all enemy vessels, isolating the Channel Islands from all food or escape of the German garrison.'[1] When he approved the liberation plan on 2 September he endorsed the proposal that the garrison should be starved out, and scribbled a marginal note: 'Let 'em starve. No fighting. They can rot at their leisure.' He was of course thinking of the Germans, but the implications for the civilian population did not escape him. He wrote in a minute of 27 September:

I am entirely opposed to our sending any rations to the Channel Islands ostensibly for the civil population but in fact enabling the German garrison to prolong their resistance. I therefore prefer to evacuate the women and children at once, and I would offer that men capable of bearing arms should be bound not to take any further part in the war. It is possible that the Germans would accept this, as with the reduction of the population their existing food supplies would last them longer. I would rather face this than go on feeding them. It is no part of our job to feed armed Germans and enable them to prolong their hold on British territory. Moreover our aircraft have many other tasks to perform.[2]

When the War Cabinet next met, the Prime Minister said that the reply to the German government must be that so long as their troops remained in occupation they were responsible for feeding the people. Otherwise the British government called on them to surrender forthwith. He no longer contemplated large-scale evacuation, however. If it became clear that the Germans were not going to feed the people, food would be sent through the Red Cross. Next day the sense of this decision was passed by the Foreign Office to the British Legation in Berne for transmission through the protecting power.

[1] Churchill, op. cit. vol. vi, p. 602.
[2] ADM 116/5356; AIR 20/3354; PREM 3/87.

The British reply caused some excitement in the German Foreign Ministry. They feared – no less than the Home Office had done – that the enemy were about to exploit the situation to their advantage. Therefore, in order to prevent the British from using propaganda against them, the contents of the note had to be examined from the legal and factual point of view.

In particular it was essential to obtain precise information about the food situation in the Islands, and the possibility of evacuating the civilians.[1] A telegram was sent asking for this information on 2 October.[2] Von Schmettow replied that there were 28,500 troops: 12,000 on Jersey, 13,000 on Guernsey, and 3,500 on Alderney. There were 62,000 civilians: 39,000 on Jersey, and 23,000 on Guernsey. Food would last until the beginning of January, although there would be shortages of some things in the middle of October. Medicines were already finished. Evacuation was out of the question. Three-quarters of the people were working for the troops, in agriculture, electricity and the waterworks, mills and workshops which could not be taken over by the troops. On the other hand, if civilians remained and were supplied by the Red Cross, food would last until May. But medicines, soap, cereals, sugar, salt, and tobacco were needed immediately.[3]

So much for the facts. The Foreign Ministry studied the legal position and decided that there was no obligation under international law for an army of occupation to feed the people if it could not do so. The Hague Convention dealt with the opposite situation where the occupying army was allowed to requisition food. It was not unusual for occupied territories to be supported from outside. The United States had fed Belgium in the First World War, and Greece in the Second. The German request to Britain to feed or remove the people would certainly stand up to world scrutiny, whereas the British demand to surrender the Islands because of the food situation could not be supported by international law. But the German position would be weakened if the troops lived off the land and thereby reduced the rations of the civilian population to bare subsistence level. This was against the rules of war, and the British would make capital out of it.[4]

Führer Headquarters made their contribution. Of the civilians, 10,500 were men between the ages of 16 and 45. Rations would last for 30 days, given severe reductions for both troops and people. There could be no question of surrender, nor of removing the civilians. The

[1] MOD 490/17, 19.   [2] MOD 490/5.
[3] T 77 787/5515388.   [4] MOD 490/15.

troops had the right and duty to use all the available food for themselves, 'but on practical grounds we cannot let the civilian population starve, but must allow them a minimum subsistence ration'. A compromise solution, which would remove all the civilians not required to one Island and transfer the troops from that Island to the other two, was dismissed as likely to take too long. There was nothing for it but to order the garrison to hold out as long as possible by seizing all the food stocks and reducing the civilians to bare necessity.[1] It was estimated that if the 'non-effectives' were removed 20,000 would be involved – one-third of the total – compared with von Schmettow's figure of a quarter.[2]

The next step was considered at a conference in the German Foreign Ministry on 5 October, when it at once emerged that the statement in the note to Britain that 'food supplies for the civilian population are completely exhausted' was simply not true. 'Our position vis-à-vis the Anglo-American note is rendered difficult by this inexactitude.' The Foreign Ministry defended itself on the ground that the note was based on an OKW telegram signed by Keitel, who should have known what he was talking about. Further investigation showed that there was enough food for the troops and the civilian population to last until the end of the year. The purpose of the German note had been to ensure that the troops would be fed until the end of spring 1945, and also to ensure that the coming harvest and the civilian reserves should be kept exclusively for the troops. It was for this reason that the British government had been asked either to remove the civilians or to send in food through the Red Cross; but the point was once again made that three-quarters of the people were engaged in 'practical service to the troops, so that evacuation without damaging the troops' interest could apply only to those who cannot work – sick, children, and the aged'.

The conference concluded that the British government had turned down the German proposal because they knew the true facts of the situation. Therefore, according to the OKW representatives, the most important thing was to save face in the further handling of the negotiation. Little could be expected from counter-propaganda on the lines that the English preferred to let their people starve rather than to accept German proposals (so the Home Office had guessed wrongly on this point) because the English with their inside knowledge would reply that if the people were really starving it was because their own produce had been denied them, contrary to the rules of war. One way out would

[1] T 77 787/5515390.   [2] MOD 490/9.

be to ask the Red Cross to send medicines, soap, and other requirements which had to be imported even in peacetime; and there was a chance that the Red Cross would agree to send food as well. It was left that the Foreign Minister and OKW must decide the next step.[1]

Von Ribbentrop found this difficult. Much time was wasted sending telegrams to those concerned explaining the situation; but no progress was made on what to say to the British government. In the event the difficulty was resolved by a change of heart on the part of the Prime Minister.

The War Cabinet was told on 16 October that nothing had come in from the Germans. The Home Secretary pointed out that pressure in parliament and the press to do something for the Channel Islands would increase if relief was sent to Greece and Poland. It was, however, decided to defer action. The Chiefs of Staff would report as soon as further evidence became available.[2] On 23 October they said that even if no food was sent the civilian population would be all right until the end of the year. They could survive longer with hardship, but without starvation. Therefore no food should be sent, although there was no objection to medical supplies and soap.[3] (In a telegram explaining the position to General Eisenhower the Chiefs of Staff estimated that if the needs of the civilian population were met from outside, the garrison would hold out 4–5 months longer.)[4]

The Home Secretary argued that his information suggested that the people could not hold out beyond mid-November, and he proposed that the International Red Cross should be asked to visit the Islands and report. The War Cabinet, however, still felt that neither food nor medical supplies should be sent. The commander of the garrison should be reminded – either by radio or leaflets – that he was responsible for feeding the people; and the Political Warfare Executive were instructed to get on with this. The position would be reconsidered in a fortnight. This disappointed the Home Office, who consoled themselves with the thought that another two weeks would not make much difference, except that it would be more difficult to deal with awkward parliamentary questions.

The Minister of Information, Mr. Brendan Bracken, thought that the proposal to warn – or threaten – the garrison commander was ill-advised and should be reconsidered. The *Festungskommandant* was going to be told to do something he manifestly could not: to feed the

[1] MOD 47/757–8; 490/3.   [2] AIR 20/3354.
[3] PREM 3/87.   [4] AIR 9/257; SHAEF/501/1.

people, when he had no food. The sufferings of the civilian population were to be used as a lever to compel surrender. Moreover, the Germans could announce their offer to evacuate the people, for which there were the precedents of Calais and Dunkirk, which would be tiresome.

Members of parliament were showing much anxiety about the Islands. On 2 November the Home Secretary was asked what information he had about food shortages and for a statement about conditions. He replied that plans had been made to send food and medical supplies. A fortnight later an M.P. referred to the 'widespread public anxiety as to the position of our own people in the Channel Islands'. Another M.P. asked if the Home Secretary would consider evacuating them 'because the last people to starve in the Islands will be the Germans'. Herbert Morrison agreed that the government shared that anxiety; but he could not very well go on to say that evacuation was at that moment under discussion with the German government.[1]

On 5 November a new appraisal was prepared for the War Cabinet. There were two problems – the welfare of the people, and the 'ultimate disposal' of the German garrison. There were three possible solutions.

First, all except men fit for military service could be evacuated. Everybody except the men left behind would be saved; but it would be difficult to transport the people and to find homes for them. The German garrison would be left with all the food produced in the Islands, and resistance would thus be prolonged. This was the most important point of all.

Alternatively, relief supplies could be sent. This would 'salve our consciences of the moral responsibility to help the civilian population', since there was a chance that at least part of the food would reach the people. On the other hand some would go to the Germans. In any case the garrison was bound to be better off, since they could justify their taking a greater share of the Islands' own produce if the civilian population were being partly fed from Britain. The problem of the garrison would remain unsolved, and there would be a continuing commitment to send in relief.

The third course was to do nothing beyond stating the garrison commander's responsibility and waiting for him to surrender before the plight of the civilian population became 'actionable' in international law. It was possible that fear of retribution would make him throw his hand in, and the disadvantages of the other two courses would be avoided. All things considered this seemed to be the right line.[2]

[1] Hansard (Commons), vol. 404, cols. 947–8; 2095–96.   [2] AIR 20/3354.

The memorandum was supplemented by information from people who had escaped from the Islands, on the basis of which a Ministry of Health expert judged that they could carry on for a few more weeks, in spite of the severe shortages of everything, including clothing. But the standard of living had fallen alarmingly. The people, especially the less well-off, were near breaking point.

On 6 November, however, the Prime Minister still persisted in his hard line. He minuted the Foreign Secretary: 'I am entirely opposed to our feeding the German garrison in the Channel Islands and thus prolonging its resistance.'[1] But next day he at last overcame his scruples about helping the garrison directly or indirectly. In the War Cabinet he proposed that food parcels should be sent on the understanding that the Germans continued to be responsible for providing the basic civilian ration; and he agreed that medical supplies should be sent, even though the Germans might take them. The proposal to warn the commander that he would regret it if he allowed the Islanders to starve (the weakness of which had been shown up by the Minister of Information) was held in abeyance pending the German government's reaction to the latest British move.

The War Cabinet decision was notified to the Germans on 7 November, and their reply was received on 23 November. The German government was willing to allow food parcels to enter the Channel Islands. They had hitherto cared for all the inhabitants and they would continue to do so. If restrictions became necessary, it would be because the British government, in contravention of international law, had prevented the despatch of food from overseas. Nevertheless, the basic ration would continue to be met. The International Red Cross would supervise the distribution of parcels, and their ships would be given safe conduct.

The Germans had won a bloodless victory – for what it was worth. The British government would now increase the total food supply, and the additional imports would not have to be carried in German ships. The garrison would be able to prolong their resistance. The Islanders, who had gone hungry for nearly two months longer than they need have done, because in Churchill's view it was necessary to crush the spirit of the garrison, were saved on the brink of disaster.

During the two weeks in which the German reply was awaited, information reached the British government that the Germans had decided to confiscate all the food stocks of the civilian population, and to

[1] PREM 3/87.

reduce their rations to the minimum required to support life. General Ismay suggested on 15 November that the purpose was probably to extend the garrison's resistance beyond the end of 1944. He added that since the information had been received from most secret sources the Prime Minister might consider that it should not be communicated to the War Cabinet. In his reply, which was given four days after the Germans had agreed to the British proposals, the Prime Minister said that the matter must be brought up to the Cabinet. He went on to ask what threats had been made to the Germans concerned. It had been decided months ago that they should be held responsible for the condition of the civilian population and that if there was any failure in this respect the ten leading officers would be placed on the list of war criminals. But this idea was not followed up.[1]

In fact the information received from secret sources echoes a report from von Schmettow to MOK West[2] of 31 October, which recorded that the garrison's food supplies would last until May 1945, and that there would be nothing left for the civilian population after January since all stocks were earmarked for the troops. The garrison could hold out until October 1945 provided that the civilians were given nothing but vegetables. If the civilians were to be evacuated, it would be essential to retain all farmers and their wives; but evacuation seemed unwise since it would reveal to the enemy the situation in the Islands, and it would mean transferring fighting men to work on the land. Rations had now fallen below the level prescribed for home troops, and they would have to be further reduced to the level allowed for civilians in Germany.[3] Next day Krancke's War Diary set out the weekly rations for the troops and the civilians. The former had been cut to 2100 g. bread, 245 g. fat, 500 g. meat, and 2,800 g. potatoes. The latter were only 500 g. bread, 125 g. fat, 20 g. meat, and 500 g. potatoes. OKM had been requested to seek authority from OKW to seize all food by 15 November. The fate of the civilian population must be left to the International Red Cross.[4]

The Islanders were unaware of all the moves in this game of diplomatic blind man's buff. Neither side knew fully what was in the other's mind, and a propaganda success (or at least the avoidance of a propaganda defeat) seemed to be just as much the prize as the survival of the garrison (from the German point of view) or the welfare of the Islanders

[1] PREM 3/87.   [2] *Marineoberkommando West.*
[3] T 77 787/5515370.   [4] MOD 509/26, 29.

(from the British). The Islanders were, however, only too well aware of the realities of the situation.

On 13 October they were brought half into the picture by a German press announcement that food for the civilian population was being sought through the protecting power and that therefore the occupying power was no longer responsible for feeding them. This, coupled with the fact that the Germans had already begun to requisition food, provoked a strong reaction in both bailiwicks. It seemed to be the beginning of the end. The Island authorities could not bring themselves to believe that the Germans had fully exposed the dangers of the situation to the British government, and they searched for ways and means of getting the facts to London. There were two courses open to them: to communicate direct with the International Red Cross, or to send their own secret envoys to England.

The Bailiff of Guernsey had already written to the Red Cross at the end of July but it seems unlikely that the Germans sent on his letter. They said later that it must have been intercepted by enemy action. Carey and Leale wrote to von Schmettow on 21 October referring to the press notice and also to a letter from Oberst von Helldorf, von Schmettow's Chief of Staff, which stated more explicitly that responsibility for feeding the people no longer rested with the army of occupation. They complained that the Germans were using the Hague Convention to take civilian food, while ignoring the provisions which required them to keep the people fed; and they demonstrated that the quantities being taken were far greater than the Convention permitted.

Von Schmettow replied in a remarkably emotional letter. The Bailiff did not do justice to his efforts to help the people, even when the enemy were sinking ships bringing food to the Islands. They had tailored agricultural production to meet the needs of the times, in spite of little co-operation from the Island authorities, who had no inkling of the suffering that war had brought to other countries. The troops had been forbidden to buy fruit and vegetables – a measure unprecedented in the history of occupations. It was now necessary to draw on civilian stocks to maintain the Island fortresses' power to resist. Germans did not build mighty fortifications without holding them to the bitter end. They would do so even if it meant disaster for the Islanders – and the besiegers alone would be to blame. He reminded the Bailiff that the German commander at Le Havre had thrice been refused permission to send away the French civilians, as a result of which thousands had died. There was no question of making contact with the protecting power.

It was physically impossible, and in any case could not be allowed.

There now seemed to be no alternative but to send someone to England with the facts – a dangerous course in the light of von Schmettow's letter. Years earlier Sherwill had deprecated escapes on the ground that they caused trouble for the community at large, and Carey seems to have shied away from advocating so bold a step, even in the serious plight in which the bailiwick found itself. The job was done for him, however, by a group of private individuals who thought that the Controlling Committee was not taking a strong enough line with the Germans. They wrote to the Bailiff on 16 September saying that he was no doubt aware that the administration of the bailiwick would be investigated after the war and that it would be to his advantage 'to shift the onus of responsibility on to the German authorities'. They called on him to demand that the Germans should either give them the food they needed, or allow them to import it. Carey replied that the Germans were well aware of their responsibilities, and added that the reference to a post-war investigation was insulting. The group wrote again to the Bailiff on 29 September and made the point that the Germans might well be aware of their responsibilities, but there was ample evidence that they were not acting in accordance with them.

They collected together all the information they could lay their hands on, including a detailed statement about the food shortage made in the States on 1 November, and entrusted these to one of their members, Fred Noyon, a retired merchant navy captain. Noyon left Guernsey by night on 3 November 'after a normal afternoon's fishing expedition' with a single companion. They were spotted by an American warship, which towed them to Cherbourg, and eventually arrived in the United Kingdom on 12 November.

Noyon was duly interrogated but he did not add materially to what was already known in Britain. In any case the War Cabinet's decision to allow food into the Islands had been taken several days before he arrived. He had arranged with friends that he would ask the B.B.C. to broadcast a message to show that he had arrived safely – which had seemed simple enough in St. Peter Port. Those who interrogated him said it would not be easy and gave him no help. Ever since the evacuation the B.B.C. had turned down innumerable requests to send messages to the Channel Islands. Noyon wrote on 20 November to 'the Chief Inspector, Broadcasting House', and when that produced nothing wrote a week later to the Director General, Sir William Haley, himself a Channel Islander. Haley commented: 'Everybody now escaping from the Channel Islands comes with the same request. I had a man here only the other day wanting me to play a tune as a message to my own father!' However, an exception was made, in spite of the absence of official sponsorship, and at one minute past 8 a.m. on 9 December 'Personal message to George. The answer is Yes', was broadcast in the Allied Expeditionary Forces programme. Noyon's friends knew that he had arrived safely, and when the Red Cross supplies found their way to Guernsey they assumed – wrongly – that it was due to their enterprise.[1]

When von Schmettow told the Bailiff of Guernsey that there must be no communication with the protecting power he was guilty of an error of judgement. German policy was to persuade Britain to supply the Islands so that the occupying forces would be absolved of any charge that they were starving the people and so that they could hold out longer. What was more likely to soften the hearts of the British government than a desperate appeal for help from their own people? Not only was it physically possible to communicate with the Red Cross, it was politically desirable. MOK West overruled von Schmettow and ordered that Carey's message should be got through immediately 'since the supply of food to the civil population has great bearing on our own ability to hold out'. The call was made on 7 November – while Noyon, the self-appointed saviour of Guernsey, was still en route for England – and was reported to Hitler's headquarters in the *Wolfsschanze*.[2]

Meanwhile Jersey was playing its part. Coutanche's comprehensive memorandum on the food situation prepared at the end of August was taken to England by an escaper, and was in the hands of the authorities on 23 September. The Island authorities could not know this, however, and Coutanche asked Norman Rumball, a former member of the purchasing commission in Granville, to take another copy with him. This was successfully delivered in the middle of November. On 7 November, the day on which Carey was allowed to telephone to the International Red Cross, Coutanche handed to the *Platzkommandant* for transmission to the protecting power a request for an assurance that Britain was in full possession of the facts. Two days later he was told that the information he had provided had been 'directed from German sources to the protecting power and had reached the hands of the British government'.[3] This gobbledygook stretched the facts as the Germans knew them. It was virtually impossible for one belligerent to communicate with another through the protecting power within 48 hours; but the

[1] B.B.C. written archives 830/306.
[2] MOD 490/26; 509/48–9; T 77 787/5515365.   [3] Coutanche, p. 48.

Germans may have been pretending that their own approach to Britain – or perhaps Carey's telephone call – could be regarded as having made Jersey's points as well.

The possibility of evacuating the civilians continued to be very much in the mind of the garrison command. Hüffmeier reported to *Marinegruppe West* on 17 October that von Schmettow was considering evacuating one-third of the population – 20,600 people. He disagreed with this. All the civilians should go except 'peasants, fishermen, and those who were essential for food production'. The only others to be retained were artisans whose job could not be taken over by the Wehrmacht. Von Schmettow estimated that with 2,400 farmers, the whole of the Wehrmacht and half the population could be fed; but if the Wehrmacht took over all farming they could provide enough for only a total of 10,000 – which was less than their own needs. In short, it seemed right to dispense with four-fifths of the civilian population.[1]

The Germans had, of course, achieved their object without the help of Carey's message, or Coutanche's contribution of 12 November, which eventually came within judicial knowledge; but it was not until after Christmas that the S.S. *Vega* arrived in St. Peter Port with over 100,000 food parcels, 4,200 invalid diet parcels, and consignments of soap, salt, medical supplies, and cigarettes. Although it was very much in the German interest that the food should come in, they were highly suspicious of the transaction, and went to great lengths to ensure that the Allies were not using it for their own purposes. On 5 December it was agreed that there was nothing against Colonel Iselin and Mr. Callias, who had been chosen by the International Red Cross to accompany the relief supplies and supervise their distribution.[2] Ob. West nevertheless ordered that they must be kept under surveillance, and further that there was to be no communication between the crew and the civilian population. The unloading would be carried out by the Wehrmacht, and the Red Cross parcels would be carefully checked for sabotage and intelligence equipment.[3] On 9 December Ob. West reported that one of the two delegates was positively suspect; but as it was now too late to have him changed he would have to be watched particularly carefully. He must have no contact with the civilians.[4]

Two days later the news came that the *Vega* would be delayed, which gave the Germans the chance to demand that the suspect delegate,

[1] MOD 111/418.   [2] MOD 490/50.
[3] MOD 509/128.   [4] MOD 509/136.

whose offence was that he had served with the British Council in Warsaw should be replaced.[1] It was suggested that the British Council was not a central government agency, but this made no difference. He was still a security risk. In any case, there might be other agents or saboteurs on board, and the whole crew must be closely watched.[2] As it turned out there was time to replace the former British Council man with someone against whom the Germans had nothing.[3]

Von Schmettow was able to report on 27 December, when the *Vega* had finished discharging in St. Peter Port and was about to leave for Jersey, that the plan to get the Islanders fed from outside had succeeded. The International Red Cross delegates had sent a message to Geneva asking that relief supplies should be extended to cover the basic civilian ration. Admiral Krancke concluded that this meant that the Red Cross would now have full responsibility for the civilians. In that case the garrison would be all right until after the next harvest.[4] The *Vega* sailed for Jersey at dusk on 29 December carrying two lieutenants as security officers.[5]

The Wehrmacht clearly intended to hold the Island fortresses for the Führer as long as humanly possible, whatever the cost to the civilian population. Von Schmettow would no doubt have carried out his orders, perhaps with misgiving, but his attitude became academic when, in the autumn of 1944, Vizeadmiral Hüffmeier, *Seekommandant*, Channel Islands, emerged as the power behind the throne in the Islands. Von Schmettow became more and more of a figurehead until he was finally removed from the scene on 'health grounds' at the end of February 1945.

Hüffmeier's influence began to make itself felt in September 1944, when he told Admiral Krancke, then in command of *Marinegruppe West*, that in his opinion measures ordered by the army would shorten the resistance of the fortresses. The troops' rations were too high and the civilians also were being treated too generously. Electricity was wasted, which could affect the repair dockyards. Von Schmettow had failed to get across the message to his men that come what might they were to hold out till doomsday. Part of Hüffmeier's evidence was a memorandum taken from a would-be escaper which asserted that the garrison did not intend to resist after January 1945. Krancke decided to do nothing for the time being – there were already difficulties between the army and naval officers under his command, and it was better to hasten slowly in putting them right.[6]

[1] MOD 509/146. [2] MOD 490/62. [3] MOD 509/154.
[4] MOD 509/182. [5] MOD 653/193. [6] MOD 508/727.

Hüffmeier, however, was impatient. He demanded the removal of a number of senior army officers and also that the navy should assume command of the Islands by stages. Krancke was taken aback. He respected Hüffmeier's passionate desire to hold the Islands, but considered his proposals beyond the realm of possibility. The garrison consisted of 3,500 naval personnel and 32,000 soldiers and airmen.[1] To make a naval man *Befehlshaber* would be disastrous for army morale. He put this to his superior, Ob. West, who agreed. Von Schmettow must remain in command of the Islands;[2] but if Hüffmeier was appointed his Chief of Staff he could exert 'naval influence' on von Schmettow's decisions.[3] This arrangement was announced right away by Ob. West, since Krancke, who was about to be given command of the newly-established *Marineoberkommando West*, did not want to start his new job by making changes at the top. He did not get off so lightly, however, for von Schmettow immediately protested at Hüffmeier's appointment, and Krancke himself was forced to spell out the new position.[4] The feud between von Schmettow and Hüffmeier was watched with interest by their fellow officers, one of whom scribbled on a report from Hüffmeier of 17 October, 'They don't even speak to each other now!'[5]

Having thus wormed his way in, Hüffmeier proceeded to consolidate his position. His zeal was praised at a Führer conference on naval affairs on 1 November, when his proposals for prolonging the occupation of the Islands 'by means of drastic confiscation and by severely reducing consumption' were studied with approval. The conference acknowledged that his recent assignment to the additional post of Chief of Staff to the *Befehlshaber* was 'a happy choice and the proper way to give this energetic personality a voice in the overall command of the Channel Islands'.[6]

The Island authorities at first refused to believe that the Germans had asked Britain for food. Krancke deprecated this, for he thought that only when they realized what the occupying authority had done for them would they increase their own production.[7] He therefore urged that the Red Cross supplies should be brought in as soon as possible.

---

[1] These figures are substantially higher than those used about this time for calculating how long food would last.

[2] MOD 508/813.   [3] MOD 508/872.

[4] MOD 509/8.   [5] MOD 111/418.

[6] *Führer Conferences on Naval Affairs 1944* (Admiralty, London, 1947), p. 63.

[7] MOD 490/35.

The next step was to ensure that the garrison had a generous share of the increased production, and the Germans went to some trouble to convince themselves that they were entitled to commandeer from the Islanders anything they produced. Hüffmeier reported that von Schmettow was uncertain 'even on military grounds' about his right to seize enemy state property (i.e. food controlled by the Islanders) on the ground that there were specific agreements on the subject. OKW ruled that even if these agreements existed, which they doubted, they were valueless in the changed situation. There was nothing against seizing enemy property when carrying out military objectives. Von Schmettow was duly informed of this ruling, which represented yet another victory for his Chief of Staff.[1]

With Hüffmeier standing over him armed with the judgement of OKW, von Schmettow could do little to help the Islanders, whatever his inclination may have been. At the beginning of December Coutanche protested about the requisition of potatoes and cereals. When the Red Cross delegates met the Island authorities and the representatives of the *Platzkommandantur* in Jersey, the German side announced that the British government had been informed that the occupying authorities could not guarantee more than 2 ounces of fat and 2 ounces of meat a week, plus a small quantity of vegetables. Coutanche, to whom this was news, immediately leaped to the attack. 'In spite of efforts to muzzle me I protested at length in French to the Red Cross representatives against this declaration by Baron von Aufsess; drew attention to the large requisitions which had been made of potatoes and cereals in breach of Article 52 of the Hague Convention; and asked that Colonel Iselin and Mr. Callias would take note of my protest and bring it to the notice of His Majesty's government in the United Kingdom.' Nevertheless the requisitions continued unabated. Now that the British were committed to send in supplies to the civilian population, the Germans were not going to let them live in comparative affluence while the garrison sank below the subsistence level.

The ruthless line followed by the occupying authority much improved the garrison's chance of survival. Von Schmettow was able to report at the end of 1944 that he had enough food of all sorts to last until 1 June 1945. Cereals would be sufficient until the next harvest. If the meat ration was to be maintained after September 1945 it would be necessary to kill dairy cattle, which would lead to a reduction in the fat ration; but on the whole there seemed to be a good chance of holding out to the end of 1945.[2]

[1] MOD 490/44; 509/125–6. [2] MOD 509/173–4.

In addition to the stocks of food held by the Island authorities the Germans made an onslaught on private hoards. The *Festungskommandant* in Jersey, Oberst Heine, announced on 9 January 1945 that the serious food situation justified public claims even on private stocks. The free gifts of the International Red Cross, and the promise of further supplies, could be accepted with decency only if there were no large private stores. Households with more than 10 tins of meat or 20 tins of fruit must surrender the excess, ostensibly for distribution to the soup kitchens or to needy civilians, although inevitably much of the 'surplus' food found its way into the possession of the troops. Four days after the order was issued it occurred to the Germans that it might be used as a justification of the possession of black market food up to the prescribed limits; and a further order was issued laying down that a serious view would be taken of any black market dealings brought to light. The original order applied only to the fortunate few whose stores had been legally acquired, but which in the circumstances must be regarded as excessive.

Shortly afterwards the *Platzkommandantur* in Guernsey followed suit. If their order was not complied with there would be house to house searches, and goods in excess of the permitted quantities would be requisitioned. This order, which seemed almost to legalize the armed robbery of which many soldiers at this time were guilty, was defended by the Germans on the ground that it was necessary to spread the available food evenly over the civilian population; and in fact some remarkable hoards were brought to light. One unfortunate man had to surrender 186 tins of soup, vegetables, and fish out of a stock of 363. More painful was his loss of 286 bottles out of his cellar of 365 bottles of cognac, whisky, vodka, liqueurs, and claret. It was probably only a small consolation that he was left with his nine sticks of shaving soap. One householder had to give up 108 of 235 tins of soup, and another, two dozen of his five dozen bottles of port. The Royal Hotel lost nearly 300 bottles of spirits, 360 tins of vegetables, and considerable quantities of soap and cereals. Another individual had to hand over 42 bottles of spirits, 197 of wine, 50 of champagne, and 170 of cider. In all these cases it was explicitly stated that the goods were requisitioned for the troops.[1] The police who carried out the searches included the *Feldgendarmerie*, the *Geheime Feldpolizei*, who were not in uniform but carried documents to establish their identity, and members of the Wehrmacht *Hilfspolizei* (auxiliary police); but it was difficult for the

[1] GF 7/1/35.

SIEGE 279

people whose houses were raided to know whether or not the men who visited them were working under even the suspect authority of the *Festungskommandant* or *Platzkommandant*. Needless to say, von Schmettow expressed great astonishment at the hoards brought to light, especially when the people were now having the benefit of Red Cross parcels.

The decline and tame capture of the Wehrmacht in the Channel Islands in May 1945 were due in part to the German troops' failure to become efficient market gardeners and peasant farmers. They could never have become completely self-sufficient, but if they had looked ahead they could have put themselves in a position to survive much longer. If Hüffmeier had commanded 30,000 reasonably well-nourished men infected with his fanatical will to resist instead of semi-invalids who were praying with what little energy they had left for a speedy end to the war, the Allies would have been faced, long after victory had been achieved in Europe, with the problem of starving out the garrison and almost certainly also the civilian population. The only other alternative would have been to mount the sort of assault which Mountbatten had envisaged earlier – with shocking loss of life on both sides and among the civilians, for whom there was no escape. Hüffmeier probably saw the second alternative as the most likely, and he may have welcomed it. He would go down to posterity as the commander who fought to a finish against impossible odds and perished at the head of his troops, a new and greater Leonidas after a new and more glorious Thermopylae.

If his men had been as deft with the spade as with the rifle they might have enabled him to achieve his ambition. 'Digging for victory' helped to keep Britain's head above water. It would have had much greater significance for the Wehrmacht in the Channel Islands. At first the troops grew vegetables as a pastime. It gave them something to think about during long periods of tedious inactivity. There is a divine irony in one of the earlier ventures into husbandry. Almost at the moment when *Feldkommandantur* 515 was hunting down copies of *Guns or Butter?* (which cast some doubt on the value for mankind of Germany's pre-war armament drive) with a view to destroying them, the troops manning the four huge 'Mirus' guns asked permission to attach a cow to the battery.

The more the German forces produced for themselves the more shipping space would be released for purposes other than the transport of food. In 1943 and 1944 many properties, including glasshouses, were taken over by the troops; but the Wehrmacht had awoken too late to the importance of seeking to make the troops self-supporting. The agricultural cycle cannot be much speeded up. It was realized, with the benefit of hindsight, that if a fraction of the shipping space devoted to cement had been used to bring in fertilizers, the overall strength of the Island fortresses would have been infinitely greater.

Towards the end of 1944 there were desperate attempts to make up for lost time. In the middle of December each battalion appointed an agricultural officer, and it was announced in orders that units should order small quantities of seed from Germany – in spite of the fact that by this time it was virtually impossible to bring in anything.[1] A few days later 60 hectares of glasshouses were requisitioned for the troops in Guernsey to grow potatoes. They had 50 tons of seed potatoes, which had not sprouted, and the Controlling Committee was ordered to supply in exchange 50 tons of sprouting seed. 'In this manner the troops will also obtain an earlier crop and therefore will not need to draw again immediately on the civilian stocks.' In January 1945 instructions were issued about growing food in glasshouses, and the hope was expressed that potatoes would last until the end of March. Thereafter, until the new season's potatoes were ready, the troops would have to make do with noodles and macaroni.[2] Men were also encouraged to take up fishing, either on their own or in company with civilian fishermen who could show them the ropes. Detailed instructions were issued as to how to find the best fishing areas. As late as 27 April – within a week or two of capitulation – the *Befehlshaber* was issuing orders stressing that the troops must be self-reliant and press on with the growing of vegetables for their own use, and providing helpful gardening hints.[3]

The failure of the Wehrmacht's efforts to become self-sufficient was matched by failure to bring in food and supplies generally. Only a small amount of shipping got through before the Allies' control of the seas round the Islands became virtually complete. Therefore supplies could be sent only by air, and even that was a gamble. On 6 October two Heinkel 111s were detailed to take food to Guernsey. One crashed on take-off. The other jettisoned its load in the sea off St. Malo.[4] Two days later the operation was repeated, this time successfully. Krancke hoped that Hüffmeier would have the sense to send out his war diary and situation reports with the returning planes.[5] At this time there was

[1] NG 01/33.   [2] Ibid.   [3] Order of 27 April 1945.
[4] MOD 508/821, 824.   [5] MOD 508/825.

supposed to be a minimum of one plane a week to the Islands, but so far as Guernsey was concerned the two Heinkels were the first for four months. They brought seven bags of mail, which caused great rejoicing among the troops. When equipment was sent by air to relieve the overburdened communications system, it was dropped in France instead of the Islands.[1]

When Admiral Krancke became MOK West with responsibility for maintaining the resistance of the fortresses he decided that the most important thing was to boost morale, which could best be done by improving postal and news services.[2] Relatives of the troops in the Islands were to be given a voucher to enable them to send Christmas parcels to their menfolk; but this proved impossible 'in view of the supply situation'. Instead, 15,000 parcels containing only cigarettes and chocolate were sent by the military authorities – which suggests that every second man had to do without.[3] However, the troops could fall back on an encouraging Christmas message from Krancke, addressed to them from the comparative comfort and safety of Bad Schwalbach; and a New Year message from von Schmettow, which informed them that they had a hard year behind them, and that they must be ready for more sacrifices in 1945. They were entirely dependent on their own resources. The things that mattered were comradeship, self-discipline, belief in ultimate victory, and the will to fight to the last.[4] Krancke noted in his war diary that the enemy were hoping to starve out the fortresses, and that if they did not succeed heavy attacks were inevitable. The longer they held out, the better for the German war effort generally.[5]

The defeatist undertone in these messages was echoed when von Schmettow acknowledged a broadcast greeting from Goebbels thanking the men of the three fortresses for collecting over a million Reichsmarks for the German Red Cross. This splendid sum had caused much pleasure. It showed confidence in victory, and solidarity with the Fatherland. Von Schmettow radioed back: 'In our complete isolation on British soil for many months past we particularly appreciate the broadcast as well as your personal greetings. The three Island fortresses, conscious of their strength, and following the example of other fortresses, will faithfully hold out to the last. With this in mind we salute our Führer and Fatherland.' Not 'former British soil' as the German Foreign Ministry had been careful to say, and not 'hold out until final victory'.

[1] MOD 508/608.   [2] MOD 509/3.   [3] T 77 787/5515228.
[4] NG 01/33.   [5] MOD 509/206.

In spite of the exhortation and encouragement the morale of the troops fell steadily. In June 1944 the increasing incidence of theft, which evoked regular protests from the Island authorities, worried the German command, although they did not reveal their feelings to the Islanders. The *Befehlshaber* warned that serious cases would be court-martialled. He did not help things much by announcing a month later 'a new food plan', which meant that rations were to be cut again, positively for the last time. 'To ensure that nourishment lasts' the evening meal would be served at 7 p.m., an hour later than usual, and all ranks must retire to bed after their mid-day meal. The *Befehlshaber's* assurances meant little, for he had to announce further reductions at the end of August. On 1 September he announced that in view of the complete isolation of the Islands any infringements of the food regulations would be regarded as sabotage. He referred to a recent murder, all for two sacks of potatoes. This was disgraceful; such conduct must be wiped out by self-discipline. Shortly afterwards von Schmettow issued an order which seemed to deny his wish for stricter discipline. Soldiers sentenced to hard labour would serve only six weeks' close arrest – simply because they could not stand up to hard labour. In November there were further 'severe cuts in rations' and it was provided that serious cases of food theft would be punished with death. In December eleven men died from eating hemlock.[1]

The depths to which the troops had sunk by the beginning of 1945 are revealed by two memoranda in January, one written by an army doctor in Guernsey. The basic ration was down to subsistence level, and the odds and ends which had made it tolerable – for example the tiny weekly issue of sardines – had all stopped. Beans and peas were being held in reserve to bridge the gap between the exhaustion of potato stocks and the new harvest. There was hardly any sugar. Razor blades ran out at the end of December. Soap would disappear at the beginning of February, and skin disease was already prevalent for lack of it. There were plenty of doctors but no medicines.[2] Inevitably there was more theft, and a grenadier who was caught red-handed was sentenced to death on 5 February.[3]

The condition of the troops became a matter of grave concern. Of 99 men who reported sick in Guernsey on 13 January 1945, 24 were also suffering from malnutrition. They were being asked to do too much, and in the last few weeks the effectiveness of the army had been seriously undermined. The existing rations were only just enough to support life

[1] NG 01/33.   [2] T 77 787/5515352.   [3] NG 01/33.

if the body was at rest. Therefore the troops should be required to do the minimum duty consistent with security. The most they could safely do was five hours a day. Long marches, and work in the cold winter air should be avoided. The men should spend most of their time in courses of instruction calling for little physical effort, since brain work did not consume much energy. Duties which involved much physical effort should be assigned to small, muscular men who needed fewer calories. At least two hours' rest in bed was essential after the midday meal, preferably in a warm room.[1]

The *Vega* made her second trip at the beginning of February. She carried a large number of food parcels, but no flour, which was desperately needed. Also eight tons of soap had to be left behind in Lisbon since the Portuguese government refused an export licence. A radio message from the two Bailiffs to the International Red Cross urging that flour should be sent at once was given priority by the Germans, as it was, of course, still in their interest to step up imports.[2] The possibility of bringing in coal and of removing sick Channel Islanders and German wounded was also considered, but there was no hospital ship available.[3] At this time the Island authorities were given a good deal of latitude in the matter of food distribution; but this happy position was short-lived.

Hüffmeier's campaign to oust von Schmettow had continued relentlessly from the moment he became Chief of Staff. In December he told Krancke that the *Befehlshaber* 'felt himself somewhat restricted in his command' on the ground that the *Festungskommandanten* in Alderney and Jersey no longer came under him. Krancke thought that they were supposed to be independent only when cut off from Guernsey, but promised to find out the true position from Ob. West. In seeking to establish that von Schmettow was in sole command, Hüffmeier was not trying to strengthen the general's hand, but was looking ahead to the day when he himself would be *Befehlshaber*.

He achieved his ambition on 28 February. He announced that he had taken over from von Schmettow, who was returning to Germany for health reasons. His goal was to hold the Islands to the end. Von Schmettow issued a farewell message to 319 Infantry Division, in which he said that after four and a half years with the Division he was being transferred to the reserve. Generalmajor Wulf took over 319 Infantry Division; Generalmajor Dini became Chief of Staff to Hüffmeier; and Oberst Heine, who had been fortress commander of Jersey, was promoted

[1] Loose Guernsey paper.　　[2] MOD 47/889.　　[3] MOD 47/886–8; 509/251.

to Generalmajor and appointed tactical adviser to the *Befehlshaber*. Many naval officers whose ships were laid up were appointed to senior positions in the command, including posts in the *Platzkommandantur*, so that the army element was sandwiched between two layers of navy.[1] The troops now had at their head a ruthless Nazi who would show them no mercy if they fell short of his requirements; and the Islanders had an opponent dedicated to keeping the garrison fed even if in the long run every single civilian had to succumb to starvation.

On 2 March, as part of a campaign for raising morale, Hüffmeier ordered a daily guard of honour outside Staff Headquarters, to be taken in turn by the three services. A week later he issued a special message for Heroes' Day, and laid a wreath. Thereafter orders relating to morale flowed thick and fast. Troops were guilty of greeting their officers in the street in a slovenly fashion. This must be remedied. There was too much fraternization with local women. In future all men must remain aloof. Anyone caught stealing food would have his rations cut. In serious cases the death penalty would continue to apply.[2]

The Bailiff of Jersey learned about Hüffmeier's appointment on 1 March. Major Heider, the *Platzkommandant*, had been replaced by Korvettenkapitän Kurt von Cleve. It was rumoured that von Helldorf had been arrested by a naval patrol. Baron von Aufsess, with whom Coutanche had had many dealings, pointed out to him that of the triumvirate who had benevolently ruled the Islands – von Schmettow, von Helldorf, and von Aufsess – two had disappeared from the scene, and he (von Aufsess) was under grave suspicion. Coutanche and the Attorney General of Jersey were regarded by Hüffmeier as active enemies of Germany. Von Aufsess finished the conversation by saying '*Méfiez-vous, nous sommes des hommes suspects!*' In fact he was less suspect than he imagined. On 15 April he was given charge of the *Platzkommandantur* in Guernsey.[3] Von Cleve was highly critical of the soft line taken by von Schmettow and von Helldorf, and declared that if the latter had had his deserts he would have been shot. As time went on, however, he mellowed, having seen the inevitability of the garrison's fate long before Hüffmeier did; and the Island authorities found that he was able to modify some of the Admiral's more outrageous demands.

Hüffmeier's appointment was discussed at a Führer conference on naval affairs on 26 March, when Hitler ordered an investigation of the officers occupying the posts of fortress commander in the western area.

---

[1] MOD 509/130.   [2] NG 01/33.   [3] NG II.

He wanted these positions to be filled mainly by naval officers 'since many fortresses have been given up, but no ships were ever lost without fighting to the last man'. This observation was caused by a report from the Channel Islands that there was a difference of opinion there about holding out to the last man, but that the situation had been remedied 'by the recent appointment of Vice-Admiral Hüffmeier as Admiral, Channel Islands'.[1]

There was little more that the Islanders could do at this point other than to keep protesting about the commandeering of food in an attempt to save something from the wreck. They could try to manipulate the stock figures in the interest of the civilian population, but this did not always succeed. In March the Germans detected that 100 tons of potatoes had been left out of the Jersey stock return in the hope that they might be secretly added to the civilian ration. They were at once requisitioned. Coutanche, who had himself instructed that the potatoes should be lost from the figures, hopefully invoked the Hague Convention and protested against 'the requisition of potatoes which were clearly essential for the civilian population'; but his protest was rejected out of hand.

The legal basis for the Germans' position, in so far as they needed one, was their assertion that they had informed the British government in the autumn of 1944 that a state of emergency would arise at the end of the year, and that from the beginning of January they could no longer guarantee more than a weekly ration of 60·2 g. of fat, 56 g. of meat, and up to 3,500 g. of vegetables. As the British government had lodged no objection they had accepted responsibility for supplementing these quantities *de facto* and *de jure* – witness their agreement to the provision of Red Cross supplies. Nevertheless, the German authorities had allowed the civilian population to have flour, meat, potatoes, fat, and other foodstuffs over and above the promised minimum. 'They have even gone so far as to jeopardise the health of the troops more than that of the civilian population.' In any case, the doctrine of military necessity justified the German position. It was accepted in international law that military necessity 'allows the provisions of the laws of war to be disregarded if it is the final and only possibility of saving oneself from destruction, or for the successful operation of an undertaking decisive for the outcome of the war'. Coutanche demanded an interview with von Cleve at which he repudiated this doctrine and also denied that the British government had taken over responsibility for feeding the Islands.[2]

[1] *Führer Conferences on Naval Affairs*, 1945, p. 92.　　[2] PK 01/19.

Hüffmeier decided that the resistance of the garrison would be prolonged if the production of milk, butter, and cheese was kept at the highest possible level. He was against the slaughter of cattle to provide the troops with a meat ration. He proposed that the civilian population in Jersey should continue to receive a meat ration of 2 ounces a week, but that they would no longer receive a full-milk ration, except for children and the sick. Coutanche fought to retain full milk for all the people - although in Guernsey the adult ration had always been skimmed - but it was only when surrender became inevitable that the *Befehlshaber* dropped his plan.

Nevertheless, he did everything in his power to delay that surrender. At the end of March he visited Jersey from Guernsey, where his headquarters were, to address a representative selection of his officers and men at a mass meeting in the Forum Cinema in St. Helier. According to the report in the forces' newspaper *Deutsche Inselzeitung*, he explained the importance of defending the Channel Islands. An attack by the British and Americans might at any moment put them in the front line. They must prepare for this hour spiritually and materially; the more desperate the times the more united must they be. Conditions were being created in which they could hold out indefinitely - here he may have been thinking about his proposed milk diet. They had a mandate to keep the Islands for the Führer and he was determined to carry it out. 'I shall hold out here with you until final victory . . . we cannot be shamed before the Fatherland, which bears unendingly a much heavier burden than any one of us.' The *Befehlshaber*'s appeal was, in the words of the official war reporter, 'permeated with true national socialist feeling and with a clarity of thought and purpose which admits no compromise. We stand by him, officers and men of the fortress of Jersey!'

13

Liberation

PLANNING for the liberation of the Channel Islands began at the end of 1943 under the code name 'Rankin Case C'.

There were three 'Rankins'. 'Case A' was to be used if the strength and morale of the German armed forces had declined so much before the Allied invasion of France that it was desirable to launch a smaller earlier assault. 'Case B' was a plan to move into Europe in the event of the withdrawal of German forces. 'Case C' applied in the event of unconditional surrender and the cessation of organized resistance in Europe generally.

In the Channel Islands 'Rankin Case C's' objective was to disarm the garrison and pave the way for the establishment of civil affairs units. When there was no sign of a German collapse after the invasion of France, 'Rankin Cases A' and 'B' lost their point. 'Case C' could now only apply to the Channel Islands, and it was converted into Operation 'Nestegg' with the same general aims. Unconditional surrender was a prerequisite. To avoid heavy casualties among the civilian population and the destruction of property the Islands must not be taken by assault.[1]

It was confirmed by Supreme Headquarters Allied Expeditionary Force (SHAEF) in March 1944 that there must be no attack on the Channel Islands during Operation 'Overlord'.[2] It was possible, however, that there would be political pressure to recover them by force. A study was therefore made of the case for attacking the Islands. They were primarily a radar and coastal artillery outpost. They denied Allied shipping the use of the channel running parallel to the west coast of the Cotentin peninsula, but they did not threaten St. Malo or Granville and were little more than a nuisance so far as 'Overlord' was concerned.

[1] WO 166/2979; AIR 20/1614. [2] SHAEF 17100/1/Ops.

To capture them would take three or four divisions plus considerable naval and air strength – an unacceptable diversion of troops from the invasion of Europe. An airborne attack was out of the question because of the heavy concentration of anti-aircraft guns. This memorandum was filed away to be brought out if need be to defeat political pressure – not necessarily in Britain – to take the Islands by force.[1]

In October a further appraisal concluded that the surrender of the garrison was of no military importance whatsoever. There was evidence of a slight twinge of conscience when it was added that relations between the civil population and the garrison were said to be friendly: that is to say it would do no harm to leave the Islanders to their fate for a little longer. All efforts to induce formal surrender were to be abandoned. In the meantime Psychological Warfare Operations should play on the theme that the Germans in the Islands were prisoners of war who did not even have to be guarded.[2]

SHAEF speculated further about the position a month after D-Day. The Germans would now find it increasingly difficult to get supplies through. There would be no attempt to reinforce the garrisons, which would have no naval or air support, and would have to fend for themselves. Sound military strategy dictated evacuation, which would not be easy, but it would end the supply commitment and save the troops for use elsewhere. 'The decision, however, will presumably depend on the whim of Hitler; and it seems quite likely that he will refuse to agree to an evacuation and may order that the Islands are to be held to the last.'[3]

Lord Portsea suggested that a contingent of Islanders should undertake the 'redemption of the Norman Islands'. He was told that this would mean withdrawing men from units all over the world, which (although the Minister concerned was too polite to say so) was no more sensible than most of the ideas the noble lord had advanced during the preceding four years.[4] Shortly afterwards the Home Secretary was asked in the Commons if plans had been worked out for the return of the population after liberation. He replied that they had, but that until more was known about conditions in the Islands it was not possible to say what should be done to enable the evacuees to return.[5]

Sherwill, in internment at Laufen, also interested himself in the fate of the Islands. He wrote on 6 July 1944 to Sir Alexander Maxwell at the

[1] SHAEF 998/1.   [2] SHAEF 743/2.
[3] SHAEF 544/5.   [4] Hansard (Lords), vol. 132, col. 299.
[5] Hansard (Commons), vol. 401, cols. 1293–4.

Home Office telling him how anxious he and his fellow Islanders were about their near and dear ones. They feared that in the event of an Allied attack there would be many casualties. 'In so small an area troops and civilian population are inextricably mixed up.' It was equally worrying to think that there might be a long siege, and he hoped that the situation in the Islands might be given special consideration by the government. 'By the way, lest you should be tempted to misunderstand, I haven't succumbed to propaganda.' In spite of this reassurance the letter was treated with great caution in Whitehall. One official commented: 'It is thought that the writer got special permission from the German authorities to write the letter, which, from the contents, should not have been too difficult.' Maxwell sent a brief and non-committal reply.

Lord Portsea, who may have thought that his long campaign on behalf of the Islands should have made them one of the Allies' primary objectives, was on the warpath again at the beginning of 1945. He castigated the government for their attitude in a remarkable speech. At last there was evidence of the true situation – brought by desperate young men and women who had escaped from the Norman Islands, whose never-conquered people were now slaves by act of the government. The echoes of the cries of the children could be heard, little children dying slowly in their homes. During five awful years no single word or gesture of sympathy, of love, of praise for people of our own blood whose sons we had accepted in our armed forces. And so he continued for eight impassioned columns of Hansard, concluding with the suggestion that the Islanders should have been allowed to die decently in defence of their homes, instead of being slaves. Other noble lords pointed out that it would be more fitting if Lord Portsea thanked the government for the relief supplies now being sent; and the Earl of Munster said that he could rest assured that rehabilitation plans were being worked out.[1] Anxiety was also expressed, in rather more moderate terms, in the House of Commons.

Aerial reconnaissance and the interrogation of those who had escaped had built up a picture of the defences, and of some of the men in command. Von Schmettow was 'aged 52, probably ailing, and of no particular distinction'. 319 Infantry Division, which had never been in action, was in poor shape. The Islands were more heavily defended than any other sector of the West Wall. The beaches were blocked by anti-tank obstacles and covered by machine gun posts well forward,

<hr>

[1] Hansard (Lords), vol. 134, cols. 787-801.

and medium guns further inland. Coastal defence guns were sited on high and precipitous parts of the coast. Mining was not extensive – a seriously mistaken judgement. Although it was hoped that all this would be irrelevant, Southern Command had to assume that 'Nestegg' which they were responsible for mounting, might meet with opposition, for example because part of the garrison wanted to fight on. Even a single battery could take a fearful toll of an unsuspecting fleet. SHAEF agreed that because of the uncertainty small guinea-pig parties should precede the main force.[1] It was presumed, however, that the Islands would be taken without a shot being fired; Sherwill need not have troubled to try to influence the British government's thinking.

This left 'Nestegg' with the main objective of getting the Islands back on their feet again in the three months after liberation. It would of course first be necessary to disarm the troops, remove them from the Islands, clear the minefields, and so on; but that done, the problems would be purely administrative. The military commander was empowered to make defence regulations concurrently with the States of Guernsey and Jersey, where control would be exercised through the Island administrations. The administrative tasks were given to No. 20 Civil Affairs Unit, and the military to Force 135, commanded by Brigadier Alfred Snow, who was in charge of the whole operation.

In the months before VE-day the civil affairs unit and departments in Whitehall ensured that every possible need in the Islands had been anticipated. Food and clothing had the highest priority. So that they might be landed quickly 200 tons of specially selected items were loaded in vehicles which would drive straight up the beaches as soon as Force 135 arrived. A further 300 tons would go on the first transports. This food would be enough to raise the diet of the Islander to 2,750 calories a day for three months, after which supplies would come in through trade channels. Clothing equivalent to 15-months' ration in the United Kingdom would give the Islanders an early chance to replenish their virtually empty wardrobes; shortly afterwards a second 15-months' ration would be sent. Food and clothing would be sold through the shops. Lists showing prices current in Britain, which were often very different from those in 1940, were provided so that people would have some idea what the cost of further supplies would be. As a gesture of goodwill the British government decided to send a free gift of cigarettes, tobacco, and chocolate.

A host of articles, including pots and pans, needles and thread, and

[1] SHAEF 743/2.

boot repair outfits, were stockpiled so that they could be shipped at short notice. The Home Office and other officials working with the civil affairs unit did their best to make certain that nothing that mattered had been overlooked. Showing a humanity not usually associated with civil servants, they even proposed that a consignment of cosmetics should be included to help to rebuild the morale of the weaker sex. Assorted packs of medical supplies were prepared to bridge the gap until orders could be sent to Britain.

Arrangements had to be worked out for the restoration of sterling as the currency of the Islands. Although sterling notes and coins had for all practical purposes disappeared, the banks were still keeping accounts in sterling as book entries against payments and withdrawals of Reichsmarks; and to minimize the inconvenience in the early days after liberation it was proposed that Reichsmarks should continue to circulate. But the liberation force was to carry with it a million pounds sterling in notes and coin, and as soon as this was safely in the banks Reichsmarks could be exchanged for sterling. However, the most stringent precautions would have to be taken to prevent the smuggling of Reichsmarks from France, since it was likely that they would be valueless there at a time when they would still retain their value in the Channel Islands. Experts attached to the civil affairs unit would decide the rate of exchange, and they would advise on all financial matters, including the determination of wage levels and the price of essential commodities. On the one hand the danger of inflation must be avoided, and on the other wages must not be kept so low that the poor could not afford to buy their proper share of rationed food and clothing – objectives easy enough to define, but difficult to achieve.[1]

The civil affairs unit was not responsible for long-term reconstruction. It would remain in the Islands for only about three months. It was accepted, however, that it would become involved in long-term questions which needed to be handled in a way that would not prejudice future decisions. Experts from the Home Office would accompany the unit, and later on advisers from other departments would join them.

Sark, Herm, and Jethou would be looked after from Guernsey. Alderney, where there was no civilian population, was a special case. It would be under military government at first; and arrangements would be made by the military to feed any OT workers and other enemy aliens found there. A section of the civil affairs unit would, however, be sent to Alderney to help the commanding officer.

[1] WO 106/2991.

Essential supplies had been bought and stored at strategic points ready for shipment, the personnel of Civil Affairs Unit 20 had been appointed and briefed, expert advisers had been nominated, Task Force 135 had been assembled – and incidentally given most strenuous military training in the bombed streets of Plymouth, which suggested that the Force Commander was under the impression that his men would be required to take the Islands by assault. The planning of 'Nestegg' was complete. It remained only for the garrison to surrender or to withdraw to the Continent and thus give the signal for the operation to start; but it soon became obvious that the Germans were going to hold on as long as they could. At one point the presence in the Cotentin peninsula of a German unit suggested that there might be a general withdrawal to give 319 Infantry Division a chance to help to stem the Allied tide, but as the advance continued this became less likely, and finally impossible.[1] The psychological warfare operation which might have tipped the garrison over the brink of surrender in September 1944 had failed. The War Cabinet's decision to allow Red Cross supplies into the Islands at the end of 1944 meant in effect that the British government was prepared to leave the Germans in possession of the Islands until the general cessation of hostilities in Europe. Meanwhile Force 135 and No. 20 Civil Affairs Unit must wait patiently.

Home Office officials knew that there must be great disillusionment in the Islands, but there was little they could do about it. It was proposed in December to drop leaflets addressed 'to the inhabitants of the British Channel Islands from their fellow countrymen' adjuring them in impressive capitals to 'KEEP STOUT HEARTS' (words which the Home Secretary had suggested the Prime Minister might use in a broadcast speech), and reciting the Home Secretary's Commons statement of 12 December. Apart from letting the Islanders know that they had not been forgotten, this would have made the point once again that the Germans were responsible for keeping the people fed, and that the Red Cross supplies were supplementary. The Home Secretary feared, however, that the leaflet might make the Germans ban further Red Cross shipments. They were, of course, only too anxious to bring in the additional food, but they could conceivably have used a leaflet raid to justify taking it for themselves, or penalizing the people in some other way; and the project was wisely abandoned.

Whitehall's misgivings were in no way allayed by the report of the International Red Cross delegates, which became available in February

[1] AIR 15/447.

1945 and supplemented information brought by escapers. It led them to conclude that the Island administrations were much more closely controlled than they had thought. More serious, rations in December had been estimated at 1,137·5 calories a day, compared with 3,500 in Britain. The Germans had told the delegates that even this level would have to be reduced very soon, since they would need an increasing share of local production. Bread, cheese, fat, and sugar would run out at the end of January. Meat, however, would continue to be available at the rate of 4 ounces a head once in three weeks. When the delegates reminded von Schmettow of his obligations he said he would do his best for the people. When the War Cabinet met on 28 March they considered the case for adding the German commander to the list of war criminals, but decided that the evidence was not entirely convincing. They thought that further warnings at that stage would not be worthwhile, and that if a warning did become desirable it would be best given privately. Channel Islanders in Britain were also disturbed about the position. For example, the Horsforth Channel Islands' Society collected nearly 3,000 signatures for a petition that the government should offer the Germans 'honourable surrender' or arrange a truce for the removal of the people.

Island morale was at a low ebb on the eve of liberation. If the little children were not exactly dying slowly in their homes, as Lord Portsea believed, it was obvious that garrison and civilians alike faced serious trouble. The one ray of hope was the monthly visit by the *Vega*, but there was no certainty that the supplies she brought would continue to reach the people, and even her movements could be put at risk by events unconnected with the war, as for example when she was delayed because her master went down with mumps.

It was probably the news of Hitler's death (which they heard on 1 May) that convinced most of the Islanders that liberation was really just round the corner. They had been sadly disappointed in the summer of 1944 when they assumed that the Allied assault on Europe would take the Channel Islands in its stride; but now freedom seemed to be assured. The German rank and file had conceded defeat. When shops began to sell Union Jacks and people carried them openly through the streets the troops stood by and watched. As the days passed excitement mounted, and rumours of the surrender of the local garrisons became more frequent after the news of the final crumbling of the German armies in Europe.

In Jersey there was some trouble when the people began to taunt the soldiers, perhaps because of a B.B.C. announcement that the war would end in a day or two. The Bailiff had to step in on 7 May to ask that there should be no demonstrations. 'In town and country finishing touches were being put to flagstaffs and everyone got busy after the announcement that Victory-in-Europe Day would be to-morrow, but the position here is not clear as the Germans are still in occupation; there has been no slackening in warlike preparations on their part, for today new gun emplacements were being made in various parts of the Island . . . at night the Germans were at defence posts, guns were manned, and searchlights swept the seas.'[1]

Next day, 8 May, there was a feeling of anticlimax. The jubilation of the last week evaporated. Then came the news that changed everything. The Prime Minister would broadcast at 3 p.m. that afternoon. Coutanche announced this in a message which he had agreed with the Germans the day before. He appealed to the people to maintain calm and dignity, and to refrain from all forms of demonstration; and he expressed the hope that services of thanksgiving would be held, as they were being held in Britain and throughout the Empire. He also asked that flags should not be hoisted until after the Prime Minister had spoken.[2] In Guernsey the Bailiff and President of the Controlling Committee were informed by the Germans at 10 a.m. on the same day that the war was over. They were also told that after the Prime Minister's speech it would be in order to hoist flags. The Bailiff summoned a special meeting of the States at mid-day. These facts were reported in a tiny special issue of the Guernsey *Star* – a single sheet 8 inches by 5 – which was brought out in the course of the forenoon.

In Jersey 'the greatest crowd, of course, was in the Royal Square, which, with the windows of surrounding houses, was packed with listeners. As the Town Church clock struck three a cheer went up at the announcement that Mr. Churchill was to speak; his statement was punctuated by cheers, especially when he referred to "our dear Channel Islands"; and when at the conclusion the Bailiff hoisted the Union Jack and Jersey flag over the Courthouse, enthusiasm knew no bounds, and many wept unashamedly.'[3] In Guernsey too there were scenes of great emotion as people grasped the fact that the long night was at last over.

The Bailiff of Jersey sent a message to the Prime Minister saying that the Islands would ever remember his affectionate reference to them, and

[1] Sinel, pp. 286–7.   [2] JFW 30/149.   [3] Sinel, p. 287.

conveying in the name of the States and people of Jersey their undying gratitude for his inspiring leadership which had led to victory and the liberation of the Channel Islands. In his reply Churchill said: 'You should have heard the House of Commons cheer at the news of your liberation.'[1]

It was not until 3 May, when the end in Europe was in sight, that SHAEF alerted Operation 'Nestegg'. Two days later General Eisenhower signalled: 'Subject to your being satisfied as to intentions of German Commander, Channel Islands, you should complete mounting and launch *Nestegg* earliest practical date.' So that something might be deduced about Hüffmeier's intentions, a radio message was sent to the Islands. They were told that G.O.C., Southern Command, was authorized to receive their unconditional surrender. A 24-hour listening watch would be maintained to pick up any reply. There was silence until 5.36 p.m. on 6 May, when the German radio station at St. Peter Port acknowledged the message and announced bluntly that 'the Commander in Chief, Channel Islands, receives orders only from his own government'.[2]

This posed a problem. 'Nestegg' depended on the certainty of surrender, and here was a hint of the resistance which Southern Command had speculated about. At this point a situation report made a reference to Operation 'Omelet', which some of those concerned with 'Nestegg' had never heard about. It was in fact the pilot operation designed to land guinea-pig companies in each of Jersey and Guernsey to see whether there was going to be any resistance. This operation was in any case desirable, since the interval between surrender and reoccupation had to be kept short. It was also easier to send two companies quickly than the 6,000 men of 'Nestegg' with their mass of vehicles and other equipment.[3]

The unconditional surrender of the German High Command came on 7 May. All active operations would cease at one minute past midnight on 9 May. It was feared, however, that the Channel Islands might not have heard the news, and ships and aircraft reconnoitring in the neighbourhood were warned to be careful. In any case, Hüffmeier might elect to fight on alone. A further signal was sent to him saying that he must be aware of the German surrender and proposing that his representative should rendezvous four miles south of Les Hanois light to sign an instrument of surrender. He replied that he now had orders

[1] PREM 3/87.   [2] WO 106/2975, 2997.   [3] Ibid.

from higher authority. His accredited representative would be at Les Hanois at noon on 8 May.[1]

H.M.S. *Bulldog*, with H.M.S. *Beagle* in company, left Plymouth at 10 a.m. Brigadier Snow was in the *Bulldog*, which also carried a party of two officers and 20 other ranks – the first landing party for Guernsey. The *Beagle* had a similar party for Jersey. They rendezvoused with a German mine-sweeping trawler at noon to find that Hüffmeier had sent a junior naval officer, Kapitänleutnant Armin Zimmerman[2], who was authorized to do no more than discuss armistice terms. He was given a copy of the surrender document and a letter from Snow to the Commander-in-Chief stating that either he or his properly accredited representative must come prepared to accept unconditional surrender. There was no question of an armistice.

Before he left the *Bulldog* Zimmerman warned that his commander had guaranteed safe-conduct to H.M. ships as far as the rendezvous only. If they stayed where they were they would be fired on by the shore batteries. He pointed out that the general cease-fire was not due until 00.01 hours on 9 May and that as it was still 8 May the coastal guns would open fire. The Naval Force Commander, Rear-Admiral C. G. Stuart (who was serving as a captain), decided that it was less ignominious to retire than to run for it after a warning shot. He had been ordered by C-in-C, Plymouth, to watch for treachery, but not to man his guns unless it became necessary.[3] He withdrew to a safe distance until a signal came that Generalmajor Heine, second in command of the Channel Islands and commander of Guernsey, would come to the same rendezvous at midnight. Hüffmeier did not come himself because of unrest among his troops, but he made two points about the instrument of surrender. He could not ground his aircraft, since he had none; and he could not safeguard his records, which had been destroyed during the isolation of the Islands 'day by day and systematically'.[4]

As it was after midnight when Heine came on board, Hüffmeier could no longer threaten to fire on the destroyers. Snow therefore decided to move from Les Hanois to St. Peter Port. Southern Command were told that the surrender instrument would be signed at dawn, and they were asked to put Operation 'Omelet' in hand forthwith. The surrender was duly signed by Heine on the quarterdeck of the *Bulldog* at 7.14 a.m. on 9 May. Two small German craft were then called alongside, and after their Swastikas had been hauled down and replaced

[1] PREM 3/87.   [2] Later *Generalinspekteur der Bundeswehr*.
[3] SHAEF 171/1.   [4] WO 106/2985.

with White Ensigns the small advance party went ashore under the command of Lieutenant-Colonel Stoneman to hoist the Union Jack. They were accompanied by Colonel Power, head of the civil affairs unit.[1]

Brigadier Snow now transferred to the *Beagle*, which anchored off St. Helier at 10 a.m. to receive the surrender of the garrison of Jersey. Generalmajor Wulf, the *Inselkommandant*, was ordered on board but failed to put in an appearance. Snow said he must be found immediately. Eventually he turned up. He was at first 'somewhat arrogant and aggressive', but after Snow had expressed his severe displeasure (which he was well qualified to do) he was reduced 'almost to tears' and duly signed the surrender document. Coutanche, who was present during the ceremony accompanied by the Crown Officers, sent a radio message to the King assuring him of the devotion of the States and people of Jersey, who rejoiced that they could once more play their part within the British Empire. He sent another message to the Prime Minister to tell him that his reference to the Islands in his speech the day before would ever be remembered. Jersey promised him undying gratitude for his inspired leadership which had brought victory in Europe and the liberation of the Channel Islands.[2] The small advance party landed as soon as the surrender had been signed, and after fighting their way through enthusiastic crowds hung a Union Jack from a window in the Harbour Office.[2]

In the afternoon the larger 'Omelet' advance parties, which included civil affairs staff, representatives of the press, and a reconnaissance group to pave the way for the main 'Nestegg' expedition, arrived in both Islands. H.M.S. *Campion* escorted a landing craft with about 200 men to St. Peter Port, and H.M.S. *Cosby* another with a similar number to St. Helier.[3] 'To the great delight of the people' there was a fly-past of R.A.F. Mosquitoes and Mustangs.[3]

The following day, 10 May, the Union Jack was formally hoisted in the Royal Square in St. Helier in the presence of the Bailiff and Colonel Robinson. The National Anthem was sung with deep feeling, and the Bailiff received a great ovation from the people when he told them he had sent messages to the King and Prime Minister. The military commander praised Jerseymen for their fortitude in the last five years. There were, however, one or two discordant notes faithfully recorded by Sinel. Someone broke into the Masonic Temple, where the impounded

---

[1] WO 106/2986.   [2] WO 106/2975, 2986, 2994.
[3] WO 106/2994, 2996; ADM 199/179.

radio sets were stored, and handed them out to all and sundry. 'Since the hour of liberation there have been incidents involving females who had consorted with the German Forces and who had earned the name of "Jerry-bag" . . . regrettable scenes took place this evening when one or two of these women were severely handled, and possibly but for the intervention of the troops would have been murdered.' Known collaborators and black-marketeers also received rough treatment.[1] There was less trouble in Guernsey, although some girls lost their jobs when their employers were threatened in anonymous telephone calls.

The main 'Nestegg' force sailed from Plymouth on 11 May. Their escorting aircraft reported that white crosses were shining everywhere in accordance with the orders issued to the German commander.[2] This time it had been the Wehrmacht's job to do the painting. For the last three days mine-sweeping had been carried out in the approaches to Jersey and Guernsey to ensure safe passage for Force 135; but no mines were found. The force reached the Islands early on 12 May. The troops went ashore at once and met 'no opposition whatever except for the mobbing of the soldiers by an hilariously enthusiastic population'.[3] One landing craft beached in the Old Harbour at St. Peter Port, which was dry at low tide. Her vehicles and stores were unloaded as the tide served – 'a very thrilling sight for the enthusiastic crowd on the quayside'. St. Sampson's harbour proved unsuitable for beaching the landing craft, but the removal of the obstacles at L'Ancresse Bay made it a satisfactory substitute. Three landing craft unloaded there. When all the craft were successfully unloaded they stood by to embark the prisoners of war.

Brigadier Snow landed at St. Peter Port at 10.45 a.m. and received Hüffmeier's surrender. The Admiral explained that he could not hand over his sword as he had destroyed it in accordance with orders. He was turned over as a prisoner of war to the commander of H.M.S. *Faulkner*, who proceeded to Jersey to pick up Wulf, the *Inselkommandant*. Snow marched to the Court House attended by several staff officers 'through streets bedecked with flags and lined with a wildly cheering throng of people'. He called on the Bailiff and was introduced to the members of the States. Champagne which had been hidden for years was brought out and the arrival of Force 135 was suitably toasted. At

---

[1] Sinel, p. 289.   [2] WO 106/2986, 2994.
[3] 'The loudest cheer was for the austere London civil servant who walked off the first assault craft, bowler-hatted, clutching a rolled umbrella and briefcase.' *The Observer*, 13 May 1945.

2 p.m. Snow read the Royal Proclamation vesting in him the powers of military commander before a large and enthusiastic audience at Elizabeth College. Then the King's message welcoming the Islands back to their rightful place with the free nations of the world, and expressing the wish that their ancient privileges and institutions should be maintained, was read out.[1]

Snow then proceeded to Jersey. The landings there had gone just as smoothly as in Guernsey and the same ceremonial was followed. The commander's party marched to the Royal Court to meet the Bailiff and the members of the States. The Royal Proclamation and the King's message were read, and were no less enthusiastically received.

On 1 May the Dame of Sark heard the news of Hitler's death on her illicit radio. On 8 May, having learned that Dönitz had surrendered, she hoisted the Union Jack and the Stars and Stripes (the latter in honour of the Seigneur, her American husband, still in internment in Germany) on the tall, square, mock-Elizabethan Seigneurie tower. The whole population was summoned to the Island Hall to listen to the Prime Minister's broadcast at 3 p.m. with his reference to the liberation of the Channel Islands. 'We still had 275 Germans all around us.' There was no sign from them that they had surrendered, and there was not a single Allied soldier on the Island. Nevertheless, that evening a huge bonfire was lit. It was seen from Guernsey, where some feared that the Germans were engaging in an orgy of destruction.

At 2 p.m. on 10 May a German motor boat with three British officers and 20 men was sent to Sark. They reported that everything was satisfactory. The shortage of food and essential commodities had been no less serious than on the other Islands, but the people were in reasonably good shape. The Germans were judged to have behaved correctly during the occupation.[2] After the British party had got in touch with the Dame and the German commander, who was reluctant to appear, the officer in charge explained that he could not spare any men for Sark for the time being, and asked if the Dame would mind being left on her own for a few days. She replied: 'As I have been left for nearly five years I can stand a few more days.' She goes on record in her autobiography: 'Our Liberation Force boarded the tug and *I* was left in command of 275 German troops! Next day I gave three orders. First, to remove the mines from the harbour; second to remove the anti-glider posts from among our crops; and third, to hand back our

[1] HO 45/19851.   [2] WO 106/2968.

wireless sets. It gave me enormous satisfaction after all these years to be giving orders over the telephone to the Germans and saying "Repeat, please", and then to hear the German voice answer, "*Zu Befehl, Gnädige Frau*".[1]

The Dame was in command of the German forces in her Island until 17 May, when the whole of the garrison was removed to prisoner of war camps in England.[2]

The Home Secretary, the member of the Privy Council most concerned with Channel Island affairs, visited Guernsey and Jersey on 14 and 15 May. He had told the Prime Minister in August 1944 that he intended to visit the Islands after liberation. Churchill agreed, but added that he should wait until the Germans had been turned out. On 9 May he minuted General Ismay: 'As soon as the Channel Islands have been liberated, about which I require constant reports, arrangements should be made for the Home Secretary to visit this part of the British Isles.[3] The War Office objected to an early visit on security grounds, but Morrison said that he wanted to see the Germans being rounded up. In spite of his earlier suggestion Churchill overruled the War Office.[4]

The Home Secretary's purpose was to express to the Islanders the sympathy of His Majesty's Government and of the British people in the ordeal through which they had passed. He also wanted to see conditions at first hand and to learn how Britain could now help the Islands. He told the House of Commons after his visit that he had found things much better than might have been expected. By the time he arrived considerable progress had been made by Force 135 in distributing supplies and in removing the Germans. The Island herds were reduced, but still intact. The most cordial relations had been established between the liberation troops and the Island authorities, and they were working together in complete harmony. The cordiality of his own reception was moving in the extreme.

He had explained to the States in both bailiwicks how it had been necessary in the interests of the Islands to withdraw British troops in 1940, and why the Islands had not been taken by force after D-Day. He was able to assure the House that 'It was clear that these courses

[1] Hathaway, pp. 170–1. After his visit the Home Secretary said that Mrs. Hathaway appeared to have remained 'almost wholly mistress of the situation' throughout the occupation. PREM 3/87.

[2] ADM 199/188.   [3] PREM 3/87.

[4] The Home Secretary's party included Major Wallace Le Patourel, a Guernseyman who had won the V.C. in 1942 in North Africa at Rebourba, where he was wounded and taken prisoner.

were both understood and approved.' (Had the Islanders been in possession of all the facts about demilitarization and evacuation, and the Prime
Minister's initial opposition to sending in food supplies, they might
have been less understanding and approving, even in the euphoric
atmosphere of liberation.)

The health and physique of the people were better than he, at least,
had dared to hope. He was particularly impressed by the healthy
appearance of the children. This was in large measure due to the
supplies received from the British Red Cross and Order of St. John
through the agency of the International Red Cross, without which the
situation would have become very grave. The Germans had not
attempted to divert these supplies to their own use, although he was
told that they had been reduced to eating cats and dogs. There had been
a gratifying absence of the grosser and cruder atrocities associated with
the Nazis, but there was plenty of evidence of wanton damage. Except
for the brutal and senseless deportations, the treatment of the Islanders
had been comparatively favourable. 'But no one who has not lived
under the Nazi yoke can fully appreciate what it means to an independent and proud people, and, as I was told, the liberation came like the
awakening from a nightmare.'[1]

At the end of his statement the Home Secretary was bombarded with
questions which reflect the anxiety which the House had felt about the
Islands during the occupation. Was everything all right in Sark?
When would the telephone service be restored? Was the Minister of
Agriculture doing enough to help the dairy farmers? Were there
plenty of doctors? When would the air service to the Islands restart?
Could the House be assured that the Germans would be kept there
until allegations of mass murder had been investigated? What about
Alderney?

Alderney's turn for liberation came on 16 May. Little was known
about the state of affairs there. Some people from the other Islands had
made their escape via Alderney after working there for the Germans,
but the amount of information they provided was relatively scanty.
In October 1944, when the 'Nestegg' planning was still under way, it
was recognized that Alderney might elect to fight on, and it was decided
that when the liberation force sailed no ship should venture within
27,000 yards of the guns there.[2] In the event, however, there was no
difficulty. Troops from Force 135 crossed from Guernsey in two
landing craft, their stores being carried in the War Department coaster

[1] Hansard (Commons), vol. 410, col. 2611.   [2] AIR 9/257.

Beal. On 20 May five landing craft evacuated 2,332 prisoners of war (of whom 170 were hospital cases) to the United Kingdom. Four of the landing craft went alongside the 300-foot pier running from Little Crabby harbour, which the Germans had built and on which the Royal Navy bestowed their professional approval. It made it possible to embark the prisoners within five hours. The sick men were taken to the fifth landing craft, which had anchored in Braye Harbour, in DUKWs, which swam off the ramp at the shore end of the West Breakwater. Vehicles were disembarked and a headquarters established.[1] 500 Germans were left on Alderney to clear up the mess made in the last five years – which puts the total strength of the garrison at liberation at 2,832 men.

The British naval commander reported that the Germans did not attempt to demolish any of the port facilities in the Islands, and that they were most co-operative in indicating all the explosive charges laid in breakwaters and jetties. These had been rendered safe, as was required by the surrender terms, and they were being removed with creditable speed. There were controlled minefields guarding the harbours at St. Peter Port and St. Sampson's, which had been put to 'safe' by the Germans who had explained the firing mechanisms.[2]

On 17 May Trinity House officers visited the lighthouses in the Islands area – Les Hanois, near which the rendezvous with the Germans had taken place, the Casquets, and those on Sark and Alderney. All lights and machinery were found to be in good order and it was agreed to get them going again as soon as possible. Two German officers and 20 other ranks were removed from the Casquets and taken to Guernsey as prisoners of war. Six others were left as a maintenance crew for the time being.[3]

The final act in the round of liberation celebrations came on 7 June, when the King and Queen visited first Jersey and then Guernsey.[4] In Jersey they attended a meeting of the States where the Bailiff moved a Loyal Address, to which the King graciously replied. In Guernsey the Bailiff read a Loyal Address at an open air meeting. In his reply the King said that he had felt deeply for his people of Guernsey and Sark throughout the long years of occupation, and that it gave him great joy that the Channel Islands, the oldest possessions of the Crown, were once again restored to freedom.

[1] ADM 199/188.   [2] Ibid.   [3] Ibid.
[4] They had been prevented by bad weather from flying to the Islands on 6 June.

When the liberation of the Islands was being planned in London there was no knowledge of the conditions the troops would meet when they arrived. It was therefore necessary as a precautionary measure to arm the force commander with very extensive powers. This was accomplished by the Defence (Channel Islands) Regulations, 1944, an all-embracing code dealing with essential supplies and services, assisting the enemy, sabotage, control of communications, restriction of the movement and activities of people, and public safety and order, so that the force commander would be able to deal with virtually any situation. In the event the reoccupation was completely orderly and the Regulations were used only for technical purposes, for example changing the time back from German to British. It was provided that the States in Jersey and the Royal Court in Guernsey might make Defence Regulations applying only to their own bailiwicks, subject to the approval of the military commander.

One of the uncertainties was what had been happening to legislation. The isolation of the Islands from Britain after the middle of 1940 interrupted the normal legislative processes. In the absence of the usual sanction of the King in Council, the *Actes des États* in Jersey had in 1940 and 1941 been 'approved by the commandant of the German troops occupying this Island' and sanctioned by the Bailiff '*en ses qualités de Lieutenant Gouverneur de cette Île*' – and thereafter simply in his capacity of Bailiff. *Projets de loi* in Guernsey had in 1940 and 1941 been promulgated by 'the British Civil Lieutenant-Governor of the Island of Guernsey' in exercise of the power conferred on him by an order of the commandant of the German forces in occupation of the bailiwick of Guernsey, of 2 July 1940. After 1941 'the British Civil Lieutenant-Governor' was dropped. None of the measures passed under these arrangements had received the sanction of the King in Council, and those passed after 1941 deliberately excluded the style 'Lieutenant-Governor' because the Germans objected to the implied recognition of the Crown.

It was therefore arguable that the authorities in both bailiwicks had been *ultra vires* in acting on the legislation; and since it dealt largely with taxation matters it was essential to put the position beyond all doubt at the earliest possible moment. This could not be done under the powers held by the military commander. It was necessary for the States in both bailiwicks to pass laws re-enacting the suspect occupation measures which were sanctioned by Orders in Council of 14 August 1945. The Confirmation of Laws (Jersey) Law put 46 wartime measures on a proper footing, and a corresponding law in Guernsey dealt with 31 wartime measures.

Defence regulations made in the Islands during the occupation were in the same uncertain state as their 'statute law'. The United Kingdom Emergency Powers Act had in 1939 enabled the States of Jersey and the Royal Court of Guernsey to make their own Defence Regulations without waiting for legislation in Britain.[1] (A draft code of Defence Regulations had been agreed with the United Kingdom authorities before the war, and it was understood that the Islands would broadly follow this.) The Island authorities duly made numbers of regulations both before and after the occupation which, so far as they were concerned, were perfectly good law.

They had no means of knowing that on 15 August 1941 an Order in Council was made in Britain revoking the 1939 Orders, which empowered them to make their own Defence Regulations – the reason being the fear that the Germans would use for their own benefit assets in neutral countries of companies registered in the Channel Islands. This could be frustrated by registering these companies in Britain. To do this it was necessary to alter the law both of Britain and of the Channel Islands, and to reinvest in the King in Council the power to make Defence Regulations which had been conferred on the Islands. In the submission of the proposed Orders to the King in Council it was explained that after the invasion of the Channel Islands the continuance of the Orders giving the Islands power to make their own regulations had become anomalous, but there had been no need to revoke them earlier.

The effect of this was that after 15 August 1941 all Defence Regulations which had been made in the Channel Islands were without the support of the parent Order in Council. But since no one in the Islands was aware that the parent Order had been pulled from beneath their feet the practical position was not affected, whatever the position may have been in pure law.

On liberation, however, it was necessary to regularize matters, perhaps even more so than in the case of 'statute law'. For this purpose a new and truly splendid Defence Regulation was drafted. Whereas His Majesty the King had been pleased to extend to Jersey and Guernsey certain provisions of the Emergency Powers (Defence) Act by Orders in Council in 1939; and whereas the States of Jersey and the Royal Court of Guernsey had used the powers thus vested in them to make Defence

[1] See above pp. 18–19.

Regulations; and whereas His Majesty had been further pleased in 1941 to revoke the Orders in Council of 1939; and whereas by reason of the severance of communication between the United Kingdom and the Channel Islands the Island authorities had never heard of this revocation; and whereas in Jersey certain Orders had been made or purported to have been made under the authority which had thus been revoked; and whereas the same thing had happened with the Ordinances in Guernsey; and whereas it was expedient for maintaining supplies and services essential to the life of the community that these Orders and Ordinances should continue to have effect – Brigadier Snow made a new Defence Regulation listing all the suspect Orders and Ordinances and breathing into them renewed and undoubted virtue.[1]

[1] The Defence (Channel Islands) Regulations, 1944. (Signed 13 June, and promulgated 16 June 1945.)

14

Aftermath

THE period of military government ended on 25 August 1945 when a Lieutenant-Governor was again appointed in each bailiwick.[1]

The troops had in the meantime successfully carried out a whole range of tasks. They had processed and evacuated to prisoner of war camps in the United Kingdom all the German troops, who at the time of liberation numbered about 27,000 men,[2] except for 3,200 who were kept back to clear mines, and to remove the 'spiders' and other anti-air-landing devices from the fields, the roll-bombs from the cliffs, and the anti-tank girders from the beaches. They had also made good progress with cleaning up and rehabilitating houses and hotels occupied by the Germans, and removing those of the fortifications which seriously interfered with amenities, again using prisoner of war labour. A major task was the dismantling of guns all over the Islands and collecting them together in central depots where they could be disposed of as scrap metal. There were over 1,000, half with a calibre of 88 mm. and above; and there were 50,000 tons of ammunition to be rendered harmless and dumped at sea.[3] There were also huge quantities of rifles, machine guns, and other weapons. Evidence was taken by intelligence officers from the prisoners of war, the political prisoners, and the OT workers in an attempt to identify war criminals. A special effort was made to track down members of the Gestapo, some of whom tried to lose their identity by donning uniform for the first time, by pretending to be sick privates and disappearing into hospital, or by committing themselves to prison where they hoped to pass unnoticed. The allegations of mass murder in Alderney, where there had been few Channel Islands

[1] Lieutenant-General A. E. (later Sir Edward) Grasett (Jersey); and Lieutenant-General P. (later Sir Philip) Neame, VC (Guernsey).

[2] The recorded figures vary from about 26,000 to 28,000.

[3] WO 106/3013.

witnesses during the occupation, were the subject of a special investigation.

Good progress was also made on the civil affairs side. The immediate problems were mostly solved during the period of military government; and a satisfactory start was made with longer-term matters, which it had been accepted from the outset could not be settled within two or three months. At the end of May Snow reported that the Island administrations were coping admirably with only a small amount of help from the civil affairs unit; he was very glad to let them get on with it. Electricity and water were gradually coming back. Coal had arrived for the gasworks and the gas supply would be restored before long. There were no serious difficulties in the maintenance of law and order, although there was still a good deal of pilfering – so much indeed that it was suspected that Germans in hiding must be responsible.

The telephone and postal services to the mainland had been restarted. The clothing brought by the liberation force went on sale in the shops in Jersey on 14 June and in Guernsey two days later. Sterling again became the Islands' sole currency. In Jersey Reichsmarks were called in between 16 and 23 May and exchanged for sterling at the rate which had been current for the greater part of the occupation – 9·36 to the pound. The banks closed in both bailiwicks on 18 and 19 June so that accounts opened in Britain by customers who had been evacuated could be merged with those which they had left in the Islands. On 20 June they were back to peacetime working.[1]

Although the shape of the Islands' agriculture had been greatly changed during the occupation in order to feed the people rather than to produce early potatoes, tomatoes, fruit and flowers for the British market, it was relatively easy to change it back again. The numbers of cattle had been well maintained. In Guernsey on the eve of the invasion there were about 4,300 head, to which were added 400 rescued from Alderney, and at the liberation the number was almost exactly the same, although the average age of the animals was higher. In Jersey the herds had fallen from 9,600 to 8,250. Pigs and poultry in both Islands had virtually disappeared because of the lack of feeding stuffs, but as soon as imports of the latter became available again it was possible to start rebuilding stocks. Some pigs, however, were imported to speed up the pro-

---

[1] Arrangements were made to issue Guernsey notes to the banks on liberation. They were printed by the Guernsey Press Co. Ltd. on a press alongside one in constant use by the Germans, who were quite oblivious to what was going on. The exchange was made in Guernsey immediately on liberation under arrangements worked out by the Controlling Committee during 1944. GF 5/1/25.

cess. The civil affairs unit reported in June that agriculture and fishing were beginning to return to normal as the fields were cleared of obstructions and the slipways in the harbours were rehabilitated; but they later recorded that fishing was 'desultory and half-hearted', which showed that the malaise of the pre-war period had not been overcome.[1]

On 8 August Colonel Power summed up the position after 90 days of military government. The Crown Officers were again in charge of legal affairs, but in Guernsey the Attorney General (Sherwill) 'weakened by two years in a German internment camp' was the only law officer available. There was no Solicitor General, and no legal draftsman. The civil affairs unit had therefore detailed a legal adviser to act as assistant to the Attorney General. In Jersey the legal help originally provided had been withdrawn since the Crown Officers were well able to cope.

For the time being there was a marked difference in the earning power of the Islands. The export of potatoes from Jersey to Britain had been forbidden – no one knew for how long – because of the presence of Colorado beetle. There could be no question of resuming the tourist traffic in 1945, and the prospects for 1946 were uncertain. There was no doubt, however, that in the long run all would be well; and in Guernsey at least there was no obstacle to a rapid return to prosperity. Her tomato exports should do well in the next two or three years. There was still some danger of public discord, but in the view of the head of the civil affairs unit 'a good deal of steam had gone out of the political boiler'. This referred to the discontent felt by some who believed that the Island authorities had failed to deal adequately with the situation created by the occupation.

Although the whole population of the Channel Islands could have been evacuated in a matter of days in 1940 there was no question of bringing the evacuees back in such a short period. The main limiting factors were accommodation and jobs in the Islands. Ships could have been made available at a pinch, but although many wanted to return immediately there was no point in rushing the people back before there were homes and jobs for them. This was agreed with representatives of the Islands at a meeting at the Home Office on 1 June. It would be up to the two bailiwicks to decide on priorities. They would prepare lists of those who should have preference which would be sent to the Passport

[1] WO 106/3007. Offers of help were received from the English Guernsey Cattle Society and the American Jersey and Guernsey Cattle Clubs covering the replacement of stock, provision of food and clothing for needy breeders, and the rebuilding of homes and farms, all of which were refused.

Office in Britain for the issue of travel permits. Priority would be given to those who had jobs waiting, especially workers in the building and allied trades, and to people whose arrival 'would create no immediate problem'. There was also a special dispensation for members of parliament, trade union officials, and heads of religious denominations. Sympathetic consideration would be given to men on embarkation leave for the Far East, former prisoners of war, and people with critically-ill relatives. The plan was that a single ship would make three trips a week with 200 passengers.

The Home Secretary said in the Cabinet on 8 June that a pledge had been given at the time of the liberation that those who had left the Islands in 1940 would be given the opportunity to return. Unfortunately the vessel earmarked to carry them would not be ready for eight weeks, and it was essential in his view that something should be done at once. Since there was no ship available he proposed that Transport Command should provide enough aircraft to fly 600 people a week to the Islands. It was decided, however, that the planes could not be spared, and the Minister of War Transport agreed to divert a ship from the Dieppe service.[1] The first sailing was made on 25 June and thereafter a steady stream returned to Jersey and Guernsey week by week until the normal passenger sailings were resumed.

The liberation force commander had been armed with a financial plan, the main objectives of which were 'to assist the Islands administration as far as possible to re-establish without delay a sound and prosperous financial structure', and to help the banks 'to get into full working order as soon as possible'. One difficulty was that the levels of prices and wages in the Islands, which the financial experts on the force commander's staff had been briefed to examine carefully, had not kept pace with those in the United Kingdom; and since the Islanders were now committed to pay United Kingdom prices for their imports this meant that wages must be increased. This process, which had to be gradual, was begun during the military period. 'There was need at the same time for the imposition of fresh taxation to mop up some of the surplus spending power that had got into other hands during the occupation. The C.A. unit pressed frequently for the preparation of proposals but these were slow in coming forward and little had been done before the end of the military period.'[2]

[1] PREM 3/87.
[2] F. S. V. Donnison, *Civil Affairs and Military Government, North West Europe 1944–1946* (London, 1961), p. 181.

L

Liberation found the governments of both bailiwicks in a difficult financial position. On the one hand revenue during the occupation had been much less than normal; and on the other expenditure was greatly increased by the occupation costs which the Islands had to bear under the Hague Convention, especially during the last year. This meant that they had to borrow heavily from the banks, and at the liberation Jersey owed them £5,960,000 and Guernsey £4,232,000. There was, of course, a great deal of sympathy for the Islanders' position both on the part of the British government and on the part of the banks. They had made generous contributions towards the cost of the war while they were still in a position to do so, and a very high proportion of their men had served as volunteers in the British forces. It was accepted that they must not suffer unduly because they alone had had the misfortune to be occupied. Even the Germans had seen that the occupation costs were disproportionately heavy in the Islands, and they had tried to mitigate them. They had also argued that it would be for the British Empire as a whole to shoulder the burden at the end of the war.

The Islands were also faced with the heavy cost of rehabilitation. It was estimated that to make good damage and to catch up with maintenance which had not been undertaken in the last five years would cost £1,500,000 in Jersey and £1,750,000 in Guernsey. On top of this there was the cost of the evacuation, the financing of those evacuees who had no means of support, and the education in Britain of the children, mainly from Guernsey, which added another £1,000,000 to the bill. At the time of the evacuation both bailiwicks had given undertakings that they would be responsible for these costs; but after the liberation the British government decided that it would be wrong to hold them to this and offered to meet the whole cost of the evacuation.

The banks agreed to help by refunding the interest which had accrued on loans to the Island governments during the occupation and to waive further interest which would arise before a general settlement was made. The British government, after discussion with the representatives of the Islands, agreed to provide a capital sum of £7,500,000 – £4,200,000 to Jersey and £3,300,000 to Guernsey. It was a condition of this gift that the money should be used solely to liquidate the debts owing to the banks, and secondly that the States should ensure the strictest economy in plans for rehabilitation. To cover the balance of the Islands' debt, which was estimated at about £3,000,000, the banks accepted States' bonds. It was decided that there would be no payments for war damage but financial assistance would be given by the

Island governments in cases where the repair of war damage was
necessary for the general prosperity of the community. Assessors were
brought in from the United Kingdom to give help in this field.[1]

In the weeks after the liberation essential supplies were sent through
military channels in accordance with programmes worked out in
advance in Britain and adjusted in the light of experience. The Islanders
were grateful for this help, but their independent spirit made them
anxious to resume normal trading with a minimum of delay. It was
considered to be impossible, however, to restore accustomed trade
channels immediately, since they had been distorted in Britain by a host
of wartime controls which were still in force. With the encouragement
of the Home Office the Islands set up Purchasing Missions in London.
They worked in close collaboration with the government departments
which regulated supplies. Orders for 'producer goods' (by which was
meant food, fuel, fertilizers, and so on) which related to the pre-war
volume of business were collected from local importers and submitted
to the appropriate control in the United Kingdom. Shipments were
arranged by the Purchasing Missions in consultation with the Ministry
of War Transport, and when the goods arrived in the Islands they were
allocated to individual traders. Consumer goods, many of which were
subject to less stringent controls, were separately dealt with. Orders
were sent to the suppliers by the Purchasing Missions, and a special
branch of the Board of Trade was established 'to shepherd Channel
Island orders through the United Kingdom machine'.

The policy makers of the Board of Trade were unhappy about these
arrangements since they had assumed that private trading would be
resumed as soon as the military period ended. They saw in the establishment of Purchasing Missions a postponement of the resumption of
normal commercial relations, which it was feared would cause ill-feeling
among the United Kingdom suppliers and their customers in the Islands.
Even the severe restriction of shipping space was no reason for a delay
in the return to normal trade. The needs of the Islands were so small
that there was no reason to create special machinery to meet them.

These misgivings were expressed in a letter of 4 June to the Home
Office. The day before, the civil affairs unit had written almost lyrically
to both Bailiffs observing that the Purchasing Missions formed the
keystone on which the whole economic future of the Islands would be
built, and wishing them every success at this moment of destiny when

[1] WO 106/3007.

they were starting out on their new enterprise. The Missions would be housed at the Home Office, where Mr. J. B. Howard would act as their expert pilot through the puzzling waters of departmental purchasing procedures – even the waters round the Channel Islands did not present more difficult problems for the unwary navigator. The letter, which it is to be hoped was dictated after an ample lunch, came down to earth in its closing passages by reminding the Bailiffs that the food brought by the liberation forces would last only to the end of the first week in August, and that their representatives would have to work hard to safeguard the position thereafter.

Whether or not they were necessary, the Purchasing Missions were going concerns. The Home Office could do little more than make this point in answer to the Board of Trade's objections. They did, however, add that it would be quite impossible to allow a 'free for all' over the next month or two since departments would have to ensure that purchases were kept at a reasonable level; but they saw no case for special arrangements after this period. In the event the Purchasing Missions carried on until the end of November 1945, after which the Islands' imports were again handled by private traders.

There were demands in both bailiwicks that those who had collaborated or fraternized with the Germans should be brought to book. Arrangements for dealing with allegations of collaboration were announced at the end of June,[1] and a great deal of the time of the civil affairs officers was devoted to taking statements from men and women who suspected that some of their fellow Islanders had gone out of their way to help the Germans and deserved to be punished. An attempt had been made earlier to classify the presumed offenders. There were the women who had associated with the occupying troops. There was, for example, one 'who was, shall we say, hostess to the German general', and another who was 'on the terms of the most intimate friendship with German officers, some of them very senior, and it is considered unlikely that those friendships were purely platonic'. Then there were people 'who had entertained Germans or who had unduly friendly social contacts', war profiteers, and informers. War profiteers could best be dealt with through fiscal measures. Informers and those who had worked for the Germans might conceivably be prosecuted under the Treachery Act.

It was established that a number of people had behaved in an

[1] WO 106/3007.

'unseemly, undesirable, and even disgraceful way'; but none of those who gave evidence was able to allege anything which, if proved, would substantiate a charge of treason or treachery. The law as it stood did not provide an appropriate penalty for the actions of those who had informed, even though in some cases they had been directly responsible for the death of fellow-Islanders who were the object of their spite; and there could be no question of retrospective legislation. In any case it would have been virtually impossible to find conclusive evidence in an area where suspicion, hatred, and feuds obscured the truth. It was felt that the ends of justice would best be served if it was left to the people as a whole to ostracize those who were supposed to be guilty – an unsatisfactory solution which contained a gentle hint of the lynch law of the American West. On the strength of what evidence was ostracism to be applied? How far was it to be carried? Most important, what remedy did the innocent victim have?

By far the biggest collaborator was the Dutch national who entered into contracts with the Germans to supply vegetables, and was allocated a large acreage of glasshouses.[1] He acted as purchasing agent for the forces and scoured Guernsey for supplies, offering other growers high prices which his contractual arrangements with the Germans made possible. He was allowed to export freely to France, which the ordinary grower could not do. Had he been a native Islander he would have faced serious charges; but since he was an alien there was nothing that could be done except to relieve him through the war profits levy of the substantial fortune he had amassed during the occupation.

By the end of September most of the pressure on the Island authorities – and on the Home Office – to take action against alleged collaborators had been dissipated, although many people continued to feel bitterly about them.

A few Islanders had made a lot of money during the occupation. These profits were mostly in Reichsmarks which were made convertible to sterling after the liberation so that they were really paid out of the United Kingdom grant to put the Islands on their feet, or from their own exchequers. It was therefore all the more desirable that the excess wartime profits should return to the general revenues, and in both Islands there was legislation for this purpose. In Jersey there was a levy of 60 per cent of profits earned in 1940-1944, and a charge of 80 per cent on casual transactions not subject to tax, for example, the sale of jewellery. All profits arising from currency exchange were forfeit.

[1] See above pp. 120-1.

(Some people had bought Reichsmarks with Treasury notes during the occupation at a very cheap rate and reconverted them to sterling at the official rate after the liberation, thereby making a considerable profit.)

In Guernsey a tax was imposed on profits arising in the course of business between 1 July 1940 and 30 June 1945, the rate being 80 per cent of the first £10,000 profits in excess of a standard profit, and 100 per cent thereafter.[1]

The Attorney General of Guernsey summed up the thinking behind this legislation. The bulk of the population had suffered grievous financial loss during the occupation, and it was unconscionable that a minority of firms and individuals by reason of special circumstances, or good luck, or low moral standards, should reap a rich harvest. There was no intention that profits earned 'in pursuit of patriotic motives' should be exempt.

The last point was material in one case in which an employee of the *Soldatenkaufhaus* in St. Peter Port, who found himself in charge of large quantities of scarce and highly-prized goods not available to the civilian population, decided as a public-spirited act to divert some of these goods to them, regardless of the considerable risk to himself. Small quantities of similar things, however, were occasionally available from France at very high prices, and it was necessary to raise the prices of the *Soldatenkaufhaus* goods which were leaked to the general public 'in order that the German authorities should not trace the source'. In a period of three years goods worth well over £150,000 were thus diverted from the Germans to the Islanders. Since the enterprising individual who hit on this ingenious method of sapping German morale paid nothing for the goods he sold, substantial sums incidentally reached his own pocket.

In spite of the fact that Guernseymen as a whole – or at least those who could afford to pay the high prices – benefited from the diversion of the goods, the organizer of the leakage was required under the War Profits Law to hand over to the States Treasury the money which he had earned from his public-spirited action. He claimed that had he taken such risks on behalf of the people in Britain his services would have been officially recognized.

The problem of the collaborationists was finally settled, as far as it could be, in November 1946 – to the dissatisfaction of many in both Islands who still wanted their pound of flesh. The Home Secretary was asked in the Commons how many people resident in the Channel

[1] War Profits Levy (Jersey) Law, 1945; War Profits (Guernsey) Law, 1945.

Islands had been reported to his department for collaboration, and what action was contemplated. He said in a written reply that communications alleging unpatriotic behaviour on the part of a limited number of British subjects in the Channel Islands had been received by the Home Office and by the commander of the liberation forces. Careful enquiries were made into all the allegations, many of which were found to be based on hearsay and suspicion. In only 12 cases was there information to suggest consideration of the question of prosecution; but the Director of Public Prosecutions decided that in no case was there sufficient ground for a criminal prosecution.[1]

This did not please those eager for revenge or to see that justice was done. Many may have felt – as did one of the deportees[2] – that there was a 'conspiracy of silence and non-action' between the Channel Island and British authorities. No doubt had the Island governments been prepared to adopt the standards of justice to which the Germans had worked during the occupation, the collaborators would have been punished to the satisfaction of their accusers – perhaps at the cost of also punishing innocent suspects. Fortunately the Island authorities refused to depart from their accustomed standards.

It was inevitable that a good many Islanders should feel that they had been let down by Britain; and the failure to publicize the King's message on the eve of invasion did not help to dispel this feeling. The lack of satisfactory means of communication during the years of the occupation made it virtually impossible to show the Islanders that they were not forgotten, and that many in Britain wanted to help them. The Red Cross messages did no more than tell people that friends and relatives were still alive; and the B.B.C., whose programmes were heard throughout the occupation – most of the time on illicit radios – could not possibly convey to the Islanders one hundredth part of the sympathy for their plight which existed in parliament and among the British public.

The question of broadcasting to the Islands was examined at intervals during the war. In November 1940 the Home Office expressed the hope that the B.B.C. would not make direct broadcasts because it might lead to trouble with the Germans. There was no objection to Channel Island programmes directed to United Kingdom listeners which the Islands could pick up, but it was feared that anything in the nature of 'resistance programmes' or programmes designed to keep morale at a high level would meet with the Germans' disfavour, and perhaps lead

---

[1] Hansard (Commons), vol. 430, col. 138.   [2] Falla, p. 186.

to reprisals. The Channel Islands Refugee Committee from time to time pressed for broadcasts, but because of the advice from the Home Office, which seems to have been eminently sensible, the B.B.C. did not act on their suggestions.

It was mooted in both houses of parliament that there should be special broadcasts to let the Islanders know that they were not entirely forgotten; but these proposals were consistently rejected. The reply was given in the Lords in January 1942 that direct broadcasts might lead to the impounding of all radio sets, and thus add to the existing hardships.[1] Nevertheless the B.B.C. found it possible to cater for the Islands in a number of ways. Lord Justice du Parcq twice made appeals for the Channel Islands Refugees Fund on the weekly 'good cause' programme. The Bishop of Winchester, in whose diocese the Islands were, also made a broadcast appeal. There was a talk on the Islands by Sir Donald Banks, one of their most distinguished soldiers. There was a Channel Islands feature programme in the Home Service in October 1940, which was later repeated in the Overseas Service. The introduction of the Red Cross message scheme was announced in November 1940. Other programmes brought in references to the Channel Islands where they could. Messages to individual Channel Islanders were banned for the simple reason that they would have absorbed many hours of the B.B.C.'s time. When a single one slipped through in December 1941 there was a great inquest. Religious services in which Channel Islanders took part were broadcast, from St. Martin-in-the-Fields in 1943 and from Westminster Abbey in 1944. There was a Children's Hour programme to which children from the Islands contributed. In short, the B.B.C. did everything it could to bring the Islands into their programmes, but refrained from aiming programmes directly at them, because of the advice from Whitehall.

Nevertheless they continued to be criticized by members of parliament and by the public at large for not doing enough for the Islands, and the Director General felt obliged to take the matter up with the Minister of Information at the beginning of December 1944. He pointed out that the B.B.C. had been under Government direction since 1940, when they were told that programmes aimed at the Channel Islands might lead to reprisals. Two years later the Minister himself had questioned the wisdom of the policy, but after a review it was reaffirmed. The B.B.C. was told that it could broadcast occasional items about the Islands, but not to them; and the Minister felt that in fairness to the

[1] Hansard (Lords), vol. 121, cols. 465–7.

Corporation this position should be made clear to those who were complaining. He also asked that the existing policy should again be reconsidered, bearing in mind the fact that radios in the Islands were now so primitive that they could pick up only the Allied Expeditionary Forces programme. The Home Office consulted the War Office, which confirmed that there was no military objection to broadcasting to the Islands.

In fact the B.B.C. had put in hand a half-hour message programme by recording messages from Islanders living in Britain in August and September 1944. When the Home Office saw the transcript of these messages they asked that any which suggested that the speakers would be home 'soon' should be deleted. In spite of the general feeling that there was no objection to a programme on these lines the recording was not transmitted until 22 May – nearly a fortnight after the liberation.[1]

The Prime Minister had interested himself in the problems of the Islanders. In February 1945 he spotted in a general report on the state of affairs there the following statement: 'Our only joy is the B.B.C., but they have forgotten us too. How everyone hopes that the King will mention us at Christmas or that the B.B.C. will put on a programme for us and tell us the day before that it is coming; but no, not for us. For France, Belgium and all the rest, oh yes, but for us, who are we?' Churchill invited the Minister of Information to study this report and it was no doubt as a result of this that the policy about direct broadcasts was changed.

In March 1945 the Home Secretary drew the Prime Minister's attention to reports that the Islanders were disappointed that they were never mentioned by the B.B.C. He said that they would much appreciate some reference to them in one of his broadcast speeches, and went perilously near drafting the speech: 'You could say that their friends and relatives in this country, and the Government, have been deeply conscious of the grievous hardships and the loneliness of their fellow-countrymen in these oldest possessions of the British Crown, cut off by the fortunes of war from all contact with the Motherland, and tell them to keep stout hearts in the knowledge that our thoughts are with them.' If the Prime Minister agreed, he would be pleased to supply further material. The Prime Minister did not agree. He replied: 'I doubt if it will be possible to introduce the subject into my broadcasts. These have to be conceived as a whole, and not as a catalogue of favourable notices.'[2]

[1] B.B.C. Written Archives 6903A.   [2] PREM 3/87.

Parliament as a whole took a close interest in Channel Island affairs. Many members, not all with the same personal concern which Lord Portsea had, asked questions about them which the government often found it difficult to answer, either because they had no information, or because it was necessary on security grounds to keep silent. One member asked in August 1943 how the Islanders were being treated by the Germans, and what the Home Secretary was doing about it. The answer was that the evidence was too fragmentary to justify making a statement to the House; 'the best way to help our fellow countrymen was to bring the war to a victorious and speedy conclusion'. Shortly afterwards another member suggested that there should be early demobilization for Channel Islanders who had not seen their relatives for a long time. What was the food situation? It was believed that while the Islanders were without most of the amenities still enjoyed in Britain, they had enough food – in March 1942 – to maintain life and health.

A suggestion that the Islanders should be regarded as prisoners of war, and thus become eligible to receive parcels of food and clothing, was rejected on the ground that prisoners of war had a well-defined status under international conventions, and there was little danger that their parcels would find their way into enemy hands. These conditions did not prevail in the Islands. On another occasion the Parliamentary Secretary to the Ministry of Economic Warfare said that the deficiencies in the Channel Islands had not impaired the general health of the inhabitants. He assured his questioner that the welfare of their fellow-countrymen was a matter of deep and constant concern to His Majesty's Government 'but we are obliged to maintain the blockade of the areas occupied or controlled by the enemy powers if we are not to yield to the enemy a vital advantage in the prosecution of the war'. Could not parcels be sent through Portugal? No, the enemy would not allow it. The Portuguese government had more than once been asked to help, but without result. So it went on for the whole of the occupation. Many Islanders may have thought that they were forgotten, but this was far from the truth.

It was easier for the British Red Cross and Order of St. John than it was for the rank and file in parliament to do something practical for the Islanders. Through the International Red Cross Committee (which played an important part in making life tolerable in the internment camps in Germany)[1] they arranged a special postal message scheme

[1] See Chapter 10.

which enabled people in Britain to send messages – at first only 10 words, but later increased to 20 – to relatives and friends in the Islands, and to receive replies. Although only a few words were allowed, they were enough to tell each party how things were with the other. The Red Cross also sent – again through the International Committee – supplies of medicines, including vitamin D for the children, and insulin. Their main contribution, however, came in the middle of the siege when things were very desperate, and the British government agreed that food should be sent in. The relief ship *Vega* made five trips in all from Portugal to the Islands, in which she carried a total of nearly 460,000 food parcels (some of them contributed by Canada and New Zealand) in addition to supplies of flour, yeast, soap, and many other necessaries. The Islanders' gratitude for the help of the Red Cross was shown a few months after the liberation when they sent the organization a contribution of more than £170,000 raised by voluntary subscription.[1]

One of the important effects of the occupation was that it forced both those who were evacuated and those who remained behind to reflect on the administration of the Islands to a degree which would have been impossible in peacetime. This led to a demand for change, including the modification of the constitutions of both bailiwicks. Although it is outside the scope of a history of the occupation it is nevertheless worthwhile glancing at the factors which led to this new appraisal.[2]

The way of life for both groups was suddenly changed. For five years they could not avoid comparing their new lot – whether survival under German occupation, or in wartime Britain – with their pre-war existence. In some cases they concluded, often on insufficient evidence, that the conduct of Island affairs in normal times was capable of

[1] P. G. Cambray and G. C. B. Briggs, *Red Cross and St. John War History 1939–1947* (London, 1949).

[2] Cf. Mr. C. W. Duret Aubin's essay on constitutional changes in Jersey. 'Of the pre-war population of some 54,000 persons, approximately 13,000 had left the Island immediately before the occupation and had spent the years thereof in the United Kingdom, where the adults and adolescents among them had become accustomed to a more bracing political climate than that which they had known in the Island. For the 41,000 persons – the number is approximate – who remained in the Island all political activities became, by order of the occupying authority, absolutely forbidden. When, therefore, upon liberation political freedom was immediately restored to those who for five long years had lost it, and at the same time there began to return to the Island the evacuated Islanders, many of whom during their sojourn in the United Kingdom had acquired a more progressive political outlook, it was inevitable that the demand for reform should be made with greatly increased vigour. And it was not made in vain.' *Bulletin of the Société Jersiaise*, vol. xvi (1953–6), pp. 167–78.

improvement. Some of the unpleasantness of the occupation in the two bailiwicks was considered to be the fault of the governing bodies, and the fact that it was the Germans who most of the time were driving the Superior Council and the Controlling Committee was discounted, or not realized, by a cold, hungry, and often angry people. That the States were forced to become self-perpetuating, simply because the Germans would not allow elections, did not help.

The rigours of the occupation changed values. Men and women who in normal times would have regarded themselves as being scrupulously honest found themselves dealing in the black market and even stealing, and were able to salve their consciences by blaming it all on the Germans. It was patriotic to flout the authority of the enemy, and it was a short step to flouting authority in general. The position of the Island authorities was made the more difficult by the fact that they could not keep the people informed about many of the difficulties they faced, since it would have meant open criticism of some line taken by the Germans; and their silence was often taken to mean weakness or incompetence. Changes would have come even without the occupation, but they would have been slow and unobtrusive. As it was, the sudden enforced change in values, the sense that the 'haves' survived the occupation better than the 'have-nots', and the feeling in some quarters – however ill-founded – that the Establishments had been feathering their nests while the ordinary people suffered, all had their effect.

A major contribution to post-war planning was made by the Channel Islands Study Group, which comprised more than 20 Islanders, most of whom at the outbreak of war were following with distinction professions in Britain. They published in March 1944 a series of papers 'in the hope that as great events unfold and the liberation of our homes draws near they may help to fill a need for information about the Channel Islands and to provide some understanding of the subjects touched upon'. These covered a wide range, including agriculture, tourism, education, labour and social services, and 'democracy in the Islands'. The conclusions of the Group, which was completely independent, pointed the way to a number of changes in all the Islands.[1]

There is no doubt that their essays contributed to the general awareness of post-war problems and had some effect on the development of Island affairs. Quite a different sort of influence was exercised by the returned evacuees. They did not come back with ready-made intellectual solutions but with individual outlooks changed in varying degree by their

[1] *Nos Îles: a Symposium on the Channel Islands* (Teddington, 1944).

individual experiences in wartime Britain. It was difficult to assess at the time what several years in a different world had done to evacuees – and to the thousands of volunteers in the British forces. Would they return with a demand for violent change, or would they merely be glad to get back home again and slip comfortably into their former way of life? It is still more difficult to come to a conclusion on this point a quarter of a century later. Individual reactions varied enormously, but it seems that the majority of the evacuees returned thankfully, and with few exceptions had no great desire for political reform. Inevitably they brought with them some features of life in Britain, which in any case would have reached the Islands in the ordinary course of events; but fears that their time in Britain would make them totally dissatisfied with their lot in the Islands proved groundless. It is impossible, however, to identify single strands in the complex pattern. In the same family the father might have remained in the Islands, the mother have been evacuated to Britain with their younger children, and their grown-up son or daughter have joined the British forces. What emerged when they came together again and compared their experiences and aspirations depended on a host of factors which differed from family to family; and it is doubtful whether the computers of a later era could relate them to the course of events in the post-war decade.

Those who had remained in the Islands at the time of the evacuation saw changes of values in many spheres. They had more opportunity to ponder these matters, and found themselves speculating on the nature of the paternal Establishments which they had hitherto accepted as being divinely right, or at least which it had never occurred to them to challenge. This too helped the process of constitutional development. In October 1943 the Bailiff of Guernsey set up a Committee to consider how far the former administrative system would cope with the strain of post-war conditions. Its recommendations that some of the States' Committees should be merged and an Advisory Council established were accepted in July 1945. Shortly before this 14 members of the States, all of whom had been in the Island during the occupation, addressed a petition to the States raising the question of reform, as a result of which it was agreed to study the need for more direct representation in the States of Deliberation, and other modifications in the constitution.

At the beginning of 1946 the States in both Islands transmitted to the King in Council proposals for reform. A Committee of the Privy Council was set up 'to enquire into the proposed reforms of the States of

Jersey and Guernsey, and into the proposed judicial reform, and advise thereon'.[1]

In its report the Committee pointed out that the Islands' 'institutions, laws, and customs are held very dear by the great majority of the people' and that 'reform has, for various reasons, progressed along different lines and at different speed to the reform of our institutions in England'. Nevertheless, despite a natural desire to adhere to traditional forms, public opinion had for some time past felt a need for adaptations designed to tally with changing concepts of government. The changes finally recommended by the Committee were aimed at increasing the democratic element in the constitutions.

In Jersey the twelve Jurats, who had been elected for life by popular franchise, no longer sat in the States, but were replaced by twelve Senators elected for a term of nine years (which was reduced to six years in 1966). The Jurats remained members of the Royal Court, being chosen by an electoral college. The twelve Rectors, nominated by the Crown, no longer sat in the Assembly, although the Dean was left with the right of addressing the States, without a vote. The number of Deputies elected by popular franchise by parish ('members of parliament') was increased from seventeen to twenty-eight. The Viscount, the chief executive of the courts of Jersey, who acted as sheriff, continued to be a member with no right to speak or vote.[2]

In Guernsey the Attorney General and Solicitor General, appointed by the Crown, who had the right to speak and vote in the States, lost the right to vote. The twelve Jurats, who were appointed by an electoral assembly, and sat for life, were no longer to be members of the States. There was created a new office of *Conseiller*, twelve being elected by electoral assembly for a term of six years. As in Jersey the Rectors lost their seats, and the fifteen *Douzeniers* were reduced to ten. Finally, the eighteen Deputies, elected by parish by popular franchise for three years, were increased to thirty-three.

Alderney, of course, was a special case. There was need for constitutional reform there too, but it took longer to achieve it. The population was small and virtually all had been evacuated. The Germans had expended more effort on the fortifications there, and they had done more damage to property. Liberation had left an untidy uneconomic

---

[1] Command Paper 7074. The members were Viscount Samuel, Lord Ammon, Mr. James Chuter Ede (chairman), Mr. R. A. Butler (later Lord Butler), and Sir John Beaumont. The Secretary was Mr. J. B. Howard of the Home Office.

[2] For the constitutional position in 1939 see the Introduction.

vacuum. Unlike Jersey and Guernsey, Alderney had no base on which the returning Islanders could rebuild their prosperity.

In 1943 Judge – now Brigadier – French advised the Home Office that it would need a pioneering job to put the Island on its feet. Many evacuees would be reluctant to leave well-paid jobs in the United Kingdom; and others who wanted to return would be aged and unable to contribute anything to the economy. Further, it would take time for the farms to become productive. A 'planned replantation' was therefore necessary. This was accepted. The replanting would have to be carried out under United Kingdom auspices with a measure of collaboration from Guernsey, pending the restoration of normal relations between the Lieutenant-Governor, the States of Guernsey, and the States of Alderney. It was envisaged that while the arrangements for Alderney would differ from those for Jersey and Guernsey, their implementation would take only a matter of months longer. This proved to be over-optimistic.

French visited Alderney with Brigadier Snow and Colonel William Arnold,[1] head of the legal staff of the civil affairs unit, a week after the liberation, and decided that the Island was unsafe for any except military personnel, since it was still heavily mined. A few buildings had been completely demolished, and although the rest were in fair condition most were stripped of furniture, fittings, and domestic equipment. Partition walls had been erected in the hotels and many houses. The Church of St. Anne had been 'stripped and brutally desecrated'. All the woodwork had been removed, presumably for fuel, and the church was being used as a store for flour and empty wine barrels. The roads had suffered through heavy traffic and inadequate maintenance. The Organisation Todt farm was still operating, but elsewhere mines made cultivation impossible.

There were three phases in the rehabilitation of Alderney. The first began with the arrival of the troops on 16 May and continued until the end of the year, when several hundred civilians were allowed to return. The second ran from the beginning of 1946 to the middle of 1947, when it became apparent that despite the assistance of the United Kingdom government the Islanders could not put their house in order. The third began when the United Kingdom authorities decided that something drastic would have to be done if the Island community was to survive, and launched an investigation by a Committee of the Privy Council.

For six months after the liberation the troops, helped by prisoner of

[1] Later Sir William Arnold, Bailiff of Guernsey.

war labour, cleared the minefields, cut down the roll-bombs, removed obstructions, collected the German guns and sent them to Guernsey to be sold with the scrap metal there, repaired houses, and generally provided a framework into which it was hoped the returning Islanders would successfully fit themselves. At the beginning of December Judge French arrived with a small reconnaissance party, which was followed by two others on 4 and 6 December. On 15 December the S.S. *Autocarrier* brought more than a hundred returning evacuees, who were welcomed with great pomp by the recently-appointed Lieutenant-Governor. General Neame, who should perhaps have known better, required a 21-gun salute which, there being no guns that could be fired, was ingeniously simulated by the detonation of 21 thunder-flashes in a convenient quarry. The *Autocarrier* brought two more waves of returning evacuees later in December, and by July 1946 685 had returned out of a pre-war population of 1,442.

The theory, blessed by the Home Office, was that communal farming should become the mainspring of the economy in the initial years; but this did not work out in practice. The forces and the prisoners of war were gradually removed, and in the middle of 1946 the States were left to administer the Island without help from the military. It became more and more obvious that the economy was not being pulled together as the authorities in Britain had hoped. To add to the difficulties Judge French's austere and realistic approach to the problems of the Island's finances found little favour with the easy-going native Alderneymen. An open feud developed between them, and at the end of September 1946 the Home Secretary had to visit the Island to make a first-hand assessment of the problem. He decided that there was nothing for it but to make a full-scale investigation. This ended the second phase.

A Committee of the Privy Council was set up with Mr. Chuter Ede as chairman and Lord Ammon and Mr. Osbert Peake as members 'to enquire into the state of the said Island with particular reference to its form of government and its relationship with the neighbouring Islands, its financial position and its economic prospects'.[1]

The Committee decided that two things were essential. Alderney must offer its inhabitants 'a healthy balance of economic pursuits', and it must provide a reasonable standard of living. This meant the expansion of tourism, and the development of agriculture, horticulture, and fishing. The Insular administration, however, could not provide the

[1] *Report of the Committee of the Privy Council on the Island of Alderney.* (Command Paper 7805.)

minimum standards required, nor would it be able to cope with the problems that lay ahead. The revenues were not enough to cover the increased official salaries that would be necessary. The Island had been more and more looking to Guernsey for a lead; and there was a case for asking Guernsey to become responsible for its major services, given that Alderney was taxed on the Guernsey scale and contributed to their joint exchequer. This idea was approved by the States of both Islands in July 1948, and the final proposals on these lines were accepted by the States of Alderney in October 1948 and by the States of Guernsey in the following month. As part of the general arrangement the States of Alderney were given two seats in the States of Guernsey.[1]

Jersey, Guernsey, and Alderney now all had a fair wind for their journey into the future, away from the long nightmare of occupation.

[1] The liberation and rehabilitation of Alderney is admirably described in *The Alderney Story 1939-1949* compiled by Michael St. J. Packe and Maurice Dreyfus (Alderney 1971).

15

Conclusion

THE Channel Islands' position as effectively autonomous states within the British Commonwealth was responsible for many of their difficulties in the months before the occupation. They were masters of their destinies in most respects. In particular they were exempt from military service outside the Islands. There was no constitutional need for them to send a single man to help Britain to fight the Nazis, and the idea that they might have to be fought in the Islands never entered the collective mind of Whitehall. Planning was limited to providing the people of the two bailiwicks with the same level of rations as the civilian population of Britain, and to ensuring that their code of defence regulations corresponded to that of the United Kingdom. It was not concerned with a potential military threat, partly because it was assumed that there was none, partly because the Islands had little strategic importance, and perhaps most of all because many of those concerned in Whitehall seem to have failed to grasp that Britain was responsible for their defence.

Nevertheless, the Islanders on the declaration of war instantly and unhesitatingly reaffirmed their loyalty to the Crown, and for the second time in half a century waived their traditional right of exemption from military service overseas. They went further, and sent proportionately substantial sums to the United Kingdom exchequer as their contribution towards the cost of the war. They asked nothing in return, but perhaps Britain gave them less than they deserved. She accepted the offer of men and money with proper gratitude; but did she give the Islanders all the help to which their spontaneous generosity entitled them?

No doubt the administrators of Whitehall had more than enough on their hands preparing for the war which Neville Chamberlain had assured them would never come. The fact remains that the Islands were left out on a limb, and that their own efforts to strengthen their defences were not taken seriously by the experts in the United Kingdom Service Departments. This may well have been right from the United Kingdom point of view, but if the policy was to leave the Islands defenceless on the doorstep of a Europe at war, there was surely a moral obligation to consider what should be done if the general conflagration looked like engulfing them.

The least that was required was a contingency plan for total evacuation, agreed with the Islands; but their remoteness from Britain, which made them the easiest target for enemy occupation, also left them remote from the thoughts of the contingency planners. They had to rely heavily on their own limited resources in preparing for war and occupation, and at the end of the day they had the worst of both worlds – a chaotic partial evacuation left almost to chance.

It has been suggested by some that the decision not to evacuate the Islands completely may have compelled the Germans to keep more troops there than they would otherwise have done. There is no doubt that the Allies benefited from the immobilization of a whole reinforced infantry division, especially in the critical days after the invasion of Europe had begun, when the Germans needed in France every man they could lay their hands on; but it is equally clear that those who remained behind in June 1940 were necessary for the survival of the garrison, and that total evacuation would have left the Germans with an even greater millstone round their necks. OKW and the *Inselkommandant* often made the point that the Islanders, or most of them, were directly or indirectly essential for the support of the garrison. One estimate was that three-quarters of those trapped by the invasion – or about 45,000 people – could not be dispensed with. If we assume that Hitler would never have allowed the garrison strength to fall below an infantry division with ancillary specialist units – which, given his fixation about the Islands, is a reasonable assumption – total evacuation would have left the Germans with the need to find thousands of people, many with special expertise, to replace the missing Islanders.

There therefore seems to be no doubt that the failure to evacuate the Islands completely was a grave error of judgement on the part of the United Kingdom authorities – from their own point of view, as well as from that of the Islanders – on three grounds, of which at least two should have been readily foreseen even by the harassed men of Whitehall in June 1940. How could anyone in Britain seriously believe that the Islanders would be better off under a German regime, even if it behaved well according to its own lights? How could anyone fail to see that if the Islanders were left as hostages, sooner or later the enemy would exploit the position, as in fact they did by ordering the deportation of more than 2,000 United Kingdom-born Islanders? The third ground, which was perhaps more difficult to foresee, was that an occupied community may be essential to the occupying power. By leaving 60,000 people in the Islands Britain made available the support needed by 319 Infantry Division. At the same time she denied herself the support that many of these people could have given to her own war effort – in the factories, on the land, and in the forces – although one of the Chiefs of Staff's objections to evacuation had been that there were already too many useless mouths in the United Kingdom.[1] The fact that Alderney survived with only a few Islanders resident may be used against the argument that the Germans needed their help; but the garrison there was very small – about a tenth of the total – and they depended just as much as did their comrades in Jersey and Guernsey on the produce of the Islands as a group.

Perhaps even more to be deprecated was Whitehall's handling of the Islands' legislation to make their menfolk available for the United Kingdom forces, which, under the constitutional arrangements, had to be blessed by the King in Council. That this generous offer never became effective was largely due to muddle and laziness in Whitehall. Fortunately for the common cause, the Islanders individually did not stand on the strict letter of the law, as they were perfectly entitled to do, and they were already making their contribution in the field in disproportionately large numbers, often with distinction, while Whitehall files intended to accept their governments' offers of their services progressed leisurely from in-tray to in-tray.

If, however, the United Kingdom concern for the Islands before the invasion was less than it might have been, the position changed as soon as the occupation began – when there was little that could be done. It was not only people like Lord Portsea with a personal interest who demanded special relief measures – most of which could not be taken without impairing the United Kingdom war effort, or discriminating in favour of a small part of occupied Europe simply because the inhabitants were British. Many members of parliament and leading public figures strove to help the imprisoned Islanders, but they could do little more than urge the government to achieve the impossible. The most practical way of showing sympathy was to help the large number of

[1] CAB 80/12.

evacuees in Britain through the agency of the Channel Islands Refugees Committee and the local Channel Island societies, and these bodies were given a very generous measure of support by the community as a whole. As soon as there was a glimmer of hope that the Islands might be liberated the military authorities and the Home Office threw themselves wholeheartedly into planning for the success of Operation 'Nestegg'.

The anomalous position of the Islands – in which they were required for certain purposes to depend on the United Kingdom – came to an abrupt end when the Germans landed. The second phase of the Islands' war had begun.

There was no precedent for the occupation, a fact which critics of the Island administrations would do well to remember. They had no experience of conducting even friendly negotiations with a great power, since the United Kingdom had been responsible for their external relations. Overnight they were abandoned to their fate. They awoke to find themselves dealing on equal terms with the greatest military power the world had known, without the benefit of the long tradition and the highly-qualified staff of the Home Office and Foreign Office – a handful of public-spirited administrators, many of them only part-time, whose main qualification for the job was a generous endowment of common sense.

Against this background it would be difficult to voice any criticism of their conduct of affairs. Had they simply kept their heads above water and done what they were told to do by the occupying power it would hardly be a matter for censure; but they carried the administrative war into the enemy camp on many occasions. It is not that they made some mistakes that is surprising, but that they did so much that was right in circumstances of the greatest possible difficulty.

The Bailiff of Jersey expressed the view that while the Superior Council had its critics, in fact it fulfilled the highest hopes of its creators. It administered the government of the Island in a way that was acceptable to most people, in spite of the fundamental change from the normal system. Before the occupation, government by committee meant that every member of the States sat on at least one committee; but the concentration of the administration into eight departments reduced the number of posts to be filled, and those members of the States whose particular experience was not required found themselves with no part to play during the occupation, except when the States had one of their rare meetings.

The position in Guernsey was much the same. The streamlining of the administrative machine there also left power in a smaller number of hands. In Guernsey, however, the Controlling Committee was not presided over by the Bailiff. Coutanche was a strong character and it was inevitable that he should play the leading role in Jersey's occupation. Victor Carey, his opposite number in Guernsey, was 69 when the occupation started, and it was equally inevitable that he should stand aside to allow someone younger and more vigorous – first Sherwill, and, when he was deported, John Leale – to carry the main burden. Carey, however, did not withdraw from affairs completely. He continued, of course, to preside over sessions of the Royal Court, and also held himself in reserve as a second line of defence to deal with the Germans on matters of particular importance. This on occasion he was able to do with some considerable effect. There was, however, sometimes confusion as to what should be reserved for the Bailiff. This led to acrimonious correspondence behind the scenes which did not make the task of the President of the Controlling Committee any easier. Sometimes Carey issued proclamations in his own name in terms which seemed to make him side with the enemy. Once he used the word 'enemy' as applying to the Allied forces, which caused surprise at the time. The memory of these proclamations lingered long after liberation.

Although there was no precedent for the occupation of the Islands, the English occupation of Tournai at the beginning of the sixteenth century might have given the Island governments some pointers. The two occupations were remarkably similar. They lasted the same time. In both, the invaders – Henry VIII and Hitler – suffered from megalomania. Both built massive fortifications. The levels of collaboration and resistance in the two places were the same. Even the officials' titles coincided – Bailiff, *Greffier*, *Procureur*, *Prévôt*, and so on. There was, however, one significant difference.

Whereas the Islands by creating the Superior Council and the Controlling Committee put themselves into a position where they could take quick decisions, the Tournaisiens, whose normal administrative machinery was just as complex as the Islands' committee systems, made no attempt to simplify things. This meant that in their confrontations with Henry VIII's representatives – who dealt gently with them, just as the *Feldkommandantur* did in the Islands most of the time, in the hope that they would be won over to the English side by kindness – they were often able to take shelter behind their cumbersome administrative procedures, and to delay or frustrate decisions.

If the States and their numerous supporting committees had been retained as the administrative machine in each Island it might have been possible to resist or at least delay some of the more unwelcome German plans; but by creating the Superior Council and the Controlling Committee and giving them the power to make instant decisions the Islanders had forged a two-edged weapon which could be turned against them. It is doubtful, however, if the Islands would have been better off with the old form of government. If they had indulged in delaying tactics, as the Tournaisiens did so successfully four and a quarter centuries earlier, they would quickly have been brought to heel by the Wehrmacht.

The idea that this might have been disastrous is supported by the evidence of the Germans' own performance in the administrative field. Their incompetence manifested itself on many occasions. Examples of their total lack of imagination in managing the affairs of the Islands have been mentioned above: the panic order to bring all boats to St. Peter Port harbour to frustrate escapes to England, which almost implied that they believed that the veteran Sir Havilland de Sausmarez might paddle – or pole! – his punt from Sausmarez Manor to Weymouth; the licensing system to enable Islanders to retain their popguns and bows and arrows – a more solemn piece of bumbledom than even wartime Whitehall produced; the need for troops to obtain a formal licence every time they wanted to buy a box of matches or a button; the strict surveillance of, for example, the Jersey Chess Club and the Girls' Friendly Society, on the grounds that they might be hotbeds of subversion; new traffic control measures apparently designed to encourage head-on collisions.

The catalogue can be extended by a measure in 1942 arising out of an attempted escape from the Islands in which the escapers were caught with photographs of military installations in their possession. It was at once decreed that photographic apparatus of all kinds must be handed over to the occupying authority. The Islanders naturally assumed that the order meant what it said and showered the Germans with everything that could conceivably be classified as photographic apparatus: lenses, tripods, projectors, printing and developing equipment, and a great variety of other articles. It was only then that the *Feldkommandantur* realized that they had created yet another sledgehammer to crack a nut.[1]

It was perhaps inevitable that there should be this sort of stupidity

[1] JFW 30/97.

at the beginning of the occupation when the *Feldkommandantur* officials were without experience; but it might have been expected that with the passage of time they would begin to see the light. However, they continued to rush out unworkable orders, and to amend them only when experience had demonstrated that they *were* unworkable. This has some relevance to the suggestion that the Islanders should have indulged in delaying tactics. It makes it seem all the more probable that if the administrative machine had been deliberately slowed down the Germans would have been forced to rely much more on their own ill-digested decrees, and the Islanders would have been on balance worse off.

Much of the evidence of the *Feldkommandantur*'s lack of administrative skill lies in the papers which they left behind in the Islands. Hüffmeier ensured that the Wehrmacht records were systematically destroyed during the siege, thereby frustrating the Allied demand that he should hand over all his papers intact. The internal day-to-day records of the troops have thus disappeared, except for a few which found their way on to *Feldkommandantur* files. This is unfortunate because there is no doubt that much could have been learned about the thinking of the German command in the Islands and the state of mind of the garrison from a study of these papers; but it does not affect the general picture. Most orders affecting the garrison, many from Hitler himself, were preserved outside the Islands and still exist, often in several copies. There are still some blanks, however. For example, the central records of the Organisation Todt seem mostly to have perished, although there may still be some in the hands of firms which worked for the OT.

The fate of the many *Feldkommandantur* files is particularly interesting. In Jersey fewer than a dozen survived, none of them of great interest. In Guernsey, however, several hundred were left behind. Lists of the *Feldkommandantur* files also survive, and a comparison of these and the surviving files reveals which FK files were destroyed – presumably deliberately. Most of them are in Series 2 of the *Aktenplan* (file list) for the *Nebenstelle* in Guernsey (which follows broadly the lines of the corresponding list in Jersey) dealing with police matters. Some of them are routine files on curfew hours, price control, identity cards, and similar matters; but there are others which might have thrown light on German policies in more interesting fields. These are concerned with 'Island dwellers with the English army', Jews, Freemasons, meetings and political organizations, and so on; but they have all disappeared. They may have been deliberately destroyed to hide as much as possible about German police activities, or they may conceivably have been removed by Allied security officers investigating war crimes. Whatever the explanation, they have, alas, vanished.

Tiny though they were, and for most of the war distant from the main areas of conflict, the Islands posed problems throughout the occupation for the British and German leaders. Hitler's were largely of his own making. They would have been much smaller had he contented himself with a reasonable garrison and a more modest scale of fortification, which were all that were necessary, and which his generals urged on him as strongly as they dared. That he was ruthless in his attitude towards the Islanders from the start is witnessed by his wild order to deport ten United Kingdom-born Islanders for every German handed over by Iran to Britain, which not even the well-disposed von Schmettow could resist.

His main concern, however, was to make impregnable the prize he had won, probably more because it was British territory than because of its strategic value during the war or after. His deep interest in the fortifications from 1941 onwards suggests that his judgement was already severely impaired. He demanded that plans should be sent to him personally and he pored over them for hours, which would have been better devoted to weightier matters. But nothing his generals did could move him. In the critical weeks in the middle of 1944 when there was still time to save something from the wreck by recalling 319 Infantry Division to France – leaving only enough men in the Islands to discourage the Allies from attacking them, which implied a very small force indeed – he could not bring himself to admit that he had been absolutely wrong in building up his Gibraltar of the English Channel. As a result the whole Division went out of the war nearly a year before the end came.

Churchill, on the other hand, took a painfully realistic view. His problem was how to win the war in the shortest possible time, and if for some reason the sacrifice of the Channel Islands had seemed likely to help him towards that end, there is little doubt what his decision would have been. It was on his orders that the ill-planned Commando raids were carried out in 1940, although he must have been well aware that they would put the civilian population in great danger – a fact which Sherwill hastened to confirm. In the event no action was taken against the people, but the odds on heavy reprisals by the Germans must have been very long. Later on Operation 'Basalt' led to the second wave of deportations. Had it been strategically right to give Mountbatten his head with a version of Operation 'Blazing', which would have blasted one or more of the Islands out of the sea, it is unlikely that the Prime Minister would have hesitated long. 'Blazing' was turned down because he judged that the cost to Bomber Command would be too high – not out of solicitude for the Islanders. In the autumn of 1944, when he was being pressed by his colleagues in the War Cabinet to allow food to be sent to the Islands, he withheld his agreement in spite of the fact that he knew that the downfall of the garrison might well be brought about only at the expense of the civilian population.

It was well known that the Führer greatly prized the Channel Islands, and therefore officials at all levels studiously paid more attention to them than they deserved. A distinction was made between Alderney on the one hand and Jersey and Guernsey on the other. Alderney was to be regarded as part of France in the long term, presumably on geographical grounds, although it is strange that the one Island which became almost wholly German should not remain so. When the war was over it would be released from direct German rule, along with the mainland of France. Jersey and Guernsey, however, would not be joined with France, nor would they return to their pre-war status within the British Empire. They were to remain a German outpost, but the fate of their inhabitants was never finally agreed upon.

The Germans devoted a good deal of study to the people and the constitutions of the Islands. A propaganda unit visited Jersey early in 1941 and made a report which was not particularly flattering. Points which struck the unit were the large number of cripples and sub-normal people, which they attributed to the 'intermixing of resident families'. There was also a very high illegitimate birthrate – virginity was not very highly prized! Liquor consumption was heavy. The peasants still lived on the land in the traditional way, knowing little of comfort and hygiene. They did nothing in a hurry, except that when the potato crop was ready for harvesting a sort of fever and mania overcame them in their anxiety to be the first on the market to get the best prices. With few exceptions they were well off; but they were not much interested in events outside the Islands. Finally, there were the people who came from the Dominions, colonies, and protectorates who were enjoying their retirement, playing golf, tennis and bridge, sailing, and driving around in elegant cars.

This report, which was based on the evidence of officers and officials who had been in the Island for some time, was referred to the *Neben-stelle* in Guernsey for comment. They agreed that it had been carefully prepared, although it was incomplete. It seems likely that the propaganda unit was under instructions to make as little of the Islands as possible, perhaps so that in a year or two the Germans would be able to point to the improvements which their regime had brought about.[1]

There may be confirmation of this in an article published in Germany in June 1943 by an official of the *Feldkommandantur* describing the position as he saw it for the benefit of his fellow-countrymen. The 'constitutional nature reserve' had been left untouched but numerous other improvements were being introduced. Traffic control had been recast on the German system, and the British police had been taught to adapt themselves to the new order. Wages and working hours, formerly at the mercy of economic forces, had been brought under control. The necessary measures had been introduced to counteract the individualist attitude of the English, who did not recognize mutual help or the obligation to work.

It was claimed that the German administration was very active in every direction in which new organization was necessary because of the failure of existing institutions. 'In total war, and situated so near to the seat of the enemy's power, much that is new has to be created. The former villas and seaside resorts of the English plutocrats have been converted to German fortresses. The face of the Islands has been changed completely. It has become more serious and more European . . . The Channel Islands have their place and mission in the new Europe; and they will show themselves equal to the task.' The official also had the temerity to refer to two recent books about the Islands by Germans,[2] one of them a mere 'picture book'. 'There are no works before the German occupation equal to these . . . which is some indication of the achievement of German Kultur.'[3]

The analysis, needless to say, was just as far from the truth as the earlier report; but nevertheless there was something to be said for a new examination of the Islands' constitutions. The view was expressed immediately after liberation that the evacuees, having experienced a more modern form of government in the United Kingdom – even if more authoritarian than usual because of the war – might add to the numbers of those in the Islands who felt that something needed to be done about the system of government. Lord Coutanche, writing much

[1] Loose Guernsey paper.
[2] Dr. Hans Auerbach and Baron von und zu Aufsess.
[3] *Deutsche Verwaltung*, 15 June 1943.

later, referred with nostalgia to the advantages of central control which the Superior Council had given, and suggested that it might be worth considering the introduction of something like it on a permanent basis.

The Germans did not make a dedicated effort to 'Germanize' the Islands. Measures in this field were few and relatively unimportant. The schools were left untouched, except for the introduction first of voluntary and then of compulsory German classes. After December 1942 German place names were introduced to run in parallel with the existing names, and no doubt at some point in Hitler's future the Island names would have been dropped. Metric measure was made obligatory in all dealings with the Wehrmacht, but avoirdupois was left intact for the Islanders' own transactions. There was strict censorship of the press, so that only German news might be read, and the press was also used to provide simple German lessons for readers at large. No books on the Führer's Index could be read. New laws were printed in German as well as English, but this was probably so that the authoritative text might be available rather than a 'Germanization' measure. The rule of the road was changed. German magazines were made available in the public libraries. All communications addressed to the *Feldkommandantur* had to be in German. All in all, a very gentle Germanization programme, but carried out without prejudice to what could happen when Hitler had won his war.

The examination by the Germans of the constitutional position in July 1940[1] was followed in September 1941 by a longer and more thoughtful investigation of the state of the occupation, some of the conclusions of which became the basis of policy for the time being. It was carried out by Professor Karl Heinz Pfeffer, who visited Jersey and Guernsey to conduct research, in the course of which 'all the peculiarities of the Islands were subject to personal inspection'. The main peculiarity detected by the Professor was that the people of the Islands were originally Norman and not British. They had become properly anglicized only after the First World War, but they regarded themselves as Jersey and Guernsey folk rather than as English or French. French agricultural workers who had bought their way into Island farms had created new problems, and the presence of a very strong Irish labour force was also disturbing. The antagonisms between the local inhabitants and the French and Irish immigrants came to light on the religious plane, since the latter were Roman Catholics whereas the Islanders were mainly Anglican and Methodist.

[1] See above p. 105.

The constitutions of both Islands derived from the eleventh century. 'They stick to the form of the ancient constitution and that form is naturally employed most elastically for modern requirements. For instance a traffic accident in 1934 is judged in accordance with a document of King John Lackland, which, moreover, has long since been known to be a forgery.' The constitutions corresponded to that in England before the electoral reform of 1832. The tourist traffic, exports of potatoes, fine vegetables, and fruit to England, and cattle breeding, had made the Islands completely independent of the British world economy, but at the moment their whole economic life was facing catastrophe. There was no fuel for the glasshouses, imports of cattle for slaughter were endangering the disease-free stock, and there were no tourists. Without German help the food situation would be hopeless.

The 'picturesque historical drama' of the Islands had been changed during the last 15 months by the presence of German troops; but Pfeffer's numerous conversations with officers had revealed that no one yet knew what line to take with the inhabitants in the long term. There were several possibilities. The 70,000 [sic] still remaining could be evacuated, leaving a free field for German reconstruction. This, however, could wait until the end of the war, and in the meantime the post-war plan could be shaped. (The Professor was thus less impatient than the Führer.) A solution on these lines would destroy the existing economy, especially cattle breeding. 'It would be of comparatively small importance if one worked with the traditional constitutional machinery or without it.' But if it was decided to get rid of the population it could be done ruthlessly on the ground of military necessity 'without taking into consideration the significance of the inhabitants'. Pfeffer thought that there might be some danger of passive resistance, and he pointed out, as the generals were to do later, that if the people were removed en masse the Reich would have to become directly responsible for farming and food supplies.

An alternative would be to copy the British policy in Malta, which had been to support the Maltese rather than the Italian population, for example by encouraging the use of the Maltese language. If this was done it would be necessary to accept that the native Channel Islanders had every right to be there and to promote their independence as far as possible. Either the British immigrants would have to be expelled or things made so unpleasant for them that they would be glad to leave of their own free will. This would mean appealing to the native Islanders' Norman heritage, treating the Islands as if they were little Germanic states, carrying on their existing constitutions, maintaining and fostering their economies, and trying not to humble their pride but rather arranging to exploit it in the interests of Germany. The people had no wish to be French. There was plenty of evidence that they would far rather be German.

The advantage of allowing the native Islanders to remain was that the Islands would retain their economic strength, and they could readily be incorporated into the German defence system. So far, however, the garrison command had shied away from putting this solution into practice, and no great harm had been done. The ordinances of the occupying authority were still passed by the Island parliaments. The prevailing system of indirect control (that is to say, the *Feldkommandantur*'s supervision of the Island administrations) left the occupation forces free to carry out their proper tasks. The Island farmers were contributing materially towards the support of the fighting strength of the troops. There had not been a single case of real sabotage. It seemed best, therefore, not to deport the whole population. This would leave the economy intact and provide a breathing space in which the longer-term policies could be worked out. If the production on which the forces depended so heavily was to be maintained or increased, the senior members of the garrison would have to combine 'tact and self-confidence' with stern measures when they became necessary.

Pfeffer stressed the importance of regarding the occupation of the Channel Islands as a dry run for the occupation of Britain. (That the Wehrmacht had shot its bolt had not become apparent in September 1941.) 'The Islands naturally have an importance for us as a test case for meeting an English population.' For the time being it was a matter of complete indifference what the English thought about the Germans, but the relationship between the troops and the civilians in the Channel Islands so far had been excellent. 'If, however, after victory we intend to draw part of the British people over to our side, the prevailing conduct of the German occupation troops can be abundantly employed as propaganda.'

For the moment the inhabitants should be regarded as hostages for the British people 'although one only needs to consider the real Englishmen as hostages'. If, however, it became necessary to punish the Islanders, for example as a reprisal for British actions against Germans, the whole situation would be altered. Political or military events elsewhere might lead to a need for sudden change. Nevertheless, it seemed commonsense to try to arrive at an agreed policy for the Islands which would look beyond the exigencies of the short term. Pfeffer has an interesting passage on the British determination to resist where he makes an assessment of morale in the Channel Islands. In general the inhabitants were co-operating loyally with the occupation authorities 'because they believe that in this way they can best endure the war, without thereby forfeiting any of their patriotism'. He had come across no case in which the people had refused to deal with the troops. It was true that since the start of the war in Russia the ordinary people were less well-disposed towards the troops, and indeed ever since Dunkirk the attitude of the man in the street had reflected the line taken by the British radio news. At first there had been 'great alarm and a reckoning with the worst, then a spontaneous tightening up, deep depression after Crete, and great hopes on the outbreak of war in the east. While we were there the high-flying balloon of these great hopes had not yet burst. In our interest it should rise as high as possible so that the fall is all the more precipitous.'

Some of the ideas in Pfeffer's study were acted on, in particular the suggestion that the occupying authorities should support the native-born Islanders and try to drive a wedge between them and 'the English immigrants'. The outstanding example of this policy of divide and win over came in 1942, when the belated deportations were restricted to English-born Islanders. (The date of Pfeffer's report – September 1941 – may be significant. It was in that month that reprisals against the Channel Islanders were first suggested; and Hitler may have picked up the idea of discrimination from the report.) The hostile reaction of the native Islanders must have come as a surprise and a disappointment to the advocates of the policy.

The States in both bailiwicks made it clear that they recognized no distinction between the two classes of citizen, and their protests left the Germans in no doubt about how they felt. The native Islanders as a whole demonstrated by their actions and expressions of sympathy that the rift which the Germans believed could be exploited to their own advantage did not exist. Discrimination was also imported into the German courts, where United Kingdom-born Islanders were given much heavier sentences than native men for identical offences tried at the same time in the same court, simply because they were British. In other cases men who were equally guilty in the eyes of the court served their sentences in the Islands if they were natives, but were sent to France – where prison conditions were much harder – if they were from the United Kingdom.[1] In 1942 the German decree that the style 'Lieutenant-Governor' (which implied subordination to the British Crown and which until then had been freely used in public documents) should be dropped, was probably regarded by them as another measure to improve the status of the native Islanders, and thus to make them more susceptible to a policy of eventual Germanization.

Had the native Islanders come willingly into the German fold it would have provided a useful precedent for the occupation of Britain. If discrimination was to be the order of the day there would be plenty of scope for it. For example, Irish residents might be 'drawn over to the German side' to use Pfeffer's expression, not only to facilitate the occupation but to bring nearer Germany's eventual takeover of the Irish Republic. The willing collaboration of the Irish community in the Channel Islands may have put this idea into the heads of the German planners. Alternatively, it might have been the German policy to favour the Scots. When Lord Boothby met Hitler before the war and made a lighthearted reference to the traditional enmity of the English and Scots the Führer took the idea seriously; in the event of a German occupation of Britain there might have been an attempt to win over the Scots by discriminating against the English. The native Channel Islanders, however, refused to provide an encouraging precedent, and their attitude must have carried some weight with the planners.

Pfeffer's other main proposal, which could not be reconciled with a policy of discrimination, also seems to have had some support. If one of the Germans' objectives in the Channel Islands was to stage-manage an occupation which could be represented to the people of Britain as being tolerable, if not actually desirable, it would have been foolish to discriminate openly against United Kingdom citizens who had chosen to settle in the Islands, or indeed to do anything that would get a bad press in Britain. This line of thought may have softened policies in the Islands in the years before the rigours of the siege forced the Germans to be tough. Von Schmettow's gentle approach, which the Islanders attributed to his natural kindliness, may have stemmed rather from the orders he received. When the authorities in both bailiwicks congratulated themselves at the end of the occupation for the part they had played in moderating the policies of the Germans, their self-congratulation may perhaps have been less well-deserved than they imagined.

[1] SHAEF/501/1.

In the first years of the occupation there was some point in regarding the Channel Islands as guinea-pigs. Although the occupation of Britain had not happened according to plan, it was assumed that it must be accomplished sooner or later. But by 1943 the philosophizing of the planners had become academic. It was no longer a question of running a model occupation in the Channel Islands to be studied as a precedent for Britain. The problem was how to enable the occupation to survive in any form at all.

The change in the German attitude is illustrated by a statement by von Schmettow on the third anniversary of the invasion of the Islands. It had only been a small enterprise, he said, but of singular importance. The oldest possession of the British Crown had been lost. By entering British territory for the first time the German soldier had begun the dissolution of the British Empire, the break-up of which was becoming more evident every day. He had formed a new bulwark for Europe, which he was defending against the Bolshevik hordes in the east and the Anglo-Saxon powers in the west and south. The enemy were proclaiming that zero hour for the attack on the Continent had arrived. Each attempted landing would be another Dieppe. The German soldier, helped by the Organisation Todt, had made the Islands impregnable. The Atlantic Wall, the mightiest defence work in history, had risen in answer to the Führer's order. When the attack came the garrison of the Channel Islands would be ready for it.

This statement was echoed in a newspaper article. Behind the wall of iron stood the German soldier, quietly conscious of his power. Day and night the hammers had rattled, the machines had pounded, and the engines had smoked to make the tomato and potato Islands part of the impregnable Atlantic wall. If the enemy tried to land, the green curtains[1] would fall, the batteries would open up, and a thousand rounds would be let loose. The agitating Jews on the other side of the English Channel might sound invasion trumpets, but the German soldier, who had righted a freak of history by setting foot in the Norman Islands, knew his task. Dieppe was a small foretaste of what would happen to the English invaders.

Fine words, no doubt, but lacking any suggestion that Operation 'Sealion' would ever be revived. They were a clear admission that one day the Islands must again be free.

[1] I.e. the camouflage netting.

M

SUPERIOR COUNCIL OF
THE STATES OF JERSEY 1940–1945

President	A. M. Coutanche Esq., Bailiff of Jersey.
Attorney General	C. W. Duret Aubin Esq.
Solicitor General	C. S. Harrison Esq.
Essential Commodities	Jurat E. P. Le Masurier
Transport and Communications	Jurat J. M. Norman
Finance and Economics	Jurat E. A. Dorey
Agriculture	Jurat T. J. Brée
Public Health	Jurat P. M. Baudains
Essential Services	Deputy W. S. Le Masurier
Public Instruction	Jurat P. E. Brée
Labour	Deputy E. Le Quesne

CONTROLLING COMMITTEE OF
THE STATES OF GUERNSEY 1940–1945

President	Major Ambrose J. Sherwill (H.M. Procureur) to October 1940. Jurat the Rev. John Leale, from January 1941. (Acting President from October 1940.)
Vice President and in charge of Essential Commodities	Jurat Sir Abraham J. Lainé, K.C.I.E.
Health Services Officer	Dr. A. N. Symons.
Horticulture	Jurat A. M. Drake, to May 1941. Percy Dorey Esq., to May 1945. H. R. Bichard Esq., from May 1945.
Agriculture	R. O. Falla Esq. W. Sayer Esq., from January 1941 until his deportation in 1942.
Labour	Deputy R. H. Johns.
Information	Deputy Stamford Raffles (died January 1942).
Housing	Jurat Pierre de Putron, from June 1945.
H.M. Comptroller	G. J. P. Ridgway Esq., from December 1940 (died September 1942).
Acting Attorney General	J. E. L. Martel Esq., from March 1943.

Major Sherwill attended meetings of the Controlling Committee in his capacity of Attorney General from July 1942 to his deportation at the beginning of 1943.

SOURCES

---

(1) MANUSCRIPTS

(a) *Channel Islands' papers*

1/1/5	Police reports
1/1/6	Pilfering
1/1/8	Arms
1/1/10	Census
1/1/16	Internees and evacuees
1/1/17	Fishing boats
1/1/18	Administration: general
1/1/19	Horticulture
5/1/8	Black market
5/1/23	Auction sales
7/1/3	German occupation: general
7/1/25	Cameras, photographic materials
8/1/2	Health services: general
8/1/2	Health services: milk board
12/1/14	Labour: general
16/3/1	Purchasing commission: general
CCM	Controlling Committee minutes

MILITARY GOVERNMENT FILES (NG)

Civil Administration

01 *Verwaltung, allgemeines.* (General administration).

01/1 *Allgemeine Erlasse für die Militärverwaltung, deren Wirkungskreis und Personal, Verschiedenes.* (General orders for the military administration).

01/2 *Einrichtungen und Dienstbetrieb der Nebenstelle, Dienstellen-Gebäude, Unterkünfte und Personal der Nebenstelle.* (Establishment, duties, buildings, quarters and personnel of the Nebenstelle).

01/3 *Aufsicht über die Landesverwaltung, Landesbeamten, Landesbehörden (Allgemeines).* (Supervision of the local administration, officials and departments).

01/9 *Sammlung von Bekanntmachungen der Feldkommandantur. (Feldkommandantur* public announcements).

01/30 *Kommandantur-Befehle der FK 515.* (FK 515 Orders).

01/31 *Kommandantur-Tagesbefehle der FK 515.* (FK 515 Orders of the Day).

01/33 *Divisions-Befehle der 319 I.D.* (319 Infantry Division, Divisional Orders).

01/34   *Inselkommandantur-Befehle.* (Island Commander's Orders).
02/23   *Fällen von Bäumen.* (Tree felling).
03/7   *Besatzungskosten.* (Occupation costs).
03/7a   *Quartierleistung.* (Billeting).
03/8   *Kriegsschäden.* (War damage).
10/7   *Soldatenkaufhaus.* (Soldiers' shop).
05/1   *Schule und Kultur.* (Education).
15/5   *Anbau für die Truppe.* (Cultivation for the troops).
18/6   *Zivile Hilfskräfte für die Truppe.* (Civilian auxiliaries for the troops).

MILITARY COMMAND

I a 1   *Militärische Angelegenheiten auf Alderney und Sark.* (Military affairs in Alderney and Sark).
I a 3   *Waffenablieferung und Waffenarsenal.* (Surrender and stocks of weapons).
I d   *Truppenbetreuung.* (Troops' welfare).
I d 1   *Soldatenheime auf Guernsey und Alderney.* (Soldiers' hostels in Guernsey and Alderney).
I f 1   *Feldgendarmerie und Geheime Feldpolizei und deren Tätigkeit.* (Field Police and Secret Field Police and their activities).
II   *Personal der Nebenstelle.* (Personnel of the Nebenstelle).

(b) Public Record Office

ADM 116	Admiralty and Secretariat cases.
ADM 199	War of 1939–1945, war history cases.
AIR 8	Chief of Air Staff.
AIR 9	Director of Plans.
AIR 15	Coastal Command.
AIR 37	Supreme Headquarters, Allied Expeditionary Force.
AIR 20	Unregistered papers from Air Ministry branches.
CAB 79	War Cabinet, Chiefs of Staff Committee, Minutes.
CAB 80	War Cabinet, Chiefs of Staff, Memoranda.
DEFE 2	Combined Operations Headquarters.
HO 45	Home Office registered papers.
FO 371	General correspondence, political.
FO 916	Reports on internment camps.
PREM 3	Prime Minister's papers.
WO 106	Directorate of Military Operations and Intelligence.

(c) *The National Archives of the United States* (microfilms)

T 77 787   *Oberkommando der Wehrmacht (OKW)*: Supply situation
in west, including Channel Islands, July 1944–April 1945.

T 77 788   *OKW*: Defence of the Channel Islands, and evacuation
plans, October 1941–October 1943.

T 77 789   *OKW*: Supply of fortresses and Islands, February 1944–
April 1945.

T 78 317   *Oberkommando des Heeres (OKH)*: Correspondence with
OKW *Wehrmachtführungstab* on defence of Channel
Islands, June–December 1941.
Correspondence etc. concerning defence and organization
of Channel Islands, March 1941–September 1942.

T 78 318   *OKH*: Photographs and maps of defences of Channel
Islands, April–July 1941.
Correspondence with OKW and OB West, March–May
1942.

T 311 16   *Heeresgruppe D* (Army Group D): Minefields on Guernsey
and Jersey 1942–1944.

T 311 19   *Heeresgruppe D*: Guernsey and Jersey minefield charts,
1940–1941.

T 312 500   *Armeeoberkommando 15* (15th Army): Reports on
supplies in Channel Islands, July–December 1941.

T 312 512   *AOK 15*: Correspondence about supplies for troops on
Channel coast and Channel Islands, January–December
1941.

T 314 444   *X Armeekorps* (10th Army Corps): Enclosures to
Kriegstagebuch. (War Diary).

T 314 445   *X Armeekorps*: Reports from subordinate headquarters,
including Guernsey, 25 June–31 July 1940.

T 314 1603   *LXXXIV Armeekorps* (84th Army Corps): Activities
and coastal defence in Channel Islands, April–December 1941; reports on fortifications of Channel Islands,
January–September 1942.

T 314 1604   *LXXXIV Armeekorps*: Operational reports on construction of fortresses, coastal security etc.

T 315 1639   216 Infantry Division, *Kriegstagebuch*, July 1940–June
1942.
Divisional orders, security measures, July–November
1940.

T 321 44   *Oberkommando der Luftwaffe (OKL):* Reports of suspected espionage in Channel Islands and France, 1940–1944. (Probably *Kriegstagebuch* of *Luftflottenkommando* 3).

(d) Ministry of Defence

(i) *Naval Historical Branch* (microfilm series)

MOD 37   *Kriegstagebuch 1 Seekriegsleitung (KTB 1 Skl.) C II b.* (War Diary, Naval Staff Operations Division).

MOD 38   „   „   „

MOD 47   *KTB 1 Skl. C VIII.*

MOD 95   *1 Skl. Akte VI 2, Küstenverteidigung.* (Coastal defence).

MOD 96   „   „   „

MOD 106   *1 Skl. Handakte I 0, Besetzung der Kanalinseln.* (Occupation of Channel Islands).

MOD 110   *1 Skl. Handakte, Invasion.* (Invasion).

MOD 111   „   „   „

MOD 490   *Akte 1 Skl. C 9 4.*

          C. *Völkerrecht.* (International law).

          9. *Ernährungshilfsaktionen.* (Relief supplies).

          4. *Versorgung der Zivilbevölkerung der Kanalinseln.* (Supplies for the civil population of the Channel Islands).

MOD 506   *KTB Marinegruppenkommando West, 1942–3.* (War Diary, Naval Group Command, West).

MOD 508   „   „   *1944.*

MOD 509   „   „   *1944–5.*

MOD 518   *Marinegruppenkommando West, Akte Chefsache, 15 XI 1 & 2. Operatione Frankreich.* (Operations in France).

MOD 581   *KTB Admiral Frankreich 1940.* (War Diary, Admiral Commanding, France).

MOD 583   *KTB Admiral Frankreich, 1942; Akten Allgemeines.* (Miscellaneous).

MOD 584   (i)   *Admiral Frankreich, Akte A III 4, Abwehr.* (Intelligence).

        (ii) *KTB Marinebefehlshaber Nordfrankreich, 1940.* (War Diary, Flag Officer, Northern France).

       (iii) *Grüne Pfeile: Besetzung der Kanalinseln am 30. Juni 1940.* (Operation Green Arrows: occupation of the Channel Islands, 30 June 1940).

MOD 586   *KTB Admiral Kanalküste, 1942–3.* (War Diary, Admiral Commanding, Channel Coast).

MOD 588   *Akten Admiral Kanalküste, 1942–3.*

MOD 591   *Marinebefehlshaber Westfrankreich.* (Flag Officer, Western France).
    1. *Akte Chefsache 8.*
    2. *Akte geheime Kommandosache 2.*
    3. *Akte geheime Kommandosache 13.*

MOD 650   *KTB Kommandant der Seeverteidigung Normandie 1940–44.* (Senior Officer, Sea Defences, Normandy).

MOD 653   *KTB Kommandant der Seeverteidigung, Kanalinseln 1941–45.* (Senior Officer, Sea Defences, Channel Islands).

MOD 653   *KTB Hafenkommandant.* (Naval Officer in Charge, Jersey, Guernsey, Alderney, St. Malo).

MOD 752   *Befehlshaber der Sicherung West.* (Flag Officer, Commanding Western Sea Defences): *Geleite* (Convoys).

MOD 753   *Befehlshaber der Sicherung West: Geleitverkehr Kanalinseln 1941–43.* (Convoy traffic, Channel Islands).

(ii) *SHAEF papers*

171/1 no. 1144   Operation 'Nestegg'
501 no. 1565   Operation 'Nestegg'
544/5 no. 1659   Joint Intelligence Committee, political intelligence appreciation.
743/2 no. 2137   Operation 'Nestegg'
998 no. 3086   Operation 'Overlord': policy on liberation of the Channel Islands.
1232/1   Operation 'Nestegg'
17100/1/Ops. no. 2176   Operation 'Nestegg'

All the above papers are included in Class WO 219 in the Public Record Office.

(e) *Foreign and Commonwealth Office Library: German Foreign Ministry photostats*

GFM 98   Bureau of Secretary of State: German-English relations, vols. 4–6, 1 January 1941–31 October 1943.

GFM 280   Bureau of Under-Secretary of State, Iran I, vol. 13, 1 August 1941–7 September 1941.

GFM 281   Bureau of Under-Secretary of State, Iran II, vol. 13, 7 September 1941–21 July 1942.

GFM 1808   Legal Department, England, Channel Islands 1943–1945.

(2) PRINTED SOURCES

COUTANCHE   Lord Coutanche, *The Government of Jersey during the German Occupation* (Bulletin of the Société Jersiaise, 1965, pp. 33–53).

DURAND   Ralph Durand, *Guernsey under German Rule* (London, 1946).

MOLLET   Ralph Mollet, *Jersey under the Swastika* (London, 1945).

SINEL   Leslie Sinel, *The German Occupation of Jersey, 1940–1945: a complete diary* (Jersey, 1945).

NEBEL   Gerhard Nebel, *Bei den Nördlichen Hesperiden* (Wuppertal, 1948).

WOOD   Alan and Mary Wood, *Islands in Danger* (London, 1965).

(3) PEOPLE WHO PROVIDED INFORMATION ABOUT THE GERMAN OCCUPATION

Mr. W. J. Allez
The late Sir William Arnold, K.B.E. (Bailiff of Guernsey, 1960–73)
Mr. F. de L. Bois, O.B.E.
Mrs. B. Bois
Mr. P. Bradshaw
Mrs. P. Broome
Mr. de V. G. Carey
Major C. E. Carrington, M.C.
Mrs. J. Coles
The late Lord Coutanche (Bailiff of Jersey, 1935–61)
Mr. V. Coysh
Mr. A. H. S. Dickinson
Deputy Cecil de Sausmarez, M.B.E. (President, States of Guernsey History 1939–1945 Committee)
Mrs. C. de Sausmarez
Mr. Frank Falla
Mr. Raymond Falla, O.B.E.
Mr. Raymond Falle
Mr. F. R. Font
Mr. Peter J. Girard
Mr. R. S. Gray
Mr. Louis Guillemette, O.B.E.

Mr. Ted Hamel
Miss J. E. Harris
Mr. R. G. Harwood
The late Dame Sibyl Hathaway, D.B.E., Dame of Sark
Mr. W. Hibbs
Mr. W. D. Hooke
Mr. J. B. Howard, C.B.
Mr. J. T. D. Hubert
Mr. Arthur Kent
Miss A. Le M. Lainé
Mr. A. P. Lamy, M.B.E.
Mr. A. le Brun, O.B.E.
Deputy Miss E. Le Feuvre
Sir Robert Le Masurier, D.S.C. (Bailiff of Jersey, 1962–1974)
Mr. V. Le Maitre
Sir John Loveridge, Kt., C.B.E. (Bailiff of Guernsey, 1973–)
Group Captain A. H. S. Lucas
Mr. Vernon Luff, M.B.E.
Mr. Colin Marie
Mr. A. T. Mahy
Mr. Ronald Mauger
Mr. O. Le Q. Mourant
Captain Hubert Nicolle, M.C.
Mr. T. X. Pantcheff

Colonel M. St. J. Packe
Captain John Parker, M.B.E.
Mr. Edward Potter
(Greffier, Jersey)
Mr. R. Pujalte
Mr. F. L. Raimbault
Mrs. F. P. G. Reynel
Mr. J. P. Robert
Mr. W. F. Robin
Miss B. Salmon
Mr. Rollo de B. Sherwill

Mr. R. T. Short
Mr. L. P. Sinel
Mr. Frank Stroobant
Dr. R. B. Sutcliffe, F.R.C.S.
Major J. M. Symes, M.C.
Mr. A. Timmer
Mr. Carel Toms
Mr. F. W. Veale
Mr. A. Verini
Mr. E. N. Walker
Miss J. Walker

Mr. Michael Ginns

SELECT BIBLIOGRAPHY

ALDERNEY SOCIETY AND MUSEUM, *Bulletin.*

ANTILL, J. KENNETH, *A Bibliography of The German Occupation of Jersey and other Channel Islands* (Jersey, States Greffe, 1975).

AUERBACH, SONDERFÜHRER DR. HANS, *Die Kanalinseln: Jersey, Guernsey, Sark* (The Channel Islands: Jersey, Guernsey, Sark). Published by order of the Commanding Officer (Jersey, 1942).

AUFSESS, FREIHERR VON UND ZU, *Ein Bilderbogen von den Kanalinseln* (A Picture Book of the Channel Islands). Published by order of the Feldkommandant (n.d.).

BALLEINE, G. R., *A History of the Island of Jersey* (London, 1950).

BONSOR, N.R.P., *The Jersey Eastern Railway and the German Occupation Lines in Jersey* (Lingfield, 1965).

CHANNEL ISLANDS STUDY GROUP, *Nos Îles: a Symposium on the Channel Islands* (Teddington, 1944).

CORTVRIEND, V. V., *Isolated Island* (Guernsey, 1947).

DONNISON, F. S. V., *Civil Affairs and Military Government, North West Europe 1944–1946* (London, 1961).

DURAND, RALPH, *Guernsey under German Rule* (Guernsey, 1946).

FALLA, F. W., *The Silent War* (London, 1967).

HATHAWAY, SIBYL, *Dame of Sark* (London, 1961).

HOOKE, W. D., *The Channel Islands* (London, 1953).

LEMPRIÈRE, RAOUL, *Portrait of the Channel Islands* (London, 1970).

LE PATOUREL, J. *The Medieval Administration of the Channel Islands* (Oxford, 1938).

MARSHALL, M., *Hitler invaded Sark* (Guernsey, 1963).

MOLLET, RALPH, *Jersey under the Swastika* (London, 1945).

MORDAL, JACQUES, *Handstreich auf Granville* (Paris, 1964).

NEBEL, GERHARD, *Bei den Nördlichen Hesperiden* (Wuppertal, 1948).

NEWPORT, WILLIAM, *Stamps and Postal History of the Channel Islands* (London, 1972).

PACKE M. ST. J., AND DREYFUS, M., *The Alderney Story 1939–1949* (Alderney, 1971).

SINEL, L. P., *Diary* (Jersey, 1945).

SOCIÉTÉ GUERNESIAISE, *Report and Transactions* (Guernsey, 1938–65, vols. xiii–xvii).

SOCIÉTÉ JERSIAISE, *Bulletins* (Jersey, 1940–68, vols. xiv–xix).

STROOBANT, F. E., *One Man's War* (Guernsey, 1967).

TOMS, CAREL, *Hitler's Fortress Islands* (London, 1967).

WADSWORTH, JOHN, *Counter Defensive: being the story of a bank in battle* (London, 1946).

WILSON, FRANK E., *Railways in Guernsey* (Guernsey, 1970).

WOOD, ALAN AND MARY, *Islands in Danger* (London, 1965).